Roman Law and Latin Literature

Also available from Bloomsbury

Studying Roman Law by Paul du Plessis
Landscapes of War in Greek and Roman Literature edited by Bettina Reitz-Joosse, Marian W. Makins and C. J. Mackie
Anticipation and Anachrony in Statius' Thebaid by Robert Simms

Roman Law and Latin Literature

Edited by Ioannis Ziogas and Erica Bexley

BLOOMSBURY ACADEMIC
LONDON • NEW YORK • OXFORD • NEW DELHI • SYDNEY

BLOOMSBURY ACADEMIC
Bloomsbury Publishing Plc
50 Bedford Square, London, WC1B 3DP, UK
1385 Broadway, New York, NY 10018, USA
29 Earlsfort Terrace, Dublin 2, Ireland

BLOOMSBURY, BLOOMSBURY ACADEMIC and the Diana logo are
trademarks of Bloomsbury Publishing Plc

First published in Great Britain 2022
This paperback edition published 2024

Copyright © Ioannis Ziogas and Erica Bexley, 2022

Ioannis Ziogas and Erica Bexley have asserted their right under the Copyright,
Designs and Patents Act, 1988, to be identified as Editors of this work.

For legal purposes the Acknowledgements on p. vii constitute an
extension of this copyright page.

Cover design: Terry Woodley
Cover image © Giuseppe Arcimboldo, *Ulrich Zasius, The Lawyer*, 1566. Oil on
canvas. Photo by: Sepia Times/Universal Images Group via Getty Images

All rights reserved. No part of this publication may be reproduced or transmitted
in any form or by any means, electronic or mechanical, including photocopying,
recording, or any information storage or retrieval system, without prior permission
in writing from the publishers.

Bloomsbury Publishing Plc does not have any control over, or responsibility for,
any third-party websites referred to or in this book. All internet addresses given
in this book were correct at the time of going to press. The author and publisher
regret any inconvenience caused if addresses have changed or sites have ceased
to exist, but can accept no responsibility for any such changes.

A catalogue record for this book is available from the British Library.

Library of Congress Cataloging-in-Publication Data

Names: Ziogas, Giannes, editor. | Bexley, Erica M., 1982-editor.
Title: Roman law and Latin literature / edited by Ioannis Ziogas and Erica M. Bexley.
Description: New York: Bloomsbury Academic, 2022. |
Includes bibliographical references and index.
Identifiers: LCCN 2021052179 | ISBN 9781350276635 (hardback) |
ISBN 9781350276673 (paperback) | ISBN 9781350276642 (ebook) |
ISBN 9781350276659 (epub) | ISBN 9781350276666
Subjects: LCSH: Latin literature–History and criticism. |
Roman law. | Law in literature.
Classification: LCC PA6029.L39 R66 2022 | DDC 870.9/3554–dc23/eng/20220105
LC record available at https://lccn.loc.gov/2021052179

ISBN: HB: 978-1-3502-7663-5
PB: 978-1-3502-7667-3
ePDF: 978-1-3502-7664-2
eBook: 978-1-3502-7665-9

Typeset by RefineCatch Limited, Bungay, Suffolk

To find out more about our authors and books visit www.bloomsbury.com
and sign up for our newsletters.

Contents

List of Contributors   vii
Acknowledgements   x

1 Introduction: Roman Law and Latin Literature *Ioannis Ziogas and Erica Bexley*   1

Part I Literature as Law

2 The Force of Literature *Michèle Lowrie*   25

3 Saturnalian *Lex*: Seneca's *Apocolocyntosis* *Erica Bexley*   45

4 *Iustitium* in Lucan's *Bellum Ciuile* *Thomas Biggs*   67

Part II Literature and the Legal Tradition

5 Terence's *Phormio* and the Legal Discourse and Legal Profession at Rome *Jan Felix Gaertner*   89

6 Beachcombing at the Centumviral Court: Littoral Meaning in the *Causa Curiana* *John Dugan*   106

7 Marcus Antistius Labeo and the Idea of Legal Literature *Matthijs Wibier*   125

Part III Literature and Property Law

8 Poetry, Prosecution and the Author Function *Nora Goldschmidt*   147

9 The Sea Common to All in Plautus, *Rudens*: Social Norms and Legal Rules *Thomas A. J. McGinn*   169

10 Intellectual 'Property': Ownership, Possession and Judgment among Civic *Artes* *John Oksanish*   189

11 Seneca's Debt: Property, Self-Possession and the Economy of Philosophical Exchange in the *Epistulae Morales* *Erik Gunderson*   207

Part IV Literature and Justice

12 Law in Disguise in the *Metamorphoses*: The Ambiguous *Ecphraseis* of Minerva and Arachne Stella Alekou   227

13 What the Roman Constitution Means to Me: Staging Encounters between US and Roman Law on Equality and Proportionality Nandini Pandey   249

Bibliography   270
Index   297

Contributors

Stella Alekou is elected Assistant Professor of Latin in the Department of Philology at the University of Ioannina. Her main research interests focus on Roman law in Latin literature and the representation of women in Ovidian poetry. She is the author of *Médée et la rhétorique de la mémoire au féminin (Ovide, «Héroïde» XII)*, 2018, and 'Medea's Legal Apology in Ovid's *Heroides* 12' (*Latomus*, 2018) and co-editor, with M. Vöhler and M. Pechlivanos, of *Concepts and Functions of Philhellenism. Aspects of a Transcultural Movement* (2021).

Erica Bexley is Associate Professor of Latin in the Department of Classics and Ancient History at Durham University. Her research specializations include Seneca (prose and verse), Roman drama and performance culture, and Neronian literature. She is the author of *Seneca's Characters: Fictional Identities and Implied Human Selves* (2022), alongside numerous chapters and articles.

Thomas Biggs is Lecturer in Latin at the University of St Andrews. He is the author of *Poetics of the First Punic War* (2020) and co-editor of *The Epic Journey in Greek and Roman Literature* (2019). He has also published over twenty articles and chapters. His research interests include Latin literature of the republic and early empire, verse depictions of history and the complex cultural interactions between Rome and North Africa.

John Dugan is Associate Professor of Classics at the State University of New York at Buffalo. His primary areas of research are Roman oratory and rhetorical theory, particularly Cicero. He is the author of *Making a New Man: Ciceronian Self-Fashioning in the Rhetorical Works* (2005), as well as articles and book chapters on Cicero's reception in ancient scholarship, fragmentary Roman literature and ancient hermeneutics.

Jan Felix Gaertner is Professor of Classics at the University of Cologne. His publications include a commentary on Ovid's *Epistulae ex Ponto* (2005), a collective volume on the discourse of exile (2007), the co-authored monograph *Caesar and the Bellum Alexandrinum* (2013) and numerous articles and reviews. His Habilitationsschrift was dedicated to law and legal language in Graeco-Roman New Comedy.

Nora Goldschmidt is Professor of Classics and Ancient History at Durham University (UK). She has published extensively in the areas of early Latin poetry and poetic biography, including *Shaggy Crowns: Ennius' Annales and Virgil's Aeneid* (2013), *Afterlives of the Roman Poets: Biofiction and the Reception of Latin Poetry* (2019) and (with Barbara Graziosi) *Tombs of the Ancient Poets: Between Literary Reception and Material Culture* (2018).

Erik Gunderson is Professor of Classics at the University of Toronto. He is the author of six scholarly monographs and a number of articles. Areas of emphasis include technologies of the Roman self, the intersections between literature and politics, as well as intellectual culture in general and rhetorical culture more specifically. His most recent book is *The Art of Complicity in Martial and Statius: The Epigrams, Siluae, and Domitianic Rome* (2021).

Michèle Lowrie, Andrew W. Mellon Distinguished Service Professor of Classics and the College at the University of Chicago, has published monographs and edited volumes on Horace, Augustan literature, the reception of Vergil, figuration and exemplarity. *Civil War and the Collapse of the Social Bond: The Roman Tradition at the Heart of the Modern*, jointly authored with Barbara Vinken, is forthcoming. *Security, Safety, and Care: A Roman Political Discourse* will receive final polish, she hopes, soon.

Thomas A. J. McGinn is Professor of History at Vanderbilt University where he has taught for over thirty-five years. He is the author of numerous books and articles on ancient Roman law and society. His interests embrace such subjects as marriage, prostitution, the family, and the status and role of women. His most recent book is *Table IV of the XII Tables* (2017).

John Oksanish is Associate Professor of Classics at Wake Forest University in North Carolina (US). The primary focus of his research is the literary culture of Rome as it is represented in both poetry and prose. His recent book, *Vitruvian Man: Rome Under Construction* (2019), integrates the work of the Augustan architectural writer Vitruvius into the broader literary context of late Republican and early Imperial Rome, with particular emphasis on metaphors of the body. His most recent projects explore notions of sufficiency and satiety in Roman literature.

Nandini Pandey, Associate Professor of Classics at the Johns Hopkins University, specializes in the literature, culture and reception of early imperial Rome. She is author of *The Poetics of Power in Augustan Rome: Latin Poetic Responses to Early*

Imperial Iconography (2018) as well as numerous scholarly and public-facing articles for venues including *Eidolon* and the *Los Angeles Review of Books*. She is currently completing a book-length project on Roman diversity and another on classics' relevance to modern life.

Matthijs Wibier is a lecturer in Ancient History at the University of Kent, Canterbury (UK). His research has focused primarily on the legal culture and legal literature of the Roman Empire. He is currently completing a monograph on Roman legal scholarship in the Early Empire and, with Dario Mantovani, a large volume that traces the circulation and reception of Roman legal literature in late antiquity. Earlier work includes 'The Topography of the Law Book' (in L. Jansen (ed.), *The Roman Paratext*, 2014) and 'Cicero's Reception in the Juristic Tradition of the Early Empire' (in P. du Plessis (ed.), *Cicero's Law*, 2016).

Ioannis Ziogas is Associate Professor in the Department of Classics and Ancient History at Durham University (UK). His main teaching and research interests revolve around interactions between law and literature in ancient Greece and Rome. His recent book (*Law and Love in Ovid: Courting Justice in the Age of Augustus,* 2021) explores the juridico-discursive nature of Ovid's love poetry. He also published a chapter ('Law and Literature in the Ancient World: The Case of Phryne') in Dolin (ed.) *Law and Literature,* 2018.

Acknowledgements

We are grateful to Durham's Department of Classics and Ancient History and the Faculty of Arts and Humanities for their financial support of our interdisciplinary conference on Roman Law and Latin Literature that took place in Durham in September 2019. We are very grateful to all the colleagues who participated in the conference. The intellectual generosity, depth and kindness of the participants were incredibly inspiring. We would also like to thank our Bloomsbury editors, Georgina Leighton and Alice Wright, and their excellent team. We are also grateful to two anonymous readers for their supportive and constructive feedback.

Ioannis Ziogas and Erica Bexley
Durham, UK

1

Introduction: Roman Law and Latin Literature

Ioannis Ziogas and Erica Bexley

What has law got to do with literature or literature with law? Law, it would seem, claims dispositive powers and aspires to intervene in the world around it by regulating behaviour, framing constitutions, establishing rules and punishing transgression, while literature constructs fictional worlds through which it explores – without any definitive goal – the permutations of what may broadly be called the 'human condition'. This distinction is more apparent than real, however. Closer inspection reveals that law and literature have a lot in common: both are grounded in language (oral or written), which invites interpretation and dispute; both engage in acts of persuasion; both vacillate between being reflections and projections of the world around them. Literature, like law, aspires to intervene in people's actual lived experience from the micro level of affecting its audiences to the macro level of dictating normative behaviour and instigating cultural change. Shelley's claim that 'poets are the unacknowledged legislators of the world' (1994: 660) celebrates precisely this ability of literature to interrogate and propose ways – or in Shelley's words, *laws* (1994: 637) – of social conduct.

From the other side, law, like literature, is deeply invested in the creation of alternative worlds. Far from being concerned with unimaginative practicalities, law pursues the dream of a utopian society, whether as a future projection of cultural ideals or a wish to return to a prelapsarian state of absolute justice. Law and literature are deeply and inevitably entangled with the origins of morality, even though, if not especially when, they are trying to break free from sociomoral conventions and feature as self-regulated discourses. Nor is law more hermeneutically stable than literature, despite its ostensible striving to suppress ambiguities and separate right from wrong. Against literature's shades of grey, law might be expected to stand out in black and white, but the reality is much murkier. Laws are redefined continually, their every enactment an act of interpretation. Like any other text, they accrue meaning over time, and context affects their content. One need look no further than the debate between originalist and textualist interpreters of the US constitution for a clear view of the hermeneutic struggles embedded in the legal profession.

Law and literature have a special interrelationship. This is not simply a case of comparing apples with oranges on the basis that both are round. Derrida's *Before the Law* (2018: 46) argues that law and literature share a particular 'narrative' quality, not just in the sense of their arising from and telling stories, but also in their aspiring to universalizing force, largely cut off from historical referents. Derrida contends that law and literature have a common origin in the form of mythological narrative (he cites Freud's analysis of Oedipus), which is 'without an author or end, but ... inevitable and unforgettable' (2018: 46). Both are stories predicated on an originary judgment, both contain the seeds of moral regulation, both appeal to a reality beyond mere fact.

At a simpler level, we may just say that law exhibits literary qualities and literature legal ones. The former of these two assertions is the mainstay of the Law and Humanities movement, which arose from study of the literary – chiefly, rhetorical and narrative – features of legal texts, and the reading of literature to augment law's ethical component.[1] 'Law *as* literature' and 'law *in* literature' were the discipline's foundational concepts, the former represented by scholars as diverse as James Boyd White (1973), Stanley Fish (1989) and Peter Goodrich (1990), while the latter has been championed by Richard Weisberg (1984) and Ian Ward (1999), among many others. The two approaches have a lot in common and frequently overlap, as for instance in Aristodemou (2000). Both categories of analysis are represented in our volume, too. On the side of 'Law *in* literature', McGinn in Chapter 9 below ('The Sea Common to All') discusses the possible presence in Plautus' *Rudens* of the legal concept *res communes omnium*; Bexley in Chapter 3 ('Saturnalian *Lex*') investigates Claudius' role as judge in the *Apocolocyntosis*, and Alekou in Chapter 12 ('Law in Disguise') traces Ovid's ambivalent use of legal language in *Metamorphoses* 6.1–145. For 'Law *as* literature', Dugan in Chapter 6 ('Beachcombing at the Centumviral Court') examines the rhetorical and metaphorical qualities of Crassus' legal reasoning, and Wibier in Chapter 7 ('Marcus Antistius Labeo and the Idea of Legal Literature') investigates how one of Rome's most famous jurists combined legal with literary learning. In keeping with the core principles of the Law and Humanities movement, all of these papers show legal and literary concepts shading into each other, so that law resembles literature and vice versa. The two disciplines, the two endeavours, combine in fruitful marriage.

Until recently, however, law has been the dominant partner in this marriage, with literature playing an ancillary role as a repository of rhetorical techniques and/or a supplement to legal knowledge. Work by Fortier (2019) attempts to shift the balance more towards literature, and the edited collection by Dolin (2018) places the two fields on a more even par. As Fortier (2019: 13–15) acknowledges, the 'and' in 'law *and* literature' conveys a lot: does it designate a harmonious relationship, or a conflict? Does it establish balance, identification, or a hierarchy? A major aim of our present volume is to continue this growing emphasis on the *literary* side of the law and literature debate by showing how literature anticipates, imitates, supplants or complements law's role in constituting rules and norms. To paraphrase Northrop Frye (1970: 70–7), literature is the basis of the social imagination that produces law and guarantees its respect. A more recent claim by Reichmann (2009: 5) also encapsulates our volume's central concerns: 'the texts of law and literature jointly contribute to … a normative universe'. To the aforementioned categories of 'law *as* literature', 'law *in* literature', and 'law *and* literature', we add: 'literature *as* law'.

At this point it is worth pausing to consider how law and literature are defined, where their boundaries lie – not easy questions for a Roman context. An obvious answer is that law comprises codified statutes and offers a basis for adjudication, but the line between legal concepts and social norms is not always clear cut. The technical language of Roman law disperses into discourse. To what extent is law synonymous with sovereign power, or behavioural precepts, or certain forms of reasoning (e.g. from precedent)? As Lowrie's contribution ('The Force of Literature') demonstrates, Rome's unwritten 'constitution' often acquired legal force despite its lack of codification. A similar if not greater range of definition confronts the category of 'literature', especially in an ancient Roman context where 'fiction' was sometimes an inadequate classificatory principle (Lowrie 2009a: 67; 2016: 75; in this volume). Latin epic was inextricably related to history and contemporary politics. Elegy, lyric, and epigram frequently addressed contemporaries and conveyed lived experience (Lowrie 2016: 75). The Romans defined literary production broadly, as *litterae* ('letters'), and included in this category a wide range of written work from courtroom speeches to historiography and technical treatises; the very discipline of 'Latin literature' reflects this diversity. So, rather than close off any avenues of potentially fruitful analysis, this volume does not police the boundaries of law and literature too strictly; doing so would risk silencing too much of the dialogue between law and literature that we wish to promote. Although a lot of the literature covered in this volume is, by modern definition, 'fictional' (*comoedia palliata*, epic, satire) and although we sometimes refer to it as such, we stress that it does not inhabit an enclosed sphere, cut off from the everyday social realities with which the law is deeply engaged. Literature has as much bearing on the actual world as law does on imaginary ones.

Hence, arguments for a special interrelationship between law and literature are all the more pertinent in the context of ancient Rome, where the two pursuits often overlapped, their production arising from roughly the same group of upper-class individuals, schooled in rhetoric and 'letters' (*litterae*). Notably, the Romans were fully aware of literature's importance in fleshing out concepts of legality. As Clifford Ando (2015a) demonstrates, interaction between fiction and social reality was crucial to the functioning of Roman law. Legal fiction extended Roman law beyond the original scope of any individual source of law. Since imaginary stories, plots, archetypes and stock characters make what is particular universal, fictional narratives became the foundation of Roman legal discourse rather than its reflection.

The genre of Roman declamation, for instance, highlights the importance of fictional laws and trials not only for training young Romans for a career in the courtroom, but also for educating them about the controversial origins of taboos and morality. The plots and stock characters of declamations strongly evoke those of Roman comedy and tragedy (see Gunderson 2016; cf. Langlands 2006: 250–1). The laws quoted in the declamations are imaginary, yet many of them clearly evoke early laws, praetorian edicts or Greek laws (see Lowrie 2016: 76; Bonner 1949: 83–132). Declamatory plots and laws are fictional, yet they feel real; they are outlandish, yet familiar; they are at once culturally specific and universal. In the end, it is the *idea* of law that matters and not its specific directives. And that is why we need to take law and literature in Roman declamations seriously (cf. Gunderson 2003).

A division between law as factual and literature as fictional clearly cannot be sustained. Although critics of the law and literature movement, such as Richard Posner (2009), aver that legal scenarios presented in literature have little bearing on actual legal practice, or on legal history, fictional narratives are in fact major sources of legal consciousness. Kafka's *The Trial* may not increase our understanding of Austro-Hungarian criminal procedure, as Posner (2009: 143) maintains, but it substantially increases our *concept* or *impression* of law's depersonalizing effect in modern, bureaucratic societies. Like Roman declamation, the importance of the narrative's legal material lies in its articulation of an *idea* rather than a specific rule set.

Literature is also capable of producing legal consequences outside the text itself, for example, in cases of libel or censorship. The situation is even more striking in ancient Rome, where interaction between the two spheres was not so strictly delineated. Catullus' poetry, for instance, not only addresses several of his contemporaries (e.g. the poet Licinius Calvus or Cicero), but is also presented as powerful speech that can injure its targets.[2] The poet's iambic attacks on Caesar are a case in point: Catullus 57 did not simply refer to an extra-textual reality, but hurt its addressee. Suetonius (*Julius Caesar* 73) tells us that Caesar considered this poem about Mamurra 'an indelible mark on his body' (*sibi ... perpetua stigmata*). The word *stigma* is significant here because its primary meaning is a mark of infamy tattooed with a hot needle on runaway slaves or criminals. Thus, for Caesar, Catullus' *stylus* has the force of law since the poet can punish his targets with the hot needle of his poetry; his writing is not just analogous to but practically indistinguishable from the slave's tattoo. Iambic verses have the power to degrade the most powerful man and brand him with the scars of infamy forever.

Additionally, Latin literature often aspired to create a socio-political reality in ways that parallel the scope and aims of Roman laws. Ovid, for instance, in his *Art of Love* assumes the voice of an authoritative legislator, in order to lay down the laws that regulate love affairs (see Ziogas 2021). He is thus creating or reflecting a social reality in contrast and parallel to Augustus' moral legislation. We should never underestimate Ovid's ambitions. He writes poetry in order to create a world and by creating a world he simultaneously legitimates it. Literature, like law, is both inspired by and inspires reality.

To the extent that law and literature are bound up with textuality, they are scripts that are fixed. They can be copied and imitated, though all acts of reproduction encourage instead of compromising an obsession with the original. Textual stability goes hand in hand with interpretative instability. The meaning of written laws and literary texts depends on context, media, method, readership and performance.[3] Legal and literary texts are hotly disputed. By being repeatedly interpreted and reinterpreted, they are repeatedly renegotiated, revised and reaffirmed.

A neat example of this confluence is the Latin word *iudex*, which describes both a judge and a literary critic. A defining characteristic of both law and literature is that both discourses have their 'guardians' or 'gatekeepers' (critics, experts, authors, lawyers) who can pass laws and judgment only by referring to a pre-established and thus more powerful set of rules and conventions (cf. Derrida 2018: 67–8). In sum, law and literature require an *auctor*, a word which in Latin describes both the author of a literary text and the proposer of a law. When Roman authors describe themselves as *auctores*, they claim that the nature of their work is simultaneously literary and juridical. They are creators, owners and guarantors of literature that has the force of law or law that has the force of literature.[4] At the same time, both law and literature constantly question, revisit and revise established norms. They are simultaneously fixed and living texts: they operate within prescribed boundaries and frameworks which they constantly push and redefine.[5]

As Kieran Dolin points out, law and literature are adjoining fields, divided by a boundary fence that keeps breaking down, despite regular maintenance (Dolin 2007: 8). In his fine introduction, Dolin (2007: 1–16) discusses how the American Supreme Court's decision of the case of *Plaut v. Spendthrift Farm Inc* (1995) revolved around interpreting Robert Frost's poem 'Mending Wall'. Justice Antonin Scalia cites Frost's poem in order to support his formulation of the law: 'separation of powers, a distinctively American political doctrine, profits from the advice authored by a distinctively American poet: 'good fences make good neighbors' (240)'. Scalia assumes that his readers will recognize his allusion to Frost's poem. He also assumes that this literary allusion has the power to legitimize the judgments of the Supreme Court. As Dolin (2007: 2) puts it, 'Political theory, history and literature combine to authorise and authenticate this law, and locate it in a larger narrative.'

But another member of the Court, Justice Stephen Breyer, questioned the understanding of the poem, noting: 'One might consider as well that poet's caution, for he not only notes that "Something there is that doesn't love a wall," but also writes, "Before I built a wall I'd ask to know / What I was walling in or walling out"' (359). Thus, Breyer points out that it is a mistake to assume that Frost endorses the line from his poem. Scalia neglected the context of the poem and simplified the thorny issue of authorial intention. Breyer's juridical critique is literary criticism. Interestingly, Dolin (2007: 3–4) argues that Scalia and Breyer uncannily re-enact the roles of the two farmers from Frost's poem. We can push his argument further: not only did the interpretation of a poem become inextricably entangled with the judgments of the Supreme Court, but the dramatization of its two opposing views is now reflected in the debate between Scalia and Breyer. The Justices are created in the image of Frost's poetry.

If intertwining legal and poetic judgments is rare in our times, it was far more common in the Roman world. We tend to think of legal discourse as specialized and autonomous, but specialization does not imply seclusion (cf. Dolin 2007: 10). The Roman jurists were indeed the group of experts which played a crucial role in the emergence of the field of law as a science. Our modern concept of law is more or less their invention (see Schiavone 2012). But the independence of legal discourse did not result in its cultural isolation. As Jill Harries (2006: 12) puts it: 'The present separation of legal discourse from the rest ... is not reflected in the intellectual approach taken by the Roman elite.' Roman authors were educated in law and saw themselves as champions of justice. Roman orators and jurists were versed in literature and used their literary knowledge in their forensic speeches and reasonings. The Augustan jurist M. Antistius Labeo, for instance, founded a school of law that emphasized the study of liberal arts. Grammar, dialectics, literary criticism and etymological analyses were keys to interpreting the law in Labeo's school. The jurists taught literature and linguistics in their schools and debated the meaning of poetry far more often than the Justices of the Supreme Court.

A telling example comes from the jurist Gaius, who, in his treatise on the Twelve Tables, quotes Homer (*Odyssey* 4.230) to support his definition of *uenena* ('drugs'). The passage comes from the *Digest* (50.16.236), in a section where jurists resemble lexicographers (*Digest* 50.16 *De uerborum significatione* 'On the meaning of words'). Gaius starts by saying that those who use the word *uenenum* should clarify whether it is 'a good or a bad drug' (50.16.236 *Qui 'uenenum' dicit, adicere debet, utrum malum an bonum*) and goes on to argue that the semantic range of *uenenum* corresponds to the Greek word φάρμακον, which describes both a noxious poison and a medicinal remedy. Gaius concludes with quoting and translating *Odyssey* 4.230 (φάρμακα, πολλὰ μὲν ἐσθλὰ μεμιγμένα πολλὰ δὲ λυγρά 'drugs, many that are healing when mixed and many that are harmful'). Homer is described as the greatest Greek poet (*summus apud eos poetarum*) who is here invoked to advise the Romans (*admonet nos*); literature lends itself to legal application.

Concomitantly, Gaius' interrogation of semantics resembles a literary pursuit as much as a juridical one. Homer was often summoned as a witness in legal disputes and his poetry was treated in the same way as law and legal documents (see Koning 2010: 76). This practice was not restricted to the Greek world, but extended to the reasonings of Roman jurists. Paul (*Ad edictum* 33; *Digest* 18.1.1), for instance, discusses whether a true sale can be made without using coins.[6] Does giving a toga and receiving a tunic instead count as sale? According to Paul, Sabinus and Cassius argue that this is a veritable sale, while Nerva and Proculus are of the opinion that this is an exchange, not a purchase. Sabinus used Homer as a witness (*Homero teste utitur*), quoting *Iliad* 7.472-5, where Homer says that the Achaeans bought wine with copper, iron, hides, cattle and slaves. But Paul challenges Sabinus' reading of the Homeric passage. In his view, what Homer describes is barter, not a purchase. Paul quotes another passage from the

Iliad to support his interpretation (6.234–5), the famous lines in which Glaukos makes an exchange of armour with Diomedes, giving gold for bronze. After criticizing Sabinus for misinterpreting Homer, Paul adds that he could have chosen a better passage in support of his *sententia*, namely the Homeric formula πρίατο κτεάτεσσιν ἑοῖσιν ('he purchased with his possessions' *Odyssey* 1.430, 14.115, 14.452, 15.483). Paul implies that his knowledge of Homer is superior to that of Sabinus, who failed to make his *sententia* convincing due to his poor command of Homeric epic.

Ultimately, Paul implies that Homer's testimony is inconclusive. Yet he takes pains to show that he is an excellent critic of Homeric poetry. Homer's authority is not simply dismissed as irrelevant. His cultural significance is beyond dispute as well as his relevance to juristic debate. This is quite striking; we would expect that Homer's poetry would be barely pertinent to Roman law. An archaic Greek epic tradition that at times reflects the world of archaic Greece and at other times the bygone world of the Mycenaean civilization it celebrates is taken into account in the works of the Roman jurists. Homer's authority exceeds national, cultural and temporal boundaries. More importantly, his authority exceeds the boundaries of literature and influences the way in which the Romans understand their legal terms and concepts.[7]

While Roman jurists debated the meaning of Homeric poetry in their reasonings, forensic orators summoned poets as witnesses to support their cases. Quintilian (*Inst.* 1.8.11–12) notes that great orators, such as Cicero and Asinius, often quoted lines from older poets, such as Ennius, Accius, Pacuvius, Lucilius, Terence, and Caecilius, in order to support their cases and please the jurors. He concludes as follows: *Quibus accedit non mediocris utilitas, cum sententiis eorum uelut quibusdam testimoniis quae proposuere confirment.* 'There is considerable practical advantage in this also, because orators adduce the sentiments of the poets as a kind of evidence to support their own positions' (see Ziogas 2021: 167). Poetry is thus quoted as legal evidence.

One of the most prominent and well-known cases of a Roman orator quoting poetry in his defence speech is Cicero's *Pro Caelio*, which we now consider as a case study for the interactions between law and literature. In this speech, Cicero casts all the main parties involved in the trial as stock characters from Roman comedy.[8] Caelius is a young man (*adulescens*) whose transgressive behaviour must be condoned; Clodia is a courtesan (*meretrix*) whose mercenary tricks must be resisted; the prosecutors resemble the stern old fathers from Roman comedy. By contrast, Cicero casts himself as the lenient father. He plays his role with flair as he enriches his speech with quotations from Roman comedy:

leni uero et **clementi patre** cuius modi ille est:
fores ecfregit, restituentur; discidit
uestem, resarcietur,
Caeli causa est expeditissima.

But if I take a mild and **indulgent father** like this one, who would say:
'He has broken a door, it will be repaired; he has torn a dress, it will be mended up,'
Caelius' case is quite without difficulty. (Loeb translation modified)

Cicero, *Pro Caelio* 38

By quoting Terence's *Adelphoe* (120–1), Cicero plays the role of the indulgent father Micio. What is more, Cicero follows the dramatic conventions of Roman comedy as an authoritative precedent that will guarantee Caelius' acquittal. As Matthew Leigh (2004a: 301) argues, Cicero aims to make the jury study the case as if they were watching a comedy, and to appeal to their deep understanding of the rules of the genre. In Roman comedy, young men's transgressive and illegal behaviour is not punished. They are typically pardoned at the end without facing the consequences of their irresponsible and often criminal actions.[9] Lenient fathers and young men in love promote the comic spirit, while strict moralists and litigious old men are blocking characters which are either humiliated and expelled from the comic stage or transformed and integrated into Roman comedy's code of conduct. In other words, legalism and litigation undermine the justice of comedy, which results from the suspension, not the enforcement, of the law.

In order to delegitimize the prosecution, therefore, Cicero relies on the nature of Roman comedy. It is, further, significant to the case that such comic performances were staged during festivals or holidays that were defined by a temporary suspension of legal action. In fact, Caelius' case takes place during the *ludi Megalenses*, a major festival that included comic performances. That a trial was held during this time is exceptional. The prosecution brought charges against Caelius under the *lex de ui*, which outlawed any act of violence against the *res publica*, and convened cases even during festivals (see Dyck 2013: 7). The accusation is extremely serious and, had he been convicted, Caelius would have most likely faced the death penalty, a closure quite unlike any ending from Roman comedy. But Cicero uses this opportunity to stage his own version of a comedy in his defence speech, thereby undermining the severity of the prosecution's accusations. The trial is far from a joke, but Cicero makes a joke out of it.

Geffcken argues that comedy in the *Pro Caelio* dismisses the accusations by diminishing their importance. In rhetoric, this is known as *minutio* or μείωσις and Cicero was a master of this trope. Similarly, comedy often made serious crimes such as theft and rape look less severe; even if their gravity was not questioned, comedy found a way to resolve these delicts without punishing the guilty. In this regard, Roman comedy is the dramatization of *clementia*, a distinctly juridical virtue that refers to the judge's power to suspend the law in the name of justice. That is why Terence's Micio, whom Cicero summons to court as the archetype of the *clemens pater*, is the embodiment of comic justice.[10] And that is why Cicero appeals to comic law. Comedy in the *Pro Caelio* is not just about making the accusations look small, but also about making comic law the sovereign adjudicator.

Cicero's forensic strategy is ingenious. His first task is to trivialize the accusations, to argue that this is not a case that threatens the existence of the republic, but a dramatic plot of a pious son caught in a greedy courtesan's trap. If the severity of the accusations is undermined, the trial is over. It is the *ludi Megalenses* and it is time for comic performances, not courtroom proceedings. Cicero makes this point by giving a comic performance that not only entertains the jurors, but also establishes comedy, with its conventional plots and stock characters, as the legal code under which Caelius' case must be tried.[11] And comic law prevailed during the *Megalensia*. No matter how irrelevant to the actual charges Cicero's histrionics seem, Caelius was acquitted in line with the conventional happy ending of a Roman comedy. The rebuttal of the accusations simultaneously restores the festive spirit of the *Megalensia*. The prosecutors are blocking characters from Plautus or Terence; they are litigious killjoys trapped in Cicero's comedy. They have simply no chance of winning their case.

Cicero virtually transforms the jurors into spectators of a comic show. But it should be noted that the reason why he draws on comedy so effortlessly is because there is significant overlap between Roman comedy and forensic rhetoric. Matthew Leigh (2004a: 315–16, 326–32) argues that comedy and rhetoric devise the same strategies of forgiveness when confronted with the problem of a wayward youth.[12] The members of the jury, like the spectators of a comedy, become complicit in the advocate's successful bid to talk the young Caelius out of a sticky situation (see Geffcken 1973: 7). The forensic orator thus becomes a comic playwright and performer. Cicero resembles not only the lenient father from Roman comedy, but also a cunning slave from Plautus, who creates a comic plot that guarantees that the young lover will have his way without suffering from the consequences of his actions.

Another, related case study of the interactions between law and literature is Terence, who achieves the inverse of Cicero's course in the *Pro Caelio* by transforming the spectators of his comedy into jurors in the prologue to the *Adelphoe* (4 *uos eritis iudices*). As we mentioned above, *iudex* means both judge and literary critic and Terence refers to both here. The prologue defends Terence's work against accusations of plagiarism, and in order to judge the case of plagiarism, a *iudex* needs to be versed in both law and literature, even more so in this case because the verdict of the jury will rely on examining issues of translation and intertextuality, areas more readily associated with literary criticism than legal judgment. The comedy that is about to be performed is introduced as evidence and the spectators need to examine it, in order to decide whether the poet is guilty or not guilty. The prologue concludes by asking the audience to give the play a fair hearing and encourage the author to continue his work (24–5). Far from being passive recipients, the audience, like a jury, has the power to condemn Terence as a playwright, if they find him guilty, or promote his career, if they approve of his comedy. This is not a joke: Terence's livelihood depends on the reception of his plays. Watching a comedy suddenly becomes the equivalent of evaluating evidence in a trial; more than 'an equivalent', it *becomes* a trial. The playwright (Terence) turns the theatre into a courtroom, just as the advocate (Cicero) turns the courtroom into a theatre.

So, the prologue to the *Adelphoe* functions like a defence speech, demonstrating that the *Pro Caelio*'s dynamic interplay between Roman law and the conventions of Roman comedy features already in Terence. The *Eunuchus*' prologue fulfils a similar function as a defence speech against accusations of plagiarism.[13] An old playwright (Terence condemns him to anonymity, but we know that it is Luscius Lanuvinus) got access to a preview performance in front of the aediles, the state officials in charge of public games. The old playwright interrupted the performance by shouting that Terence was a thief (i.e. a plagiarist), not a playwright, but that he would fail to deceive (*Eunuchus* 21–4). The prologue is a response to this accusation: a counterattack on the old playwright and a defence of Terence's work. Not unlike a forensic orator, Terence begins his prologue with a *captatio beneuolentiae*, aiming to flatter the audience and make them share his perspective (cf. Sharrock 2009: 87–8; McGill 2012: 119–20). Cicero employs this rhetorical technique at the beginning of the *Pro Caelio*; in fact, both the *Eunuchus* and the *Pro Caelio* begin with the same words (*si quis*).

In his counterattack, Terence accuses the old playwright of making bad Latin plays out of good Greek models: Luscius' translations were faithful, but his poetry poor. He then accuses him of ruining Menander's original play by not following proper legal procedure:

> atque in Thesauro scripsit causam dicere
> prius unde petitur aurum qua re sit suom
> quam illic qui petit unde is sit thesaurus sibi
> aut unde in patrium monumentum peruenerit.
>
> and in his *Treasure* he represented the defendant as putting his case for the possession of the gold before the plaintiff explained how the treasure belonged to him and how it came to be in his father's tomb. (Loeb translation modified)
>
> Terence, *Eunuchus* 10–13

In a court of law, the plaintiff usually speaks before the defendant. In his comedy, Luscius ignores this rule. Critics note a striking inconsistency in Terence's accusations: Luscius cannot both translate closely and make changes to the plot of the play he is translating (see, e.g., Barsby 1999: 84). However, as Alison Sharrock (2009: 91) points out, this inconsistency only increases the resemblance of Terence's prologue to a court case, in which *argumentatio* involves subtle sleights of hand and precise logic is less important than effective rhetoric. What is more, even though Terence presents his prologue as a defence speech in response to an accusation (6 *responsum*), the audience and readers of the *Eunuchus* do not have a chance to listen to Luscius' speech. We can merely view the accusations of the prosecution through the defence's distorting lens (20–5). In other words, the *Eunuchus* ostentatiously reproduces the fault of which it accuses Luscius. The plaintiff is deprived of his right to speak in the comic courtroom.

The main point is that the comic plot reflects and is reflected in the story of the production of Terence's play; Roman reality and comic fiction blend together. Terence's criticism may look rather pedantic and trivial, but is significant. The prologue highlights the importance of legal conflict in comedy, arguing that the well-designed plot of a play should correspond to proper procedure in a trial. A comic playwright cannot afford to be ignorant of the rituals of law and Luscius' failure to follow judicial procedure in his play seriously undermines the charges he brought against Terence. The plot of comedy should correspond to the plot of a trial and anticipate its outcome. There are transgressions and accusations, and at the end there is a verdict that aims to resolve conflict and restore justice.

While the typical prologue of New Comedy gives an outline of the play's plot, Terence's prologues outline the story of their performance. But one of the striking effects of Terence's prologues is that they still give the impression that they present the outline of a comic plot.[14] Terence and Luscius Lanuvinus correspond to stock characters from Roman comedy: the young man and the grumpy old man. As Sharrock (2009: 89) puts it, a conflict between a young man and an old man, which the young man must win, is a programmatic image for the content of comedy. More specifically, the accusation of theft (*furtum*) resonates with comic plots in which young men, usually with the help of cunning slaves, steal money, often from stern fathers, in order to obtain the object of their desires. Since the word *furtum* may also describe extramarital affairs, it further resonates with the passions of the youth that feature prominently and are prominently condoned in Roman comedy.

Luscius, by contrast, is cast as a blocking character. He is the stern old man, who will not allow our young playwright to succeed and fulfil his desires. He loudly accuses the young poet of attempting to deceive (23–4 *exclamat furem non poetam fabulam/ dedisse, et nil dedisse uerborum tamen*. 'He shouted that the play was the work of a thief, not a playwright, but that the attempt to deceive had not worked' Loeb translation). To deceive (*uerbum dare*) is one of the most distinctive characteristics of Roman comedy. But the point is that the audience takes the sides of those who deceive, not of those who are deceived. In other words, Luscius' accusations are not going to find any supporters in the context of a comic performance. The wordplay between *fabulam dedisse* ('to give a performance of a play') and *dedisse uerborum* ('to deceive') may suggest that Luscius may actually not be such a bad poet. The performance of a *fabula* (the fictitious story of a play) creates a semblance of reality that is essentially deceptive: *fabulam dedisse* is synonymous to *uerba dedisse*. What is more, dramatic deception is associated with truth and wisdom. The Sophist Gorgias famously remarks on dramatic performances that 'he who deceives is more honest than he who does not deceive, and he who is deceived is wiser than he who is not deceived' (Plutarch, *Moralia* 348c). Deception is crucial for establishing the rule of comedy. The successful playwright, like the successful comic hero, is a powerful illusionist, an archetypal trickster.[15] By attacking Terence's ability to deceive, Luscius threatens Terence's existence as a comic playwright.

As a blocking character, the old playwright literally blocks the performance of comedy by interrupting it with his incriminations. He introduces a litigiousness that is the enemy of comic justice. In order for the comic performance to resume, this grumpy old man needs to be expelled from the comic stage. This is precisely what the prologue to the *Eunuchus* does. Terence casts Luscius as a blocking character that undermines the comic spirit, and presents himself as the comic hero who always wins in the end. By weaving together the background story of the play's performance with stock plots and characters from comedy, Terence aims to guarantee the support of the audience/jury.

Luscius also functions as a foil for the members of the audience. His loud interruption of the play's preview shows that audience members of Roman comedy were not restricted to polite passivity. Luscius' shouting (23 *exclamat furem*) contrasts with the prologue's plea to the audience to watch the performance quietly (44 *date operam, cum silentio animum attendite* 'pay attention and listen carefully in silence'). Ironically, by interrupting Terence's play, Luscius enters the comic universe since he is readily stereotyped as a blocking character. By contrast, the prologue's *captatio beneuolentiae* aims to win over the spectators and make them actively support and encourage our poet's work. One way or another, spectators, like jurors, have the power to reward or punish.

In his response to Luscius' accusation, Terence argues that if he committed plagiarism, he did so inadvertently, and this admission, too, has legal ramifications. Terence maintains that his alleged transgression was the outcome of poor practice, not malicious intent; his inexperience should be taken into account. In a trial, the issue of intention (*animus* or *mens*) would be crucial for determining the severity of the crime. Further, Terence declares that if he did indeed commit a theft, this was due to ignorance:

> si id est peccatum, peccatum **imprudentia**st
> poetae, non quo furtum facere studuerit.
>
> If that was an offence, the offence was due to the **inadvertence** of the playwright; he had no intention of committing plagiarism. (Loeb translation)
>
> <div align="right">Terence, <i>Eunuchus</i> 27–8</div>

The key word in this passage is *imprudentia*. In its non-technical sense, it means 'lack of knowledge' or 'absence of intention' (see *OLD* s.v. *imprudentia*), but in its technical sense it means 'want of knowledge of law' (see Berger 1953, s.v. *imprudentia*). In its legalistic sense, lack of knowledge of the law would not be an excuse, unless the person concerned was very young or very inexperienced (see *Digest* 22.6). The jurist Paul states, 'in almost all penal cases, age and ignorance are a defence', trans. Watson (*Digest* 50.17.108 *fere in omnibus poenalibus iudiciis et* **aetati** *et* **imprudentiae** *succurritur*). Of course, the sources of the *Digest* are much later than Terence, but it is still quite striking that Terence's argument here is in line with juristic reasoning. Whether or not Terence was familiar with a version of this legal principle is most likely an unanswerable question, but the main point for our purposes is that the tenets of Roman law seem in this instance to coincide with the 'laws' of Roman comedy: the young should be forgiven due to their inexperience. The conventions of this particular literary form find a parallel in the legal rules designed to regulate social conduct.

Terence's reasoning in the *Eunuchus*' prologue also remains faithful to the spirit of Roman comedy, where law's suspension rather than its enforcement defines the plays' plots and performative context. Just as official legal business is held in abeyance for the duration of the festival, so the comic plot always avoids taking matters to court. Its arbitration scenes typically occur between family members and their primary aim is forgiveness; clemency, not punishment, is the heart of comic justice. So, when Terence asks for forgiveness at the end of his prologue, he is in effect asking for the rule of comedy to be reaffirmed:

> **qua re aequomst** uos cognoscere atque **ignoscere**
> quae ueteres factitarunt si faciunt noui.
>
> **In this case, it is only fair** that you should examine the facts and **pardon** the new playwrights if they do what the old have always done.
>
> Terence, *Eunuchus* 42–3

Terence stages a trial to signal comedy's power to suspend the law. A plea to pardon (*ignoscere*) the young at the end of the prologue corresponds to the typical happy ending of a comedy (see, e.g., Terence, *Heauton Timorumenos* 1045–67; Plautus, *Mostellaria* 1154–9). This forgiveness, which is always granted, is presented as fair and just (*aequomst*) in a performative context that evokes a trial setting that features an advocate, a defendant, a prosecutor and a judge. Terence's *qua re* actually implies the technical meaning of *res* as 'a legal case' or 'a matter at issue in a court of law' (*OLD* s.v. 11). The comic courtroom is in session and we can rest assured that it will rule in favour of the young playwright.

Cicero transforms the courtroom into a theatre, while Terence transforms the theatre into a courtroom. In our view, this is not just a case of one discourse borrowing from another. Does comedy appropriate forensic rhetoric? Does Cicero steal the plots and characters of Roman comedy? Does legal discourse borrow from literature or is it the other way around? The answer is that we are dealing with a chicken and egg situation. Law and literature derive from the same matrix and in the case of drama and courtroom rhetoric, from the same performative matrix, in which actual social roles are interwoven with their theatrical counterparts. The strict father or the wayward youth are stock characters that embody an imaginary *persona*, yet, more often than not, these stock characters are also defined by their relationship to the law: the Roman father is the embodiment of sovereignty, while the young man struggles to free himself from his legally dependent status. The stock characters of the *matrona* ('married woman'), the *uirgo* ('marriageable woman'), and the *meretrix* ('courtesan') are likewise impossible to conceive of without reference to their legal status. But their legal status is also impossible to conceive of without examining the key role of social performance in fleshing out legal *personae*. Literary and legal persons reflect each other; they are originals that are created and reproduced by a narrativity and a performativity that define both juridical and literary discourse.

We can also see in the parallel examples of Cicero and Terence how literature sometimes assumes law's role in settling disputes and regulating moral conduct. Cicero structures his *Pro Caelio* according to the stock characters and rules of Roman comedy not just to entertain jurors who are missing out on the *ludi Megalenses*, nor just to diminish the apparent severity of the prosecution's case, but to produce an actual real-world result in the form of Caelius' acquittal. Comic tropes are not ancillary here; they are fundamental to the jurors' assumptions about the case. True, literature may not have quite the dispositive power as law, but in an example such as the *Pro Caelio* it is hard to say where the distinction lies. Similarly, the prologue to Terence's *Eunuchus* employs a clever combination of *palliata* motifs and legal language to persuade the audience of a particular outcome, namely their favourable reception of the play. Of course, this is not a real trial or a real acquittal, but it is undeniable that the legal and literary confluence in Terence's prologue is aimed at extra-textual results, whether in the form of clearing his name, promoting his play, or – as may have been the case – winning a dramatic competition. His audience of *iudices* certainly appear to have been persuaded and to have taken a positive view of the work: the *Eunuchus* was awarded 8,000 sesterces and allowed an encore performance on the very same day (Suet. *Vit. Ter.* II). Law is not ancillary here, just as Roman comedy is not ancillary in Cicero's *Pro Caelio*, since, by framing his play with this charge of plagiarism, Terence draws his audience's attention to the everyday world lying beyond the fictive one they are about to enter. Imaginative fiction is rendered indistinguishable from the circumstances of its composition, and from the playwright's intent for his production to succeed. For Cicero and Terence, law and literature operate side by side, with powerful results.

* * *

This book is the first edited volume to challenge the disciplinary boundaries between law and literature in Roman Studies. While experts in Roman law and history often discuss law in Latin literature (e.g. Badian 1985; Treggiari 1991) and experts in Latin literature study Roman law (e.g. Kenney 1969; Gebhardt 2009), each group of scholars uses the other group's work as a means to an end. For Romanists and Roman historians, literature is a source of information about the realities of Roman law. In fact, it is sometimes regarded as a necessary evil, given that, although literary texts may include indispensable information about Roman law, historical accuracy is not their primary concern. Literary scholars, on the other hand, tend to treat law's appearance in literature as a literary effect – a trope, a metaphor, or even a consequence of Roman writers' schooling in rhetoric. This book aims to challenge these approaches by inviting scholars of Roman law and Latin literature to consider more meaningful and productive points of contact between legal and literary discourse.

To this end, the book engages with the interdisciplinary field of 'Law and Literature', which, although well-established, is relatively new in Classics. Within this interdisciplinary context, we aim to show how indispensable the Roman world is for Legal Humanities. While excellent studies explore law and literature as force fields of mutual contestation (e.g. Aristodemou 2000; Sarat 2008; Dolin 2007; 2018), they tend also to be broad and eclectic, moving rapidly from discussion of Sophocles' *Antigone* to Shakespeare's *The Merchant of Venice*. The Roman Republic and Empire have been mostly overlooked, despite their being periods of massive tectonic shift in the legal and literary landscape. The discipline of Classics has a lot to contribute to this lively debate about legal and literary interactions but, to date, the topic remains underexplored.

As Klaus Stierstorfer (2018) argues in a recent chapter, this connection between law and the humanities is not a recent invention, but goes back to classical antiquity. It features prominently both in Hesiod, whose poetry revolves around an overlap between poetic and juridical discourse, and in Hebrew cultural history, where the closely allied corpora of *halachah* and *haggada* could be translated as 'law' and 'literature' respectively. In regard to ancient material, it may be more accurate to characterize the study of law and literature as a *revival* of legal humanism. This book aims to contribute to that revival.

Despite such intriguing interactions between law and literature in the ancient world, appreciation of this field in Classics has been limited. It is indicative that in the recent *Oxford Handbook of Roman Law and Society*, there is only one chapter on 'Roman Law and Latin Literature' (Lowrie 2016). The field of law and literature often acknowledges the importance of the ancient Greek world, but rarely invites classicists to contribute to the debate. It is even rarer to find scholarship on Roman law and Latin literature. In a recent volume on *Law and Literature*, there is only one chapter on 'Law and Literature in the Ancient World' (Ziogas 2018), which mostly covers Classical Athens. While recent work by Lowrie (2009a; 2016) and Gunderson (2015a: 85–107) suggests a paradigm shift, such theoretically nuanced approaches still represent a very small portion of classical scholarship. Experts in Roman law rarely engage in constructive dialogue with specialists in Latin literature and vice versa.

This volume aims to bridge that divide and the conference from which it originates showed that the project is timely.[16] The lively dialogue during the production of this volume between experts in Roman law and Latin literature demonstrated that there is a real desire to bring these two worlds together. On the one hand, scholarship on Latin literature is increasingly focusing on the historical, social, and political backgrounds that shape the production of literary works, in contrast with the older trend of studying literature as a closed universe unrelated to historical realities. On the other hand, scholarship on Roman law has recently been emphasizing the fact that legal discourse was not culturally isolated (e.g., Harries 2006, Wibier forthcoming). In other words, literary scholars are eager to examine the importance of law in literature or the juridical nature of Latin literature, while Romanists are ready to embrace the interactions between literary and legal discourse. This volume capitalizes on the right moment to open a fruitful dialogue between scholars of Latin literature and Roman law and thus aims to make a major and much overdue contribution to this interdisciplinary field.

The chapters in the volume are arranged thematically in four parts that cover a broad chronological range – from Naevius and the Twelve Tables (Goldschmidt) to comparisons between US and Roman law on equality and proportionality (Pandey). Part I, 'Literature as Law' opens with Lowrie's chapter ('The Force of Literature'), which argues that stories in Republican Rome assumed a force approximate to law's binding power without its dispositive capacity. Next, Bexley's chapter ('Saturnalian *Lex*: Seneca's *Apocolocyntosis*') examines how Seneca's satire claims the quasi-legal power to judge and punish Claudius. Finally, Biggs ('*Iustitium* in Lucan's *Bellum Ciuile*') studies the importance of the 'suspension of the legal' (*iustitium*) at key textual moments in Lucan's epic, arguing that its occurrence generates a literary as well as juridical zone of indistinction.

Part II, 'Literature and the Legal Tradition', opens with Gaertner ('Terence's *Phormio* and the Legal Discourse and Legal Profession at Rome'), who shows how Terence mocks the authority of legal experts and uses this humour as a defiant act of social correction. Themes of legal exegesis provide links to Dugan ('Beachcombing at the Centumviral Court: Littoral Meaning in the *Causa Curiana*'), who argues that the *Causa Curiana* marks a convergence of legal and literary discourses, effectively becoming an allegory for how readers of all texts generate meaning. Legal expertise is also the focus of the last paper in this section: Wibier ('Marcus Antistius Labeo and the Idea of Legal Literature') examines the work and *nachleben* of this prominent jurist as a case study for the connections between legal and literary learning.

Part III focuses on 'Literature and Property Law'. It begins with Goldschmidt ('Poetry, Prosecution, and the Author Function'), who investigates Foucault's 'author function', which presupposes modern copyright law, against the background of the Roman Republic. For Goldschmidt, dialogues between literature and law contributed to the emergence of an 'author function' in this period. Next, McGinn ('The Sea Common to All in Plautus, *Rudens*: Social Norms and Legal Rules') suggests that the scene between Trachalio and Gripus in the *Rudens* anticipates the Roman legal category of *res communes omnium*, thereby exploiting a concept of public property that owes as much to social norms as to legal strictures. Following on from McGinn, Oksanish ('Intellectual 'Property': Ownership, Possession, and Judgment among Civic *Artes*') takes Roman law's distinction between title and possession, and its mechanisms for property transfer, as points of departure to show how these principles undergird arguments over disciplinarity and civic influence in Cicero and Vitruvius. Rounding out Part III, Gunderson ('Seneca's Debt: Property, Self-Possession, and the Economy of Philosophical Exchange in the *Epistulae Morales*') shows how Seneca challenges the law's supreme position as a master discourse. The literary work of the *Letters* teaches the reader how to transition away from everyday legalisms and towards higher concepts.

In Part IV, 'Literature and Justice', Alekou ('Law in Disguise in the *Metamorphoses*: The Ambiguous *Ecphraseis* of Minerva and Arachne') focuses on the weaving competition in Ovid's *Metamorphoses* 6, arguing that it evokes a trial setting in which the tapestries embody the literary re-enactment of a quasi-legal spectacle, and the episode overall becomes a critique of legal injustice. The volume's final paper (Pandey 'What the Roman Constitution Means to Me: Staging Encounters between US and Roman Law on Equality and Proportionality') is inspired by Lowrie's chapter which explores a broad definition of Rome's unwritten constitution. Pandey offers a comparative analysis of Roman and

American law and discourse regarding enfranchisement and advancement across race and gender, with a focus on statutes and stories that assign some groups lesser value than others. Pandey asks whether law accretes prior uses and interpretations, as reception theorists argue for literature, and discusses how laws that embed histories of oppression can still be tools for social justice.

The scope and themes of the volume revolve around the quintessentially normative nature of Latin literature vis-à-vis the literary character of Roman law. We examine the interactions between legal texts (e.g. laws, edicts, statutes, courtroom speeches, *responsa* of jurists) and literary works (e.g. comedy, epic, satire, letters). The chapters engage with legal and literary theory, the philosophy of law, and the history of Roman law and literature. Thematic connections include law and authoritative power (Biggs, Oksanish, Gunderson, Goldschmidt, Alekou); storytelling between law and literature (Lowrie, Dugan, Pandey); constructions of sovereignty (Biggs, Bexley, Gunderson); law in comedy (Gaertner, McGinn, Pandey); the jurists between law and literature (McGinn, Wibier, Dugan, Gaertner); legal and literary forms of interpretation (Dugan, Oksanish, Pandey) and the potentially literary origins of Roman legal concepts (Lowrie, Goldschmidt, McGinn).

Stories, plots, and myths that are crystallized in literary media not only have the force of law, but also influence laws and statutes. In the absence of a codified Roman constitution, storytelling, especially narratives of exemplarity, played an active role in shaping concepts of legality (Lowrie). Literature comes before the law both in the sense that it anticipates the law and in the fact that it is subjected to the law. It is literature's position as simultaneously inside and outside the juridical order that endows it with sovereign authority.

Latin literature often advertises its distance from the litigious world of the *forum*. From Plautus' comedies and Ovid's love poetry to Lucan's *Bellum Ciuile* and Seneca's *Apocolocyntosis*, the suspension of the juridical order is a prerequisite for the production of dramatic, poetic, and satiric performances. Literature thrives in a 'state of exception' (Agamben 2005a), in order to establish its alternative, often utopian, jurisdiction. Drawing on Giorgio Agamben, two papers in the volume (Bexley, Biggs) examine the ways in which authors pronounce a legal standstill and thus appropriate the power of the sovereign legislator. For Gaertner, the humour of Roman comedy can be interpreted along Freudian lines as a defiant act of independence or sovereignty. Similarly, Gunderson argues that Seneca presents philosophical self-emancipation as a sovereign suspension of the institutions of human law.

Literature's claim to sovereign legislative powers often goes hand in hand with its attempt to give voice to marginalized groups and subvert gender dynamics. It is not a coincidence that courtesans, slaves and other legally disabled groups are given legal rights in Latin literature. Our volume focuses on Latin literature's attempt to legally empower the outcasts (Alekou, Pandey). This move is more often than not related to debating and revising property laws (slaves), rights of citizenship (foreigners, women, slaves), and rights of marriage (foreigners, courtesans). Literature, like law, applies precedent in order to expand the horizons of legality and thus create a more just and inclusive society. From that perspective, literature is not unlike law – the projection of an imagined future upon reality (cf. Cover 1986: 1064).

Notes

1. Ward (1995) 3–27; Fortier (2019) 3–11.
2. On injurious speech, see Butler (1997) 43–70. On the law as speech that can injure, see Cover (1986).
3. Lowrie (2009a), Part IV 'Reading and the Law' is important.
4. In Roman law, *auctor* describes a guarantor who approves the transference of property.
5. See Dolin (2007) 6–9 for a fine discussion of the importance of boundaries in law and literature. Law attempts to create, police and occasionally transgress social, spatial and temporal boundaries; see Sarat et al. (1998) 3–4. Literature, like law, depends on internal and external boundaries for its identity and its everyday functioning. Yet these boundaries are made to be transgressed.
6. See Wibier (2020) who argues convincingly that quoting Homer in the context of economic exchanges was widely practised in the juristic tradition.
7. See also Wibier (in this volume) on poetry in juristic debate.
8. On the importance of Roman comedy in the *Pro Caelio*, see Geffcken (1973); Leigh (2004a). Also Goldberg (2005) 87–97, who discusses the role of comedy, tragedy and other dramatic genres in Cicero. On comedy in Cicero: Karakasis (2014) and Polt (2021) 45–69. Batstone (2009) 218–19 argues that Cicero reconstructs a question of fact as a question of representation and, in so doing, reconstructs a legal case as a comic drama. Hanses (2020) 130–55 examines comedy, tragedy and mime in the *Pro Caelio*.
9. Leigh (2004a) argues that comedy sets limits and establishes fundamental generic controls to unruly behaviour. This is indeed what the genre does, but note that comedy often pardons serious crimes, such as the rape of a freeborn citizen.

Comedy's power to understate the consequences of criminal acts may be greater, and more problematic and controversial, than what Leigh suggests. It is precisely this understatement of serious crimes that serves Cicero well in the *Pro Caelio*.

10 Cf. Terence, *Adelphoe* 42–3 *ego hanc **clementem** uitam . . . secutu' sum*.
11 According to Hanses (2020) 145–6, Cicero highlights that Caelius' life follows the pattern of the *adulescens* from Roman comedy, which foresees that the young man will eventually move on from his comedic lifestyle. Hanses rightly adds, 'if the jurors accept this superimposition of a comedic structure onto Caelius's life . . . they also have to accept that according to the rules of Roman comedy, the defendant has to be acquitted.'
12 On Roman comedy and oratory, see also Sharrock (2009) 83–93.
13 On plagiarism in Latin literature, see McGill (2012), especially Chapter 4, which deals with Terence, and Goldschmidt (in this volume).
14 Sharrock (2009) 87–92 is important. See also Gunderson (2015a) 55–79. They both focus on Plautus, though Terence deserves more attention.
15 On the importance of deception in Roman comedy, see Sharrock (1996).
16 The volume originates in an international conference on 'Roman Law and Latin Literature' (Durham, 2–4 September 2019).

Part One

Literature as Law

2

The Force of Literature

Michèle Lowrie

To say something has the force of law presumes the law has the ability to get things done, to create realities. It also presumes that law grants legitimacy to the exercise of force in the sense of violence by an authorized agent of the state. Something only has the force *of* law if it is not in fact law, so whatever force it may have is understood to be analogous to or parasitic on the law's force. My title, 'the force of literature', calques 'force of law' and thereby hints that literature is among those things of which we may say – or might want to say, but hold back from saying – that it has the force of law. This volume is devoted to outlining the contours of the ambivalent relationship between Roman law and Latin literature as each other's opposites, analogues and sometimes twins. Beyond such ambivalence, my title primarily asserts that literature has its own force. Both law and literature may sit inertly on the page or spring to life through performative enforcement or enactment. But literature plays a role in shaping and transmitting the political imagination independent of law's dispositive force. An essential difference is that law should provide stability, while literature drives toward conflicted interpretation.

Life and death

In the classical period, Latin had no word for what moderns call literature. *Litteratura* meant writing or the science of language in the sense of grammar or philology. Closer is the plural, *litterae*, a collective body of verbal compositions recorded in writing, but the social institution such writings participate in lacked a name. Cicero reaches for some equivalent category when he claims his adolescent readings instructed him in politics.

> Sed pleni omnes sunt libri, plenae sapientium uoces, plena exemplorum uetustas: quae iacerent in tenebris omnia, nisi litterarum lumen accederet. Quam multas

nobis imagines – non solum ad intuendum, uerum etiam ad imitandum – fortissimorum uirorum expressas scriptores et Graeci et Latini reliquerunt? Quas ego mihi semper in administranda re publica proponens animum et mentem meam ipsa cognitatione hominum excellentium conformabam.

But books, the words of wise men, and antiquity are all full of examples, which would all lie in the shadows unless the light of letters were added. How many images of the bravest men, expressed not only for contemplation but also for imitation, have authors both Greek and Roman left behind! By bringing these images before me in administering public affairs, I used to mould my mind and spirit in accord with my thinking about the most excellent men.[1]

Cicero, Pro Archia 14

The listed terms – *books*, consisting of *letters*, written by *writers*, and the *words* of the wise – define a literary sphere formally. Stress on the normative weight such writings and words bear identifies their social function. Their didactic value derives from their transmitted content: they are a repository of images from antiquity of excellent men earning praise for acting honourably, whose *exempla* embody socio-political and, I argue, even legal norms. That Cicero moulds himself according to these men's model turns what might otherwise be idle words into a socio-political space whose dynamism finds grammatical expression in a gerundive: *in administranda re publica*. He instantiates Bonnie Honig's stress on the importance of stories to politics: 'As is so often the case in democratic politics, how we tell the story matters a great deal. It also matters what stories we tell.'[2] Cicero's letters bring examples into light; he enacts these performatively: his moulded spirit directs political action according to transmitted norms. Cicero presents a rosy picture of unity in the tradition and in the application of principles excellent men represent.

This passage instantiates several constitutive contrasts, parallels, and pairings: speech and writing, form and content – more precisely medium and transmitted norm – past and present, contemplation and action. Words – speech and writing taken together – share a mediating function. The performative re-enactment in politics of transmitted norms reanimates models from antiquity recuperated through contemplating what letters bring to light.

The passage's first sentence specifies a crucial aspect of this literary sphere's role in politics: letters are a matter of life and death. Cicero refers to his quelling the Catilinarian conspiracy as consul in the previous year. His facing down attempted assassination and willingness to throw his person into struggle depend on what he learned from reading. Although moderns often poo-poo

Cicero's boasting, we should never forget the extraordinary violence of Roman politics in this period. Cicero in fact underwent exile a few years later and was assassinated twenty years after his consulship. He faced, he says, bodily torture in the pursuit of praise and honour, which led him to fight *pro salute uestra*, 'for your safety and wellbeing,' where 'your' means the Roman people, at risk of his own life. Cicero highlights his defence of what he later identifies as the highest constitutional norm: *salus populi suprema lex esto* ('let the people's safety be the highest law', *Leg.* 3.8). Without literature's persuasive force, Cicero suggests he might not have obeyed the call to enforce this legal mandate during his consulship. Doing so risked his life and inflicted capital punishment on others.

I aim to show how Latin 'precepts and letters', to use Cicero's phrase, played a constitutional role in ancient Rome. They filled a hole in Republican Rome's famously unwritten constitution – not just because they were written. They transmitted norms, among only functions, and were not the only institution to do so – law being another – but without the medium, the exemplary message could not go through. Roman law and Latin literature both responded dynamically to politics on the ground. Literature served as no static repository of timeless images, stories, or norms. It continually updated constitutional processes. After reviewing elasticity in the Republican constitution, I analyse literature's role in transmitting norms, and finally show that during the Catilinarian conspiracy, stories – as much as, perhaps more than, law – supplied the authority backing the constitutional norms Cicero enforced. Furthermore, the processes used against the Catilinarians and during parallel political crises changed the constitution, with the result that subsequent literary texts, specifically Livy's history, updated stories to reflect the changes and thereby provided a new constitutional template, if not a constitution per se.

Constitution

The lack of codification, namely systematic arrangement, in the Roman Republican constitution and the absence of a central document recording such a system are not the same thing, although writing is certainly a potent tool for giving stability to systems. The lack of either codification or writing hardly means no constitution existed at Rome, but it does mean their constitution, like any oral tradition, was fluid[3] – not to say chaotic. Even written constitutions admit of flexibility, not only in being subject to formal amendment, but in requiring interpretation. In Cicero's *De re publica*, Cato's judgment of the superiority of the Roman constitution to those founded at one time, by one founder attests to its organic growth, in response to historical events. Unlike the constitution of the single *nomothetes* who 'had equipped his state with laws and institutions' (*rem publicam constituisset legibus atque institutis suis*, *Rep.* 2.2), apparently *ex nihilo*, Cicero's account of the Roman constitution depicts a constitution determined not by laws, but rather the progressive standardization of institutions following upon political determinations. He identifies the auspices and the senate, for example, as Romulus' 'founding-stone' contributions to the 'republic' – *firmamenta rei publicae* (*Leg.* 2.17). In both Cicero and Livy, the law follows a living constitution rather than vice versa.

Such dynamism leaves open a space for literature or at least a literary sphere. In *The Constitution of the Roman Republic*, Andrew Lintott makes a remarkable claim:

> The constitution of the Republic consisted of far more than statutes: it was based on traditional institutions defined by precedents and examples. These were above all embodied in stories, whether these related to more recent events and had good claims to historicity or were reconstructions of distant events with a strong element of myth.[4]

It is hard to imagine a constitutional lawyer saying something similar about a modern constitution. The Roman Republican constitution rested on stories beyond law in that they provided precedents and examples, which defined the traditional institutions that paralleled and reinforced statute. Like the books that educated Cicero, like the poetry to which Horace attributes a utilitarian as well as an aesthetic function (*Ars poetica* 99–100, 343–4), these stories serve a didactic purpose, to undergird the traditions grounding the institutions on which the Republic was constituted.

The stories recording precedents and examples were transmitted by oral tradition and in writing. Scipio in the *Somnium Scipionis* (*Rep.* 6.23) assumes children hear the praise of the past from their fathers. Cicero could have read such stories in epic and history: Ennius' *Annales*, Cato's *Origines*, and Hostius' *Bellum Histricum* among numerous others, mostly lost. In Augustan times, Vergil's *Aeneid* fills in Rome's prehistory. Mytho-historical tales crop up also in genres further afield, such as elegy (Propertius' Tarpeia poem, 4.4) and lyric (Horace's Regulus ode, 3.3; Hannibal's long speech in *Odes* 4.4). The large body of tales told by Livy, that is, in historiography, and in collections gathered for rhetorical use, such as Valerius Maximus, assemble them in one place. That such stories are transmitted through verse and in highly aestheticized genres hardly impedes their constitutional importance, provided they define and transmit the necessary norms.

Lintott's inclusion of myth beyond history as material for precedents and examples recognizes the irrelevance of facticity as a criterion for setting norms. Quintilian's definition of the *exemplum* similarly discards a cited deed's need to have actually occurred:

> quod proprie uocamus exemplum, id est rei gestae aut ut gestae utilis ad persuadendum id quod intenderis commemoratio.
>
> what we properly call an *exemplum*, that is, the narrative recollection of a deed done, or *as if done*, that is useful for persuading what you intend.
>
> *Institutio oratoria* 5.11.6

The *exemplum* pertains to the speaker's argument, provided it conveys some higher truth. Latin calls this higher truth not *ueritas*, but *ius*.[5] Unlike modernity, where fiction is one predominant criterion for classifying a verbally crafted artefact as 'literature,' much of Latin literature does not look 'literary' by this standard. Even Horace's *Odes*, spoken in the first person by a historical author to historical addressees, qualify neither as fiction, however many layers of ventriloquism, persona, or implied author intervene, nor as fact or non-fiction, because poetic communication occurs via extra-ordinary language.[6] The Romans felt more comfortable assigning a didactic function to literature than post-Romantic moderns. Although Horace's *Ars poetica* does not identify poetry's utility beyond warning (*monendo*, 344), its didactic function is clear. Furthermore, he understands poetry to have some pragmatic force. It should lead the listener's spirit (*animum auditoris agunto*, 100) in a way that corresponds well to Cicero's statement in the *Pro Archia* that he formed his spirit by reading exemplary stories. These guided his administration of the state according to a constitutional norm, namely *salus populi*.

Not all stories providing a basis for the Roman constitution concern the form of government, but there are many such. Livy's account of how Brutus, among others, expelled the tyrannical Tarquins and founded the Roman Republic is a good example: the new institution breaks up kingly power by dividing it between two consuls and establishing term limits (2.1). Further stories narrate foundational rights and institutional structures, e.g., how the right to appeal and the establishment of the tribunate provided the political solution to the first secession of the plebs (2.32); how law was established at Rome by the decemvirs who wrote the Twelve Tables (3.34), and so on.[7] These aetiological stories not only tell the history of origins, but also have a kind of force: the description defines those institutions, often better or at least more fully than descriptions attested elsewhere, however much historians quibble about details.[8] This may be all Lintott means: stories provide a record of institutions and their processes.

I would press stories' constitutional function further. The language Cicero uses to characterize Scipio's history of early Roman institutions in *De re publica* 2 suggests his narrative inches closer to a codified constitution – without being one – than the mere transmission of past events. To quote Laelius, Scipio is to reduce 'to a reasoned account the things that Romulus did by chance or necessity' (*ad rationem quae a Romulo casu aut necessitate facta sunt*, *Rep.* 2.22). Scipio reasons about the institutions whose origins he narrates with commentary and evaluation. Commentary and interpretation belong as much to law broadly defined as formal statute. The debate and commentary in the Talmud, for example, belong as much to Jewish law as the Torah's precepts. Similarly, dissenting opinions published by the American Supreme Court do not create binding precedent or become part of case law, but have authority, namely, a kind of legal force. In Latin, the commentary in the *Digest* belongs to Roman law without bearing the dispositive force of statute. The constitutional weight of stories surpasses the formal description of institutions in that they transmit norms.

What is a constitution? Merriam-Webster's dictionary definition reveals it is no one thing.[9]

> 1a: the basic principles and laws of a nation, state, or social group that determine the powers and duties of the government and guarantee certain rights to the people in it.
>
> 1b: a written instrument embodying the rules of a political or social organization.
>
> 2a: the physical makeup of the individual especially with respect to the health, strength, and appearance of the body: "a hearty constitution."
>
> 2b: the structure, composition, physical makeup, or nature of something: "the *constitution* of society."
>
> 3: the mode in which a state or society is organized especially: the manner in which sovereign power is distributed.
>
> 4: an established law or custom: ordinance.
>
> 5: the act of establishing, making, or setting up: "before the *constitution* of civil laws."[10]

This list is hierarchical: principles come before laws; the powers and duties of a government and the rights of the people precede the written instrument; a strong sense of embodiment, whether of a person or a corporate body, inheres in the concept; only then come organization, established law and custom, and last, establishment as a foundational act. To avert confusion, scholars should specify which type of constitution they mean.

The study of the Roman constitution has since Mommsen traditionally entailed compiling lists of public law statutes, providing schemata of assemblies and offices and assessing the powers of particular magistracies.[11] Such scholarship has focused on the shape of governmental structures and Lintott's book provides an accessible modern synthesis in English. These structures determine the 'mode' or 'manner' of organization of Merriam-Webster's section 3. They follow in a tradition started by Plato, developed in Aristotle and Polybius, of 'descriptive constitutionalism.'[12] Aristotle's definition of *politeia* begins by describing a form:

> A constitution (*politeia*) is the arrangement (*taxis*) of magistracies in a state (*polis*), especially of the highest of all.
>
> *Pol.* 3.1278b 9–15

Thomas Wiedemann has stressed, however, that while Greek constitutional thought from Aristotle to Polybius prioritizes the form of constitutions (kingship, oligarchy, democracy, their perversions, or mixed constitution), the Romans concentrated more on power and norms,[13] that is, Merriam-Webster's 1a. This tendency is no exclusive dichotomy. Aristotle continues by defining government (*politeuma*), for instance, according to the location of sovereignty, a question of power; his examples are in the people (democracy) or the few (oligarchy). And Cicero's *De legibus* (3.6–11), one of few interventions in political theory in Latin, documents the formal organization of republican order with the names, powers, and duties of the magistracies.

Benjamin Straumann's recent analysis of Roman Republican constitutionalism shifts the focus away from governmental shape to the determination and application of norms.[14] In substance, the highest norm, for Cicero, is protection of the *salus populi*, before whose imperative Romans in the Late Republic became creative about legal process. The source of such norms is *ius*, particularly, again for Cicero, natural law. I submit that the reason why the Roman Republican constitution rested, according to Lintott's formulation, on stories beyond statute is threefold. 1) Stories offered a potent medium for the definition of *ius*, constitutional norms in Straumann's sense. 2) As Lintott says, they transmitted the precedents and examples that defined institutions, what Latin calls the *mos maiorum* (customs of the ancestors). 3) Stories define institutions not abstractly, but through concrete, embodied instances, according to the preference of Roman political thought.[15] It follows that their constitution rests in part not on abstract definition, but on records of examples showing the pragmatic application of principle.

The legal categories most central for the republican constitution are *mos* and *ius*, much more than *lex*. Just as modern 'literature' does not map neatly onto the broad sphere of Latin *litterae*, Roman law exceeds statute. The breadth of both spheres, law and literature, allows for surprising overlap viewed from the perspective of modern constitutional thinking.

Of the words that can be translated into English as 'law,' Latin distinguishes between *scitum* (statute, ordinance, decree, act, *Gesetz*, *loi*), *consultum* (decree), *lex* (statute narrowly understood, but also law conceived in its broadest sense), and *ius* (right, justice, legal power or authority, *Recht*, *droit*, *justice*). *Ius* can mean the justice system, as when one 'goes before the law' or 'calls someone before the law' (*ire/uocare in ius*), but its basic meaning, 'what is right or just,' broadens the law's scope to the normative system that provides the standard against which to judge the legitimacy of statute or decree, which could otherwise be unjust. Cicero insists that *lex* is not merely a *scitum* (Marcus), nor does it depend on writing (Quintus).

> **Marcus**   ...legem neque hominum ingeniis excogitatam, nec scitum aliquod esse populorum, sed aeternum quiddam, quod uniuersum mundum regeret imperandi prohibendique sapientia....
>
> **Quintus**   Adsentior frater, ut quod est rectum uerumque, <aeternum quoque>[16] sit neque cum litteris, quibus scita scribuntur, aut oriatur aut occidat.
>
> **Marcus**   Law has not been thought out by the minds of men nor is it some statute of peoples, but something eternal, which rules the whole world through the wisdom of ordering and prohibiting....
>
> **Quintus**   I agree, brother, that what is right and true is eternal and does not arise nor fall with the letters with which statutes are written.
>
> *De legibus* 2.8, 11

Cicero names the law's broader sphere *ius naturale*. Although this phrase is conventionally translated as 'natural law,' its meaning is less reified in Latin than the English: a better translation would be 'what is naturally just or right,' that is, what everyone by virtue of being human senses to be just. Cicero adds the Stoic qualification 'according to reason'. Natural for Cicero typically means universally conventional or social, rather than rooted in either biology or in a transcendent conception of the divine. The divine mind that is the source of natural law in *De legibus* is synonymous with reason, a universal human faculty given by and shared with a god conceived as part of the world rather than existing apart from it. Just as the semantic field of literature is not confined to the aesthetic, but encompasses utility, the semantic field of law surpasses formal statute or decree (*scitum* and *consultum*). Both spheres encompass what is normatively right. The stories guide the application of principle pragmatically, especially when interpretation is conflicted.

Form and norm, *ius* and *mos*

Latin letters fill in, to some extent, for the missing Republican Roman 'written instrument embodying the rules of a political organization' (Merriam-Webster's 1b). On the formal level, they supply a written record of institutions and process, but more dynamically, they transmit norms. The norm has priority over process and therefore outweighs any pre-existing record. This spawns revisions in the stories that appear to falsify history, judged by a standard of truth. Recognizing the constitutional weight of story-telling, however, lets us appreciate revisionism according to a different measure. Law and literature both operated responsively in this period, more like oral tradition than fixed document.

A poet provides the earliest and most economical instance of constitutional thinking: Ennius' line *moribus antiquis res stat Romana uirisque* (the Roman state stands on ancient customs and men, *Annales* 156 Sk). Our 'constitution' derives from the verb used here: *stare*. All of the *-stituere* compounds entail making something stand. The *con-* prefix implies togetherness. The verb *constituere* means to make stand, to set up, to establish, and the noun *constitutio* means, among other things, the established arrangement of a state or a set of principles.[17] According to it, a society stands together. Law may be missing here, however, Ennius' description of the 'faithful friend' closely conjoins knowledge of custom and law as pillars on which his capacity for prudence rests.[18] Custom may not be synonymous with law, but points to it. Ennius is less interested in constitutional form than in enactment. The conjunction of 'customs' with 'men' conceptualizes constitution as a shared and embodied performance of politics. Individuals continually reenact and thereby transmit and reinforce ancient customs honed through practice.

Aristocratic agents who grew up in the system lived and breathed their constitution without needing to study a written record. They learned received process, how best to argue in court and before political bodies, the shape and powers of the magistracies, and the limits on these powers through the *tirocinium fori*, that is, via apprenticeship rather than book learning. An occasional, brilliant new man – Cato, Cicero – broke into the club, but success was rare. It therefore makes sense that it was one of these new men who composed a pair of texts that comes closest to recording the Roman Republican constitution and thereby made it more accessible. If Ennius describes how the system worked, Cicero's *De re publica* and *De legibus*, as Elizabeth Asmis has suggested, approximates the constitution itself.[19] Scipio's narrative and commentary in *De republica* book two records and transmits institutions and laws and *De legibus* book three enumerates offices and their respective powers. These descriptions do not have the force of law, but they do have a kind of force. In a continually re-enacted constitution based on performance, a description in a literary medium, especially by a respected author, has the power to shape the understanding of the elite readers who were these dialogues' audience.

Even in a robustly codified constitutional system, literature brushes up against law.[20] It is a question of how much and how. In the Roman republican constitution, where right prevailed over legal form, Cicero's approximations still lack the force of law. His texts – like all literature – are neither legislative bodies nor participate in a legislative body with the authority to pass statute. Their job is one of political imagination: they think up and give form to what the constitution is at that moment, but also to what it could be. Beyond substantive work, they invite contemplation on the affordances and limitations of literature's discursive force. *De legibus*, for instance, creates productive ambivalence about its own degree of performative power. Cicero's speaker Marcus playfully adopts the role of the lawgiver. His use of legal style skirts the grey zone between legally dispositive language (statute) and fiction (literature in its strongest, modern sense), precisely the overlap this volume explores. Given the potential confusion in textual transmission, Marcus may give a mere *descriptio* (description) or a performative *discriptio* (distribution or assignment) of the magistrates' powers and duties.[21]

> **Quintus** Quam breui frater in conspectu posita est a te omnium magistratuum descriptio/discriptio, sed ea paene nostrae ciuitatis, etsi a te paulum adlatum est noui.
>
> How succinctly, brother, have you placed before our eyes a description/ assignment of all the magistracies, but this is almost that of our city, although you've added a few new things.
>
> *De legibus* 3.12.2

This textual indeterminacy is symptomatic of ambivalences in performative force. *Descriptio* would keep his textual speech act this side of 'inert' fiction, *discriptio* would tilt toward the force of law. Marcus' ventriloquism of the lawgiver similarly produces another productive ambivalence. *He* has set the dialogue's notional law code[22] and his invitation to his interlocutors at the passage's end to depart and vote on his law likewise flags the text's status between law and literature.[23] Is the gesture playfully imitative without performative force or does it seriously imagine that Cicero's code could be made dispositive?[24] The code's simultaneous accord and slight non-accord with the actual assignment of powers and duties of magistracies at Rome keeps the text in a liminal discursive place. If Quintus uses *discriptio*, the thought experiment is potentially transformative; the writing of new laws intimates their possible enactment.[25] Constitutions need to be imagined before they can be instituted.

If legal force is limited to statute, the enactment of Cicero's constitution as described in these texts would depend on his authority to bring law before a formal legislative body and on his actually doing so, but since the Republic's constitution was never formally enacted, but grew organically and was furthermore based on stories as well as statute, it then becomes hard to exclude the stories told in these texts from having some kind of force. For instance, the senate maintains its power on the authority vested in the story of Romulus' establishment of it. The question becomes what kind of authority lies behind the stories that undergird the institutions of the state. Does this authority lie in any concrete narration of the story, such as the one Scipio tells in *De re publica*, or only in the story as an abstract cultural given? Is Scipio's version only parasitic on some potent ur-story? If so, then how could scholars retrieve the ur-story, lost in the mists of oral tradition? If Scipio's version has its own authority, then how dispositive is it? These questions circle around the problems of performative discourse Jacques Derrida outlines in his seminal article, 'Signature, évènement, contexte,' where the actual source of authority behind performative language remains potent, but always seems to reside elsewhere.[26]

A further problem is that authority bears stylistic markers, which, being imitable, can be deployed in literature without having dispositive force. The legal style Cicero uses for his description/assignment of functions, with its frequent future imperatives (*esto, sunto, redeunto*), also skirts the grey zone between citation and performative discourse. Legal style conveys authority. For pontifical law, Cicero 'will propose laws in the voice of the laws'[27]; the *legum uerba* are not as antique as those of the Twelve Tables, but a bit older than ordinary, quotidian language.[28] What kind of authority does Cicero reach for? Given the constitution's lack of formal codification or enactment, it is hard to pin down the exact place on the spectrum where authority passes from merely citational to actual.

It is tempting to dismiss the legal style in *De legibus* and Marcus' adoption of the voice of the laws as a playful literary game. What makes this game more serious is first, the strong role of natural law in both *De re publica* and *De legibus*, and second, the actual role stories played in justifying capital cases. In his explanation of natural law's role in the Roman Republican constitution, Straumann stresses the distinction between *ius* and *lex* and that when *ius* conflicts with statutory law, it 'assumes the rank of a source of superior constitutional norms' that 'win out over statutory law'.[29] What is right according to natural law, especially safeguarding *salus populi*, prevails over formal process. Actions taken under the legitimating authority of extraordinary offices (dictatorship, master of the horse) and decrees (*senatus consultum ultimum*, senate's ultimate decree), which were used to address emergencies where ordinary process was felt to grant insufficient power, had to meet the standard of a higher norm, *ius*, namely what is right judged according to reason. When Cicero and others say the Gracchi were killed *iure*, Straumann to my mind goes too far in translating 'constitutionally' rather than merely 'rightly'. Given the lack of a codified constitution, injecting such legally formal language into Latin conveys an impression of greater notional stability than warranted. To unpack his shortcut, I suggest, 'in accord with higher constitutional norms,' when the context suggests that these contravene statute. A higher order legal sphere steps in when mere law fails. Cicero's argument for natural law in his political theoretical works is no merely theoretical exercise, but explains and justifies how Roman politics actually worked.

As for stories, in the spirit of Roman political thought, let us consider an example.

Constitutional revisionism

In Cicero's first Catilinarian oration to the senate, he recommends putting Catiline to death on the basis of constitutional norms.[30] His legal ground consists of not statute, but a list of *exempla* and an extraordinary decree, the *senatus consultum ultimum* (ultimate decree of the senate = SCU), bearing the force of law (*Cat.* 1.3-4).[31] The precedents of Tiberius Gracchus, Spurius Maelius, Gaius Gracchus and Marcus Fulvius, Saturninus and Gaius Servilius (*Cat.* 1.3-4) fit a pattern: populist overreach with tyrannical ambition. Cicero assumes his audience's cultural knowledge. Naming, a mere hint of narrative, activates recognition of the story each senator had heard from his father – as Scipio

Africanus avers in the *Somnium Scipionis* (*Rep.* 6.23) – or read in lost histories. The *exemplum* of Gaius Gracchus bears especial weight, because the SCU was a legal innovation that authorized putting him to death. The decree and the precedents together countervail normal constitutional process, namely the right to appeal and to a trial before the people. The familiarity and normative weight of the *exempla* diffuse the extraordinary nature of the decree.

Letters, in one form or another, validate the senate's decision. In the end, they reached consensus and voted to condemn the Catilinarians to death because Cicero had the good fortune to produce the smoking gun of incriminating letters written by Catiline's associates.[32] While the documents provide convincing evidence of the fact of conspiracy,[33] the stories articulate both a political framework for adjudication and the norms that legitimate the senate's decision.

The first *Catilinarian* highlights a performative problem: the SCU, which charges the consuls, including Cicero, to see to it that the state receive no harm, is inert. It is 'closed up in tablets, as if hidden in a sheath' (*inclusum in tabulis uelut in uagina reconditum, Cat.* 1.4). The metaphorical sword has no force because it is stuck in writing. Cicero accuses himself of inertia. According to Ennius' formulation, the stories make the *mos maiorum* clear, but the second half of the equation, the *uir* – in this instance Cicero – is needed to keep the state standing by putting the SCU into use. We can be confident of the influence of Ennius' model on Cicero because he is, in fact, the primary ancient source for the archaic Latin poet's hexameter, which his speaker Scipio quotes at the beginning of *De re publica* book 5. Scipio, whose own cousin Scipio Nasica killed Tiberius Gracchus, laments already in the dialogue's dramatic setting (129 BCE, after Tiberius' but before Gaius' death) that the *mos maiorum* has become obsolete through oblivion and the lack of upstanding men (*Rep.* 5.1–2). Writing in the mid-50's, Cicero puts himself in the same rank as Scipio Nasica, among others, who had 'saved' the state (*Rep.* 1.6), with significant overlap of the heroes who stopped the villains listed at the beginning of the first *Catilinarian*. The historical layering in both dialogue and speech spells out the *mores* to be enacted. Psyching himself up to act accordingly in the speech, Cicero demonstrates the process, conveyed abstractly in the dialogue's citation of Ennius, by which a man brings to life the norms, encoded in the stories, that justify taking the legal remedy out of its sheath.

Literature, at the margins of law, steps in to articulate norms where exceptional challenges strain ordinary process. Cicero's *exempla* at *Cat.* 1.3–4 all entail extraordinary crises, whose political solutions laid strict interpretation of legal process aside before a higher norm.[34] For the Catilinarians, the SCU was the political measure that legitimated the senate's arrogation of decision-making and the consuls' execution of their will, given the absence of trial before the people. There is no intimation in our sources that the form of these measures lacked legitimacy. The personal nature of Clodius' attack on Cicero, which resulted in his being exiled for putting citizens to death without trial, is generally viewed as disqualifying his arguments.[35] In a contest between political expediency and formal process, traditional stories, especially amassed in a weighty list, put meat on the bare articulation of principle.

The differing legal and political contexts of the deaths of Cicero's catalogue of transgressors reveal that, despite the fact that the consuls were authorized by the same decree to counter Gaius Gracchus, Saturninus, and Catiline, the *senatus consultum ultimum* was no privileged means for coping with crisis. The formula typically identified with the SCU, *ne quid res publica detrimenti caperet* ('that the state receive no harm'), articulates the norm underlying all the cases, even where the SCU was not used, namely, *salus populi*. For Spurius Maelius, dictatorship was responsible for enforcement. The circumstances of Tiberius Gracchus' assassination by the *pontifex maximus*, acting as *priuatus* outside political office, set the case on sufficiently shaky constitutional ground that his brother Gaius Gracchus passed a statute, the *lex Sempronia de capite ciuis*, reaffirming that no Roman citizen should be put to death without trial, to prevent a repeat occurrence. The senate, ever creative, invented the SCU as a legal workaround against him. The fact that the norm's executors, Scipio Nasica, Cicero, *et al.* faced their day in court and endured exile because of their actions, even if in the end they were recalled, shows that the extraordinary measures were vulnerable to legal challenge.[36] Their actions had to face adjudication, but in every case, the constitutional norm prevailed over strict law.

Cicero's treatment of the Maelius story, set in *praeteritio* as *nimis antiqua* (*Cat.* 1.3), demonstrates that his stories' normative weight supersedes facticity. As Quintilian tells us (above), an *exemplum* did not need to have happened, but only be *uelut facta*. Cicero does not make it clear whether he brackets Maelius because the antiquity of myth posed a problem of fiction or that the precedent had expired, a question of temporal limitation. The *praeteritio* floats the story in a limbo, where its force falls short of full legal precedent, but the episode nevertheless deserves mention because of the cultural authority borne by ancient things in Rome as the expression of shared values.

Our most extensive source for Maelius, Livy 4.13–16, postdates Cicero's First Catilinarian.[37] Maelius belongs to a trio, often cited together, whose stories' narration shows traces of the constitutional challenges posed by the Catilinarian conspiracy. In them, as in Cicero's list, law repeatedly cannot provide the tools sufficient to the crisis. Political legitimacy, however, comes from adherence to the norm of defending the people's safety – ironically against populists acting for the benefit of the people. Spurius Cassius, the first, proposed agrarian legislation reminiscent of the land reform attempted by the Gracchi, was accused of aspiring to sole rule (*regnum*), lost the favour of the plebs, was put to trial and executed in 485 BCE. Livy says the method of the trial is uncertain. The similarity of the land legislation to more recent conflicts makes Livy's version historically suspect. Spurius Maelius, the second, sold grain at a low price during a shortage, stockpiled weapons, was accused of *regnum* and executed by Servilius Ahala, serving as master of the horse for the dictator Cincinnatus, who was appointed to deal with the crisis – *exsoluto legum uinclis* ('unshackled from law', 4.13) – in 439 BCE. Manlius Capitolinus is the third. He had saved the Capitoline from the Gauls, later became jealous of Camillus' station as Rome's leading man, promoted populist debt relief, was charged with *regnum*, tried by the *comitia* – they had to move the trial to where the people could not see the Capitoline Manlius had saved – and thrown off the Tarpeian rock on the very Capitoline in 384 BCE. Some of these dates are more squidgy than others, much uncertainty clouds every story even in antiquity. Of Manlius, for instance, Livy cannot find strong evidence to support the traditional charge of *regnum* (6.18.16). Modern standards would set these stories under the category of myth at best, fiction at most unreliable.

And yet they have a kind of force. In Livy, Cassius and Maelius recur repeatedly as parallels for Manlius. The people upbraid each other for abandoning their champions in need (6.17.1–2). Their examples are Cassius and Maelius. When Manlius is released from imprisonment for accusing the senate of hoarding Gallic gold that could have been used for debt relief, he is emboldened because the dictator has not treated him like Maelius (6.18.4). In a speech, he asks if he should await their fate (6.18.9). The senate says they need a Servilius Ahala to cope with Manlius (6.19.2–3). Narratively, these repeated *exempla* foreshadow Manlius' demise, a formal function. Within the story, they are a call to action. Their role in Livy's history, as in Cicero's use of Maelius, has the further pragmatic force of recording precedents that justify state-sponsored violence against citizens charged with violating the constitution.

Cicero pays at least lip service to process: of the trio, only Maelius is cited in the opening of the First Catilinarian, the closest parallel in that he was the only one not to receive a proper trial. By emphasizing his authorization by the SCU, as in the cases of Gaius Gracchus and Saturninus, he keeps mostly to the same formal legal ground. But his citation of Tiberius Gracchus and of Maelius, however distanced, sets the norm above legal process. Livy also cares to some degree about process. His doubt about the allegation of *regnum* calls into question the constitutionality of Manlius' trial and execution. This is the force of citing the stories: to evoke a higher norm against which to judge the case at stake. While Cicero takes the examples as proving his point, the complexity of Livy's narration maintains a non-ideologically driven 'even-handedness'.[38]

These stories show Romans thinking about process and its limitations within the sphere of letters. Cicero and Livy both measure particular cases against the norms embodied in mytho-historical stories. Straumann shows that deferring to a higher norm in emergencies *was* the process.[39] It could take the shape of dictatorship or the SCU among other extraordinary measures. In these stories, formal process ends up being re-inscribed after the fact. Livy includes a highly anachronistic detail in his account of Manlius. With the senate's call for a Servilius Ahala to eliminate Manlius, Livy not only evokes Maelius explicitly and Catiline implicitly, but attributes to the senate a formula that had not yet been invented.

> Decurritur ad leniorem uerbis sententiam, uim tamen eandem habentem, ut uideant magistratus ne quid ex perniciosis consiliis M. Manli res publica detrimenti capiat.
>
> They took recourse in a verbally gentler decision, nevertheless having the same force, that the magistrates see to it that the state receive no harm from the pernicious plans of Marcus Manlius.
>
> Livy 6.19.2–3

This is the wording of the SCU, retrojected backwards not only from the time of its actual invention for Gaius Gracchus, but also from its more recent use for Catiline and Caesar.[40] The norm underlying the Maelius story, the Manlius story, and the SCU are the same. Livy may elide them in that they have the same force.

Livy's normalizing gesture, however, runs up against literature's inherent ambivalence, which destabilizes the secure application of norms. By placing Cicero's famous opening to the First Catilinarian, *quousque tandem* ('how long, damn it', *Cat*. 1.1) at the start of one of Manlius' rabble-rousing speeches (6.18.5), Livy signs his allusion to the speech and its long history of citation, by Clodius, among others. As Christina Kraus has noted, Manlius echoes both the consul and the revolutionary in his dual role as *seruator patriae* and *patronus plebis*.[41] These echoes raise questions whose interpretive instability challenges the story's ability to serve as a constitutional model. How can the same figure replay opposing sides? Do Livy's doubts about Manlius' aspiring to *regnum* retrospectively attach to Cicero's use of the SCU and the senate's condemnation of Catiline? Livy raises such parallels to spur us to think, as he suggests in his preface, to reach our own judgments without giving away his own.[42] The interpretive instability of *exempla* derives in large part from literature's inherent openness to ambivalence. Livy sometimes, but rarely imparts authorial commentary. His text throws readers into the position of deciding constitutional questions without transparent guidance.

If the Maelius story bears normative force, what kind of force does Livy's Manlius story, with all its ambivalence, bear? Judged simply as history, the anachronistic retrojection of the SCU into the story falls short of the standard of truth.[43] Judged, however, in Merriam-Wester's definition, as a 'written instrument embodying the rules of a political or social organization', Livy's written history amends Republican Rome's unwritten and uncodified constitution to bring it up to date with current processes. How far can the definition of constitution be pressed? The exemplarity of Roman history certainly lent it the quality of an instrument. I would say that the stories historiography records embody the rules, rather than that the written document does. Livy comments less on the stories he tells than Scipio does in his history of early Rome in the *De re publica*. His approximation of a constitution comes less close than Cicero's. The important question, however, is less of form, but of operation. Both texts attest to the normative weight of stories in decisions about life and death without relieving readers of the responsibility of making those decisions. Their interpretation of the meaning of these exemplary stories leads to judgments as momentous as those made in a court of law.

Closing thoughts

Two models for the constitutional force of Latin letters deserve consideration. 1) Literature supplies the functional equivalent of the uncodified constitution. 'Equivalent' insists that literature is not the constitution and 'functional' means it performs at least some of its work. 2) Literature supplements the uncodified constitution. Where Rousseau saw a supplement as 'an inessential extra added to something complete in itself', Jacques Derrida pointed out in *On Grammatology* that what is complete in itself cannot be added to, so a supplement indicates an originary lack.[44] Such supplements are often dismissed as 'inessential' or even 'frivolous,' the way literature is dismissed as play before the authority and power to make realities generally attributed to law.

The difference between these two models for ancient Rome depends on how much a constitution actually existed. 'Functional equivalent' implies there was no constitution and that literature performed some of its expected function, while 'supplement' implies something existed to have an originary lack. Given the Republican constitution's performative nature, I affirm that it existed and operated despite lacking dispositive documentation or codification. Although I insist that literature performed some of the function of a constitution, that does not mean there was no constitution at all, however unstable it may have been. The Romans constantly invented new instruments and forms, and how to apply agreed principles was fiercely contested. The instability literature's malleability imparted to the republican constitution affected the norms' application, not the norms themselves. Recognizing aspects of each model, I incline to 'functional supplement'. The supplement performs some of the work – the transmission of norms – needed for the constitution to operate without bearing all the work.

Could the constitution have done without the stories? The Roman propensity to concrete examples, to embodiment rather than abstraction – actual men enacting ancient customs in Ennius' formulation – means that a constitution without particular instances revealing norms in action, would lack the force supplied by literature. The textual descriptions of an actual state, Cicero's *De re publica* and Livy's history, fill in once the performative constitution was fading. Codification comes late, after the fact, as a record without the force of law once practices took a different turn.

Notes

1 All translations are my own.
2 Honig (2009) 64.
3 Lintott (1999a); Straumann (2016); Bhatt (2017) 77.
4 Lintott (1999a) 26.
5 Straumann (2016) 55–62.
6 Horace offers a test case for the liminal space between fiction and non-fiction, Lowrie (2009b) 2–3; on *carmen* as ritual, non-ordinary language, Habinek (2005) 1–4.
7 Vasaly (2015).
8 For the underestimation of Livy's political thought, Miles (1995) 3–6; of early Roman historiography generally, Cornell (1986) 74.

9 The law dictionaries are less informative because they come too quickly to particular instances – the American, the British – without defining the genus to which the species belong.
10 https://www.merriam-webster.com/ (accessed 2 November2020).
11 Ando (2013) 919–20.
12 Schütze (2019) Section 1.
13 Wiedemann (2000) 520–1.
14 Straumann (2016) follows in a Germanic tradition contrary to Mommsen. Nippel (2008) 123–4, 140 reviews Christian Meier's appreciation of *mos* and *exempla* and stresses these were not rules, but sites of contestation.
15 For Roman aversion to 'explicit theorizing', Wiedemann (2000) 517; Hammer (2014) 7; Lowrie and Lüdemann (2015) 1–15; Lowrie (forthcoming). Pandey's paper in this volume embodies the Roman commitment to embodied approaches to thinking.
16 Dyck (2004) 272 defends Vahlen's supplement.
17 *OLD ad loc.*
18 *et mores ueteresque nouosque tenentem / multorum ueterum leges diuomque hominumque / prudentem* ('and a prudent man, comprehending customs old and new, laws of many old gods and men', *Annales* 283–4 Sk.).
19 Asmis (2005).
20 The introduction of this volume reviews law and literature as a field.
21 Also at *Leg.* 3.12.8, 3.13.4. Dyck (2004) 481 prefers *descriptio*, as parallel to *compositio* in the following speech.
22 Compare, *ut in lege posui* ('as I set in the law', *Leg.* 2.47.18).
23 Marcus: *Lex recitata est: discedere et tabellam dari iubebo* ('The law has been read out: I will order you to depart and the voting-tablets to be distributed', *Leg.* 3.11).
24 Dyck (2004) 480 dismisses the gesture as 'witty'.
25 Quintus: *non recognoscimus nunc leges populi Romani, sed aut repetimus ereptas aut nouas scribimus* ('We are not now reviewing the laws of the Roman people, but we're either fetching back those that have been snatched away or writing new ones', 3.37).
26 Derrida (1972).
27 Marcus: *legum leges uoce proponam* (*Leg.* 2.18.5).
28 For style, Dyck (2004) 288–9.
29 Straumann (2016) 54.
30 For the conflict between law and overriding norm and its antique reception, see La Bua (2019) 218. Cicero repeatedly returned to the question of the legality of killing politically dangerous citizens not merely to justify his actions, but to tease out the relationship between norm and law. For Cicero's analysis of the same *exempla* as cited in the first *Catilinarian* according to *status* theory, Wisse (2007) 49–51.
31 For the commemorative and normative burden of traditional *exempla*, see Roller (2018) 6–8; Langlands (2018) 4.

32 Dyck (2008) 165: the senate's meeting on 3 December, when the letters were disclosed, 'took on the aspect of a trial'. He stresses that legally, oral oaths were primary, while written documents provided 'mere confirmation' (*Cat.* 3.10.6–8).
33 The distinction between law and fact postdates these events; Cornu Thénard (2020). What the evidence proves is the *factum*. What the stories evince is *ius*.
34 For the production of norms from *exempla* through analogy, Ando (2015b).
35 Mitchell (1971); on Clodius, 60–1, although Cicero's account is indisputably biased.
36 Fiori (1996); Lowrie (2007).
37 On alternative versions by Calpurnius Piso, Cincius Alimentus, and Dionysius of Halicarnassus, Lowrie (2010) 179–80.
38 Kraus (1994) 247.
39 Straumann (2016) 63–118.
40 Momigliano (1942a) 113.
41 6.17.5; 6.18.14; Kraus (1994) 200.
42 Chaplin (2000).
43 Henderson (1989) 68 queries history's resistance to iterability on the assumption that truth lies in the unique; the counter-movement is the desire for the paradigmatic (75).
44 Derrida (1967).

3

Saturnalian *Lex*: Seneca's *Apocolocyntosis*

Erica Bexley

Introduction: Who guards the guards?

Holding people to account is a large part of the law's job. Assigning doers to deeds, ensuring the appropriate punishment of transgressions and transgressors, recommending processes of reparation, regulating the conduct of public bodies, organisations, governments, and nations: each is an example of the law apportioning and policing responsibility, individual and collective. As a regulatory force, though, the law, too, must be held accountable, which means that any justice system must incorporate sufficient checks and balances to ensure that it remains just; otherwise it loses all credibility. Urgent enough in parliamentary democracies and constitutional monarchies, the task acquires another layer of difficulty in more autocratic contexts, where a single ruler embodies the ultimate (terrestrial) source of legitimacy.[1] *Quis custodiet ipsos custodes*? A major problem of sovereign legality is its self-legitimizing nature: the sovereign is subject to the law, but in deciding what counts as law, he also transcends its framework, making law by his very ability to exceed it. The pressing question then becomes whether and how such an arrangement can guarantee the sovereign's being held to account.

This paper examines the twinned issues of sovereignty and law in Seneca's *Apocolocyntosis*, combining ancient Roman – specifically, Senecan – concepts of sovereign power with theoretical approaches formulated by Carl Schmitt and Giorgio Agamben. As summarized in the preceding paragraph, Schmitt's 'paradox of sovereignty' maintains that the sovereign 'stands outside the normally valid legal system [but] nevertheless belongs to it' for he is the one with the power to suspend and reformulate the constitution in times of emergency.[2] Sovereignty, for Schmitt, represents 'not ... the monopoly to coerce or to rule, but ... the monopoly to decide'.[3] Writing at the opposite end of the twentieth century,

Agamben transforms Schmitt's idea from a temporary, emergency measure into the ongoing state of modern biopolitics, and regards the paradox of sovereignty as inherent in the very operation of the juridical order: 'the sovereign, having the legal power to suspend the validity of the law, legally places himself outside the law. This means that the paradox can also be formulated this way: "the law is outside itself".'[4] For Agamben, the sovereign exception – i.e. whatever is acknowledged as excluded from the juridical order – becomes the rule, included by its very exclusion, and authority 'proves itself not to need law to create law'.[5] Not only does no-one guard the guard in this case, but the guard's role entails its own negation.

Notwithstanding their modern grounding, these ideas are also applicable to the Roman principate, where the conflation of legislative and executive functions meant 'the emperor was simultaneously above the law, within the law, and the law itself'.[6] An oft-quoted phrase from Ulpian provides the perfect example, acknowledging the ruler's legally sanctioned exemption from law in a paradox reminiscent of Schmitt's: *princeps legibus solutus est* ('the emperor is not bound by the laws' *Dig.* 1.3.31). In other words, the emperor's freedom from legal strictures is legitimated via its very codification: the *princeps* is simultaneously inside and outside the juridical order. The law authorizes its own suspension.

In the case of Claudius, and the *Apocolocyntosis*, this issue of legal anomie is thrown into particularly sharp relief, because as *princeps*, Claudius coupled supreme political and legal authority with his own, obsessive interest in legal proceedings. Although it was usual for emperors to sit in judgment,[7] and to formulate new laws, Claudius' constant, visible meddling with the justice system drew attention to the emperor's – and indeed, the law's – accountability. How could the law self-regulate when the ultimate source of its regulation was so erratic? And could the ruler ever be held legally responsible for his imputed travesties of justice? The *princeps*' ability to pass judgment on others while escaping it himself is a problem at the heart of the *Apocolocyntosis*. Not only does Seneca's satire subject Claudius to a posthumous trial and punishment, and mete out a poetically appropriate sentence, but it also enacts, through its genre and narrative voice, the dialectic of lawmakers being both inside and outside the juridical order, specifically, of someone being able to hold others accountable without himself answering to the law.

Curiously, this aspect of the *Apocolocyntosis* has received hardly any scholarly attention. While Classicists acknowledge the text's legal imagery and language,[8] they are more likely to classify the *Apocolocyntosis* either as a nonsensical Menippean romp[9] or a piece of political criticism[10] than an insightful assessment of Rome's legal problems under the principate.[11] Granted, what Claudius suffers in this satire *is* funny, and it *is* a comment on the indiscretions of his reign and a possible lesson for Nero, but it is also shorthand for the emperor's broader role in the juridical order, especially his position as judge. In the course of ridiculing Claudius, the *Apocolocyntosis* comments on the principate's legal structure, the emperor's monopoly of legal decision-making and the consequent problems of judicial responsibility. The text reflects the concerns of its era, a time when the *princeps*' centralization of legal authority was becoming all the more apparent. Further, the *Apocolocyntosis* does not just document the principate's legal failings, but actively intervenes in them by imagining its narrative, and the narrator's voice, as having the force of law. The satire judges Claudius and invites its audience to do the same. This means that we, as readers, are granted the opportunity of performing what the law failed to do during the emperor's lifetime: we hold Claudius to account; we guard the guard.

Trial and punishment 1: Olympus

The first such judgment in the *Apocolocyntosis* is the *concilium deorum* (8.1–11.6), the longest section of the work's extant text,[12] where the gods debate Claudius' admittance to divine status. Like many such *concilia*, the scene is imagined as a meeting of the Roman senate.[13] Claudius arrives at Olympus' threshold and convinces Hercules to admit him and champion his case. Some gods are persuaded, but the majority vote against the motion. Framing the debate are two denunciations of Claudius' conduct as emperor. The first speaker, rendered anonymous by a lacuna, condemns him for enforcing the suicide of his prospective son-in-law, Lucius Silanus Torquatus, and for his hypocrisy in posing as a moral reformer while the worst breaches of marital law happened in his own household (8.2–3). The final speaker, Augustus, follows the first deity/senator in denouncing Claudius for executing fellow aristocrats (10.3) and, more importantly, members of the imperial family (10.4; 11.1–6) and for doing so without first hearing both sides of the case (10.4). These two speeches, especially Augustus', transform the scene from a senatorial *relatio* into a full-blown trial,[14] as Claudius is charged on multiple counts of judicial murder and failure to follow correct courtroom procedure.

Thus, the episode poses as repayment for Claudius' judicial misconduct. The main motif is reversal, which unites the scene's satirical requirements with its role as a piece of 'poetic justice'. Instead of presiding over the gathering, Claudius plays the hapless petitioner; rather than acting as a judge – one of his favourite occupations while in power (Suet. *Cl.* 14–15; Tac. *Ann.* 12.43.1) – he is subjected to others' judgment; in place of sentencing family members, he is sentenced by a family member. On the surface, this looks like a reinstatement of legality, with Claudius finally being made to answer for his deeds, if only in fictional terms.[15]

Augustus' speech plays a large role in creating this impression, as it appears to deliver a decisive 'message' about the dangers of emperors disregarding the law.[16] Among the several self-promoting claims of its preamble is the phrase *legibus urbem fundaui* ('I gave Rome a foundation of laws' *Apoc.* 10.2). This clear allusion to Vergil's Numa (*qui legibus urbem / fundabit*; 'who will give Rome a foundation of laws', *Aen.* 6.810–11) casts Augustus in his favourite role as guardian and (re)originator of ancestral – in this case, specifically legal – tradition.[17] Augustus poses as a yardstick by which the gods are encouraged to measure Claudius' aberration, and his position as founder imbues his opinions with a high level of judicial authority.

Such seeming legitimacy is further enhanced by Augustus' ostensible disavowal of absolute power. When he cites with approval the *sententia* of Messala Corvinus, *pudet imperii* ('I am ashamed of my *imperium*' *Apoc.* 10.2), he implies a talent for self-restraint that Claudius apparently lacks. As the guardian of Roman law, Augustus is presumed capable of controlling himself, that is, of generating from his own conscience the checks and balances necessary to the exercise of justice. Only the emperor can set limits on his own *imperium*, which includes his juridical powers. This would be a situation with worrying consequences were it not for the fact that Augustus professes to submit himself willingly to his own limitation.[18]

As a result, Augustus' verdict acquires significant moral and legal force. His condemnation of Claudius is couched in explicitly legalistic terminology: **pro sententia mea** *hoc censeo ...* **placet mihi** *in eum seuere animaduerti nec illi rerum iudicandarum* **uacationem** *dari eumque quam primum exportari et caelo intra triginta dies excedere, Olympo intra diem tertium* ('**I propose** this **according to my opinion** ... **I decree** that he be dealt with severely, nor should he be granted **exemption** from due process of law, and he should be banished straightaway, having to leave heaven within thirty days and Olympus within three' 11.5–6).[19] Such terminology casts Augustus not just as the law's representative, but as its *voice*, a cipher for law's lexical power to define, judge and punish. Further, it hints at his role as (former) imperial lawmaker, since the phrase *placet mihi*, besides referring to individual opinion, also evokes in this context the legislative formula *principi placuit* ('it has pleased the emperor' cf. *Dig.* 1.4.1 *quod principi placuit legis habet uigorem*; 'what has pleased the emperor has the force of law'). Effectively, Augustus' utterance *is* law, and it is imbued with such authority that it is easy to interpret his judgment as the text's own. In contrast, Claudius seems more of an imperial lawbreaker than maker: he is portrayed as incapable of following official procedure, and the stuttering unintelligibility of his voice prevents it from acquiring any judicial force.[20] While the Claudius of Seneca's *Apocolocyntosis* may talk endlessly *about* the law, he cannot, it seems, *embody* it in the same way that Augustus does.

Justice, therefore, is presumed to have been served: following Claudius' abuse of it, the law has been reinstated through the person of Augustus, and Claudius' erstwhile sovereign power has been curtailed by the superior power of heaven. The unfettered judicial behaviour of the sovereign has finally been called to account. Moreover, as the medium for Augustus' judgment, the text, too, formulates a verdict on Claudius' conduct. Calling the work a 'verdict' is no mere metaphor, either, for although the *Apocolocyntosis*' condemnation of Claudius is not the same as a courtroom decision, the text's mimicry of official discourse draws attention to law's primarily verbal existence, its grounding in authoritative and persuasive language, its textual form and need for interpretation.[21] The *Apocolocyntosis* opens with the narrator's promise to report *quid actum sit in caelo ante diem III idus Octobris* (1.1 'what went on in heaven on 13 October'), where the official formulation allows the satire to pose as an authorized record, and suggests not just 'what happened in heaven', but 'what was *decreed*' and the precise date of its ratification.[22] In other words, the text (jokingly) claims legal status for its pronouncements. The same applies to Augustus' verdict at *Apocolocyntosis* 11.5–6: the prominence of legal language highlights law's enactment as and through words, meaning in turn that a literary work can approximate to if not appropriate law's regulatory authority.

In submitting Claudius to Augustus' judgment, the *Apocolocyntosis* also highlights the larger issue of the audience's and of history's verdict on the emperor. A trial scene invites readers to take sides, to draw their own conclusions; at very least, it makes readers aware that their consumption of the text is also a process of decision-making, in this case, about Claudius' apparent disregard for Roman legal norms. And such decision-making on the audience's part, whether positive or negative, represents a curb on Claudius' self-substantiating power. He no longer exercises a sovereign monopoly over decision-making; he must bow to others, to the force of public opinion. The audience, rather than Claudius, assumes the position of judge.

Equally, the scene can be read as reinstating the senate's decision-making power by undermining the official proclamation of Claudius' godhead. In laughing at Claudius' *consecratio*, the text appears to challenge the public narrative of the emperor's deification and to give the 'senate' a chance to revisit its original decision. This problem has long vexed scholars because the text's mockery threatens to destabilize Roman traditions of emperor worship, with attendant consequences for Nero styling himself *diui filius*.[23] Ittai Gradel's distinction between absolute and relative categories of divinity comes closest to resolving the issue: Claudius has been consecrated a god of the Roman state and the *Apocolocyntosis*, Gradel maintains, does not question this. Instead, it ridicules Claudius' bid to become an absolute divinity, a matter which the gods, not the Roman state, must decide.[24] Although neat, the solution has one sticking point, and that is Gradel's all too swift dismissal of the *concilium deorum*'s resemblance to a senate meeting.[25] This detail is crucial because it implies the senate's *reconsideration* of Claudius' godhead just as much as it implies Olympus' initial consideration of the issue. And herein lies the senate's potential freedom, because it (re)gains the power to decide Claudius' fate, albeit in a fictional context. If, as Kaius Tuori claims, Claudius' reign represented 'the decisive ending of the senate's influence as a court of law',[26] then the *Apocolocyntosis* resurrects that influence. Its fictional context is not so very far removed from the everyday realities of Roman life, either, for if one of the *consecratio*'s aims was to establish how Claudius would be remembered, then the *Apocolocyntosis*, too, claims that function, even if it falls short of enforcing obedience. This does not, of course, solve the problem of the *Apocolocyntosis* mocking Claudius' divinity, but finding a solution is not my current aim. Instead, I want to show how the text subverts the emperor's monopoly of decision-making by subjecting him to others' judgments, particularly to the judgment of law-making bodies such as the senate.

According to Suetonius, the historical Claudius was a keen but erratic judge, 'sometimes prudent and perceptive, sometimes thoughtless and hasty, often trivial and like an insane person' (*modo circumspectus ac sagax, interdum inconsultus ac praeceps, nonnumquam friuolus amentique similis, Cl.* 15.1). He seems to have acted without regard for principle and precedent: in making decisions, 'he did not always follow the letter of the law' (*nec semper praescripta legum secutus, Cl.* 14.1) and he appears to have marginalized the role of professional juriconsults (as the adjective *inconsultus* at Suet. *Cl.* 15.1 may imply).[27] Although his zealous courtroom attendance was probably due to a backlog of cases that had accumulated under Tiberius and Caligula,[28] it could easily appear as a desire to monopolize legal business, especially when coupled with Claudius' inconsistent verdicts. It is this image of Claudius the idiosyncratic and over-enthusiastic judge that Seneca tackles in his *Apocolocyntosis*, chiefly by asserting the law's independence from its main imperial administrator. Seneca's satire holds out the hope that Claudius will be made answerable for his actions in the afterlife, whether in the imaginary setting of Olympus or, more literally, in the text's promulgation of the emperor's failings. Both scenarios assume the existence of a power higher than Claudius', a power that imitates and may even be said to usurp law's function in making Claudius answerable for the 'crimes' committed in his role as *iudex*. It is about bringing Claudius' sovereign authority within the law's orbit, however fictively and belatedly.

Judging Olympian judges

There is, however, an added layer of complexity to Seneca's *concilium deorum*, because it portrays a senate almost as shambolic and corrupt as the petitioner it seeks to deny.[29] Jupiter is depicted as having forgotten correct procedure by allowing Claudius to attend the senatorial debate (9.1). The king of the gods also criticises his fellow 'senators' for their disorderly conduct: *uos mera mapalia fecistis* ('you have made a real pigsty of it' 9.1). Diespiter, who speaks in support of Claudius, is introduced as 'consul designate, a petty money-changer ... [who] used to sell citizenship rights' (*consul designatus, nummulariolus ... uendere ciuitatulas solebat*, 9.4) and to prevent readers from ascribing such unprincipled activity *only* to Claudius' allies, Seneca similarly portrays Janus, an opponent of Claudius' godhead, as a lazy consul designate appointed by a debased system (9.2).[30] How can this degenerate deliberative body be expected to deliver any kind of justice?

Augustus' speech, too, is problematic because of its blatant self-interest. He admits to feeling *indignatio* (10.2) and focuses his condemnation on *iniurias meas* ('wrongs done to me' 11.4), which he demands the senate avenge (11.4). As Katherine Aftsomis observes, this is not the image of an impartial judge, but of 'an enraged emperor seeking vindication', an emperor who has, moreover, power to sway the senate's decisions.[31] Initial impressions of the senate's freedom begin to seem pretty illusory in this light, and Augustus emerges not as the law's disinterested voice but as a sovereign leader capable of manipulating judicial proceedings for his own satisfaction. The judicial abuses attributed to Claudius, then, appear to be perpetuated on Olympus.

Jupiter is a prime example, since details of his caricature recall Claudius' own: he is an absent-minded *princeps senatus* (9.1) in an incestuous marriage (8.2), who acts aggressively – though not murderously – towards family members (11.1). This mild resemblance to the erratic *princeps* undercuts Jupiter's mythological status as a dispenser and guarantor of justice. Notably, his breaking of Vulcan's leg (11.1), which anticipates Claudius' own limping dismissal from Olympus, is presented as an act of arbitrary violence involving serious if unstated ramifications for the divine council's treatment of the dead *princeps*. To the extent that Claudius becomes a victim of his own capricious behaviour, therefore, justice may seem to be served, but to the same extent, Jupiter cannot really be said to embody it. Can this impasse be resolved?

We could chalk it up to satire's love of inversion: the narrator reprimands injustice only to reprimand the reprimanders and we are all left wondering whom and what to laugh at.[32] This may be true of Seneca's *Apocolocyntosis*, but I think there is a further purpose at work here, because in exposing the moral weaknesses of this particular 'senate', Seneca once again invites questions about the law's overall ability to self-regulate under the principate. How can justice be guaranteed or the legal system maintain credibility when it has been designed in such a way that the ultimate source of law, the emperor, cannot be held accountable except by his own willing submission? If Jupiter's conduct in the *concilium deorum* seems a reflection of Claudius' own, that is a consequence both of its being fitting punishment for Claudius' misdemeanours (a 'taste of his own medicine') and of its epitomizing the deeply problematic paradox of the *princeps* transcending the law at the same time as deciding and enforcing it. As a Claudian figure, Jupiter evokes this uneasy marriage of intra- and extra-juridical status: he has the authority to convene proceedings and to judge Claudius, but that very authority also permits him to act capriciously.

The same paradox applies to Seneca's portrayal of Augustus, who commandeers senatorial procedure, allows his own grievances to intervene and produces a verdict primarily out of anger; this is not the conduct of a good judge, especially not by Seneca's standards.[33] As much as Augustus in the *Apocolocyntosis* enforces the law, he also seems to stand beyond it. If such observations seem to contradict my earlier assertions about the Olympians' judgment of Claudius, that is due to the text's multi-layered approach, its portrayal of apparent Olympian justice undercut by the very same problems that Claudius exemplifies, namely, the self-regulating nature of sovereign power. The satire's questioning of Jupiter, Augustus, and the senate's judgment does not, therefore, invalidate its main theme of the *princeps*' extra-judicial position. The *Apocolocyntosis* still addresses the issue of the emperor's legal accountability, only from a more complex standpoint. We can say that the satire encourages readers to judge not just Claudius but Augustus, Jupiter, and the entire trial depicted at 8.1–11.6.[34] We can also say that it handles the issue of sovereign legality with depth and sophistication; it doesn't propose any easy solutions.

To illustrate this paradox more fully, I draw attention to the opening of Seneca's *de Clementia*, a text scholars often pair with the *Apocolocyntosis*.[35] It begins with Seneca's promise to 'perform the function of a mirror' (*speculi uice fungerer, Clem.* 1.1.1) in order to display Nero to himself (*ut . . . te tibi ostenderem, Clem.* 1.1.1), and underscore the pleasure involved in gazing upon and examining a good conscience (*Clem.* 1.1.1). For Peter Stacey, the mirror's significance lies in its construction of a 'self-reflecting moral *persona*' for the Senecan sovereign.[36] Effectively, Nero is urged to act as a mirror for himself and to scrutinize his actions, just as Seneca's text uses the rhetorical strategy of posing as a protreptic mirror for the young *princeps*. Self-government becomes the foremost ingredient in good government; self-rule guarantees the rule of law and the sovereign's legitimacy. But the metaphor of the mirror has a flipside as well, because it also shows how 'nothing except the emperor defines the limits of jurisdiction'.[37] The only person to whom Nero can be held responsible is Nero himself, and although his moral guidance is supposed to stem from the external, universal standards of Stoic natural law, his earthly conduct is essentially free from supervision. Moral checks and balances, however superior in origin, seem weak when faced with Nero's capacity for self-determination. Like Augustus and Jupiter in the *Apocolocyntosis*' *concilium deorum*, the Nero of *De Clementia* 1.1 is imagined as being simultaneously inside and outside the juridical order, able to suspend the law's validity in the name of justice (e.g. in acts of clemency), and thereby to create new legal standards. He embodies the law just as he embodies his own reflection. For the *Apocolocyntosis*' Olympian 'senate', visiting justice upon Claudius involves a similar – albeit more glaringly irresponsible – dismissal of good judicial practice: Augustus and Jupiter are depicted as having judged Claudius correctly despite (or because of?) their erratic, irate, 'Claudian' behaviour as judges. They transcend and therefore remake the law as needed.

The overall effect is of Seneca and his audience adopting the role of judges and discerning the right and wrong not just in Claudius' conduct but in that of the text's other juridical figures, too. (The same could be said of the *de Clementia*: it is the text itself, Seneca as author and, above all, the audience's expectations of the *princeps* – his mirror standing in for his 'reputation' – that are meant to keep Nero in check.) This approach enables Seneca to dissipate the problem of sovereign power by creating a *community* of judges whose diversity of perspectives and eras prevents any one of them from monopolizing the decision-making process. The text itself becomes a legal artefact, simultaneously evidence and verdict, and it is a clear example of literature intervening actively in legal problems. The *Apocolocyntosis* weakens Claudius' sovereignty by making him the object of others' judgments and, at the same time, a butt of ridicule.[38] Claudius is no longer in control; Seneca and the audience are. In the world of the *Apocolocyntosis*, the *princeps*' authority is no longer legally independent and underived: it is checked, curtailed, regulated by others, a job performed by the text itself as much if not more than by the characters within it. The sovereign power of decision-making passes from Claudius as *princeps* to Seneca as author, and to his readers. Although it is still quite a step from putting the emperor on trial in fiction to putting him on trial in actuality, the *Apocolocyntosis* opens the door to this possibility, by intimating that people other than the emperor can interrogate and place limits upon his power.

Trial and punishment 2: The underworld

If this paradox of sovereign legality receives light inflection in the *concilium deorum*, it is brought to fuller prominence in the subsequent underworld trial, where Claudius is charged with murder under the *lex Cornelia* (14.1). Aeacus conducts proceedings in true Claudian fashion, denying the defendant an adjournment and then, his right of reply (14.2). Claudius is condemned without a hearing; Aeacus decides *altera parte...audita* ('with one side of the case heard', 14.2), a direct echo of Claudius' own practice, as reported at *Apocolocyntosis* 12.3.19–21: *quo non alius / potuit citius discere causas / **una tantum parte audita*** ('no-one could decide cases faster, **with only one side heard**' cf. Suet. *Cl.* 15.2). Aeacus' ensuing citation of a Hesiodic maxim, 'should you suffer what you have done, this would be true justice' (αἴκε πάθοις τὰ ἔρεξας δίκη εὐθεῖα γένοιτο, 14.2; fr. 286.2 M-W) confirms that the very *form* of the trial, not just its outcome, functions as punishment for Claudius.[39] While this wilful disregard for procedure seems shockingly novel to the assembled crowd, Claudius himself merely thinks it unfair, rather than unprecedented (14.3) – partial recognition of his own erratic conduct as judge, even if he does not think it worthy of punishment.

The result is that Aeacus embodies *both* a just judge *and* a Claudian travesty of justice. It is significant that the narrator calls him *homo iustissimus* at precisely the moment he forbids the defence counsel from speaking (14.2). This label is at once an ironic acknowledgement of Aeacus flouting accepted legal procedure and genuine praise for his treatment of Claudius.[40] Essentially, Aeacus contravenes the law in order to apply it better, and his status as the law's guardian enables him to overstep its jurisdiction, to create it by suspending it. The scene is a brilliant miniature illustration of law's paradoxical dialectic: Aeacus has to override official procedure in order to be just; he must imitate Claudius in order to show how unlike Claudius he is in his ruling; he must break with precedent in order to adopt a sufficiently Claudian precedent to ensure not only Claudius' but the law's own accountability. Inasmuch as he, like Jupiter, is a quasi-Claudian figure, Aeacus embodies the problems inherent in sovereign power's relationship to the law: he is all at once above it, subject to it, and its point of origin. Only in this case, in implied contrast to Claudius' own courtroom conduct, abuse of the law happens for a good purpose.

Following the trial, Claudius undergoes two stages of punishment, each designed to match and therefore repay his particular personal failings. The first is the sentence handed down by Aeacus: eternal gambling with a broken dice box (14.4), a witty spin on Sisyphus' endless labour (15.1) and the Danaids' hopeless water-carrying. The punishment's significance lies in its evoking one of the historical Claudius' favourite past-times (Suet. *Cl.* 33.2), and in its being an essentially Saturnalian activity, for only during the short period of this festival was gambling sanctioned by Roman law (though those laws appear to have been largely ineffectual in preventing its practice at other times).[41] In being condemned to rattle and lose his dice *semper* (14.4), Claudius performs the penal equivalent of his time spent as *princeps*, which Seneca characterizes as an ongoing Saturnalia (8.2; 12.2: *semper*). I address this theme fully in the next subsection; for now, it suffices to say that Claudius' lonely, one-man Saturnalia in the afterlife mirrors and inverts his equally singular conduct as the *Saturnalicius princeps* (8.2).

The second stage of punishment arrives along with the work's abrupt conclusion: Caligula turns up and claims Claudius as his slave; the judgment is made in Caligula's favour, and 'he hand[s] [Claudius] over to his freedman, Menander, to be his secretary for petitions' (*is Menandro liberto suo tradidit, ut a cognitionibus esset*, 15.2).[42] The scene is obviously formulated as a response to the historical Claudius' notorious over-reliance on freedmen and their unprecedented level of influence at the imperial court. Claudius remains dependent upon them in the underworld, but from a position of social subservience rather than one of authority.[43] In a basic sense, Claudius' relegation to this category is typical of comedy's 'monde renversé' where social hierarchies are temporarily disturbed (though we should note that, in Claudius' case, the reversal is supposed to be permanent).[44] Yet the punishment also entails deeper thematic significance because Claudius' slave status inverts and corresponds to his former position outside the juridical order. Just as the emperor stands above the law, so the slave, in Roman society, stands below it. Slaves are defined largely by their exclusion from the law's protection: they cannot bring lawsuits, nor prosecute on someone else's behalf; they are objects, property rather than 'people'; they can be assaulted with impunity.[45] So Claudius, as a slave, continues to inhabit an extra-juridical realm, just without the privileges he used to enjoy.

His allotted task of dealing with *cognitiones* is also relevant, at the most literal level because the position of *libertus a cognitionibus* appears to have been established under Claudius (*CIL* vi.8634),[46] and more figuratively, because the legal process of *cognitio*, where the same magistrate or judge presided over the case from beginning to end, is thought to have evolved in tandem with the principate, as a consequence of Rome's increasingly centralized governmental structure.[47] This centripetal movement appears to have culminated in Claudius' reign: we know from Suetonius that Claudius frequently attended (*Cl.* 12.2) and held *cognitiones* (*Cl.* 15), and Tacitus complains of Claudius' having 'concentrated all the functions of the laws and magistracies in his own hands' (*cuncta legum et magistratuum munia in se trahens princeps*, *Ann.* 11.5.1). Significantly, the *cognitio* allowed judges to exercise more discretion than the older formulary process did,[48] which meant that it afforded Claudius more scope for his idiosyncratic interpretation and application of the law, a situation that further highlighted the problems of his sovereign power as judge. The *Apocolocyntosis*' reference to *cognitiones* therefore achieves a neat inversion, for Claudius remains absorbed in the same kinds of legal proceedings he once pursued as emperor, but without his previous level of executive control.

In sum, both Aeacus' decision and Claudius' punishment focus attention on the sovereign's problematic use of his legal powers, and on the need for their external regulation. Once again, it is the text, author and audience that perform this function by submitting Claudius to (quasi-)legal scrutiny. It is particularly significant that Seneca situates this trial in the Underworld and brings Claudius before a jury of his victims (13.6), since this move allows him to invoke the idea of collective judgment as counterweight to the sovereign's self-legitimization, and equally, the idea of Claudius' real punishment being his historical reputation, the verdict placed upon the past by those able to right (and rewrite!) its wrongs in the present. Seneca, too, occupies this role, as one of Claudius' more fortunate victims. Hence the text itself acquires the status of a trial and assumes the judicial power to decide Claudius' (posthumous) fate. Where the law is presumed to have failed during Claudius' lifetime, the *Apocolocyntosis* offers an alternative form of justice.

The Saturnalian *princeps*

The final key element in the *Apocolocyntosis*' critique of sovereignty is its Saturnalian leitmotif, its 'comic anchor', which Seneca uses to characterize Claudius' reign as an extended period of social role-inversion and clownish misrule.[49] Everything about the emperor, from his physical handicaps and incontinence to his erratic behaviour and his tendency to fill the imperial court with ex-slaves casts him as a topsy-turvy Saturnalian figure. His role as an arbiter of law also fits within this theme and not just because his capricious conduct is well known to have extended to the courtroom. The Saturnalia's real significance, in this regard, lies in its simultaneous negation of and obsession with legality, for this festival was a time of legally sanctioned anomie in which court business was suspended and various actions otherwise forbidden by law were permitted.[50] It was not, however, a time of pure lawlessness; rather, it resembled a parodic reflection of legal activity, when mock laws were promulgated,[51] and festivities demonstrated acute fascination for juridical issues. Like the sovereign, therefore, the Saturnalia is defined by law as being outside the law; it creates a legal framework by means of law's suspension and/or negation, effectively occupying a zone of indistinction between norms and anomie.[52]

In the *Apocolocyntosis*, Saturnalian themes map neatly onto Claudius' juridical waywardness, itself a form of institutionally protected arbitrariness. The theme implies that Claudius inhabits a kind of juridical limbo in which he may pursue a variety of anomalous legal activities without being brought to account. Only once he has died and his Saturnalia come to a close can his actions be evaluated in light of the law's reinstatement. Although recognised by scholars, this interrelationship between law and the Saturnalia in the *Apocolocyntosis* has not received anything approaching detailed attention.[53] The present subsection, by contrast, explores the theme in full, concentrating especially on how Seneca uses Saturnalian motifs to comprehend and evaluate the *princeps*' exceptional role in the Roman legal system.

On two occasions, the *Apocolocyntosis* refers explicitly to Claudius as a Saturnalian ruler. The first occurs at 8.2, when a member of the *concilium deorum* protests that not even Saturn would consent to deify Claudius: *si mehercules a Saturno petisset hoc beneficium, cuius mensem toto anno celebrauit Saturnalicius princeps, non tulisset* ('if by Hercules he had asked this favour from Saturn, whose festival he celebrated year-round, as a Saturnalian *princeps*, he would not have received it'). The second is during Claudius' funeral, where one of the pale, emaciated jurists emerging from the shadows says to the grieving barristers, *dicebam uobis, non semper Saturnalia erunt* ('I kept telling you it wouldn't be the Saturnalia forever', 12.2). The idea behind both references is not just that Claudius' rule represented a travesty of regular imperial government, but more precisely, that it constituted a legal 'no man's land', which normalized the flouting of judicial norms.

To take the second passage first: here Seneca establishes a contrast between the jurists, who found themselves out of work during the Claudian Saturnalia, and the orators who lament their loss of business as a consequence of Claudius' death. The division encapsulates Saturnalian versus non-Saturnalian forms of legal activity. The jurists' fundamentally procedural and scientific relationship to the law casts them as anti-Saturnalian figures, people who respect and uphold, even formulate, the rules –a direct contrast to Claudius' freewheeling, idiosyncratic approach to legal matters. Their retreat into hiding (12.2) signals the irregular 'legality' of the Claudian Saturnalia; only once it is over can juridical normality be resumed. The *causidici*, on the other hand, fit well within a festival context. As witnessed by Terence's prologues and Cicero's *Pro Caelio*, analysed in the introduction to this volume, oratory and comedy make good bedfellows. Oratory and performance likewise: when Seneca describes the barristers crying at Claudius' funeral, the addendum *sed plane ex animo* ('but obviously with sincerity' 12.2) highlights their more usual practice of performing this emotion in court. Although such displays were well recognised as part of the orator's repertoire and training,[54] Seneca suggests that the *causidici*'s professional insincerity represents a travesty of legal processes. It becomes, in other words, another aspect of Claudius' Saturnalia: a false or flippant version of law, a parody of it, parasitic upon the real task of administering justice.

The former example, at *Apocolocyntosis* 8.2, illustrates a similarly Saturnalian paradox, for here Claudius' imperial authority is assumed to incorporate its own negation. As a *Saturnalicius princeps*, Claudius is at once a travesty of imperial *auctoritas* and the ultimate expression of it because he stands outside the world of everyday norms and is answerable to no-one. The phrase is obviously a play on *Saturnalicius rex*, the title given to those who, appointed by lot, oversaw the Saturnalian festivities in individual households. These 'kings' would dispense for the festival's duration jovial and arbitrary orders (e.g. Epict. *Diss.* 1.25.8; Luc. *Cron.* 4), which the household or group of *conuiuae* was bound to obey. Their being called *reges* emphasized their anomalous status as chief representatives of the Saturnalia's parodic government and therefore, as inversions of the real state of affairs.[55] By substituting *princeps* for *rex*, however, Seneca implies not just that Saturnalian misrule becomes the norm under Claudius, but that such governmental anomalousness is built into the emperor's role, namely via his continuous lack of accountability. Like the Saturnalian *rex*, he may devise arbitrary laws without fear of legal repercussions, and he far exceeds the *rex*'s power in being able to set the terms of his rule.

Hence Claudius' characterization as a Lord of Misrule, like his treatment on Olympus and his Underworld trial, encapsulates his problematic role as sovereign lawmaker, his legally sanctioned ability, as *princeps*, to flout and remake the law, to stand both inside and outside the juridical order. The Saturnalia is a particularly apt means of examining this issue because its celebration entails a marked exploration of juridical limits. For example, a passage from Seneca, *Epistles* 47.14, suggests that even slaves could be granted the carnival privilege of being *reges*, since the rules of the Saturnalia, as established by Rome's *maiores*, 'permitted them to assume honours in the household and **to pronounce judgment**' (*honores illis in domo gerere **ius dicere** promiserunt*). If this passage is reliable,[56] it is an excellent example of the Saturnalia's legal inversions, whereby those who are all but excluded from the lower end of juridical order suddenly and briefly occupy a position at the opposite end, both roles entailing the ambiguous stance of being simultaneously inside and outside the law. As a parody of the lawmaker, the slave-cum-king flouts the law and institutes it; he does the former, in fact, in order to perform the latter. What is more, his exceptional extra-legal status is itself condoned by religious custom. In this respect his conduct mirrors the problem of legal and sovereign self-legitimation explored throughout this paper: how can law be constituted if not by its own overturning, and to what extent are those creating the law also subject to it?

As much as this Saturnalian motif deals with Claudius' own, peculiar abuse of justice, it also tackles the broader problem of the *princeps*' legal status, and law's status under the principate; Claudius simply happens to be an apposite example. Notably, the work persists in aligning kings with fools, again, not only because Claudius appears to unite the two categories, but also because their union evokes a Saturnalian 'state of exception': neither figure can be held accountable; each exists at the fringes of the juridical order, included by their exclusion and denoting the upper and lower limits of law's functioning. In the *Apocolocyntosis*' opening paragraph, Seneca refers to Claudius as *ille, qui uerum prouerbium fecerat, aut regem aut fatuum nasci oportere* ('he who made true the proverb that one must be born either a king or a fool' 1.1). Significantly, the Latin adage derives from a Greek saying, and this is where we can see Seneca's subtle ideas about law and autocratic government emerging: μωρῶι καὶ βασιλεῖ νόμος ἄγραφος ('for the fool and the king the law is unwritten' cited by Porphyrion on Hor. *Sat.* 2.3.188). The phrase implies that regular, codified law cannot encompass kings or fools; they operate according to a different set of rules, if they follow rules at all. Augustus makes a similar claim in his speech at the *concilium deorum*, describing one of Claudius' aristocratic victims as *uero tam fatuum ut etiam regnare posset* ('indeed such a fool that he could even have been king' 11.3). Clearly, the combination of fool and supreme ruler is not restricted to Claudius, even if he represents its prototype. By making the *fatuus* a prerequisite for the *rex*, Augustus suggests that both are made of the same Saturnalian material. It is not just the idea that being incompetent qualifies one for rulership, as per the Claudian model, but also that rulers and fools occupy the same sphere: they are beyond the law's reach.

In a broader application of the Saturnalian theme, Claudius is also portrayed as sitting in judgment during periods of recess, such as the summer, as he tells Hercules at the entrance to Olympus (7.4–5).[57] His boast of diligence is cast in ludicrous terms, as Claudius compares his work to Hercules' cleaning of the Augean stables (7.5). Making the activity seem doubly laughable, moreover, is the fact that Claudius' diligence appears misplaced: it happens at the wrong time of the year, an application of law during a period of (relative) recess, like the Saturnalian practice of misrule. Seneca may be alluding here to the historical Claudius' habit of trying cases *etiam suis suorumque diebus sollemnibus, nonnumquam festis quoque antiquitus et religiosis* ('even on his own anniversaries and those of his relatives, and on old festival days and days of religious ban' Suet. *Cl.* 14.1). While this most likely refers to Claudius following Augustus' example in removing some minor celebrations from the Roman festival calendar in order to make more room for court business,[58] nonetheless it characterizes the *princeps* as engrossed in legal proceedings to the point where he seems to contravene their customary suspension during *dies festi*. The continued practice of law in such circumstances risks making a mockery of law itself – again, a ready parallel for the mock-government of the Saturnalia.

As this last example demonstrates, the *Apocolocyntosis* depicts Claudius' 'Saturnalian' reign as a paradoxical period in which the emperor cannot be held accountable but can himself pursue seemingly limitless judgment of others. In calling Claudius a *Saturnalicius princeps*, Seneca simultaneously invalidates the emperor's legal activity and affirms that his victims have no recourse. Law is hamstrung under Claudius, just as it is during the Saturnalia. But this means that literature can step into the void and assume the mantle of justice.

Conclusion: The sovereign narrator

Having invoked throughout this paper the idea that Seneca's text mimics the law in its judgment of Claudius, I want to conclude with a brief glance at its narrative voice, specifically, its opening claim to evade accountability:

> si quis quaesiuerit unde sciam, primum, si noluero, non respondebo. quis coacturus est? ego scio me liberum factum, ex quo suum diem obiit ille, qui uerum prouerbium fecerat, aut regem aut fatuum nasci oportere. si libuerit respondere, dicam quod mihi in buccam uenerit. quis umquam ab historico iuratores exegit?
>
> if anyone asks the source of my information, first, if I don't want to, I won't reply. Who will force me? I know that I have been freed from the moment he died, that man who made true the proverb that one must be born either a king or a fool. If I feel like responding, I'll say whatever comes into my head. Who ever asked a historian for sworn witnesses?
>
> Apoc. 1.1–2

The declaration obviously plays on the trope of the historian's impartiality,[59] but it is more than light-hearted mockery or an admission of the satirist's unreliability as a narrator,[60] for here we see the same paradox that Seneca pursues throughout his characterization of Claudius: someone who judges others without himself being held accountable. The *Apocolocyntosis*' narrator asserts his underived power to say whatever he likes, without the need for oaths or proof, without, in other words, the quasi-legalistic framework of evidence and interrogation. This is the satirist in his dual role as prosecutor and defendant, bent on attacking whomever he pleases but also having to ward off the risk of offending the powerful.[61] His main means of achieving this protection, moreover, is to highlight the blatant fictitiousness of his account, the impossibility of its being taken seriously. It is the literary nature of Seneca's/the narrator's accusation that grants him both the underived power to accuse and a refuge from potential retaliation.

Yet this distance only intensifies rather than minimizes literature's relationship to the law, because the narrator himself assumes the position of a sovereign, claiming a monopoly over decision-making and an attendant freedom from legal strictures. The narrator creates and imposes his own laws, suspending or changing them at will, a condition that applies in greater or lesser degrees to all literature, but which the *Apocolocyntosis*' introduction brings home with especial force. Thus, Seneca's judgment of Claudius is the equivalent to his asserting legal and sovereign control: he sets the parameters, decides the verdict, and inhabits a quasi-Saturnalian realm – in a manner of speaking – where his judgments become untouchable. Literature in this case does not usurp law's power so much as create an equally powerful alternative, a process that mirrors actual legality and even claims to achieve more.

This theme of judicial accountability is a central issue in the *Apocolocyntosis*, from its opening all the way through to Claudius' final punishment. It is the primary method by which Seneca evaluates Claudius' actions as emperor, and even more fundamentally, the means by which he interrogates the sovereign's relationship to the law (for despite its overt status as an occasional piece,[62] the *Apocolocyntosis* deals with enduring issues at the heart of Rome's imperial government). It is also the major means by which the text itself engages with the limits and possibilities of legal power, as Seneca's narrator assumes the sovereign ability to judge Claudius and invites his audience to do likewise. Impossible as it may be to bring Claudius into a real court, this posthumous attack serves the equivalent and perhaps more enduring purpose of tarnishing his memory, vindicating his victims, and granting a community of readers the opportunity to curb the emperor's power. Literature does not just assume law's role in this case, but actively displaces it.

Notes

1 The only higher source of legitimacy being divine; see Stacey (2011) for its role in Seneca's political thought.
2 Schmitt (2005) [1922] 7.
3 Schmitt (2005) [1922] 13.
4 Agamben (1998) 15. On Agamben's 'state of exception', derived from the Roman legal concept of *iustitium*, see Biggs (in this volume).
5 Agamben (1998) 16.
6 Tuori (2016a) 11. The theories are also applicable because of their ancient background: Schmitt was influenced by Roman concepts of dictatorship, on which see Tuori (2016b), and Agamben's work developed from his study of Roman law: see Ziogas (2021) 10.

7 On the significance of the emperor's role as judge, see Aftsomis (2010) and Tuori (2016a).
8 Eden (1984); Kaplan (1991); Braund and James (1998) 306–7; Robinson (2005); Paschalis (2009); Aftsomis (2010).
9 Paschalis (2009) 202, and to a lesser extent, Relihan (1993) 75–90. Osgood (2007) 329 similarly maintains that the narrator's 'patently playful voice ... allows Seneca to claim some distance from the contents of his work.'
10 E.g. Momigliano (1934) 76–7; Griffin (1976) 129–30; Leach (1989); Braund and James (1998) 291–300; Whitton (2013); Panayotakis (2014). See Coffey (1961) 261–2 for older political approaches to the text.
11 Only Aftsomis (2010) tackles this issue.
12 There is a small lacuna between 7.5 and 8.1: see Eden (1984) *ad Apoc.* 8.1 for details.
13 Aftsomis (2010) 109.
14 Aftsomis (2010) 134.
15 In favour of this interpretation is the parallel case of Lucilius' *concilium deorum* (fr. 5–46 Warmington), which attacked Lucius Cornelius Lentulus Lupus for corrupt conduct that, in life, had not prevented him from attaining the rank of *censor*. Freudenburg (2015) 98–105 is an appealing argument for close thematic connections between Lucilius' and Seneca's *concilia*, though Eden (1984) 16–17 cautions against the potential circularity of such views, because Seneca's satire is typically used as a guideline for reconstructing Lucilius. On the content of Lucilius' *concilium deorum*, see Manuwald (2009) 51–4.
16 The speech has long been taken as key to the text's serious purpose: Momigliano (1934) 76–7; Eden (1984) *ad Apoc.* 10.1; Leach (1989) 200–16; Binder (1999) *ad Apoc.* 10.1–11.6; Aftsomis (2010) 128; Vannini (2013); Green (2016) 685.
17 A role reinforced by the preceding claims, in which Seneca's Augustus alludes to his own *Res Gestae*. See Green (2016) for discussion.
18 An idea that permeates Roman thinking about the emperor's relationship to the law. For example, Pliny *Pan.* 65.1 notes that Trajan's conduct generates a new adage, *non est 'princeps super leges' sed 'leges super principem'. idemque Caesari consuli quod ceteris non licet.* 'it is not "the *princeps* is above the law", but "the law is above the *princeps*"'. The same limits applied to other consuls are also applied to Caesar as consul.' Pliny implies that Trajan behaves this way purely out of self-restraint. In other words, the *princeps* is the only one who can make himself accountable to the law, bring himself within its compass. The same idea emerges from *Cod. Iust.* 6.23.3: *licet enim lex imperii sollemnibus iuris imperatorem soluerit, nihil tamen tam proprium imperii est, ut legibus uiuere.* 'although the law of *imperium* has set the emperor free from formal laws, nonetheless nothing is so proper to *imperium* as the fact of its living by the laws.' Here, the emperor's supra-legal power is recognised in law and, one could say, made *possible* by it, while at the same time transcending it.

The *princeps* is included in the judicial system via his exclusion and his accountability is revealed as entirely self-directed.
19 Berger (1953) 386 on *censere*, 632 on *placet*, and 757 on *uacatio*. Legal and procedural language in this passage is noted by Eden (1984) *ad Apoc.* 10.1–11.5 and collated by Kaplan (1991) 105–6. Also relevant to the legal timbre of Augustus' speech is his reciting from a notebook (11.5) since the verb *recitare* is often used of legal pronouncements, e.g. Pliny *Ep.* 10.56.2, and Berger (1953) 669.
20 Claudius' voice is ridiculed at *Apoc.* 4.3; 5.2; 7.3; 11.3. Braund and James (1998) and Osgood (2007) show how the satire links Claudius' unsteady voice to his professional/moral failures as emperor. For the satire's more general combination of Claudius' bodily and moral failings, see also Panayotakis (2014) 155–6.
21 Manderson (2019) 260–71. See also White (1981–82).
22 Eden (1984) *ad Apoc.* 1.1 with comparanda.
23 See Eden (1984) 9–10 and Whitton (2013) 155–7 for summaries of the problem. For more specific treatment of the issue: Griffin (1976) 129–31; Price (1987) 87; Nauta (1987) 75; Gradel (2002) 325–30.
24 Gradel (2002) 327–30.
25 Gradel (2002) 326.
26 Tuori (2016a) 155.
27 On Claudius and the jurists, see Levick (2012) [1990] 117, and below.
28 Levick (2012) [1990] 116; Hurley (2001) *ad Cl.* 15.2. See also Suet. *Cl.* 23.1
29 Thus Relihan (1993) 81: 'a council of unworthy gods'.
30 Janus' position as *designatus . . . in kal. Iulias postmeridianus consul* implies that he is consul for only one afternoon, a clear allusion to the habit, adopted under the principate, of shortening consuls' terms of office so that more individuals could achieve this honour over the course of a calendar year. Further, the appointment for the *afternoon* coincides with traditional Roman siesta time, so Janus' role entails no work.
31 Aftsomis (2010) 135–6. Rudich (1997) 39 likewise notes Augustus' self-centredness in the *Apocolocyntosis*. O'Gorman (2005) 105 remarks that Augustus' *indignatio* 'makes him a quasi-satirical speaker'.
32 Relihan (1993) 89–90, Paschalis (2009) 202–4. On the text's seemingly self-contradictory inversions, see Nauta (1987).
33 Aftsomis (2010) 136. Cf. Seneca's description of judgments formed in anger at *Ira* 1.17.7 (which recalls his portraits of Claudius in the *Apocolocyntosis*) and of the need for judges to be calm at *Ira* 1.19.2.
34 Cf. Aftsomis (2010) 137.
35 Leach (1989); Braund and James (1998).
36 Stacey (2011) 22.
37 Hammer (2014) 281–2.

38 The idea comes from Kastan (1986), who argues for a fundamental, conceptual link between monarchy's representation on stage in Renaissance England, e.g. in Shakespeare's history plays, and the eventual execution of Charles I.
39 Robinson (2005) 235. The line may also reflect Claudius' own purported fondness for quoting Homer (e.g. *Apoc.* 5.4), especially when dispensing verdicts (Suet. *Cl.* 42.1).
40 *Pace* Paschalis (2009) 209, who reads it only as ironic.
41 On gambling during the Saturnalia, see Versnel (1993) 147–8.
42 The line is problematic, but this is its most commonly accepted form. See Eden (1984) with discussion *ad loc.*, Binder (1999) and Schmeling (2020).
43 Knoche (1975) 105; Coffey (1976) 166: 'having been the dupe of freedmen in his lifetime, he becomes a slave of a freedman in the underworld. . . . His degradation is thus complete.'
44 The concept of the 'monde renversé' comes from Bergson (2005) [1911] and has been a staple of Plautine scholarship since Segal (1986). It works equally well as a theoretical paradigm for the *Apocolocyntosis*, with the obvious caveat that satire and comedy are not identical genres.
45 Though some imperial legislation was meant to protect slaves, it was fairly ineffectual. Joshel (1992) 28–32 is a helpful summary.
46 Eden (1984) *ad Apoc.* 15.2
47 Mousourakis (2007) 127–9; Rüfner (2016).
48 Aftsomis (2010) 104.
49 The quotation is from Braund and James (1998) 298. Versnel (1993) 205–10 was the first to explore the work's Saturnalian motif in depth, followed by Nauta (1987).
50 On the Saturnalia's relationship to the law, see Agamben (2005a) 71–3 and Ziogas (2021) 62–5.
51 Such as the comical *lex Tappula*: see Nauta (1987) 86; Versnel (1993) 161–2.
52 Agamben (2005a) 73.
53 Braund and James (1998) 306–7; Robinson (2005) 249.
54 Gunderson (2000); Fantham (2002).
55 Nauta (1987) 85.
56 See the caveats of Nauta (1987) 87 n.57 and Versnel (1993) 150 n.81. Edwards (2019) *ad loc.* does not flag any problems.
57 Not an official time of holiday for the law courts, but a less busy period, as Pliny *Ep.* 8.21.2 notes: *Iulio mense, quo maxime lites interquiescunt.* 'in the month of July, when legal business is at its quietest.'
58 Hurley (2001) *ad Cl.* 14.1.
59 Compare *Apoc.* 1.1 – *nihil nec offensae nec gratiae dabitur* 'nothing will be granted to animosity or favour' – with Tac. *Ann.* 1.1.1: *sine ira et studio* 'without anger or partisanship.'

60 An argument pursued by Paschalis (2009) 202, and Relihan (1993) 17 and 35.
61 Keane (2006) 73–4, drawing on Knight (1990) 143–4. The satirist's outspokenness could, of course, have real-world repercussions, in the form of breaking libel laws, or in the *Apocolocyntosis*' case, risking a charge of *maiestas*. See Goldschmidt (in this volume) for more on poetry and prosecution.
62 Possibly presented at the Saturnalia of 54 CE: see Griffin (1976) 129 n.3 and (1984) 96–7; Eden (1984) 4–5; Nauta (1987); Graf (2005) 204. See Nauta (1987) 69 for the origins of the hypothesis. Whitton (2013) 155 cautions against giving the hypothesis too much weight.

4

Iustitium in Lucan's *Bellum Ciuile*

Thomas Biggs

Legality dominates the second line of Lucan's *Bellum Ciuile*, where it emerges from a perverted declaration: *iusque datum sceleri canimus* ('legality conferred on crime we sing'). From this point forward, the epic activates several powerful concepts drawn from the legal sphere. One of the most important is *iustitium* ('cessation of the legal'). In this chapter, I argue that Lucan stretches *iustitium*'s meaning beyond the uses attested in other extant Roman texts. In the epic, *iustitium* contributes to the creation of a liminal zone where the senate, the Delphic oracle, and the city of Rome fail to function according to their past laws. *Iustitium* in Lucan's poem is at once (1) a Republican institution, signifying a cessation of civil and state-level affairs, and (2) at the same time fully imperial, indicating the funereal cessation made for mourning the death of a prince, attested first for the young heirs apparent of Augustus. By pushing the *iustitium* to such ends, Lucan presages later developments in political thought. Accordingly, the vision I offer of a textualized political space suspended in the light of emergency is at times predicated on a dialogue between Roman thought and modern political philosophy, especially that of the contemporary Italian philosopher Giorgio Agamben in his *Homo Sacer* project. Like the sublime in Henry Day's study of Lucan, the *iustitium* offers a way of thinking through the text that held meaning for Romans but has also spurred contemporary theoretical developments.[1]

Iustitium is essential to Agamben's state of exception (*Stato di eccezione*), itself the temporary suspension of the rule of law to preserve a state in the case of an exceptional and legally unanticipated threat.[2] For several twentieth-century thinkers, the ability to declare something similar to a state of exception supplied the very definition of sovereign power. The Wex dictionary of the Legal Information Institute at Cornell defines sovereignty as 'a political concept that refers to dominant power or supreme authority', noting that '[t]he Sovereign is the one who exercises power without limitation. Sovereignty is essentially the power to make laws.'[3] The influential though tarnished German jurist Carl Schmitt's conception of sovereign power informs this framework ('Sovereign is the one who decides on the exception'), but the idea is already found in certain strands of ancient political thought.[4] For example, Archytas of Tarentum (fourth century BCE) argued that life and law meet in the sovereign who cannot therefore be subjected to law, itself a view in dialogue with Aristotle's 'supremely virtuous king' who 'marks the threshold between the inside and the outside of the political order both above and below the law.'[5] As I will argue in the pages that follow, the *Bellum Ciuile* shows readers a Caesar linked to the standstill of *iustitium*, a character who articulates and then embraces the functions of the sovereign relative to the state of exception, one who inhabits the paradoxical position inside and outside the juridical order.[6] This may seem a contradiction, but the simultaneous existence of opposites is one result of the politico-juridical anachronism that *iustitium* brings out in the poem. Indeed, it is to a multiform, anachronistic Caesar that the poem ultimately subjugates its characters and readers in what I view to be a biopolitical act. This Caesar, whose sovereignty takes shape in the epic, even shapes the poetic world. Hence his *potestas* has (meta)literary implications as well. And by way of conclusion, I will show that although Caesar is made sovereign by the epic, the narrator elevates readers to the position of sovereign judgment by invoking along with *iustitium* the similarly suspended state introduced by the so-called *senatus consultum ultimum* ('final resolution of the senate'), thereby replicating a situation where every Roman (and reader) is empowered to act.[7]

Paying attention to Lucan's unique use of *iustitium* helps us to articulate, to unpack, and to redescribe some aspects of the epic's infamous breakdown or confusion of *leges*. It lets us see the textual world as a 'state of limbo' or a state of suspension, at times expressed on syntactical, grammatical, social, religious, legal, and political terms.[8] This suspension appears a reflection on the legal and political sphere's mutation under Caesar and his successors as well as a comment on poetics in line with Jacques Derrida's remark that literature is '"an institution which tends to overflow the institution", whose law "tends, in principle, to defy or *lift* the law"'.[9] Scholars have long remarked upon the dislocations of Lucan's text, from syntactical subject–object reversals in verses of violent action (for example, the Caesarian Scaeva's cry at 6.160–1), to weddings that lack all features of a wedding (see the negative catalogue of Cato's empty wedding at Book 2.350–79). On stylistic grounds, the epic is 'defined by discontinuity and diversion ... contortions in sentence structure, the highs and lows of ... [a] variable pitch', as

Gareth Williams recently put it.¹⁰ Theorists and historians of civil war have highlighted the impossibility of discerning good and bad or virtue and vice when friends and family are the enemy.¹¹ *Iustitium* in particular furthers our discussion of these central points. Viewing the poetic world and its grammar in relation to the vacuous standstill of *iustitium* sheds new light on how multiple temporalities, statuses, and multiple states of ruination can coexist in the narrative but never reach their final form, a dynamic that results in the very abeyance that holds off empire while simultaneously enabling it.

Part I

We begin with definitions. According to the *Oxford Latin Dictionary*, *iustitium* was a 'cessation of judicial and all other public business, in the event of national calamities, riots, etc. (latterly perh. only on the death of an emperor or one of this family). b (transf., of any suspension of activity)'.¹² In Republican Rome, the *iustitium* enacted an official suspension of business either to prepare for an emergency or to observe public mourning. As for what could be expected at the experiential level, the sources include the change from civilian to military dress and the mustering of soldiers; the suspension of public business, which includes the senate; the closing of the shops and private business; the suspension of jurisdiction and the closing of the courts.¹³ The declaration of *iustitium* is sometimes even tied to a special prerogative of the dictatorship during the Republic, a potentially intriguing linkage of cessation with the singular entity (a sovereign?) who is, in a sense, *solutus legibus* ('not bound by the laws').¹⁴

Beyond the tangible effects of *iustitium*, namely the series of actions one can order and organize into lists, Agamben offers some illuminating abstractions. He argues that

> the *iustitium* was not simply a suspension in the administration of justice, but an abeyance of the law as such ... [a] juridical institution that consists solely in the production of a juridical vacuum [*un vuoto giuridico*], of a space entirely devoid of *ius*.¹⁵

For Agamben, *iustitium*'s essence is visible in its etymological formation from *ius* and *sistere*. It means literally 'to bring to a stop, to suspend the *ius*, the juridical order.' On this point, Agamben can quote Aulus Gellius, who states it is 'as if it were an interval and a sort of cessation of the *ius*' (*iuris quasi interstitio et quaedam cessatio*).¹⁶ Agamben even cites anonymous 'grammarians' who 'explained etymologically, *sicut solstitium dicitur* (*iustitium* means "when the law stands still, just as [the sun does in] the solstice")'. Yet he seems to miss the fact that this explanation is transmitted not by some random 'grammarian' but by the scholiastic comments on Lucan's epic found in a tenth-century medieval manuscript (*Commenta Bernensia*, Cod. 370). The analogy was passed down from antiquity specifically to explain Lucanian *iustitium*. At any rate, these grammarians and antiquarians often miss the mark. In their interpretations of the term and its meanings they rely too heavily on etymology and analogy or overstate the nature of legal suspension at Rome, offering Agamben the appearance of evidence in support of his more sweeping claims about total juridical vacuity. Roman legal historians largely do not support the notion that law itself was suspended *in toto*. Nonetheless, if these ancient authors have led Agamben into excesses of interpretation, his claims actually line up with what I propose Lucan's poem suggests about the transformations at Rome that led from Republic to Principate. Agamben's misreadings, if that is what they are, elucidate Lucan's poem.

We now have some sense of the Republican *iustitium*, but what of the funereal dimensions that took shape under the pressures of nascent empire? Let's briefly consider a few examples starting from the late-Augustan or Tiberian consolation by 'Pseudo-Ovid' for Livia, the wife of Augustus, on the death of Drusus the Elder in 9 BCE ('the untimely end of yet another imperial favorite and possible successor').[17] The elegiac poem notes that during this *iustitium* (*Epic. Drusi* 185–7)

> iura silent mutaeque tacent sine uindice leges;
>   aspicitur toto purpura nulla foro.
> Dique latent templis...

The *iura* are silent, and the muted laws are hushed without a defender; no purple is spotted in the entire Forum. The gods are hidden away in their temples...[18]

These lines are of extreme scholarly importance among the pre-Lucanian sources for *iustitium*. In fact, the first attested use of *iustitium* for funereal mourning concerns an heir apparent of Augustus. Subsequently, *iustitia* were somewhat regular during the Julio-Claudian dynasty. Extant inscriptions record the funereal *iustitia* for the death of Augustus' adopted sons Gaius and Lucius (cf. *CIL* VI 895=31195 and *CIL* IX 5290).[19] Tacitus's account of the later death of Drusus' son Germanicus at *Annals* 2.82 is representative: a declaration of *iustitium* (*sumpto iustitio*) is followed by several months of empty courts and a vacuum in public affairs (*desererentur fora*); closed homes; silence and lament rule the day (*passim silentia et gemitus*). An extant bronze tablet of the *rogatio* on Germanicus' death, the Tabula Hebana, notes the closure of the temples. Moreover, several ancient authors consider the *iustitium* of Drusus the Elder in particular to be a distinctly notable moment of transition. While pseudo-Ovid's *consolatio* certainly shows up in several Lucanian intertexts, I suspect an important influence on Lucan's broader thinking was Livy's likely decision to end (or nearly end) his histories with the death and funeral of this same Drusus, i.e. to conclude the *Ab urbe Condita* with the *iustitium* that functioned as a period of mourning a lost prince *and* as a transitional zone between Republic and dynastic imperial monarchy.[20]

In an important 1980 study Henk Versnel explored how social mourning and *anomia* define the response to a *princeps*' death, ushering in a liminal or marginal period, a quasi-interregnum, wherein the *iustitium* sits at the centre and is defined by a complex of mourning acts. Illuminating for the world of Lucan's epic, these critical periods are said to be marked by 'temporary substitution of order by disorder, of culture by nature, of *kosmos* by *chaos*, of *nomos* by *physis*, of *eunomia* by *anomia*', a series of inversions that present a society in chaos, a period of license and legal anarchy defined by its 'in-betweenness' on cosmic and terrestrial planes.[21] In the epic's opening, Lucan hints at *iustitium*'s relevance for such a liminal period as he more generally depicts a discordant Stoic(ish) cosmos and destabilises (or perhaps simply redefines) *ius* itself, creating, in Agamben's words, 'a space devoid of law, a zone of anomie in which all legal determinations ... are deactivated ... an absolute non-place with respect to the law.'[22] As noted already, the poem begins 'Of wars across Emathian plains, worse/more than civil wars, and of legality conferred on crime (*iusque datum sceleri*) we sing.' The meaning of *iusque datum sceleri* in line 2 is key, if admittedly elusive.[23] In his commentary, Paul Roche translates 'legality imposed upon criminality,' and he underscores the fact that '[t]he notion of legal authority is [a] ... thematic preoccupation of the text.' According to his statistics, '*ius* appears 75x in *BC* and is the first of many legal words, phrases, and allusions to feature in the poem.'[24] The second line of Book 1 inverts the meaning of *ius* and the verses to come highlight the impotence of *leges*, but it is at the start of Book 2, after Caesar has crossed the Rubicon and portents have revealed the anger of the gods, that Lucan explicitly introduces *iustitium* (*BC* 2.16–21):

> ergo, ubi concipiunt quantis sit cladibus orbi
> constatura fides superum, **ferale per urbem**
> **iustitium**; latuit plebeio tectus amictu
> omnis honos, nullos comitata est purpura fasces.

tum questus tenuere suos magnusque per omnis
errauit sine uoce dolor.

So realization that the world would pay with great calamities
for the gods' truthfulness enacted a **funereal suspension
throughout Rome**; every magistrate lay low, clad in
ordinary dress, no purple robe accompanying the Rods of office.
Then their complaining they suppressed, and **deep and voiceless
grief pervaded** all.

What follows the declaration of *iustitium* in line 18 is the official cessation writ large of what makes Rome Rome. The *iustitium* functions on a local level within Book 2: the shops and courts are shut; the treasury (the Temple of Saturn) is locked until Caesar opens it impiously in Book 5. These are tangible markers of the cessation of the legal and the suspension of the religious sphere during *iustitium*. The funereal dimensions of this scene simultaneously draw upon the later imperial/dynastic developments.[25] In this pivotal moment there is an impossible coexistence of the distinctly Republican and imperial aspects of *iustitium*.

Immediately after the declaration of *ferale iustitium*, a lamenting Roman matron emerges from the shadows to define the political pause placed upon the principate's emergence that *iustitium* creates through suspension.[26] The delay is key to creating imperial sovereignty – it foreshadows the installation of hereditary dynasty (think of Germanicus or Drusus and their *iustitia*) – but it is also a delay to empire's emergence. Hence the poetic state of exception that plays out in the remaining books suspends the teleology of Republican history, granting a juridico-political aspect to the often divine or fatalistic delays (*morae*) well known from Lucan's epic predecessors (2.36–42):

> Quarum una madentis
> scissa genas, planctu liuentis atra lacertos,
> 'nunc', ait 'o miserae, contundite pectora, matres,
> nunc laniate comas neue hunc differte dolorem
> et summis seruate malis. Nunc flere potestas
> dum pendet fortuna ducum: cum uicerit alter
> gaudendum est.'

> One of them spoke, with torn
> and dripping cheeks, her arms black and blue from her blows:
> 'Now bruise your breasts, O miserable mothers,
> now tear your locks; do not defer your grief

or save it for the last disaster. Now, while the leaders' destiny
is in suspension, you may weep; once one of them has conquered,
you must rejoice.'

Already at the opening of Book 1 (*iusque datum sceleri*) and here at Book 2's beginnings, the *Bellum Ciuile* introduces *iustitium*, a declaration of a poetic state of exception, a literary manifestation and figuration of what Agamben defines as the temporary suspension of the rule of law. And Lucan is at once innovative and traditional in thematizing 'suspension' as a crisis of content (the crossing of the Rubicon, the outbreak of civil war, and the need to judge, *krinein*, to choose sides) and a crisis of craft (how to shape a chaotic and strained poetics capable of relating the *anomie* of civil war).

In his 2013 book, *The Poetics of Consent: Collective Decision Making and the Iliad*, David Elmer proposes that a similar nexus of conflict and crisis is enacted at the opening of Homer's *Iliad*. Hence such exceptional states may draw upon a unique epic inheritance as well, building upon the tradition's ur-text. Elmer argues that a suspension of normal political function and even of linguistic expression/narrative protocol is enacted by the conflict between Achilles and Agamemnon, claiming specifically that '[t]he *Iliad*'s opening scenes provide a kind of dramatized symptomatology of the crisis opened up by the state of exception.' In Elmer's words, '[w]hether as a matter of law or of language –or indeed of any coherent system –the suspension of norms brings about as an immediate consequence a certain crisis of uncertainty.'[27] For audiences, the crisis between Achilles and Agamemnon that sets the *Iliad* spiralling into suspension is not bound to a timeline of recent historical events. Essential, however, to Lucan's *ferale iustitium* in Book 2 are the fictive dimensions of the *iustitium*'s place in the epic's narrative chronology. As Fantham notes in her commentary, '[t]here is no record in the historical sources of such a suspension in 49.'[28] And despite her attempt to work around this contradiction, it is clear that there was truly no *iustitium* declaration during Caesar's march south.[29] Lucan invents *iustitium* when it wasn't actually declared and, as we can now explore, takes the very idea of its power to suspend and silence and makes it a driving thematic force in the epic, giving a juridical term the power both to describe the Roman world he inhabits and to recast the dynamic of crisis and conflict found already in the *Iliad*.

Upon his arrival in Caesar's camp after fleeing from Rome, the (former) tribune Curio delivers an important speech (see especially 1.272-9). To his mind, *ius* remained so long as he could speak from the *rostra*, but war has now compelled laws to be silent (*at postquam leges bello siluere coactae*, 277). At first glance, perhaps the clause simply displays a vivid use of language. The silence of law is, however, more intricately tied to the suspension of *ius* Curio has just recognized: recall pseudo-Ovid's consolation for Livia ('the *iura* are silent, and the muted laws are hushed without a defender'). The suspension of *ius* is constantly marked by the literal silence of legality and of people. Lucan clearly plays with this dimension of the term.[30] He already noted that 'grief wandered without voice' (*errauit sine uoce dolor*) during Book 2's *ferale iustitium*. A basic depiction of silent grief? Within a view of the text that notes the political *potestas* of silence, the link between *sine uoce* and *iustitium* must carry greater meaning (see discussion of the Pythia below).

By this point in my reading, we have seen that the transformation of *ius* is prominent both in Book 1's opening and in Curio's speech, where it is ultimately negated and then subordinated to Caesar's sovereignty, which is to say his power to reshape status and meaning within the poetic state of exception, to make *hostis* ('enemy of the state') into *ciuis* ('citizen') once again.[31] *Ius* also returns at the beginning of Book 2 as the fully developed *ferale iustitium*. But before the close of the first book, the words of the late-Republican polymath, antiquarian, and astrologer Nigidius Figulus prefigure the *iustitium* to come (1.666–70).[32]

> inminet armorum rabies, **ferrique potestas**
> confundet **ius** omne manu, scelerique nefando
> nomen erit uirtus, multosque exibit in annos
> hic furor. et superos quid prodest poscere finem?
> **cum domino pax ista uenit**. duc, Roma, malorum   670
> continuam seriem clademque in tempora multa
> extrahe ciuili tantum iam libera bello.

> war's frenzy is upon us: **the power of the sword**
> shall overthrow **legality** (*ius*) by might, and impious crime
> shall bear the name of heroism, and this madness shall extend
> for many a year. And what use is it to ask the gods to end it?
> **The peace we long for brings a sovereign**. Rome, prolong your chain
> of disaster without a break and protract calamity
> for lengthy ages: only now in civil war are you free.

Like the poet and several other characters, Lucan's Nigidius Figulus is aware of civil war's status as suspension, a temporal and aesthetic exception that defies structures of domination, that slows movement toward an imperial *telos*. The lines contain a 'longed-for endlessness', to use Day's words, a part of the poem's sublimity that is itself further enacted by the poem's fragmentary, abrupt closing in Book 10 with Caesar under siege.[33] (The state of the poem's conclusion, intentional or not, also contributes to the epic's poetics of suspension and delay, specifically the delay of the imperial future/Neronian present's arrival.) We might also conclude, as Duncan MacRae does in a nuanced reading, that Nigidius' characterisation highlights his links to empire:

> despite his expertise and 'Republican' politics, the theologian can only predict a monarch (*dominus*). This forecast of a *dominus* alludes to an Augustan-period story that Nigidius had predicted, on the birth of Octavius (the future Augustus) in 63, that a *dominus terrarum* had been born. The allusion introduces an ambiguity into the identification of this *dominus*: Julius Caesar, Augustus, even Nero?[34]

This shifting *telos* for Nigidius' speech can also be expressed as the rise of the sovereign that the state of exception enables, a princeps who is truly legion within Lucan's historical palimpsest. And *this* is a dimension of late Republican history scholars have illuminated in recent work, a dimension Lucan dramatizes in the epic.

In an excellent series of studies, Michèle Lowrie has articulated the shift in political power that I see at the core of Lucan's thinking on *iustitium* and exception. Lowrie has begun to spell out how sovereignty at Rome was forged in the late Republican period by repeated states of exception that led to the principate.[35] This focus on exception as the pathway to sovereignty links Lucan's forebodings of Agamben with key dynamics of the actual transformations that occurred in late-Republican Rome. Lowrie retools Schmitt's famous dictum: '[t]he sovereign was created by the decision on the state of exception' and Augustus' sovereignty is that defined by Schmitt and expanded on by Agamben; 'Augustus may in fact provide the foundational model for this problematic.'[36] In his hunt for foreknowledge in a late-Republican world-in-suspension, Lucan's Nigidius Figulus expresses this outlook in pithy Neronian terms: at present, *iustitium* and *bellum ciuile*; soon enough, *cum domino pax ista uenit*. Long before Agamben or Schmitt, Lucan makes the same argument through his depiction of the emergence of sovereignty in the figure of Augustus, a story told through the epic's protreptic and anachronistic depiction of Julius Caesar as a character who is always already his imperial successors, and who acts in an epic world that is experiencing a 'temporary' emergency that for Nero's readers had become a permanent state of exception.

Beyond Nigidius Figulus' vision of Roman history, *iustitium* and prognostication are especially important for Book 5. As the book opens, the senate in exile convenes in Greece. Caesar has marched on Rome; Pompey, the senate, and their allies have scattered across the Mediterranean. It is telling that the senate here – in a sense the Republic itself – meets for a final time.[37] A short way into his opening speech, Lentulus makes this idea explicit (5.27–37):

> Tarpeia sede perusta
> Gallorum facibus Veiosque habitante Camillo
> illic Roma fuit. non umquam perdidit ordo
> mutato sua iura solo. **maerentia tecta**
> Caesar habet **uacuasque domos legesque silentes**
> **clausaque iustitio tristi** fora; curia solos
> illa uidet patres plena quos urbe fugauit:
> ordine de tanto quisquis non exulat hic est.
> ignaros scelerum longaque in pace quietos
> bellorum primus sparsit furor: omnia rursus
> membra loco redeunt.

> When the Tarpeian sanctuary
> was burnt by Gallic torches and Camillus lived at Veii–
> there, was Rome. Not ever has our Order lost
> authority by change of soil. **The mourning houses,**
> **empty homes, the silent laws, and Forum closed**
> **in grim suspension** – those are Caesar's; that Senate-House
> sees only those Senators whom it expelled when Rome was full:
> from such a mighty Order whoever is not an exile is here.
> War's first frenzy scattered us, ignorant of wickedness,
> reposing in long peace: now all the limbs return
> to their place again.

uacuasque domos: Hyperbole drives the depiction of an empty city. Historians will object that many remained in Rome, but quibbling misses the point. Vacuity is the key. Caesar's Rome is no Rome, and its houses are empty. They are reduced to faint line drawings of a spectral city. Indeed, the *ferale iustitium* noted in Book 2 is here reintroduced by *maerentia tecta*. Funereal mourning becomes relevant once again. It foreshadows Caesar's death through a scene of Rome in mourning that only becomes possible with *his* demise - and especially so with the deaths of Augustus and his numerous heirs apparent before him.[38] ***legesque silentes***: The vacuous city is depicted with its laws silenced. We recall Curio from Book 1, where he explicitly noted *ius* was no longer in force and that war compelled laws to be silent (*leges bello siluere coactae*). I suggested that we connect the image of silent laws with Pseudo-Ovid's understanding of the *iustitium* itself as *iura silent mutaeque tacent sine uindice leges*. Lentulus thus strengthens this understanding of a suspended legal sphere within the epic. ***clausaque iustitio tristi fora***: Finally, the sad *iustitium* Lentulus depicts reaffirms the funereal one in the second book. The senate, like Caesar's Rome, is defined by its suspended state. A reader might also think of the role *iustitium* plays not only in pressing pause on Republican Rome but also in signalling the emergence of dynastic empire.

From this vision of *iustitium* in an ersatz senate, the epic immediately turns its narrative gaze upon Appius, the senate's proconsul in Achaia. Appius travels to Delphi to find out the future, but the oracle, Apollo's mouthpiece, is on vacation. Because of regal fear of the future, the shrine of prophetic Phoebus has apparently been closed for many years[39] (***multosque obducta per annos***, 5.69; cf. Figulus' words etc cf. Figulus' words at 1.668), so Appius tries to compel the priestess. Lucan continues (5.111–18),

non ullo saecula dono
nostra carent maiore deum, quam Delphica sedes
quod siluit, postquam reges timuere futura
et superos uetuere loqui. nec uoce negata
Cirrhaeae maerent uates, templique fruuntur   115
iustitio. Nam si qua deus sub pectora uenit,
numinis aut poena est mors inmatura recepti
aut pretium...

        Our generation lacks
no greater gift of gods than that the Delphic sanctuary
has fallen silent, ever since kings feared the future
and forbade the gods to speak. And Cirrha's prophetesses
do not grieve that voice is denied (*uoce negata*), but enjoy the temple's
suspension (*iustitio*). Because, if the god enters any breast,
an early death is the penalty of taking in the deity,
or the reward.

The poet addresses the prophetess as Figulus did Rome and the reader: enjoy the state of suspension while it lasts. Yet the Delphic priestess is soon said to be lying about her inability to access the divine through communion with Apollo. She appears, when forced, to be inspired and relates pages of the history which have yet to be revealed by the narrator (though she truly only speaks for a moment). Does this alter *iustitium*'s force in the epic?

Deceit undermines a reader's view of this admittedly anomalous instance of *iustitium*. It is also the final use of the term in the epic. Tellingly, in the OLD entry for *iustitium* included at the beginning of this chapter, option b 'of any suspension of activity' is propped up by this passage alone. A reader might wonder what the priestess' refusal to gaze upon the future has to do with the various characters who attempt the same, succeed, but recoil from revelation.[40] One of the most striking examples of this sort of declaration comes from the narrator himself in Book 7 (his famous *tacebo* at 556 concerning Pharsalus, 'I will be silent'), and it is surely not irrelevant that the Delphic priestess here is called *uates*, like Vergil's sibyl who foresees *bella, horrida bella* in Italy (*Aen.* 6.86), hence a poet-figure, a prophet of civil war.

To conclude Part I of this chapter, a reader could do worse than to recall Nigidius Figulus, who like the Pythia seeks knowledge of the epic's discordant world by utilising a prognostic system itself in a state of suspension. Figulus, along with the Etruscan haruspex Arruns, who is called a *uates* in Book 1 as he refuses to interpret the entrails, and the inspired matrons, prophets, and prophetic gods who populate the poem, especially the Delphic priestess and the necromancer Erichtho, all have a purchase on defining the emerging political sphere. They import the imperial future into the fictive, uncertain late-Republican outlook of the narrative's constructed temporality. In a study of divinatory practice, liminality and boundary transgression in the epic, Federico Santangelo remarks that Lucan's 'world has lost its proper order, natural and political alike', hence the compulsion felt by so many characters to seek the future out through striking but flawed means.[41] I suggest that Lucan's insertion of *iustitium* into prophetic and religious spaces signals the origin of this disorder.

Part II

Following Schmitt, Agamben stresses that

> The paradox of sovereignty consists in the fact that the sovereign is, at the same time, outside and inside the juridical order. If the sovereign is truly the one to whom the juridical order grants the power of proclaiming the state of exception and, therefore, of suspending the order's own validity, then [he now quotes from Schmitt], 'the sovereign stands outside the juridical order and, nevertheless, belongs to it, since it is up to him to decide if the constitution is to be suspended *in toto*'.[42]

Lowrie has subsequently reaffirmed that Roman law, in select instances, can back up Agamben's argument on this particular matter. She introduces, among others, a passage in Gaius that shows the emperor was both outside the law in his ability to create it, but subject to the law since his power derived from it.[43] It is this very matter that Lucan underscores during Caesar's encounter with the spectral, grief-stricken *imago Patriae* at the Rubicon in *BC* 1 (1.183–92). When personified Patria says, 'Where further do you march? (*quo tenditis ultra?*) if as citizens, this far only is allowed (*si ciues, huc usque licet*)', she appeals to an understanding of the legal that has already been suspended. She is made ignorant of what the Neronian reader cannot but recall: Caesars decide on such matters. Caesar comes *iure* because he is already the decider of the constitutional sphere in the silence of *leges*, during the suspension of *ius*. Impossible, yes, but not in Lucan's poetic world.

At the Rubicon, Caesar even informs a reader of the relationship his actions have to the *iustitium* (225–7):

> 'hic' ait 'hic pacem temerataque iura relinquo;
> te, Fortuna, sequor. procul hinc iam foedera sunto;
> credidimus satis <his>, utendum est iudice bello.'
>
> Here I abandon peace and desecrated *iura*;
> Fortune, it is you I follow. Farewell to treaties from now on;
> I have relied on them for long enough; now war must be the judge.

To repeat, 'the sovereign, having the legal power to suspend the validity of the law, legally places himself outside the law.' *iura relinquo* indeed.[44] So too, Lucan's Caesar, as the sovereign force that dictates the dimensions of the state in the poem, can be thanked and blamed for playing a major role in shaping the grotesque and perversely attractive aesthetics of the poetic world. On this reading, his phrase *iura relinquo* also carries a metapoetic force. But an important qualification is needed immediately. On at least one key level, Lucan depicts Caesar as always already the possessor of sovereign power, even from the outset of the narrative. This is one of the paradoxes I discussed earlier in the chapter. It enacts a collapse of the Caesarian future into Republican past; or rather, it highlights the a/pantemporality of the text. In the story of the emergence of the sovereign through the Republic's descent into states of exception (following Lowrie), Lucan already grants Caesar that power. Caesar performs the declaration and places himself outside the law, but he is already sovereign: state and Caesar are one. An anachronistic paradox, perhaps, but the narrator's retreat into an historically contingent outlook allows for this bifurcation.[45]

As noted already, Caesar's crossing of the Rubicon did not actually prompt a *iustitium* declaration. That is Lucan's invention. There was, however, a motion of the senate to recognise the situation as a *tumultus*.[46] Moreover, at the moment of Caesar's crossing the senate had already activated the emergency measure of the so-called *senatus consultum ultimum* (*SCV*). Alongside *iustitium*, this rather opaque and shifty concept, famously exploited by Cicero for the Catilinarians (see Sallust, *Bellum Catilinae* 29.2–3), helps us to understand Lucan's meditation on sovereign power. Caesar's own *Bellum Ciuile* (1.5) even describes the *SCV* declaration that enacted the unique suspension Lucan recreates in the epic. In general, the resolution calls on Romans to act to save the state, a charge often thought to legitimize all Romans to perform violence outside of normal legal bounds in order to stop individuals (likely citizens now deemed to be *hostes*) from doing harm to the Republic.[47] So, in order to grasp what Lucan is up to by engaging with the suspended legal sphere of *iustitium* and to a less explicit degree the *SCV*, we need to think a bit more about emergency declarations and how they affect the individual biopolitically.

Engaging closely with Adolph Nissen's study of *iustitium* (1877), Agamben suggests that 'ancient authors and modern scholars seem to oscillate between the idea of a total anomie, in which all juridical powers or features are abolished, and the opposite conception of legal plenitude, in which the law seems to coincide with the whole of reality'.[48] Agamben here adduces Livy's claim that during *iustitium* the consuls are reduced to the state of private citizens (*in priuato abditi*) alongside a slightly different case, that of the private citizen, Scipio Nasica. In 133 BCE, following a *SCV* declaration, Nasica killed Tiberius Gracchus under the pretence that the current legal situation granted him magisterial *imperium*; the example regularly returns in late-Republican accounts of the *SCV*.[49] In this context, Agamben also reads Theodor Mommsen's conception of the *SCV* as a quasi-dictatorship and, more importantly, as something like the release of a floating *imperium* that could be taken on by anyone (e.g. Nasica) during the *Notstand*, a state *außerhalb des Rechts*, 'outside the rule of law'.[50] And it is here, in the light of *iustitium* and Mommsen's somewhat misappropriated formulation of the *SCV* that I begin to see a way of reading Lucan's epic on juridical grounds: a poetics based on the State of Exception, not just a poem *about* a state of exception.

Like Caesar's sovereign declaration, the act of reading depends on the sovereign power of judgment.[51] It is also derived from the reader's unique, paradoxical position both inside and outside the world of the text. Readers of the *BC* are told by the narrator how to think and how to feel, yet they are never fully bodies in (textual) space, like those subjected to the violence of war and

Caesarian domination on the fields of Pharsalus. They exist in a threshold. They are extratextual Neronian readers who are also made into paratextual characters that peer in from the margins. They are pressured to collapse fully into the poetic world as embodied agents, especially when apostrophized into action. Despite only being ghostly presences, readers are still subjected to the biopower of Caesarism and of Lucan's text, to its biopolitical programme. This is so because they are made to feel a part of the poem's unfolding world, and because their 'real' world is also that of Caesar: a new ruler with the same name.

Biopower is a concept Agamben and especially Michel Foucault have explored to somewhat differing ends. For our present purposes it can be defined as Foucault does: the 'subjugation of bodies and control of populations', and 'the set of mechanisms through which the basic biological features of the human species became the object of a political strategy, of a general strategy of power'.[52] Shreyaa Bhatt has recently argued that the theory illuminates the bodily politics of Augustus, whose acts, of making his body the site of sovereignty and of regulating the fertility, reproduction, safety, and security of Romans (think of certain *leges Iuliae*), show us a developing set of ideas and practices concerned with the state's 'control of the biological'.[53] The *BC* explores this political revolution in the body of Julius Caesar, in addition to the often-fragmented bodies of the epic at large. It grapples with the biopolitical regulation of citizens to what Agamben calls 'bare life' (using a reductive view of Aristotelian *zōē* versus *bios*), which is the state that emerges from asking 'how life itself or natural life is politicized' ... [to which] the answer is 'through abandonment to an unconditional power of death, that is, the power of sovereignty'.[54] Lucan's epic thus narrates the citizen body's (/the body politic's) movement from Republic to Empire (capitals R and E). It narrates both the collective and the individual Roman *corpus*' transformation. And I here speak not just of its institutional transformation. It tells of the individual's subjugation to the sovereign body of a Caesar, which, as Lucan declares, is everything (*omnia Caesar erat*, 3.108).[55] In a state of exception, in the aftermath of the sovereign declaration, a citizen is reduced to bare life in the face of the emergent transformation in power. From this perspective, the poetic state of exception brought on by *iustitium* becomes an *aition*, an origin story for how the Neronian reader became subject to the probing and invasive compulsion of Caesarian rule and for how the individual is interpolated into a body politic coterminous with the princeps. A reader may very well be granted the position of a Scipio Nasica within a zone of legal plenitude; they may become a figure seemingly invested by a sovereign authorization to act against Caesarism through the instrument of interpretation. At the same time, however, a reader is shown to be part of a poetic world that is Caesar, hence part of a body politic defined and dominated by the body of the *princeps*.

The poem thus suggests that the Roman Empire is a continual exception that comes into existence through 'exception.' The text is also a potential site of resistance to sovereign power, to power embodied in the singular Caesarian ruler. If the empire is permanent *iustitium*, the/a Republic remains on standby. As long as the textual war still rages – as long as a reader keeps reading – sovereign power is not yet placed in the hands of an individual, an idea that stands improbably alongside what Lucan also says of Caesar's grip on power from the very beginning. Sovereignty remains divided among citizens/readers, who are called upon to take action, but *iustitium* also enables dynastic monarchy's emergence out of the Republic, a reality that remains inescapable for Neronian readers.[56]

Notes

1 Day (2013). For Roman culture and Agamben, see Lowrie (2007) and (2010); Willis (2011). Cf. Weiner (2015) on Sophocles' *Antigone*. For law and Latin poetry, see e.g. Kenney (1969); Videau (2004); Gebhardt (2009); Lowrie (2016); Ziogas (2016a) (2016b), (2018), and esp. (2021).
2 Agamben (1998) 15; Lowrie (2010) 174.
3 https://www.law.cornell.edu/wex/sovereignty. See Bexley (in this volume).
4 Schmitt (2005) 5.
5 Gower (2015) 13.
6 Anzinger (2007) 122: '*iustitium* ist für Lucan ein Stichwort für den Ausnahmezustand.' Willis (2011) is essential reading.
7 For the *SCV*, see Lintott (1999a) 89–93; Arena (2012) 200–19; Straumann (2016), which takes a limited view of the *SCV*'s legal impact. The essays in Buongiorno (2020) appeared too late for consideration.
8 The poetic world and the empire are akin to Agamben's 'regularized state of exception', which is (Lowrie [2010] 178) 'a paradox whereby exceptional arrangements, by definition temporary, become the regular constitution, although the fiction is that the old constitution still operates.' She calls the contradiction a 'state of limbo.' Cf. Rich (2012).
9 Derrida (1992b) 36 via Davies (2016) 20.
10 Williams (2017) 99–100. See Henderson (1987).
11 E.g. Armitage (2017).
12 Cf. *TLL* 7.12.717–18. See also the more conservative understanding in Berger (1953); Nissen (1877) with caution.

13 Golden (2013) 87. The sources record at least 23 *iustitia* from 465 BCE to 23 CE. For example, Liv. 4.31.9: 'armed men were stationed on the walls, in the forum a *iustitium* was declared and the shops were closed. Everything became more like a camp than a city.' Cf. Liv. 9.7.8; Cic. *Phil.* 5.12; *Har. resp.* 55.11–22. For an illuminating treatment that touches on *iustitium* and late-Republican politics, see Russell (2016a).
14 Cornell (2015) 120–1 rightly cautions against this view.
15 Agamben (2005b) 286.
16 Agamben (2017) 201.
17 Jenkins (2009) 3. See Schrijvers (1988) 349–50; Schoonhoven (1992) *ad loc.*; Anzinger (2007) 121ff.; Brännstedt (2016). Cf. the *iustitium* of Drusus (*officium lugubre*) at Sen. *Marc.* 3.1–2.
18 All translations are my own unless otherwise noted.
19 See Lott (2012) for these texts and discussion.
20 Cf. Jenkins (2009) 6. When Lucan depicts Caesar's meeting with Patria at the Rubicon in Book 1 (see discussion in Part II of this chapter), he may allude to a similar scene linked to Drusus' demise once found near the conclusion of Livy's text. Drusus is elsewhere reported to have encountered a female spectre in Germany who declared he could go no further, after which he soon died (cue the *iustitium*). If Drusus were known to Lucan as an heir apparent who fully signalled the end of Republican history ('real' and Livian), and his meeting with a ghostly allegory led to death and *iustitium*, it is hard not to see Caesar in *Bellum Ciuile* 1 as already characterized by this background, one that foreshadows his own death and the worldwide *iustitium* to come. Cf. discussion in Narducci (1989); Radicke (2004).
21 Versnel (1980) 584–5. Cf. Agamben (2017) 84; 222–4.
22 Agamben (2017) 209.
23 Translations of Lucan in the current chapter are after Braund (1992).
24 Roche (2009) 103.
25 For the subsequent comparison of Rome's mourning and a matron's loss of a child, see Keith (2008) 234–5; Blaschka (2014) 186–8. On women, lament, dynasty and the poetic world's various disruptions, Gillespie (forthcoming).
26 Cf. Anzinger (2007) 122 (and ff.): '*ferale iustitium* kann verstanden werden als der Stillstand, der in einem Trauerfall eintritt – in diesem Falle die vorweggenommene Trauer über die bevorstehenden Toten des Krieges.' On Lucanian innovation in these lines, Schrijvers (1988) 349.
27 Elmer (2013) 69.
28 Fantham (1992) 83.
29 A recent commentary reflects the confusion of the historical tradition: Barrière (2016) 22 and 26. See Schrijvers (1988) 347–8.
30 Anzinger (2007) 122. Gowing (2005) 91: 'silence is one means of denying memory'.

31 On *hostis/ciuis* in the epic, see Roller (2001), with definitions at 28 n. 25; Willis (2011) especially chapter 3. In general, Lintott (1999a); Allély (2012); Straumann (2016) 95f.; Cornwell (2017) 21–3, 50–3.
32 MacRae (2013) 272–3; Volk (2017) 342–7.
33 Day (2013) 92.
34 See MacRae (2013) 274–5; Volk (2017) 343–6.
35 Lowrie (2007); (2010). Cf. Rich (2012).
36 Lowrie (2007) 55.
37 Henderson (1987) 147: '[a]lready Republican *ius* is "drawn to a close".'
38 On the civil war as Rome's funeral and the role of *iustitium*, see Blaschka (2014) 185–8.
39 Barratt (1979) 40.
40 Cf. Day (2013) 100.
41 Santangelo (2015) 184. On this matter, we might compare the *BC* with Thomas Hobbes' meditation on sovereignty, *Leviathan* (1651). Hobbes treats the tension between prophetic power and sovereignty as one that destabilises power (on analogy Figulus and others thus pose a threat for the emergent Julio-Claudian sovereign). We should also connect the Apollonian *iustitium* of Book 5 and the god's role in inspiring the Pythia with the Lucanian narrator's complex statement in the infamous 'Praise of Nero' in Book 1.
42 Agamben (2017) 17.
43 *Inst.* 1.5. See Lowrie (2010) 183 n. 13 Cf. *Digest* I.3.31: *Princeps legibus solutus est* ('the princeps is not bound by the laws'). See relevant discussion in Bexley (in this volume).
44 Spentzou (2018) 249–50; 268: 'His sublime excess is contagious; everything and everyone in touch with him is "absolved from limits", to use Eagleton's striking observation.' See Rimell (2015) 241 n. 19.
45 For anachronism, see now Rood, Atack and Phillips (2020). Gowing (2005) 97: 'it is very difficult to resist reading Lucan's *Pharsalia* as anything but a provocative commentary on the genesis of a Julio-Claudian autocracy and Nero.'
46 *OLD s.v.* 2a; Berger (1953) *s.v.* (746). For *tumultus* in the epic, Schrijvers (1988) 343.
47 See Cornwell (2017) esp. 50–3.
48 Agamben (2005a) 287.
49 It even appears explicitly in Lucan's epic as a precedent for the senate's suspension of *ius* (1.266–7). See Agamben (2017) 203–5.
50 In *Römisches Staatsrecht*, Mommsen even renders *iustitium* through related terms, *Aussetzung der Rechtsprechung*, what we might translate 'the suspension of jurisdiction or the power of the legal'. Mommsen (1888) 1063–4.
51 See also Bexley (in this volume).
52 Foucault (2007) 1. Agamben's recent comments and publications concerning the Covid-19 pandemic have sparked an often-heated series of debates and condemnations. What damage 2020 will do to his legacy remains to be seen.

53 Bhatt (2017). Cf. Habinek (1998) 29 and *passim*; Milnor (2006).
54 Catherine Mills, *Internet Encyclopedia of Philosophy* https://www.iep.utm.edu/agamben/. She continues: 'It is in this abandonment of natural life to sovereign violence ... that "bare life" makes its appearance. For bare life is not natural life *per se* ... but rather, it is the politicized form of natural life. Being neither *bios* nor *zoe*, then, bare life emerges from within this distinction and can be defined as "life exposed to death," especially in the form of sovereign violence. (compare HS 88).' Cf. Agamben (2017) 9. Brooke Holmes' recent interrogation (2019) of the weaknesses in Agamben's binary is necessary reading.
55 Cf. Connolly (2016) 294. As Leigh puts it, 'Lucan's Caesar sees himself, and is seen by his supporters, not as a citizen, but as a king. He thus arrogates to himself the status of kingship which Seneca confesses in the *De Clementia* as the reality of Nero's rule.' Leigh (1997) 57. For a new take on the epic's social compact, see Fertik (2018).
56 This chapter developed from conversation at a meeting of Yale's Classics and Theory colloquium held in 2010. I have benefited from the opportunity to share this research at the University of Warwick, Durham University, Marshall University, and Brown University. For comments and discussion, I am particularly grateful to Nora Goldschmidt, Peter Heslin, Elena Giusti, Victoria Rimell, Christina Franzen, John Bodel, Jay Reed, and the editors of the present volume.

Part Two

Literature and the Legal Tradition

5

Terence's *Phormio* and the Legal Discourse and Legal Profession at Rome

Jan Felix Gaertner

The comedies of Plautus and Terence are the most extensive body of non-fragmentary Latin texts from the late third and early second century BCE. Since all the surviving comedies are based on works of Greek New Comedy,[1] they are an important testimony to the reception of Greek literature in Rome and offer a good starting point for investigating how Rome interacted with other cultures and what might be the peculiarity of the Romans or specifically Roman. On the other hand, the comedies also contain many pieces of information on various details of everyday Roman life such as food, clothing, social interaction, or religious customs. Particularly frequent are references to Roman law and Roman legal terminology: the plays allude to Roman legal norms or procedures, and often apply (more or less jokingly) legal ideas and legal terminology to entirely non-legal matters such as, e.g., a love affair.[2]

Over the last 150 years, several studies have dealt intensively with the legal contents and legal terminology in the Roman comedies of Plautus and Terence. To this day, two main approaches are prevalent: on the one hand, legal historians exploit the comedies as sources for the reconstruction of Attic and Roman law,[3] and on the other hand, classical philologists use our knowledge of ancient Greek and Roman law to determine how closely the comedies of Plautus and Terence are based on lost models of Greek New Comedy. These two approaches are methodologically problematic, because they assume that literary texts generally provide a faithful representation of the world in which we live or the laws that we are supposed to follow. Nevertheless, the two approaches have vastly improved our understanding of the legal contents of Roman comedies and their relationship to the historical reality in Athens and Rome.[4] The literary and sociological dimension of the topic, however, has not yet been fully grasped. Three questions seem particularly important and interesting.

To begin with, theatre performances – like every other act of communication – take place in a context of social and legal norms, e.g. rules regarding the freedom of speech or intellectual property.[5] This immediately raises the question how Graeco-Roman comedy has been shaped by legal parameters such as the legal norms of theatre performances or the legal status of actors and authors.

A second important question, which has not yet received sufficient attention, concerns the influence of Roman comedy on the perception of the legal system, its norms and its principal actors (judges, lawyers, legal experts). Philosophers and sociologists such as Bourdieu and Habermas have convincingly demonstrated that legal norms do not simply exist and are obeyed, but presuppose a social consensus that is negotiated through communication.[6] Consequently, Graeco-Roman comedies do not simply "reflect" the legal reality, but they recall, imprint, or challenge legal norms.[7]

Thirdly, there are also a number of fundamental literary and philological questions: Where, how and why do literary texts adopt expressions, thought patterns or structures from legal texts or procedures?[8] Is there such a thing as a typical legal comedy? Is the way law is dealt with in comedy different from that in other literary genres?

The present paper will address the second set of questions, i.e. the influence of comedy on the perception of the Roman law and legal system, and it will focus on Terence's *Phormio*. This play, which was first staged in 161 BCE, is an adaptation of the lost Greek comedy *Epidikazomenos* by Apollodorus of Carystus. Its plot is comparatively complicated, and legal issues play a greater role than in any other Roman comedy. Hence, it may be helpful to recall the key elements of the plot.

The play is set in Athens, and a central character is the old citizen Chremes. Besides his Athenian wife Nausistrata and his Athenian son Phaedria, he secretly has a second family on the island of Lemnos, consisting of an unnamed second wife and the beautiful daughter Phanium. At the time of the play the aforementioned daughter Phanium has reached marriageable age, and Chremes and his brother Demipho want to discreetly marry the young woman to Demipho's son Antipho, so that no one will ask too many questions about the girl's pedigree. While Chremes sails to Lemnos to fetch his daughter, however, Phanium has already come to Athens with her mother to look for her father. The search is unsuccessful, the mother dies and the destitute orphan mourns her death. By chance, however, the young Antipho sees her and immediately falls in love with her. Since his father Demipho would never agree to marry a destitute orphan, Antipho's friend Phormio devises the following plan: while Antipho's father is on a business trip, Phormio will take the young Antipho to court, claiming (a) that the girl has lost both parents, (b) that Antipho is the girl's closest male relative, and (c) that he must marry her in accordance with the Attic epiclerate or 'heiress law';[9] if Antipho does not deny the kinship in court, he will automatically be sentenced to marry the young woman.

At the beginning of the play, this plan has already been carried out, and Antipho's father Demipho has just returned home. He does not know that his son's wife is Chremes' Lemnian daughter Phanium and that the marriage he and his brother were planning has already been brought about. Thus, while his son has gone into hiding out of fear and shame, Demipho tries to get rid of the young woman: Accompanied by three legal advisors, Demipho confronts the cheater Phormio. When this confrontation ends merely in mutual threats, Demipho is at a loss, but Phormio unexpectedly changes his strategy and offers to marry the girl himself in exchange for a large dowry.[10] Demipho and his brother Chremes gladly accept, but, after the money has been paid, they learn that Antipho's current wife is Phanium and want to cancel their agreement with Phormio and get their money back. In the last scenes of the play, they try to drag Phormio to court, but he calls on Chremes' wife, Nausistrata, and exposes the bigamy. Since a divorce would ruin Chremes financially, the two old men beg for Nausistrata's forgiveness and accept the loss of their money.

There are few overall interpretations of the play, and of the few interpretations that exist, only two (if I am right) take into account the importance of legal issues: in 1978, Segal and Moulton argued that the play was mocking Roman lawyers and siding with Terence's friend and patron Scipio Aemilianus, who had been criticized for not appearing as a lawyer and for having little interest in Roman law and litigation; and in 1983 David Konstan accentuated the contrast between legal norms and humanity and stated that the play advocated love, humanity, and a neglect of social and legal barriers.[11]

Both interpretations contain good observations, but they pay too little attention to the perspective of Terence's Roman audience. The play is set in Athens, all the characters have Greek names, and central elements of the plot, such as the marriage between Antipho and his cousin Phanium[12] or the Attic concept of *epikleroi* must have seemed very alien to a Roman audience: in fact, Terence felt that he had to explain this foreign legal concept to his audience, cf. *Phorm.* 125-6: *lex est ut orbae, qui sint genere proxumi, / is nubant, et illos ducere eadem haec lex iubet* ('there is a law that female orphans must marry their closest male relatives, and this same law orders those male relatives to marry them').[13] These and other features distance the action from the Roman audience's world of experience. It must therefore have been more natural for the spectators to understand the bizarre court case and the turbulent negotiations between Phormio and the old men as depicting Attic law. If the plot had any Roman legal significance at all, it probably would have reinforced common Roman prejudices against Greek *leuitas*[14] and legal incompetence.[15] Hence, contrary to what Segal and Moulton (1978) and Konstan (1983) have claimed, Terence's *Phormio* would have hardly motivated Roman spectators to question law or legal norms in Rome, but would have rather strengthened their confidence in the superiority of their legal system.[16]

However, there is one scene in Terence's *Phormio*, which clearly refers to the Roman legal system, but has received little attention by Segal and Moulton or Konstan, and that is the scene which follows Demipho's first confrontation with Phormio. The old man complains about his situation and then turns to his three legal advisers Hegio, Cratinus and Crito:

> 446 DEMIPHO: uidetis quo in loco res haec siet:
> quid ago? dic, Hegio. HEGIO: ego? Cratinum censeo,
> si tibi uidetur. DEMIPHO: dic, Cratine. CRATINUS: mene uis?
> DEMIPHO: te. CRATINUS: ego quae in rem tuam sint ea uelim facias. mihi
> 450 sic hoc uidetur: quod te absente hic filius
> egit, restitui in integrum aequomst et bonum,
> et id impetrabis. dixi. DEMIPHO: dic nunc, Hegio.
> HEGIO: ego sedulo hunc dixisse credo; uerum itast,
> quot homines tot sententiae: suos quoique mos.
> 455 mihi non uidetur quod sit factum legibus
> rescindi posse; et turpe inceptust. DEMIPHO: dic, Crito.
> CRITO: ego amplius deliberandum censeo:
> res magnast. HEGIO: numquid nos uis? DEMIPHO: fecistis probe:
> incertior sum multo quam dudum.

DEMIPHO: You see the situation. What do I do? Speak, Hegio.

HEGIO: Me? I suggest Cratinus, if that's all right with you.

DEMIPHO: Speak, Cratinus.

CRATINUS: You mean me?

DEMIPHO: Yes, you.

CRATINUS: I would want you to do what is to your advantage. In my opinion it is right and proper for what your son did in your absence to be rendered null and void. And you'll win your case. That is my advice.

DEMIPHO: Now you, Hegio.

HEGIO: I'm sure that he (*pointing to Cratinus*) has given you excellent advice. But the truth is, there are as many opinions as there are people; everyone has his own way of looking at things. My own view is that what has been done in accordance with the law cannot be rescinded, and it is dishonourable to try.

DEMIPHO: Now you, Crito.

CRITO: I suggest that this needs further deliberation. It's a weighty matter.

HEGIO (*to Demipho*): Is that all?

DEMIPHO: (*ironically*) You've been very helpful. (*aside*) I'm even more uncertain than I was before.

trans. J. Barsby (2001)

Although the Greek names of the characters suggest a Greek setting, this whole scene cannot be based on Apollodorus' *Epidikazomenos*, but must have been inserted into the plot by Terence.[17] First, the scene violates the dramatic conventions of Greek New Comedy: unlike in the surviving plays of Greek New Comedy, there are more than three speaking characters on stage at the same time. In addition, there is an obvious inconsistency in Demipho's stage movements: in verse 314, the old man has gone into his house, but in verse 348 he returns from the marketplace with the three legal advisors without having left the house in the meantime. Such inconsistencies were carefully avoided in Greek New Comedy.[18] In Apollodorus' *Epidikazomenos* the old man probably entered his house and stayed there until Geta had fetched *Phormio* and knocked on the door.[19]

Secondly, the consultation with the legal advisers clearly reflects the Roman, not the Athenian legal reality.[20] Although the Greeks made highly complex considerations about state and law, they did not develop a separate legal discipline with specialized legal experts.[21] In Rome, on the other hand, there had been a professional interpretation of law since the end of the third century BCE at the latest.[22]

Thirdly, the comments of the legal advisors are clearly based on Roman, not Attic law. Cratinus' legal opinion that the son's actions during his father's absence can easily be reversed is difficult to reconcile with the legal situation in Athens, where men who had reached the age of majority were, at least legally, completely independent. Cratinus obviously has the Roman *patria potestas* in mind here, according to which a Roman adult citizen was still subject to his father's authority and required his father's consent for many legal transactions.[23] In addition, Cratinus' words also bristle with Roman legal terminology: *restitui in integrum* is a technical term well documented in Roman legal texts (see below for its exact meaning), and *aequum et bonum*, *impetrare*, and *rescindere* are likely to have been common in contemporary forensic speeches.[24]

Thus, Terence has grafted a typical Roman *consilium* with Roman legal experts and Roman legal arguments onto a case which is completely un-Roman because it presupposes the Attic concept of *epikleroi*. Unlike the other scenes in *Phormio*, this passage clearly urges the Roman audience to relate the events on stage to their own lives. Hence, we may ask: How could this scene have influenced the Roman audience's attitude to the Roman legal system?

In a paper of 1954, which has been quoted again and again,[25] Hildegard Kornhardt correctly stated that Cratinus and Hegio represent two positions of the Roman legal discourse: Hegio stands for legal formalists who consider everything that has come about in formal compliance with the law to be legally correct; Cratinus advocates a more modern view of legality and justice, according to which the intention of the legislator and the respective legal actors must be taken into account. According to Kornhardt, Terence takes the side of the 'modernists' and the *restitutio in integrum*, which (according to Kornhardt) was only recently included in the praetorian edict. If Kornhardt's argument is correct, Terence would have tried to win over his Roman audience for the *restitutio in integrum*, and we would have here clear evidence that the poets of Roman comedy tried to influence the contemporary discourse on law and legality.

But let us take a closer look at Kornhardt's argument. A first problem concerns our sources. The Roman *restitutio in integrum* is known to us primarily from the fourth book of the *Digest*, in which five reasons for a *restitutio in integrum* or 'restoration to the previous state' are given: first, intimidation or coercion (Ulp. *Dig.* 4.2.1); secondly, *dolus malus*, i.e. deception or fraud (Ulp. *Dig.* 4.3.1.1); thirdly, non-age (Ulp. *Dig.* 4.4.1.1); fourthly, civil death or *capitis deminutio* (Ulp. *Dig.* 4.5.2.1); and fifthly, absence (Ulp. *Dig.* 4.6.1.1). Kornhardt (1954: 67) argues that (a) Demipho's son is probably younger than 25 years, (b) Phormio acted deceptively, and (c) Cratinus explicitly refers to Demipho's absence. Consequently – according to Kornhardt – Terence alludes to three of the five known reasons for *restitutio*.

However, Terence and the legal sources compiled in the *Digest* are several centuries apart, and it is unlikely that all five reasons for *restitutio* mentioned in the *Digest* were included in the praetorian edict at the same time.[26] In view of these (and other) problems, some scholars (e.g. Klingmüller 1914: 683) have categorically rejected Terence as a source and avoided clear statements as to when *restitutio in integrum* was introduced. This scepticism obviously goes too far, because Cratinus' words clearly presuppose the existence of a legal remedy called *in integrum restituere* and it can hardly be a coincidence that absence is explicitly mentioned both by Cratinus and in the *Digest*. Equally implausible, however, is Kornhardt's assertion that Terence also alludes to non-age and *dolus malus*, for Cratinus' words contain no reference at all to the son's age or to the family relations invented and presented by Phormio in court.[27]

Another problem concerns Terence's attitude to *restitutio in integrum*. It is certainly true that the poets of Greek comedy sometimes question Attic legal rules and practice,[28] and it is conceivable that Terence would take up this tradition. Thus, Kornhardt's assumption that Terence takes sides against legal formalism may sound plausible at first sight. On closer examination, however, there are strong arguments against this interpretation.

First, Cratinus is hardly a suitable mouthpiece for the poet, for he is closely connected with the antagonist or blocking character Demipho, and the *restitutio in integrum* he recommends would destroy the marriage of the young lovers Antipho and Phanium. All this makes Cratinus rather disagreeable. Moreover, the advice of all three counsellors is expressly qualified as unhelpful in verses 458–9. Had Terence really wanted to advertise the *restitutio in integrum*, he would have designed a more convincing and likeable advocate for his legal views.

A second objection concerns the absurdity of Cratinus' advice. As has been said above, *restitutio in integrum* concerned the 'restoration to the previous state' in case that someone had not voluntarily consented, had been deceived, could not have consented because of his age, had lost his legal capacity, or had been absent. This is not very appropriate to the case in *Phormio*, where an adult Athenian citizen with legal capacity was convicted in court and accepted the judgment, but his father, who was not involved in the trial at all, wishes to annul the judgment retroactively. In addition, Antipho's father Demipho was absent on private business, and such absence for private business is likely to have become a reason for *restitutio* only at a comparatively late stage.[29] Furthermore, practically-minded Roman spectators must have asked themselves what a *restitutio in integrum* should look like in the case of a sexual relationship: the marriage between Antipho and Phanium seems to have existed for some time, Phanium has probably lost her virginity, she may be pregnant, and there is no way to restore the original state.[30] The fact that Cratinus nevertheless proposes *restitutio in integrum* shows that he does not grasp the realities of the current case, but mechanically thinks in legal terms and plays out his legal programme.

A third and final concern relates to the social and legal position of Roman actors. Roman citizens lost some of their civil rights if they appeared on stage.[31] Consequently, actors – including the first stage poets, many of whom also worked as actors – were exclusively slaves, freedmen and foreigners.[32] They risked physical punishment for bad acting or other misconduct,[33] and the theatrical groups (*greges*) were financially dependent on the magistrates, who hired them to perform at one of the religious festivals. A self-confident interference in the legal-theoretical dispute between formalists and intentionalists, as Kornhardt assumed, or a fundamental criticism of the legal system or its norms – such as Konstan or Segal and Moulton suspected – seems quite unlikely in view of the low social status and high degree of dependency of Roman actors and acting poets in early Rome.

Thus, on closer inspection, Kornhardt's often repeated interpretation must be modified in several respects. Although Terence's legal advisor scene does quote two basic positions of Roman legal interpretation, which later clash, for example, in the famous *causa Curiana*,[34] it was hardly meant to arouse support for or defend the *restitutio in integrum*.[35] Instead, the viewers' attention is drawn to something quite different: the absurdity of Cratinus' proposal to demand a *restitutio in integrum* and especially Demipho's words *fecistis probe – incertior sum multo quam dudum* ('You help me well. I am much more uncertain than before') raise the question of how helpful Roman legal experts were and whether legal counselling was sometimes little more than a pompous self-dramatization.

On the surface, this conclusion may resemble the interpretation of Segal and Moulton. However, there are three important differences: first, unlike Segal and Moulton, I would not refer the entire play to Roman law, but only this particular scene; secondly, I would not interpret this very scene as a criticism of the Roman legal system and legal representation in general, but only as a parody of legal advice; and thirdly, legal advice and legal exegesis do not seem to me to be criticized as a whole, but Terence mocks just a particular type of people that offer legal advice and representation.[36]

In the following, I would like to underpin this interpretation with a few further considerations and then place it in the historical and literary context. I will begin with a few observations on Terence's representation of the three legal experts. The emphatic use of the personal pronoun *ego* ('I') in verses 449, 453, and 457, which is not required syntactically, can be interpreted as a sign of self-confidence, perhaps even self-indulgence or self-importance, and *dixi* ('I have spoken'), which Cratinus pointedly places at the end of his statement, has an authoritative tone. At the same time, the proposal to request a *restitutio in integrum* is not practicable, none of the legal opinions goes into the details of the case at hand, and the fact that the lawyers try to evade giving their opinion and want to leave as quickly as possible (cf. 447–9, 458) seems downright shy or fearful. This highly contradictory presentation of the three lawyers has an amusing effect and can be compared to the mockery of other intellectuals and unpractical experts: We can think, for example, of the philosophers in the Phrontisterion of Aristophanes' comedy *Clouds*, of Molière's depiction of lawyers and doctors, or of the theoretical physicists in the American comedy series *Big Bang Theory*.

This comic effect automatically raises the question what Terence wanted to achieve with this mockery. There is no easy answer to this question, for there is a wide spectrum of competing theories of what is comic, and, depending on their personal attitudes and experiences, individual viewers may have reacted quite differently to Terence's legal experts. However, Terence, too, could not anticipate the individual sensitivities of his spectators, but had to work with generally accepted, consensual assumptions, and many theories can be safely ignored, if we are primarily interested in the social interaction between Terence, the actors, and the Roman audience. Two approaches seem particularly fruitful for our question: The first is Bergson's idea of laughter as a social corrective against behaviour that poses a threat to society;[37] the second is the view, held by e.g. Freud, that humour is a defiant act of self-assertion and independence or sovereignty.[38]

Both approaches would fit very well into the context of the 160s BCE. The time of Plautus and Terence is commonly regarded as a heyday of Roman jurisprudence.[39] In their lifetime, the fundamental institutions and laws of the *ius ciuile* were created.[40] Legal counselling and advocacy became a means of social advancement,[41] and for the first time, a significant number of jurists held the highest offices in the Roman state.[42] In addition, nicknames such as *Sapiens*, *Sophus* or *Catus* testify to the intellectual reputation of some of these early jurists,[43] and the 'awkward and clumsy, pedantically fearful style'[44] of the contemporary laws testifies to the desire to regulate human life as precisely as possible. Given the prominent role of jurists and lawyers in the late third and second centuries BCE, it is immediately understandable that Plautus and Terence engage so intensively with Roman law and legal terminology, and it is hardly surprising that Terence's three legal advisors poke fun at a jurisprudence that thinks only in legal principles and loses sight of reality. Thus, the laughter that the scene of the three legal advisors provokes can be plausibly interpreted as an act of self-assertion towards this group of influential experts and as a social corrective in the Bergsonian sense.[45]

In Terence's oeuvre, we find no other scene which alludes so precisely to Roman law and in particular to Roman legal experts. However, our scene is sometimes associated with a verse from Terence's comedy *Heautontimoroumenos* (796): *ius summum saepe summa est malitia* ('Law, if applied in the strictest fashion, is often the utmost malice').⁴⁶ According to Kornhardt (1954: 68), the verse is an attack on formal law, but this interpretation quickly proves to be quite implausible. To begin with, the slave Syrus, who utters the words in question, does not want to take up the cudgels for equity and against legal formalism, but has quite different aims: he has just told his old master that his newly found daughter Antiphila is mortgaged to the prostitute Bacchis, and now he wants to persuade him not to start a legal dispute about the debt, but to generously provide money for the daughter's supposed release. However, the money will only serve to enable Chremes' son Clitipho to pay for and enjoy the services of the prostitute Bacchis. Given this context, one can hardly speak of Syrus (or Terence) seriously advocating equity or pointing out the disadvantages of formal law. Instead, we have a very harmless joke: A slave, who is not legally competent himself, has picked up a philosophical idea about law, ostentatiously displays his 'wisdom' and, in doing so, transfers this philosophical thought in a very slanted way to an unsuitable object.

Closer parallels can be found in three of Plautus' plays. In *Epidicus*, the old Periphanes and his friend Apoecides are explicitly characterized as experienced senators:

> 184–5 EPIDICUS: sed eccum ipsum ante aedis conspicor cum Apoecide
> qualis uolo uetulos duo.
> iam ego me conuortam in hirudinem atque eorum exsugebo sanguinem,
> senati qui columen cluent.
>
> EPIDICUS (*referring to his master Periphanes and Apoecides*): But look, I can see my master himself and Apoecides in front of the house, two old men of the sort I want. Now I'll turn myself into a leech and suck out the blood of these men, who are known as pillars of the senate.
>
> trans. W. De Melo (2011)

Because of his experience and expertise, Apoecides is later asked to supervise a money payment on the forum (cf. *Epid.* 291–2). However, he fails to notice that the slave Epidicus does not use the money to buy a slave (as ordered), but hires a lute player instead. When the fraud comes to light, Epidicus' master Periphanes scolds not only his slave, but also himself and above all his moronic friend Apoecides:

> 517 PERIPHANES Quid nunc? qui in tantis positus sum sententiis,
> eamne ego sinam impune? immo etiam si alterum
> tantum perdundumst, perdam potius quam sinam

520 me impune irrisum esse, habitum depeculatui
     ei sic data esse uerba praesenti palam!
     atque me minoris facio prae illo, qui omnium
     legum atque iurum fictor, conditor cluet;
     is etiam sese sapere memorat: malleum
525 sapientiorem uidi excusso manubrio.

PERIPHANES: What now? Should I let her off without punishment, I, whose name is often to be seen as proposer of such important decrees? No, even if I had to waste the same sum all over again, I'd rather waste it than let myself be made a laughingstock and be cheated without punishing him. Dear me! To be tricked like this, in person and publicly! And yet my case is not as bad as the case of that chap [i.e. Apoecides] who has a reputation for being the maker and framer of all laws and legal principles. He even says that he's clever. I've seen a hammer cleverer than him, and that with its handle knocked off.

trans. W. De Melo (2011)

Apoecides' characterization as a legal expert and legislator can hardly go back to Plautus' Greek model, because the members of the Athenian *Boule* were chosen by lot and each served there only for a limited time,[47] so that membership was not an indication of high social status or many years of political and legal experience. Therefore, we are clearly dealing with a Romanizing change here, and Plautus must have turned a stupid old friend of his Greek model into a Roman senator, who was very well versed in legal theory, but completely naive and incompetent in practice. This is not too far away from Terence's legal advisors, who can juggle with legal terms, but fail to give Demipho any helpful advice.

An even closer parallel to Terence's legal advisors is the appearance of several *advocati* in Plautus' *Poenulus*. There, the young Agorastocles frames the pimp Lycus, by first sending his slave Collybiscus with a large sum of money into Lycus' brothel and later claiming that the pimp has stolen his slave and his money. To make this legal trap more effective Agorastocles gathers a group of *advocati* from the forum. Although their main function is to introduce Collybiscus to Lycus and later act as witnesses to Agorastocles' house search[48] and although several details point to Greek, not Roman law,[49] Plautus partly recasts the witnesses of his Greek model as Roman *advocati*. This becomes most prominent in verses 721–45, where Agorastocles not only asks them to take note of important details (723–7), but also wants to know their view of the case. As in Terence's *Phormio*, the answers given by the *advocati* are not very helpful and eventually drive him mad (cf. especially 730–1, 736–9).

The third parallel comes from *Menaechmi*. In this play, the young Epidamnian patron Menaechmus returns home from the forum and complains extensively about a client he had to represent in court (571–99). Since the verses clearly refer to the Roman patronage system,[50] we have to assume that Plautus is freely expanding here and making a point about Roman legal practice. Of course, the situation in *Menaechmi* is different from *Phormio*, because the Plautine scene is about legal representation, while Terence focuses on legal advice. Nevertheless, the passages are comparable in that both highlight the disinterest of legal professionals for their clients: just like the Terentian *advocati* impatiently ask (458) *numquid nos uis?* ('Do you still need us?'), Plautus' Menaechmus wants to solve the matter as quickly as possible in order to get back to his sweetheart, and when this fails and the matter goes to court, he has no sympathy for his client, but even curses him (596–7). In contrast to the Terentian *advocati*, Menaechmus leaves an impression of competence because of his sophisticated negotiations, but on the whole his lack of interest and commitment makes him, too, a rather negative example of legal counselling and representation.

The cliché of unhelpful or impractical legal experts can later also be found in Cicero. In his speech *Pro Murena* of 63 BCE, Cicero contrasts the militarily and politically experienced statesman Murena with the petty jurist Servius (*Mur.* 19–29) and claims that legal experts deliberately exploit the ambiguity of Roman law and the ignorance of their fellow citizens and are even responsible for the corruption of Roman laws (cf. especially *Mur.* 26–7). That these claims are not just motivated by the forensic tactics is shown by a similar statement in Cicero's philosophical dialogue *De Legibus* (2.47): There 'Marcus Tullius Cicero' assumes that lawyers are either incompetent teachers or deliberately spread confusion in order to give the impression that they are even more knowledgeable and competent. Likewise, in Cicero's rhetorical work *De Oratore*, 'Antonius' presents the typical Roman legal expert as a cautious and astute jurist (*leguleius quidam cautus et acutus*), a herald of lawsuits (*praeco actionum*), a singer of legal formulas (*cantor formularum*) and a caviller, who hunts for syllables (*auceps syllabarum*) – in short: someone who knows and exploits small details, but loses sight of the big picture.[51] These characterizations or rather caricatures resemble the legal experts of Roman comedy and are particularly close to Terence's Cratinus, who immediately brings up the *restitutio in integrum* and emphasizes the father's absence, but does not see that the *restitutio in integrum* can hardly be a solution.

The parallels in Plautus and Cicero show that Terence's advisors scene fits in harmoniously with a whole series of other passages in which legal experts are mocked for their unpractical knowledge. This consistent pattern not only corroborates our interpretation of *Phormio*, but also brings us back to the question of Roman comedy's contribution to the Roman legal discourse. The fact that, some hundred years after the first staging of *Phormio*, Cicero employs similar stereotypes about jurists and, in doing so, probably consciously draws from Roman comedy[52] shows that Terence's and Plautus' plays *did* have an effect on how Romans thought about legal norms and how they viewed their legal system. However, the comic poets are primarily interested in the human and practical aspects of law. While they rarely position themselves directly with regard to legal norms,[53] their plays imprint patterns of behaviour: just as the humiliation of the bigamist Chremes in the final scene and the emphasis on family cohesion and marriage have a stabilizing effect on the legal system and society as a whole, the skewed transfer of legal terms and the mockery of Roman legal experts function as a social corrective against petty-minded legal experts who are out of touch with the real world and whose mechanical application of law could pose a threat to social cohesion.[54]

These last observations, of course, have finally also some bearing on our picture of Roman law and legal practice. Contrary to what has been claimed, e.g., by Kunkel and Liebs, criticism of the Roman jurists does not begin with the time of the Gracchi in the 130s and 120s BCE[55] nor with a satire by Lucilius,[56] and it is not simply a result of the growing political tensions of the late Republic or the fact that advocacy becomes an important path of advancement in Roman society and politics.[57] Instead, it is already tangible in Plautus' *Epidicus*, *Menaechmi*, and *Poenulus*, fills an entire scene of Terence's *Phormio* in 161 BCE, and may have originally had more to do with the fact that the early Roman jurists were not always highly esteemed men of honour and great creativity,[58] but occasionally also narrow-minded and socially inept or unpractical specialists.

Notes

1 The attempts by Goldberg (1978), Chiarini (1979), Stärk (1989) and Lefèvre, Stärk and Vogt-Spira (1991) to demonstrate that *Epidicus, Persa, Menaechmi, Curculio, Truculentus,* and *Captivi* all lack a Greek model have not been accepted and are contradicted, among other things, by the legal contents of the plays; cf. Scafuro (1997) *passim*, Gaertner (2011) *passim*, (2014) 617–18 and see also e.g. Brown (1995) and Petrides (2014) 431–2.

2 For a quick overview see e.g. Gaertner (2014) 619–21 (Plautus), 627 (Terence). On law and the language of love see especially Zagagi (1980) 106–31.

3 Cf. the survey in Bartholomä (2019) 229–32.
4 Cf. especially Becker (1896) 35–59, Schwind (1901), Fredershausen (1906), (1912), Paoli (1962), (1976), Witt (1971a,b), Scafuro (1993), (1997); for further literature see Gaertner (2014) and Bartholomä (2019) 229–32.
5 Cf. e.g. Luhmann (1981) 53, Derrida (1992c) 185, and the Introduction and Goldschmidt (in this volume).
6 Cf. Habermas (1992) 138, 443, *passim*, Bourdieu (1986) 15, and the Introduction to this volume.
7 Cf. also McGinn (in this volume) on Plautus' *Rudens* anticipating (or paving the ground for) the Roman legal category of public property (*res communes omnium*).
8 Cf. the discussion of Terence's prologues in the Introduction to this volume.
9 According to Attic law, if a deceased had only female offspring, the closest male relatives were entitled to marry the heiress(es) or had to provide a dowry for the orphan(s): cf. e.g. Harrison (1968) 132.
10 Phormio's intention is to provide money for Antipho's cousin Phaedria, who is madly in love with a beautiful slave girl, but cannot pay the pimp Dorio. This side plot has little to offer in terms of legal analysis and can therefore be ignored here.
11 Cf. Segal and Moulton (1978) 287 and Konstan (1983) 128–9, whose interpretation partly resembles Schneider (1961); contrast Forehand (1985) 91: '[the play] does not develop a consistent philosophy about the law'. According to Büchner (1974) 359, *Phormio* generally lacks deeper significance (similarly Posani (1941) 49) and is simply an 'Intrigenstück' that celebrates the superior skill of the sycophant Phormio; similarly Lefèvre (1978) 114, but Michel (1987) emphasizes the peripatetic and stoic elements in the play. Godsey (1928) and Arnott (1970) concentrate on Phormio's characterization, Bianco (2009) on tragic elements and genre. Frangoulidis (1996), (2013) interprets the play along medical lines. Goldberg (1986) 75–90 accentuates the artful composition; similarly Norwood (1923) 74–84, Posani (1941) 29–40, Grimal (1983), Kruschwitz (2004) 113–15. Kruschwitz (1999) 142–3 rightly comments 'das Hauptanliegen ... liegt ... in der Demaskierung der Doppelmoral der Väter Demipho und Chremes', and Moore (2001) 253–65 correctly emphasizes the links to the Roman patronage system and the exchange of *officia*.
12 Marriages between cousins were considered incest and became acceptable only in the last years of the Republic and the early Principate, cf. Tac. *Ann.* 12.6, Plut. *Quaest. Rom.* 265d, Cic. *Phil.* 2.99 and e.g. Treggiari (1991) 107–19.
13 Kuhn-Treichel (2018) offers a well-informed analysis of Terence's depiction of the epiclerate and demonstrates that the Roman play is compatible with Attic Law; contrast Kamini (2015) and see also Bartholomä (2019) 232–6 on the epiclerate as a topic of Greek and Roman comedy. Hence, there is no need to assume a drastic reshaping of the legal elements of the plot by Terence as assumed by Lefèvre (1978).

14 Cf. Plautus' use of *Graeca fides* ('Greek credit', i.e. payment in cash, because one cannot trust the Greeks) at *Asin.* 199 (cf. Hurka (2010) 120 *ad loc.*), his representation of the slaves' banquet as typical Athenian practice (*Stich.* 670), or the usage of *pergraecari/congraecare* for 'lead a dissolute life' at *Most.* 20-2, *Bacch.* 742-3. Cicero, too, associates Greeks with loose morals, cf. Cic. *Flacc.* 57, 61, 71, *Sest.* 141.

15 Cf. e.g. Cic. *De Orat.* 1.197: *incredibile est enim, quam sit omne ius ciuile praeter hoc nostrum inconditum ac paene ridiculum;* ... *hominum nostrorum prudentiam ceteris omnibus et maxime Graecis antepono* ('for it is unbelievable how all civil law apart from our own is disordered and almost ridiculous; ... I consider the prudence of our men to be superior to all others and especially to the Greeks').

16 Whether Terence's Greek model was meant to question Attic law is a different question. In principle, Konstan's interpretation of Terence's play could fit Apollodorus' comedy, but caution is advisable. First, we can only speculate what Apollodorus highlighted in his play, and secondly the *Epidikazomenos* could have just as well focused on the misinterpretation of reality and false assumptions (cf. e.g. the old men's attitude towards Antipho's wife before and after they know her true identity). Furthermore, the fact that Antipho and Phanium feel naturally attracted to each other and end up marrying another Athenian citizen in accordance with Attic law can also be interpreted as legitimizing Attic law and implying a kind of biological corroboration of the exclusiveness of Athenian citizenship; for this idea cf. e.g. Lape (2004).

17 Cf. already Lefèvre (1978) 17, Blanchard (1980) 51, Braun (1999) 43, Maltby (2012) 166.

18 Cf. e.g. Duckworth (1952) 118-20.

19 Thus already Lefèvre (1978) 17, Barsby (1992) 145.

20 Cf. Lefèvre (1978) 16-17.

21 Cf. Wolff (1974) [1964], especially 83, 88-9, 91, 95-6.

22 Cf., e.g., Leo (1913) 22-3, Schulz (1961) 11-14, 70, 106-13, Frier (1985) 155-71, Wieacker (1988) 318-40, 519-51.

23 Cf., e.g,. Kaser (1971) 64, 343.

24 Cf. Kornhardt (1954) 66 and Massioni (1993) 170-1.

25 Cf., e.g., Gaiser (1972) 1093-4, Lefèvre (1978) 15 n. 40, 16-17, 20, (1994) 180, 203, (2008) 203 n. 252, Bartolomä (2019) 240.

26 Klingmüller (1914) 678, 680, Schulz (1922) 222-3, and others assume that non-age and absence had been the earliest grounds for *restitutio in integrum*.

27 Besides, *dolus malus* and *metus* may have become reasons for *restitutio in integrum* at a rather late stage, cf. Kupisch (1974) 158-9, 166-7, 242 n. 9, who dates them to the first century BCE. Also, the *restitutio minorum* would presuppose that Antipho is *sui iuris*, while Cratinus' comments about the father's absence imply that he is still under *patria potestas*: cf. Kaser (1955) 488.

28 The best example is, of course, Aristophanes' *Wasps*, but cf. also the role of the epiclerate in Menander's *Aspis*.
29 Cf. Kaser (1955) 487. At Ulp. *Dig.* 4.6.1.1 the acceptable reasons for absence are primarily *rei publicae causa* ('for the sake of the republic') and *inue uinculis seruitute hostiumque potestate* ('or in captivity, enslavement or power of the enemy'). The general clause *si qua alia mihi iusta causa esse uidebitur* ('if some other reason will appear just to me') towards the end of the quotation at Ulp. *Dig.* 4.6.1.1 is likely to have been introduced at a much later date: see, e.g., Klingmüller (1914) 683, Kaser (1955) 457.
30 Already Kaser (1955) 488 hints at this problem.
31 Cf. Lebek (1990) 48–9, 52 with reference to Cic. *Off.* 1.150, Ulp. *Dig.* 3.2.2.5; see also Kaser (1956) on *infamia* in general and Spruit (1966). On the history of acting and the social status of actors see Leppin (1992).
32 Cf. Leppin (1992) 30–5 (foreign origin of actors), 36–44 (legal status) and Brown (2002) 225, 233–6.
33 On this *coercitio* of Roman actors see Mommsen (1899) 47 n. 5, Leppin (1992) 76. An important precedent was the punishment of Naevius in the late third century BCE: although the details are difficult to establish (cf., e.g., Goldschmidt in this volume), our ancient sources suggest that some sort of punishment took place (cf. especially Plaut. *Mil.* 210–12, Gell. 3.3.15).
34 See, e.g., Wieacker (1988) 581 n. 45 and Dugan (in this volume).
35 Incidentally, the passage is also unlikely to have promoted Hegio's formalistic interpretation of the law. His opinion (455–6) *mihi non uidetur quod sit factum legibus / rescindi posse* ('it seems to me that what has been done in accordance with the laws cannot be nullified') would be in line with the objective of the plot (preserving the marriage of Antipho and Phanium) and the fact that the audience's sympathies are directed towards the young couple and their friends, but the lines focus on something else: see below.
36 In view of what has been said above about the social and legal position of early Roman poets and actors it is unlikely that Terence's criticism was aimed at jurists of high social status. It is a plausible, but not verifiable hypothesis that his main target were contemporaries of a lower social status who used legal expertise and advocacy as means of social advancement: cf. n. 41 below.
37 Cf. Bergson (1995 [1899]) 103: 'le rire est véritablement une espèce de brimade sociale'.
38 Cf. Freud (2009 [1927]) 254–5: 'etwas Großartiges und Erhebendes'.
39 Cf. e.g. Wieacker (1988) 519.
40 Cf. e.g. Wieacker (1961) 171–3, 186, (1970) 183, Kaser (1967) 169–70, 177, Dulckeit, Schwarz and Waldstein (1989) 170–1, 243.
41 Cf. Wieacker (1970) 186: 'Für Männer ohne andere Beziehungen zu alten Familien war Konsultationspraxis der sachlichste (und für unsere Begriffe verdienstlichste)

Zugang zur geschlossenen politischen Gesellschaft der Nobilität'; see also Wieacker (1988) 529–30.
42 Between 201 and 95 BCE, sixteen jurists reached the consulate (two of them even twice), four jurists became censors, five attained the praetorship but not the consulate: cf., e.g., Kunkel (2001) 41–4 and Schulz (1961) 48–9, Bauman (1983) 5–6, Wieacker (1988) 528–30, Lehne-Gstreinthaler (2019) 82–3.
43 Cf. Jörs (1888) 256.
44 My translation of Schulz (1961) 113; cf. also Wieacker (1988) 521 n. 9.
45 Given the social and legal parameters of acting in Rome (see above with nn. 31–3), this criticism is unlikely to be an act of self-assertion of slaves or ex-slaves vis-à-vis freeborn Romans, but probably reflects tensions among the Roman citizens and looks towards the social competitors of the caricatured jurists.
46 The two passages are associated e.g. by Kornhardt (1954) 68, Lefèvre (1978) 20, Michel (1987) 123. On the meaning of *summum ius* see Kornhardt (1953). Cf. also Cic. *de off.* 1.33 and see Jörs (1888) 260, Stroux (1949) [1926], Büchner (1957), Fuhrmann (1971).
47 Cf. e.g. Hansen (1991) 247–9.
48 This difference from Terence's *Phormio* is highlighted by Lefèvre (1978) 16 n. 43.
49 Cf., e.g., *Poen.* 800 and Scafuro (1997) 433–4.
50 Cf. the references to clients (574) and patrons (581, 585).
51 For further (and also later) parallels of this cliché see Dyck (2004) 94 on Cic. *Leg.* 1.14.
52 Cf. Cicero's use of comic motifs and techniques in *Pro Caelio*: see the Introduction to this volume.
53 A rare exception is Curculio's attack on the ineffective regulation of the financial sector at Rome, cf. *Curc.* 506–11 and Gaertner (2014) 626.
54 Cf. the remarks about the non-independence of the legal discipline and discourse in the Introduction to this volume.
55 Cf. Kunkel (2001) 58–9.
56 Cf. Liebs (2006) 2 and Lucilius frr. 56–96 Krenkel. In addition, judging from the fragments, Lucilius' poem about T. Albucius' prosecution of Q. Mucius Scaevola does not seem to have focused on Scaevola's legal expertise, but on his conduct in the province Asia and Albucius' silly love for everything Greek.
57 Cf. n. 41 above.
58 Cf. Jörs (1888) 258: 'ehrenhafte Charaktere', Schulz (1961) 117: 'die schöpferischen Geister großen Stils', and Wieacker (1988) 521 n. 8.

6

Beachcombing at the Centumviral Court: Littoral Meaning in the *Causa Curiana*[1]

John Dugan

In the *causa Curiana*, a 90s BCE court case involving the interpretation of a disputed will, the law and literary analysis converge. This legal action turns upon conflicting views of how to determine a text's meaning. At its crux is no less a matter than how the living may divine the meaning of the words of the dead, and how to interpret a text in a way that maintains justice, to both the deceased author and the living affected by that interpretation.[2] The case is therefore about the profound question of how texts convey sense, and a rich meditation on the ethics of reading. The longevity and reach of the case rests on its canonization within rhetorical theory, and, from there, its introduction into the hermeneutical and exegetical traditions. In the words of Hans-Georg Gadamer, 'the theoretical tools of the art of interpretation (hermeneutics) have been to a large extent borrowed from rhetoric'.[3] The *causa Curiana*'s investigation of the relationship between authorial intention and text (*uoluntas* and *scriptum*) became part of the basic conceptual frameworks of subsequent hermeneutical thought: a legal case that casts a long shadow on the interpretation of literature.

Its reception made the *causa Curiana* a 'literary' phenomenon; yet there is no point at which it was a purely legal as opposed to literary entity. This case was argued before a jury at Rome's centumviral court, the body that heard disputes over inheritances. Any court case involves rhetoric: figurative, literary language. Further, the *causa Curiana* is 'literary' in how it is preserved. We have no unmediated access to the *causa Curiana*; it exists only within other authors' texts, fragmented and represented to serve the expressive, literary objectives of their excerpters. Ironically, for a case much preoccupied with scrutinizing the exact wording of a will, our understanding of this case relies upon hearsay. Therefore we must read the surviving traces of the case knowing they perform literary functions within these intermediary texts.

The case can be read as a crude allegory of a rhetorical (as a proxy for 'literary') approach vanquishing a legal one at court (though we would be mistaken to do so).[4] Yet, the legal and the literary are intertwined throughout: a legal case resolved through rhetorical argumentation, and surviving to us within literary texts that shaped the form it would take within subsequent traditions. The *causa Curiana* is both about textual interpretation and a 'text' that is itself the product of interpretive processes. There is no 'outside' of the literariness and interpretation when one is dealing with the *causa Curiana*.

I use the term 'literary' in a provisional, scare-quoted way. Literature (and the literary) are fluid concepts. Michèle Lowrie reminds us there is no single Latin equivalent to our 'literature'; Romans used the plural '*litterae*' to encompass a multiplicity of different textual expressions.[5] 'Literary' in this essay designates both certain texts that employ figurative language and certain modes of reading that embrace figurative and associative interpretation. Legal discourse can position itself as opposed to unruly figurative and associative valences, though that posture can prove unstable. Legal discourses rely upon the notion of the 'literal' to give solidity to their claims; yet the figurative can reassert itself, and wend itself past such attempts at fixed delineation. The difference between the legal and literary is not the extent to which these texts are susceptible to tropical, figurative readings, but rather how far figurative expression and interpretation is deemed legitimate within their respective interpretive communities.

In the *causa Curiana* the eminent jurist Quintus Mucius Scaevola advanced a strictly literal interpretation of the provisions of the wording of the will. In opposition, the orator Lucius Licinius Crassus claimed the jurors should take into account the manifest intentions of the dead testator and not just adhere to the letter of the text.[6] Our evidence emphasizes the abstractions that animate the dispute (*scriptum*, *uoluntas* and *aequitas*) and the professional identities of the advocates – one jurist, one orator.[7] Rather than scrutinize these monumental forces and characters that have dominated the scholarship on the case, or the details of Roman testamentary law in the *causa Curiana*, this essay instead reads the case for its literary dimensions and focuses upon the simile that Crassus uses to begin his speech in response to Scaevola's meticulous argumentation. Cicero mentions as an aside – though in a specific and detailed way – that Crassus compared Scaevola's construction of his defence of a strictly literal reading of the will to a capricious beachcombing youth. Although seemingly tangential to Crassus' arguments, this image plays upon specific meanings that the shore has within both the Roman legal and literary imaginations. This image activates associations that redound to the larger interpretive questions of the *causa*

Curiana.⁸ Further, this episode's specificity stands in contrast to the general loss of detail in Cicero's account. Yet Cicero preserves a fully developed conceit of Crassus' speech that we can subject to a literary analysis.

Crassus' detour to the shore is a literary and rhetorical counter to Scaevola's more strictly legalistic approach, one that contains ideas and images that activate intertextual connections with literary texts. This passage also signals a hinge point in the case itself: the moment (according to Cicero) when the momentum shifts in favour of a more expansive notion of textual meaning, one that is not wedded to an unreasonably literal interpretation. This part of Crassus' speech symbolizes a mode of reading and interpretation that trumps strict literalism and considers the contingences that frame interpretive choices. Further, Crassus' persuasive gambit is not simply a crude admixture of 'literary' figures and techniques into a legal context. The meanings at play in Crassus' introduction of this seashore anecdote activate associations that are both literary and legal, and simultaneously literary and legal. This is therefore a vivid instance of the interpenetration of legal and literary strands of thought within Roman legal and rhetorical culture.

Cicero's *Causa Curiana*

Scholarship tends to treat the *causa Curiana* as a discrete free-standing historical entity, but our knowledge of the case depends upon Cicero.⁹ We must consider the specific reasons that drive his uses of this case within his works.¹⁰ Two interconnected concerns shape his narratives: he presents the case as a classic exploration of tension between interpretations based on literal reading vs those considering implicit authorial intentions (a conflict monumentalized within *status* theory);¹¹ and he uses the opposing advocates as representatives of their respective professions. For Cicero, Scaevola is the best orator among jurists, and Crassus the best jurist among orators,¹² and these roles correspond to their interpretative approaches to the disputed will. Scaevola's juristic precision, however, ultimately fails when confronted by Crassus' powers of oratorical persuasion.¹³ Cicero wants the *causa Curiana* to be a test for determining the relative merits of juristic and oratorical approaches, likely leading him to omit details that wouldn't substantiate that thesis.

Cicero's specific preoccupations regarding the *causa Curiana* have left us with an unsatisfying and incomplete understanding of both the underlying facts and the full array of arguments employed at trial.¹⁴ Sometime in the 90s BCE, a

Roman named Marcus Coponius drew up a will in the expectation that he would soon become a father. This testament left his estate to this yet-to-be-born son, while taking the caution to name a certain Manius Curius as a substitute heir in the event this son died before reaching the age of maturity. Coponius died. The son was never born. The will fell into dispute, with Coponius's kinsmen claiming that Curius was not the legitimate heir to this estate since the conditions of the will had not been fulfilled.

Cicero's account of the *causa Curiana* appears to avoid narrative aspects of the case not pertinent to the central question in dispute: did Coponius mean for Curius to be his heir even if his expected son were not born? His focus upon this limited legal question leads to an enigmatic account of the facts of the case. We hear nothing of agency of Coponius' wife – in fact, only one source deigns even to mention her existence.[15] We don't know why Coponius was so sure that he would have a child, and that his child would be a suitable male heir. We do not know Curius' relationship with Coponius, or if Coponius' kin had any grievance against Curius that might have given them further reasons to sue for the estate. We do not know why Coponius died, and under what circumstances.

By omitting these details Cicero ignores their pathos, and leaves unwritten a literary account of the case highlighting the emotional dimensions of this story. Cicero presents the *causa Curiana* as dealing with powerful and disembodied hermeneutical ideas that are untroubled by narrative specificities. A potentially deeply human narrative has been drained of its blood. There is a marmoreal, monumental quality to Cicero's representation of the case: for him Crassus' speech is a significant national accomplishment, one that bests military triumphs.[16] And while this speech survives as a fragmented monument, Crassus' exordium is still legible, an inscription on that monument we can interpret in some indirect, raking light.[17]

The implicit plot follows the melancholy narrative of a father crafting a will in the too-robust faith that he would soon have an heir; the disappointment that no baby was ever born, a non-event that places the meaning of will in dispute, pitting the father's friend and apparently intended beneficiary against the claims of that father's kin. The story could have been told as a cautionary tale of the perils of excessive care in drafting a will – anticipating the birth of a son who never appeared – or of insufficient foresight in accounting for the possibility that a son might not be born within the conditions of the will, and thus fail in his duty to look after the interests of his friend Curius. Cicero ignores such affective dimensions latent within this case, and in their place emphasizes abstract disembodied vectors: text – intention – equity.

Crassus' depiction of Scaevola as a boy beachcomber, and the associations that this depiction activates (specifically, the shore as a liminal, ludic place where signs are found and interpreted), can be read as a return of these repressed literary dimensions. Except the narrative that reappears is not of events of the case itself but in the form of an allegory of interpretive method, as suits the case's hermeneutical preoccupations. This return occurs, depending upon how one conceives of the exordium of the speech, either as a throw-away reference meant to move beyond Scaevola's successful opening speech, or as an image that sets a tone for Crassus' whole argument. Of course, these interpretive choices needn't present a dilemma, since something presented as tangential and apart from the gist of the case can nonetheless get firmer purchase upon the minds of the jurors because it is not a legal argument that would invite logical scrutiny. This vivid send-up of Scaevola could linger in the minds of the jurors over the course of Crassus' own speech, opening persuasive space for his own interpretation of the story.[18] This account of Scaevola's quixotic interpretive moves invites the jurors to consider the range of contingencies that shape hermeneutical decisions and welcomes consideration of landscape, humour, the senses, materiality, and chance. Scaevola's legal technicalities yield to Crassus' vivid, embodied exordium.

Scaevola at the beach

Cicero presents Crassus' humorous takedown of Scaevola's interpretive method as a refusal to engage directly with Scaevola's masterful defence of a literal reading of Coponius' will (*Brut.* 197):[19]

> ut contra Crassus ab adulescente delicato, qui in litore ambulans scalmum repperisset ob eamque rem aedificare nauem concupiuisset, exorsus est, similiter Scaeuolam ex uno scalmo captionis centumuirale iudicium hereditatis effecisse.

> Crassus, however, in rebuttal, began with a story of a self-indulgent young man, who, walking along the shore, had found a tholepin and because of that matter become eager to build a boat; in a similar manner, he argued, Scaevola, from the basis of a single tholepin of fallacious argument had created a case of inheritance for the centumviral court.

Cicero's version of Crassus' exordium shows obvious signs of compression and simplification. Crassus was known for highly polished beginnings to his speeches.[20] We should therefore read this as a telegraphic account of what likely was a fully developed and detailed burlesque of Scaevola's interpretive approach.

Crassus' opening gambit plays an obvious tactical role. He knocks his opponent off his sure stance, and diminishes the status that Scaevola had so carefully enacted as part of his legal tour de force performance. In the prestige game so carefully attended to in the Roman courts, Crassus needed to strike a swift blow against Scaevola's authority as an expert jurist. And he does so with something memorable and enduring and that would appeal to the visceral connections of the jurors' thoughts. Crassus's use of humour plays upon associated ideas that transport them into aesthetic delight and cognitive assent.[21]

Tholepins act as a ship's oarlocks, the pivot point for directing the oar's energy into the water. The oar was attached to the pin by a leather strap.[22] Likely ancient beaches were littered with such pegs. Given their small size they make a suitably trivial part of a boat relative to the whole ship, thus underlining the absurdity of the analogy. Elsewhere, Cicero uses a tholepin as a synecdoche for a ship: a man expecting to find a boat 'sees not so much as a tholepin'.[23] This expression suggests that the specific figurative use of *scalmus* for 'the least part of a ship' was already part of Romans' image repertoire.

As the cardinal element of a boat's oarage the tholepin is an apt representation of the cognitive shape, as it were, of the stipulation on which Scaevola's understanding of the will pivots. Scaevola's 'tholepin of verbal trickery' turns upon the fact that, in order for a son to die, he must first be born.[24] Using this quibble he has distorted the clear intention of Coponius – that his estate should go to Curius in the event that Coponius did not have a son. By making this condition in the will into a tholepin, a text becomes a material object. Crassus's simile thus tangibly represents his and Scaevola's opposed positions within the hermeneutical circle. Scaevola starts with a part of the text to achieve the meaning of the whole. While Crassus starts with an overall conception of the case – that Coponius would have wanted Curius to be his heir – and subordinates the details of the will to fit this interpretation.

The shore in the Roman imagination

So why does Crassus start his case by taking the centumviral jurors to the shore? Why liken Scaevola to a spoiled capricious youth beachcombing and dreaming big boat dreams based on humble flotsam? The shore – *litus* – is an area of fascination within the Roman mind, making important appearances in both literary and legal texts. When Crassus summons the shore as the imaginary topography for his depiction of Scaevola, he is not simply engaging in a variety of literary allusion – a departure that interrupts the flow of his legal argumentation. Instead, the shore is always already simultaneously a legal and literary concept, one with specific associations that pertain to the *causa Curiana*'s property disputes. It is a site for writing and the workings out of intellectual problems. It is a place associated with youth, play, and improvisations of meaning. And it is a liminal space between the legally unregulated expanse of the sea versus the legal and topographical surety of *terra firma*. The shore is thus a landscape that activates ideas – ones that find expression in both literary and legal texts – that are quietly supporting the case's hermeneutical operations.

Representations of beach-combing in Roman literature place Scaevola's depiction as a day-dreaming, tholepin-fondling youth in a broader cultural context. Shell collecting appears as benign ludic release in the *De oratore* where we learn Laelius and Scipio used to regress to boyhood in their shell gathering by the shores at Caieta and Laurentum (2.22):[25]

> saepe ex socero meo audiui, cum is diceret socerum suum Laelium semper fere cum Scipione solitum rusticari eosque incredibiliter repuerascere esse solitos, cum rus ex urbe, tanquam e uinculis, euolauissent. non audeo dicere de talibus uiris, sed tamen ita solet narrare Scaeuola, conchas eos et umbilicos ad Caietam et ad Laurentum legere consuesse, et ad omnem animi remissionem ludumque descendere.

> Often have I heard my father-in-law[26] say that his own father-in-law Laelius almost invariably had Scipio with him upon his country excursions, and that the pair of them used to become boys again, in an astonishing degree, as soon as ever they had flitted from the prison of town to rural scenes. I am afraid to say it of personages so august, but Scaevola is fond of relating how at Caieta and Laurentum it was their wont to collect mussels and top-shells, and to condescend to every form of mental recreation and pastime.
>
> Trans. Sutton and Rackham 1942

While this passage hesitates over the question of the seemliness of such important men regressing to boyhood play on the seashore, it presents this activity as harmless form of recreation freed from the strictures of adult responsibility. The difference between Scaevola's beachcombing regression and that of Scipio and Laelius is clearly one of occasion: the former interrupted the seriousness required of the centumviral court with whimsical impulsiveness. When Crassus calls Scaevola a *delicatus* in the *causa Curiana* this term brings a freight of pejorative associations that diminish his authority: 'addicted to pleasure or ease'; 'self-indulgent'; 'fastidious'; and 'particular about trifles, pernickety'.[27] The semantic range of this term spans notions of being spoiled, dissipated and frivolous to being difficult to please and overly precise. As such it seems apt both for a youth engaging in pointless play and the mature jurist captivated by pointless stipulations.[28]

Beachcombing without proper regulation and boundaries can spin out of control. Caligula notoriously ordered his soldiers to fill their helmets and clothing with seashells as offerings owed to the Capitol and Palatine. In this compulsory game directed by the mad emperor, the shells are capriciously given symbolic value, becoming tokens like coins or gems.[29] While this is a far darker scene of shore play than Scaevola's, they both include the act of wilfully imposing far-fetched meanings upon artefacts found on the beach.

We elsewhere find the shore as the place where signs present themselves from the sea, as in the fish that leapt to Augustus' feet as he wandered the beach and presaged his defeat of Sextus Pompey.[30] The chaotic expanse of the sea can yield materials on the shore, which becomes the site for the interpretation of such signs for the person happening to be wandering there. The act of walking upon the beach seems a part of nexus of thought linked to the interpretation of found objects.[31]

From a broader perspective, the shore appears within Latin texts as a place of impermanent writing, a slate for the working out of provisional thought which one may chance upon. The *litus* therefore occupies an intermediary space between the chaos of the sea and the fixity of solid land. The shore can present signs and portents to castaways emerging from the chaos of the ocean. Vitruvius and Cicero preserve the story that geometrical designs drawn in the sand gave evidence to a shipwrecked philosopher that he had landed in a civilized place (Virtruvius 6.1):[32]

> Aristippus philosophus Socraticus, naufragio cum eiectus ad Rhodiensium litus animaduertisset geometrica schemata descripta, exclamauisse ad comites ita dicitur: 'bene speremus! hominum enim uestigia uideo.' statimque in oppidum Rhodum contendit et recta gymnasium deuenit, ibique de philosophia disputans muneribus est donatus, ut non tantum se ornaret, sed etiam eis, qui una fuerunt, et uestitum et cetera, quae opus essent ad uictum, praestaret.

> The philosopher Aristippus, a follower of Socrates, was shipwrecked on the coast at Rhodes, and observing geometrical diagrams drawn upon the sand, he is said to have shouted to his companions: 'There are good hopes for us; for I see human traces!' Forthwith he made for the city of Rhodes and came straight to the gymnasium. There he disputed on philosophical topics and was so richly

rewarded that he not only fitted himself out, but supplied his companions with clothing and other necessaries of life.

Trans. Granger 1934 slightly adapted

Here the sand of the beach is both a medium for the working out of intellectual problems, and itself an intellectual problem for the philosopher to unravel. After drawing the proper inference from that symbol, Aristippus advances beyond the shore into the regulated space of the island to conduct his intellectual business within the solidity and articulation of the gymnasium's dimensions, reaping his material rewards. The structured institutional space of the gymnasium allows transactional exchange within a regulated framework. The anecdote highlights the liminality of the *litus*: a place for serendipitous intellectual discoveries and play, intermediately placed between the fluidity of the sea and the civilized regulated domain of manmade structures inland.

Within the Roman literary imagination, the shore becomes the place of failed writing. To plough the shore is a Roman proverb for futility: the furrows don't last; the sand is infertile.[33] Ovid in *Epistulae ex Ponto* uses the convergence of the plough and pen, and the futility of tilling the shore, to construct this metaphor for pointless writing and the exhaustion of inspiration (4.2.15–16):[34]

> nec tamen ingenium nobis respondet, ut ante,
>   sed siccum sterili uomere litus aro.

> Yet my talent does not answer the call as of old,
> for I am furrowing a barren shore with an ineffective plough.

Trans. Wheeler 1924

Here, and in the preceding examples, the *litus* is a space for provisional and potentially futile sense making and intellectual activity. There is an inherent semiotic instability to this space, one that undermines both making signs and interpreting them.

In moving from these various refractions of the *litus* to specifically legal ones, we see distinct continuities of thought. The law also treats the shore as a space that resists definition.[35] Yet while literary texts show a fascination with the expressive possibilities of this instability, the law seeks to regulate and rationalize this space that defies delineation. Quintilian classifies the *litus* as a commonly used word whose meaning is open to debate.[36] The *Digest* defines the shore following the inevitably inexact measure of highest reach of the sea's waves.[37] The play in this definition becomes explicit in the jurist Gaius Aquilius Gallus' designation of the shore (Cicero *Topica* 32):

saepe etiam definiunt et oratores et poetae per translationem uerbi ex similitudine cum aliqua suauitate. sed ego a uestris exemplis nisi necessario non recedam. Solebat igitur Aquilius collega et familiaris meus, cum de litoribus ageretur, quae omnia publica esse uultis, quaerentibus eis quos ad id pertinebat, quid esset litus, ita definire, qua fluctus eluderet.

Again, orators and poets often define by using a word in a metaphorical sense, taking their cue from a certain similarity, and that with a certain charm. But I shall not move away from your (i.e., legal) examples unless I have to. So when shores were the issue, which you jurists want to be public property, and people who were concerned with this asked what a shore was, Aquilius, my colleague and friend, used to define 'shore' as 'where the wave plays.'

Trans. Reinhardt 2003

Here Cicero discusses metaphor with the jurist Gaius Trebatius Testa, the dedicatee of the *Topica*. To keep his example suited to Trebatius' profession, he uses the legal definition of shore advanced by Aquilius, a friend of Cicero's who had served with him as praetor in 66.[38] This use of metaphorical language within law, as Quintilian's reference to this passage makes explicit, is an uncharacteristic deviation from jurists' usual practice of using precise literal terminology and into a figurative expression better suited to oratory or poetry.[39] Aquilius resorts to literary language to define the fluid boundary between the shore and sea. The 'play' in this definition shows both the inevitable ambiguity of what constitutes the *litus*, but also marks as a place where the border between literary and legal language is permeable. Metaphor, a figure that passes over boundaries, seeps onto the ludic space of the shore via the play of language.[40] The form *fluctus* can be explained as a 'collective singular' (Reinhardt 2003 *ad loc.*) yet, combined with the semantic range of *eludere* ('to defeat expectations,' 'evade,' 'mock' [OLD]) suggests a personification in which the sea confounds attempts at stabilizing the definition of the shore.[41] Aquilius' choice of this specific metaphor to designate this intrinsically liminal space shows an awareness that the *litus* eludes definition.

Roman law found the shore to be a site of conflicting public and private concerns that required careful delineation.[42] Here the shore is public space, like the air, flowing water, and sea (*Digest* 1.8.2). Yet the shore, unlike the unregulated expanse of the sea, falls within the reach of Roman dominion. One may build on the shore so long as the structure does not impede its public use (*Digest* 43.8.3-4). One may use the shore, so long as one keeps distance from private property (*Digest* 1.8.4). One may build onto the sea, but should the sea overtake that structure it becomes public (*Digest* 1.8.10).[43] In the event of a shipwreck, goods found on the shore are up for grabs provided some time has elapsed since the event of the wreck. Items found on the blank slate of the shore apart from specific chains of events and ownership appear free for the taking (*Digest* 47.9). Natural materials found on the shore become the property of whoever finds them (*Digest* 41.2.1.1.4).[44] These legal provisions for the status of matter found on the shore provide a cultural context for Scaevola's use of the tholepin. According to Roman legal thought, the person who found something on the liminal space of the *litus* may employ this object as he wishes. The *scalmus* is free for Scaevola's taking and use, though of course Crassus criticizes the liberties he takes in disproportionate synecdoche.

Plautus' *Rudens* is the Latin text with the richest engagement of the legal and literary dimensions of the seaside. This play is the only Roman comedy set on the shore, and the *litus* plays a crucial role within the drama.[45] The sea is an engine of chance whose dice-throw causes the evil pimp Labrax's boat to be shipwrecked in a storm.[46] In contrast to the sea's chaos, the shore becomes the setting for the workings out of property rights and, through the reading of tokens, for sorting out proper familial relationships and ownership. First, in the tug-of-war property dispute that gives the play its name, Trachalio and Gripus, like opposing advocates, advance different understandings of the law of salvage to sort their ownership of the trunk containing the tokens that will eventually lead to the reunion of the prostitute Palaestra and her long-lost father Daemones.[47] Then the tokens (*crepundiae*) contained within the trunk are methodically interpreted to establish the relationship of father and daughter.[48] This play therefore enacts many of the themes implicit within Crassus' anecdote: the *litus* as a site for the working out of property rights and familial relations, and for the interpretation of signs.

Synecdoche in Roman legal practice: parts and wholes in property disputes

When Scaevola uses a tholepin as a representation of a notional whole boat, he engages in a parodic version of practices already seen within Roman courts. Here I refer to the archaic practice, preserved in Gaius and Aulus Gellius, of bringing to trial a portion of a property that has fallen into dispute: a clod of earth from a plot of land; a broken bit from a boat or a roof tile from a house to symbolize the whole.[49] So this synecdoche, the kind of artefactual, symbolic thinking that Crassus has Scaevola engage in, was already part of the latent intellectual coding of Roman legal practice, though Scaevola takes it to ludicrous extremes.

The specific relationship between a part of the boat and its whole was also a preoccupation within Roman law. Jurists debated what portions of a ship should be regarded as intrinsic to a ship (that is, part of its *instrumenta*). According to Labeo, a mast should be considered an essential part of a ship but not a sail since ships without masts are useless, while a sail was more of an addition to a ship than a part (*Digest* 50.16.242). Similarly, jurists debated whether the purchase of a boat should include its skiff (on the basis of its being part of the ship's tack: *Digest* 33.7.29). Within Roman legal thought, the boat was an object that called into question the relationship between parts and wholes. Crassus exploits these preoccupations in his representation of Scaevola's interpretive overreach.[50]

Conclusions

The shore sets the stage for Crassus' caricature of Scaevola, enabling a dismantling of his prestige as a jurist and the reduction of his interpretative moves to a capricious form of associative play. Scaevola pretends he can build a stable legal argument using the provisions of the will, but does so within an intrinsically unstable environment. The shore anecdote allows Crassus to establish a counternarrative to the explicit terms in which the interpretive debate is framed. And the associations that Crassus activated are a potent melding of legal and literary valences. Literary and legal conceptions of this liminal space quietly give heft to Crassus' cunning rhetorical gambit.

More generally, this episode offers a mode of analysis that embraces materiality, contingency and uncertainty to counter Scaevola's more restrictive, literal and cerebral mode of interpretation. By highlighting figurative and associative dimensions of language, Crassus offers an alternative to Scaevola's constrained reading of Coponius' will. The centrepiece of this strategy is Crassus' transformation of Scaevola's cardinal argument into a material object.[51] The idea 'one must first be born in order to die' becomes a trivial token, a chanced-upon tholepin with no claim on stable meaning.[52] This symbolism itself opens up ways of thinking that are not confined by the literal but embrace figurative thinking: A can also be B, and simultaneously both A and B. In its reception, the *causa Curiana* became reduced to disembodied and de-contextualized forces – text, intention, equity. Yet court cases can turn on particularities and associations of thought. The tholepin is central material particularity on which this case pivoted.

This anecdote reintroduces materials and bodies that seem elided and suppressed in our accounts of the case – Coponius' wife, the son never born, the mystery of why Coponius' body succumbed to death – and provides the members of the centumviral court a sensory rather than a strictly logical experience. Contingency and materiality return, not as a narrative of the events of the case, but in Crassus' depiction of Scaevola's interpretive method. Crassus offers the jurors mental transport to a shore where a boy wanders and dreams boyish dreams; and that boy is the august Scaevola, whose mystified authority as a jurist gets obliterated: he is not a master-builder of speeches and argumentation, but a *delicatus*, improvising an improbable argument out of proportion with reality. Further, the anecdote reinscribes the corporeal materiality and contingency of Crassus' oratorical performance: an orator improvising solutions to unfolding persuasive challenges in real time.

Also, Crassus' transformation of Scaevola into a capricious boy permits the symbolic return of the glaring absence that gave rise to legal dispute in the first place: Coponius' never-born son. And that boy wanders a beach while toying with a tholepin which serves as the materialization of the crucial condition of the will that Coponius' non-existent son made problematic: 'it is necessary to be born before dying'. The image of a wilful and stubborn youth playing upon the expanse of the shore summons associations with the son who has capriciously refused to be born, leading to the failure to realize the conditions of the will. The *adolescens* in this image grants a fleeting glimpse of a scenario where there would be no need for hermeneutical inquiry, but an uncomplicated world of proper testamentary and familial succession. As the tholepin conjures thoughts of a missing boat, so too the boy playing with that tholepin reminds us of the absence of that child which gave rise to the *causa Curiana*.

While Crassus defeated Scaevola in this case, the underlying legal matter – the specific sort of testamentary substitution that would allow Curius to inherit Coponius' estate regardless of the birth or death of his son – was not a settled question until the time of Marcus Aurelius.[53] The legally open-ended and unresolved quality of the *causa Curiana* extends also to how the beach scene can apply both to Scaevola's and Crassus' interpretive methods. Within the larger dialectics of the case, the shore can have different allegorical applications. For Crassus, *terra firma* is the obviousness of Coponius' intentions and chaos is to be found in perverse interpretations of flotsam churned up from the disorder of the sea. Yet for Scaevola, the sea is the hermeneutical chaos of reading apart from the grounding of text, where enduring lines can be drawn and interpreted with precision. The image has a fluctuating way of being applicable to either side of the case: who is the over reader? Who is fetishizing a small detail and infusing it with meanings beyond its legitimate field of influence? The hermeneutical circle resists closure, and emphasizes the provisional nature of textual interpretation. Further, regardless of Cicero's framing of the case as clash between the advocates' professional specialties, we should not imagine their interpretations here imply immutable disciplinary commitments. Crassus' and Scaevola's rhetorical strategies could change – in fact, did change – as the circumstances required.[54]

And, finally, this image implicates us as readers of the meaning of this protean case. There is a metaliterary, recursive quality to interpretations of the *causa Curiana*. We have ultimately no escape from the hermeneutical challenges it poses. As Crassus and Scaevola struggle to divine the now obscure intentions behind Coponius' will, we likewise are trying to interpret the meaning of the *causa Curiana* from its enigmatic and fragmentary textual traces.

The anecdote warns of the interpretative peril of privileging a part over the whole: using that fragment of a boat to build a whole vessel. Am I engaging in interpretative gestures that risk reprising the complaint that Crassus makes of Scaevola: taking a small bit of an interpretive problem and treating it as disproportionately important? By taking a bit of the lost case and applying to the whole, am I performing what might seem a Scaevolan gesture of interpretative overreach that reprises his privileging of *ipsissima verba* over meaning apart from text? As so often happens with readings of this hermeneutically self-referential case, it is easy to get a sinking feeling of one's own interpretive precariousness: you think you are finding your way round the usual pitfalls, discovering a key to the case that will open more of its secret logics. We are Scaevolas seeking understanding as we wander on this beach.

And yet two paradoxical factors in the survival of this trace of the speech substantiate the interpretive approach this essay takes: Cicero presents this anecdote as both the tone-setting turning point in case, and a humorous aside that does not directly engage with the issues in play. Cicero, whether himself or in the tradition he relies upon, treats the first image that Crassus offers to the centumviral court as sufficiently emblematic to have found itself used as a token – a synecdoche – of the whole speech. In this overdetermined process of memorialization – one that includes its literary and legal resonances – we can see significances both in the original formulation of this anecdote and in the reception of it as having some kind of explanatory function for the case of which it is a part. The status of the anecdote as symbol of, and supplement to, the *causa*

Curiana – being simultaneously at its heart and on its periphery – gives it a special status as a form of commentary upon case as a whole.

Notes

1 I would like to thank the editors of this volume for their many helpful suggestions and corrections. Also, Thomas McGinn generously provided some timely bibliographical assistance, for which I am in his debt.
2 Within the massive bibliography on the *causa Curiana*, these studies are particularly important: Tellegen and Tellegen-Couperus (2016); Harries (2006) 97–102; Zimmermann (1996 [1990]) 628–32; Frier (1985) 135–8; Vaughn (1985); Tellegen (1983); and Wieacker (1967). For a systematic overview of the modern scholarship on this case see Tellegen and Tellegen-Couperus (2000) 173–81.
3 Building upon Gadamer's insight [Gadamer (1979) 23–4], Kathy Eden and Rita Copeland have explored how the hermeneutical tradition adapted rhetorical techniques for the discovery of arguments (*inuentio*) to use as interpretive categories. See Eden (1997), esp. 7–19; Eden (1987); Copeland (1991) 63–86. Cf. Dugan (2013) 218. For an overview of the theme of the letter vs the spirit of the law in ancient jurisprudence see Vonglis (1968) and cf. Moatti (2015) 199f. and n. 18.
4 On the limitations of such a view see Frier (1985) 137f. On the relationship between law and rhetoric more broadly see Tellegen and Tellegen-Couperus (2013).
5 Lowrie (in this volume) and Lowrie (2016) 70–2; see also 75–6 for how 'fiction' is not a satisfactory designation for 'literature' in Rome.
6 For a detailed account of Crassus' and Scaevola's careers, see Bauman (1983) 303–420.
7 Cicero offers these summaries of their positions: (Scaevola) [*Brut.* 196]: *quam captiosum esse populo, quod scriptum esset neglegi et opinione quaeri uoluntates et interpretatione disertorum scripta simplicium hominum peruertere?* ('What a snare was set for the People when what was written was ignored and intentions determined by guesswork and the written words of simpleminded people perverted by the interpretation of eloquent men?') (Crassus) [*Brut.* 198] *deinde aequum bonum testamentorum sententias uoluntatesque tutatus est: quanta esset in uerbis captio cum in ceteris rebus tum in testamentis, si neglegerentur uoluntates* ('He then defended right and equity, the meaning and intentions of wills: how many snares lay in words, with respect to other things and particularly in wills, if intentions were ignored.') On Crassus' use of *aequitas* [*Brut.* 144–5]: *in explicanda aequitate nihil erat Crasso copiosius* ... [145] *ita enim multa tum contra scriptum pro aequo et bono dixit.* ('in explaining equity nothing was more resourceful than Crassus ... for he said so much on behalf of what is fair and right against the written word...' trans. Manuwald

(2019b) here and throughout this chapter for the other fragments and testimonia of the case).

8 In my reading of this fragment of Crassus' speech I draw inspiration from the New Historicist approach to the anecdote: something that reveals 'counterhistories' to a dominant narrative: '[T]he anecdote could be conceived as a tool with which to run literary texts against the grain of received notions about their determinants, revealing the fingerprints of the accidental, suppressed, defeated, uncanny, abjected, or exotic – in short, the nonsurviving, even if only fleetingly'. Gallagher and Greenblatt (2000) 52. Cf. Dugan (2018) 144.

9 The major references to the case in Cicero are: *Inu.* 2.122; *Caec.* 53, 69; *de Orat.* 1.180, 238, 242; 2.24, 140–1, 221; *Brut.* 144–6, 195, 256; *Top.* 44. Tellegen and Tellegen-Couperus (2000) see Cicero's account as more faithful to historical reality than is generally accepted by scholars. On the value of Quintilian (*Inst.* 7.6.9–10) see Tellegen (2003).

10 For an attempt to show how the *causa Curiana* plays a functional role in Cicero's *Brutus* see Dugan (2012).

11 See Cicero *Inu.* 2.116–53.

12 *Brutus* 145: *eloquentium iuris peritissimus Crassus, iuris peritorum eloquentissimus Scaeuola.*

13 On Roman jurists in the time of Cicero see Harries (2006).

14 All court cases are 'literary' in that they involve story telling. These legal narratives play out on at least three registers: the events that led to the legal dispute, the facts of which the court case is seeking to represent; the events of the court itself: how the drama of the court unfolds; and, finally, the various subsequent 'tellings' of this case: how this legal action becomes memorialized in later accounts. For a discussion of the *causa Curiana* from this perspective see Könczöl 2008a. For narrative as a theme within law and literature studies see the influential collection Brooks and Gewirtz (1996) and more recently Henderson (2015).

15 *Inu.* 2.122.

16 *Brut.* 256: *malim mihi L. Crassi unam pro M'. Curio dictionem quam castellanos triumphos duo* ('I should choose for myself rather the single speech of L. Crassus on behalf of M'. Curius than two triumphs over outposts').

17 Scholarship generally passes over this episode in silence. But see Könczöl (2008a) 30–1 and Vaughn (1985) 219–20.

18 As Vaughn (1985) 219 suggests, the anecdote is 'the touchstone for an appraisal of the tone of Crassus' remarks.'

19 On the appearance that Scaevola's case could not be bested see *Brut.* 197: *quis esset in populo, qui aut exspectaret aut fieri posse quicquam melius putaret?* ('who was there among the People who would have either expected or thought that there could be anything better?').

20 *Brut.* 158: *paratus igitur ueniebat Crassus, exspectabatur, audiebatur; a principio statim, quod erat apud eum semper accuratum, exspectatione dignus videbatur.* ('Crassus, then, came always prepared, he was awaited, he was listened to. Straight from the exordium, which with him was always carefully arranged, he showed himself worthy of the expectation.')

21 *Brut.* 197: *hoc ille initio, consecutis multis eiusdem generis sententiis, delectauit animosque omnium qui aderant in hilaritatem a seueritate traduxit.* ('With this beginning, when many other comments of the same kind had followed, he delighted the minds of all present and turned them from seriousness to a mood of joyfulness.') Cf. *Brut.* 198: *haec cum grauiter tum ab exemplis copiose, tum uarie, tum etiam ridicule et facete explicans eam admirationem adsensionemque commouit, dixisse ut contra nemo uideretur.* ('Setting forth all this, at once with earnestness and abundant illustration, and with great variety of clever and amusing allusion, he provoked such admiration and won such assent that no opposition seemed possible.')

22 Vitruvius 10.3.6. See Casson (1971) 86f.

23 *Off.* 3.59.

24 *De orat.* 1.243: *cum et illud nimium acumen illuderes, et admirarere ingenium Scaeuolae, qui excogitasset, nasci prius oportere, quam emori.* ('While you were both mocking that oversubtlety of Scaevola's and marveling at his cleverness as he had worked out that it was necessary to be born before dying.')

25 On this passage see Wohlleben (1998). Cf. Val. Max. 8.8.1. Leeman et al. (1981–2008) *ad loc.* compare the setting of the *Octauius* of Minucius Felix on a riverbank, a scene that also features shell play (ch. 3).

26 Coincidentally, it is our Crassus, the *De oratore*'s protagonist, who relates this story. His reliance on his father-in-law Mucius Scaevola the Augur for this anecdote matches the claims that Crassus made use of his help also in the *causa Curiana* (*Pro Caecina* 69; *De orat.* 1.242). For a recent discussion of the cultural importance of the father-in-law/son-in-law relationship see Gowers (2019), esp 11–17 on Crassus and Scaevola the Augur.

27 *OLD* sv *delicatus* 1.

28 Cat. 50.3: presents the decision to be *delicati* as a ground rule for Catullus' and Calvus' game of poetic improvisation (*conuenerat esse delicatos*). Perhaps the term was particularly suited to ludic contexts and associated with the production of literature.

29 Suet. *Calig.* 46: *repente ut conchas legerent galeasque et sinus replerent imperauit, "spolia Oceani" uocans "Capitolio Palatioque debita."* Cf. Aurelius Victor 3. For a revisionist interpretation of this story see Woods (2000).

30 Pliny *Nat. Hist.* 9.55.2. Cf. Suetonius *Aug.* 96.2.

31 For an analysis of the cultural significance of walking in the Roman world see Sullivan (2011).

32 Cf. Cicero *Rep.* 1.29.
33 Virg. *Aen.* 4.212f.; Ovid *Heroid.* 5.115f. 16.139f.; *Trist.* 5.4.48; Sen. *De Ben.* 4.9.2; and Juv. 7.48f.
34 *OLD* sv. *aro* 1d and 3b: '[to furrow] wax or paper in writing'.
35 See McGinn (in this volume) on the vexed question of when the shore became a focus of legal scrutiny. He notes (with Gutierrez-Masson (1993) 300) that most experts think that, at least in the earliest period, Roman jurists did not distinguish the *litus* from *mare*. He observes (with Dursi (2017) 37–40) that the first attested legal definition of the shore dates to the mid-first century BCE – Gaius Aquilius Gallus' (see below). Full-blown attention to the shore by Roman jurists may postdate the *causa Curiana*. Yet we can be certain Cicero was well aware of the shore's disputed status in law; likely readers of the *Brutus* (46 BCE) were as well. And robust engagement of the shore in later legal writings attests to its intrinsic ambiguities.
36 Quint. 8.3.13.
37 *Digest* 50.16.96.pr.1: *litus est, quousque maximus fluctus a mari peruenit: idque Marcum Tullium aiunt, cum arbiter esset, primum constituisse*. ('The shore covers the area over which the highest tide of the sea reaches, and they say that Marcus Tullius first established this when he was arbiter' trans. Watson 2009 here and through this chapter); *Digest* 50.16.112.pr.1: *litus publicum est eatenus, qua maxime fluctus exaestuat*. ('The public shore extends as far as the waves reach at their furthest point.')
38 On Aquilius see Reinhardt (2003) *ad loc.* and Frier (1985) 145–53. He was a student of Scaevola Pontifex (*Digest* 1.2.2.42). Dursi (2017) 39 offers the attractive hypothesis that Aquilius may have provided this definition to Cicero to help resolve a dispute involving the shore. If so, this would make sense of the *Digest*'s enigmatic claim (50.16.96.pr.1, quoted in previous note) that Cicero was first to propose that the highest reach of the waves marked the *litus*. Perhaps Cicero is credited there with formulating a definition that Aquilius had furnished him.
39 Quint. 5.14.34.: *nam et saepe plurimum lucis adfert ipsa tralatio, cum etiam iuris consulti, quorum summus circa uerborum proprietatem labor est, litus esse audeant dicere qua fluctus eludit* ('Metaphor itself often illuminates. After all, even lawyers, who take great pains over the precise significance of words, venture to define the shoreline as the place where the wave 'plays itself out' trans. Russell 2002).
40 Cicero's discussion in *De oratore* of how metaphor ought to be a regulated form of verbal transgression calls upon the authority of legal language. His formulation for metaphor 'ought to seem to have come with permission and not by force' (*ut precario non ui uenisse uideatur* [*De orat.* 3.165]) imitates the possessory edict '*nec ui nec clam nec precario a aduersario possederit.*' ('that he neither by force nor by stealth nor by permission gained possession from the opposed party'). For Cicero, the stability and transparency of this legal formulation is a suitable check against the unruliness of metaphor. See Dugan (2005) 167–8.

41 This implicit personification of the sea recalls the formulation of Tuori (2018) 209: 'The sea was a legal actor, granting and depriving rights, but it could not be restrained under the sovereignty of even the Roman people.'
42 The following discussion is much indebted to Tuori (2018). For a rich treatment of complexities of the public/private polarity in Roman conceptions of space, see Russell (2016b).
43 See Tuori (2018) 209 on how 'the sea was not only a boundary between legal realms, but also a defining feature of ownership'.
44 See McGinn (in this volume) for further discussion of the laws governing items found on the shore.
45 As Leigh (2010) 210 notes, 'setting on a beach is distinctly atypical' for a Roman comedy. McGinn (in this volume) supplements this sketch with its rich treatment of the legal themes in the *Rudens*.
46 Plautus *Rudens* 358f.
47 *Rudens* 969–77. For a detailed discussion of this scene, see Konstan (1983) 74–82. On law in Roman comedy more generally, see Gaertner (2014), Bartholomä (2019) and McGinn (in this volume).
48 *Rudens* 1154–1159. For an illuminating discussion of birth tokens and 'the material poetics of tragic recognition', see Mueller (2016) 70–108.
49 Gaius *Inst.* 4.17; cf. Gellius 20.10.9. On the practice of *uindicatio rei* see Greenidge (1901) 56–60 and 185–8 (with specific reference to the centumviral court); Butler (2002) 9–10.
50 I am indebted to Peter Candy for bringing these texts to my attention.
51 For materialist approaches to classical texts see Mueller (2016) and Mueller and Telò (2018).
52 That this proposition was the central target of Crassus' wit is implied in *De orat.* 1.243: *cum et illud nimium acumen inluderes et admirarere ingenium Scaeuolae, qui excogitasset nasci prius oportere quam emori* ('while you were both mocking that oversubtlety of Scaevola's and marvelling at his cleverness as he had worked out that it was necessary to be born before dying').
53 *Digest* 28.6.4pr. See Wieacker (1967) 161–4.
54 See Cic. *De Off.* 3.67 for a case in which Crassus argued on behalf of the letter of the law against Marcus Antonius' defence of equity. Likewise, Scaevola defended intention in court (*Digest* 28.5.35.3). See Tellegen and Tellegen-Couperus (2000) 197 and note 44. In this light, Cicero's chiastic locking of Crassus and Scaevola together ('best orator among jurists ... the best jurist among orators') begins to suggest they are only slightly different twins rather than mirrored opposites.

7

Marcus Antistius Labeo and the Idea of Legal Literature[1]

Matthijs Wibier

Introduction

The contributions of Marcus Antistius Labeo to Roman law and Latin literature kept stirring the minds of elite Romans for generations. Active in the Augustan age, this jurist and scholar enjoyed rock star status in legal circles well into late antiquity. The surviving fragments of the Roman jurists treat Labeo as a foundational figure, a point of departure for many of the legal discussions that played out over the course of the Principate. In addition, Labeo was also showered with admiration by encyclopaedic writers such as Festus and Aulus Gellius. The latter in particular was impressed by Labeo's wide learning and his facility for integrating law, philosophy, linguistics and antiquarianism in tackling intellectual problems of any kind, including legal questions. For all these writers, Labeo was clearly an exceptional mind, but more than that, he symbolized a critical juncture in the evolution of intellectual traditions at the confluence of law and letters. While Gellius' work elevates Labeo as the embodiment and culmination of an almost extinct scholarly ideal type, the jurists cast him as the cornerstone of their specialist legal discipline.

This chapter explores Labeo's reception in the Early Empire, examining in particular how Labeo, in the hands of later authors, functioned as a vehicle to think through complex questions about the relationship between law, literary production, as well as politics. In other words, while the well-attested engagement with Labeo offers an opportunity to trace the influence of his work, my interest here is in how later writers use Labeo to make a point, to articulate their reflections on larger questions about law and literature. One of these questions is about the nature of law in relation to the literary. As the introduction to this volume discusses in detail, both law and literature constitute discursive space to think about the social world, and they are normative in the sense that they simultaneously reflect the social world that produced them and imagine what that world could or should be. If this means that both law and literature are discourses invested with normativity, we may wonder to what extent society at any given place and time perceives them to overlap or be distinct – or more precisely, to what extent the legal is considered to form a discrete, technical discourse at some remove from other areas of literary production. For the Romans, the answer to this question is not straightforward. On the one hand, focusing specifically on the (unwritten) Roman constitution, Lowrie's chapter in this volume emphasizes that the constitution and its legal force were largely conjured up by texts that modern readers will probably consider literary rather than legal. While few legislative texts articulating constitutional law were in circulation, the Romans may have absorbed their sense of the constitution from a variety of other types of writing, including historiography and collections of *exempla*. This suggests that law and literature for the Romans were not as distinct and separate as they tend to be to modern Western eyes. On the other hand, we should also keep in mind, as Frier has shown, that Roman private law saw the emergence of a specialist technical discourse in the Late Republic that was differentiated from wider textual realms in the 'disciplining' hands of the jurists.[2] This in turn indicates that the relationship between law and literature in the first centuries BCE and CE was complex and multifaceted. The picture differs depending on where exactly we direct our gaze. We will see that Labeo and his work offered later authors a way to examine the issue and express their thinking.

A further key question about the nature of legal discourse concerns control of the law: if law is in some measure a distinguishable mode of formulating norms, we may wonder whether the authority to articulate those norms is also considered to fall to a distinct individual or group (or to distinct individuals or groups). In other words, who gets to articulate the law, in what way, and why? Once again, the Roman situation is complex, and especially the Early Empire is an important moment in the history of Roman law and literature. The emergence of the Principate marked a significant shift in the way power was held and exercised. Law was one of the areas that saw gradual but significant change. Legal authority was traditionally decentralized in the sense that the praetors, assemblies, senate, and jurists were all able to formulate statements of the law that carried especially great authority.[3] But the source record indicates that a succession of emperors made attempts to gain more control over legislative processes and the justice system. For example, in addition to Augustus' introduction of a series of laws aiming to regulate many aspects of social life, Vespasian appears to have expanded the capacity of the imperial courts, and Hadrian seems to have issued substantially more rescripts than his predecessors while also ending the prerogative of praetors to draft their own edicts.[4] We will see in some detail below that Labeo's biographical tradition focuses on his defiance of Augustus and his clashes with him in the Senate. In the context of the seismic shocks to the political system and the protracted struggle over who got to formulate the law, the anecdotes about Labeo's behaviour obtain larger significance and invite the reader to reflect on the nature and ownership of law.

The Principate was a time of profound changes in the social fabric and cultural life of the Roman world.[5] When it comes more specifically to literature, there is a long tradition of studying the relations between the establishment of the Augustan regime and the production of poetry. While this discussion used to be framed in terms of 'propaganda' for the new system, thinking has evolved to emphasize the complex dynamics and mutual dependencies between poets and power holders. Poetry, or indeed any form of literature, does not simply reflect or justify underlying realities, but by projecting a certain view of the world, it can be actively implicated in forming new realities. For example, Ziogas has shown in detail how Ovid's love poetry claims for itself a position of exceptional authority to define sexual behaviour in a way that self-consciously rivals the princeps' bid to regulate sexuality through his legislation. What is more, this idea of elegiac sovereignty can be shown to predate Augustus. This suggests that Roman poets propounded and amplified notions of supreme authority of the type that Augustus eventually appropriated to shore up his regime.[6] Ovid fits a wider trend in the Augustan Age of projecting the idea of a new era, an idea with an impressive ancient and modern reception. This wider discourse about the Principate as a new era, often explored by thinking about law, is another dimension to the context in which Labeo and his early readers found themselves. We will see below that the jurists usually find Labeo a point of departure, someone at a turning point in legal history who was preceded by *ueteres* but who himself was usually not classed as such.[7]

Labeo's biographical tradition: politics, legislation, and the cultivation of *libertas*

A brief tour d'horizon of the surviving snippets of Labeo's biography is a convenient starting-point for our discussion for at least two reasons. On the one hand, the scenes give us some more background on Labeo while highlighting his ability to attract the interest and attention of those who wrote about him. On the other hand, more often than not the episodes bear on legal and legislative practice, set against the backdrop of the profound changes to the way politics and law functioned under Augustus.[8]

As already briefly mentioned, Labeo gained himself a reputation for his willingness to antagonize Augustus. One of the best-known incidents took place in the Senate and is recounted briefly by both Suetonius and Cassius Dio. Suetonius' *Life of Augustus* embeds the event as part of a series of short anecdotes about Senatorial debate under Augustus (*Div. Aug.* 54.1). We are told that Senators regularly interrupted Augustus, while he was speaking in the Senate, to indicate that they did not understand him or disagreed with him. We even hear that part of the Senate insisted on discussing the nature of the *res publica* (a term not further specified), and that these discussions more than once made Augustus run away in anger. This is the point where a brief altercation with Labeo is inserted:

> Antistius Labeo senatus lectione, cum uir uirum legeret, M. Lepidum hostem olim eius et tunc exulantem legit interrogatusque ab eo an essent alii digniores, suum quemque iudicium habere respondit. nec ideo libertas aut contumacia fraudi cuiquam fuit.
>
> Suet. *Div. Aug.* 54.1

> For the selecting process of the Senate, when one man chose one other man, Marcus Antistius Labeo chose Marcus Lepidus, [Octavian]'s old enemy who was then living in exile, and when asked by him if there were other, worthier men, he responded that each person had his own considered opinion. And not, on that account, was *libertas* or defiance a cause of harm to anyone.

The context is the review of the Senate choreographed by Octavian and Agrippa in 18 BCE. In contrast to the other purges of the Senate, this review appears to have taken the form of limited self-selection by Senators themselves.[9] Labeo proposed Marcus Lepidus the triumvir, someone who had a complicated past with Octavian. In line with the immediately preceding anecdotes in Suetonius, this episode has a punch line that is couched in terms of the freedom to speak about political affairs as one wishes. The text makes the story reflect well on Augustus. The use of the term *libertas* in particular sets up a contrast with the accounts of Tiberius' intolerance of dissenting Senators and his attempts to extort their obedience through *maiestas* legislation and informers (e.g. Tac. *Ann.* 1.72–3; cf. Suet. *Tib.* 8.2). Suetonius has styled the altercation with Labeo in such a way as to bring out the *ciuilitas* that he seeks to praise in Octavian-Augustus starting from 51.1.[10]

In Suetonius' representation, Octavian showed restraint and knew his place in the political and legislative arenas. In comparison, the Octavian in Cassius Dio's account of the same incident is much more aggressive and vindictive (54.15.6–8). Octavian contends that by suggesting the name of Lepidus, Labeo has committed a transgression and needs to be punished (ἐπιωρκηκέναι . . . καὶ τιμωρήσεσθαι). Labeo's response, too, suggests that the stakes are rather different. Instead of claiming that he should be free to think and decide as he pleases, his retort attacks Octavian by pointing out his inconsistent views regarding Lepidus: if he has let Lepidus keep the office of pontifex maximus, why would he not allow him to sit in the Senate? We are told that this was a nice save on Labeo's part (οὐκ ἀπὸ καιροῦ εἰπεῖν ἔδοξε). But the entire interaction suggests a dramatically larger power imbalance between Octavian and Labeo, and by extension the Senate. Dio's presentation appears to leave little room for *libertas* or any closely related idea of independent political activity. Rather, Octavian's presence in the political system is both overwhelming and overbearing.

Further assessments of Labeo in relation to political power can be found in the historian Tacitus, the jurist Pomponius, and in ancient scholarship on the poet Horace. In his list of notable deaths at the end of *Annals* book 3, Tacitus provides an obituary of the jurist Ateius Capito that includes a pithy *synkrisis* comparing Capito and Labeo. Other authors, most notably Pomponius, treat the two as arch-rivals (*Ench. lib. sing.* = *Dig.* 1.2.2.47). Tacitus' presentation of the two jurists is constructed around their relation to the princeps: while Capito's *obsequium* garnered the applause of those in power (*dominantibus*), the *incorrupta libertas* of Labeo's massive contributions to law provoked retaliation in the form of a blocked consulship (3.75). Labeo here functions once again as a shorthand for a configuration of the political system that constrains the manoeuvring space of the princeps. But where Suetonius focuses on politics in the Senate, Tacitus provides us with a miniature prompting his readers to think about the role of jurists in the formulation of law and about who ultimately controls that process. Tacitus emphasizes that Labeo's approach earned him widespread fame (*ob id fama celebratior*), thus nudging his readers towards taking this view very seriously.

Law is also a key area of contention between Labeo and Augustus in the ancient commentary on Horace ascribed to Pseudo-Acro.[11] The text of Horace's Satire 1.3.82 claims that its subject is 'madder than Labeo' (*Labeone insanior*). The notes of Porphyrio and Pseudo-Acro (the latter in two recensions) all offer some very basic background information about our jurist.[12] While both Porphyrio and the second recension of Pseudo-Acro connect Labeo with *libertas* and mention his defiance of Augustus,[13] the first recension provides a succinct characterization of Labeo as 'the jurist who used to carp at the statutes of Caesar Augustus' (*iuris peritus uituperabat leges Augusti Caesaris*, p.43.10 Keller). This last note casts the antagonism between Labeo and Augustus as focusing on specific pieces of legislative output. We are not given any more detail about the nature of Labeo's objections and their amplitude: were they merely directed against individual laws that he found unacceptable as laws, or should we take the note as raising a larger, more systemic critique of legal authority and the ownership of legal discourse? The answer is probably both. On the one hand, a juristic fragment of the Severan jurist Ulpian cites Labeo's negative assessment of the Augustan *Lex Iulia et Papia* in terms of its legal quality:[14]

> de uiro heredeque eius lex tantum loquitur. de socero successoribusque soceri nihil in lege scriptum est. et hoc Labeo quasi omissum adnotat. in quibus igitur casibus lex deficit, non erit nec utilis actio danda.
>
> Ulp. *Ad legem Iuliam et Papiam* 7 = Dig. 24.3.64.9

> This law only speaks about the husband and his heir. About the father-in-law and his legal successors nothing has been written in the law. And Labeo comments that this had been, as it were, neglected. Hence in these cases the law is defective, and an *actio utilis* will not even be given.

The passage tells us that Labeo pointed out a deficiency in the law, a flaw in the design that left in-laws with nothing, not even a legal remedy. Given that Augustus may have outlived Labeo, Labeo must have expressed his criticism not long after the law had come into force, and Ulpian's agreement suggests that it had stood the test time and no meaningful remedies had been introduced. The important thing to note for our purposes is that Labeo apparently criticized the law for its formulation and effects. In Ulpian's depiction, Labeo accepted that the law was indeed law, and he did not challenge Augustus' prerogative to introduce (or orchestrate the introduction of) laws that were binding. If we return to Pseudo-Acro's note about Labeo and the Augustan legislation, this point obviously fits well. But we should also observe that Pseudo-Acro claims that Labeo attacked Augustus' laws (*leges*) in the plural. Together with the imperfect *uituperabat*, this suggests that the note is channelling a wider and more fundamental critique of Augustus' legislative activities. Rather than finding fault with some of the specific laws introduced by Augustus, Labeo's opposition emerges as systematic, and perhaps principled. The note in Pseudo-Acro is thus another invitation for readers to reflect on larger questions about the nature of law and legal discourse.

The anecdotal snippets reviewed above are the surviving remnants of what must have been a much wider fascination with Labeo's role in public life. In spite of the scarcity of material, it is nonetheless clear that the episodes share an interest in exploring Labeo's position in relation to that of Augustus. While not every single one of them makes an explicit connection with questions of law, we have seen that the scenes encourage reading them as emblematic of larger structural changes to politics and law that played out under the Principate and that were still alive for writers such as Tacitus. In addition to repeatedly bringing up the notion of *libertas*, they stimulate readers to think about the struggle over the delineation of legal authority and the nature and ownership of legal discourse.

Aulus Gellius: Labeo, law and the ideal of the polymath

The passage from Ulpian quoted above offered a first glimpse of Labeo as a writer and the authority of his work as a major point of reference for later authors. In contrast to the biographical side of Labeo's legacy, we are much better informed about the reception of his written work. The work of Aulus Gellius in particular is a testimony to the interest in Labeo in elite literary circles beyond the confines of the juristic class. Gellius' work is therefore not merely an important source for Labeonic fragments; but with its sustained agenda of protreptic towards a life of letters and learning, it also provides an opportunity to capture a Roman perspective on the value of a figure such as Labeo and his expertise in and beyond law. We will see that Gellius' engagement with Labeo raises fundamental questions about law and legal discourse, especially in relation to wider forms of literary production.

Labeo was clearly a fascinating figure for Gellius. To be sure, Gellius does not neglect to include an anecdote that fits nicely with Labeo's confrontational style and his association with *libertas* that we have just seen. Purportedly quoting a letter of Capito, the text tells us that Labeo was possessed by 'some intense and senseless *libertas*' (*libertas quaedam nimia atque uecors*, 13.12.2) and, even under Augustus, would not consider anything as legally binding unless it was commanded by the Roman *antiquitates*.[15] We then hear that Labeo ignored a summons by the tribunes of the plebs, claiming that they had the power to arrest but not to summon him. Gellius quotes a passage from Varro in addition, which explains the legal details and which Gellius uses to offer gentle criticism of Labeo's over-confident obstinacy.

The entire scene provides a thumbnail sketch of Gellius' approach to intellectual life.[16] The chapters of his *Attic Nights* tend to be predicated on a question that has arisen and to which no easy answer exists.[17] The dramatized quest for an answer often involves discussions with intellectual authorities and the consultation of books. A recurrent theme is the exposure of authorities, often in public performances, by repeated questioning. Solace generally comes from unexpected corners. This might happen in the form of less narrow-minded, more widely read, and certainly less pretentious intellectuals chipping in, or it happens by pulling out and reading aloud a learned book. The scene in which Labeo refused to be summoned by the tribunes is an illustration of this setup. For Gellius, Labeo's views are worthy of serious consideration, as we will see, because of Labeo's status as a scholar and the intellectual value that Gellius has attached to his writings. But this does not mean that Labeo is always right. In searching for a solution, Gellius offers a close reading of Varro's *Antiquities* that then allows him to unpick Labeo's standpoint. Yet the gentleness of the criticism at the end of the chapter suggests that Labeo has not fallen off his pedestal.[18]

It is probably fair to say Gellius treats Labeo very seriously whenever he makes an appearance in the *Attic Nights*. Chapter 13.10, which contains the most extensive eulogy of Labeo, gives an indication as to why Gellius was so interested in him:

> Labeo Antistius iuris quidem ciuilis disciplinam principali studio exercuit et consulentibus de iure publice responsauit; ceterarum quoque bonarum artium non expers fuit et in grammaticam sese atque dialecticam litterasque antiquiores altioresque penetrauerat Latinarumque uocum origines rationesque percalluerat, eaque praecipue scientia ad enodandos plerosque iuris laqueos utebatur. sunt adeo libri post mortem eius editi, qui Posteriores inscribuntur, quorum librorum tres continui, tricesimus octauus et tricesimus nonus et quadragesimus, pleni sunt id genus rerum ad enarrandam et inlustrandam linguam Latinam conducentium.
>
> Gell. 13.10.1–2

Antistius Labeo devoted himself with the foremost zeal to the study of the civil law and he formulated opinions 'publicly' about the law to those who consulted him; but he was also not destitute of the other good arts and he had immersed himself in the study of grammar and in dialectic and the lofty literature of the olden days and he was steeped in the origins and the explanation of Latin words, and he used that knowledge in particular to untie many knots in the law. There are indeed books that were put in circulation after his death, which are entitled *Posteriores*, of which three consecutive books, the 38th, 39th, and 40th, are filled with matters of that kind useful for explaining and elucidating the Latin language.[19]

Gellius praises Labeo here for his wide learning: while his scholarly contributions in the legal sphere are foregrounded, he was profoundly knowledgeable in language, logic, and literature. What made him such a good legal scholar, we hear, is that he exploited all these various branches of learning in solving legal questions.[20] The opening sentence indicates that he was advising people who came to him with legal queries. But he also produced many writings. We should probably understand the work mentioned in the final sentence as containing at least in part a stock of opinions of the type mentioned, perhaps supplemented with views and discussions of a more hypothetical and academic character. The *Posteriores* contained plenty of legal opinions that were appreciated by later jurists: Gaius' *Institutes* as well as excerpts throughout the *Digest* cite this work of Labeo dozens of times.[21]

An example of where Gellius finds Labeo's acumen helpful is chapter 4.2, where the question has arisen as to the difference between *morbus* and *uitium* in a slave's physical body. The distinction has immediate legal application, so we are told, since it occurs in the edict of the curule aediles. Gellius explores a variety of views, starting out from Caelius Sabinus' commentary on the edict but hastening to add that this jurist is merely quoting Labeo. Throughout the rest of the chapter, Labeo serves as the main interlocutor, whose definitions and distinctions are considered carefully. One of his points is that not every defect is a defect that makes a significant difference to the condition of a slave, using the example of a missing tooth. Towards the end of the chapter, Gellius considers that earlier jurists appeared to have converged on definitions of the terms, namely that defects are chronic and diseases ebb and flow, only to add the warning that accepting their view would go 'against the view of Labeo that I have just discussed' (*contra Labeonis quam supra dixi sententiam*, 4.2.14). Here, it seems, Labeo is placed as a counterweight against an entire corpus of pre-existing legal writing, bringing out his authority. Gellius caps the chapter with a quotation from Masurius Sabinus (fl. under Tiberius). We are not told explicitly how his definitions relate to the preceding discussion, thus inviting reflection on the part of the reader. But his claim that disease and defect can only be properly assessed in relation to how incapacitating they are for the individual in question appears to start out from Labeo rather than the other jurists. Labeo is inserted here as a critical link in the history of Roman jurisprudence. His conceptual innovation is what seems to have made the difference, even though later jurists such as Masurius Sabinus and Caelius Sabinus refined the notions.

While a question about the aedilician edict can have legal import for the present, Gellius is often led to Labeo on questions of legal antiquarianism or pontifical law.[22] One example is a question 'on the taking of a Vestal Virgin' (*de uirgine capienda*) by the pontifex maximus (1.12). We hear that Labeo has written in most detail about this. Setting out from Labeo, the discussion leads us via Ateius Capito, the text of a *lex Papia*, Fabius Pictor, Sulla's autobiography, and Cato back to Labeo, this time his commentary on the Twelve Tables. The chapter begins and ends – comes full circle – with Labeo. Chapter 15.27 treats the different types of *comitia* primarily by engaging with a work of the legal scholar Laelius Felix, who in turn cites Labeo as a source for antiquarian information. In 6.15, Labeo's commentary on the Twelve Tables serves as a source for listing examples of *acria et seuera iudicia* of Republican lawyers, for which Gellius and his projected readership held a certain fascination.[23] In all these cases, Gellius is not pursuing questions with a direct bearing on an acute legal problem in the author's present. Rather, the legal scholarship of Labeo (and several others) serves him in his attempts to elucidate matters pertaining to the Roman past, ranging from public law to old-time morality. Labeo's work turns out to be a very good resource for that. Occasionally, we even find Gellius turning to Labeo for information beyond the legal. The same chapter 13.10, from which we have seen the eulogy above, proceeds to consider Labeo's thought on the etymology of the Latin word for sister (*soror*), which is then paired with Nigidius Figulus' etymology for brother (*frater*). Labeo's explanation of *soror* through *seorsum* ('outside') clearly serves as a mnemotechnic for a piece of legal basic doctrine: '[a sister] is so called, because she is born, as it were, "outside" and she is removed from that house in which she was born and moves over into another household' (*appellata est, quod quasi seorsum nascitur separaturque ab ea domo in qua nata est et in aliam familiam transgreditur*, 13.10.3). Despite encapsulating a piece of legal knowledge, however, Gellius appears to be preoccupied primarily with Labeo's virtuoso lexical analysis, just as he is with Nigidius' explication of *frater* as *fere alter* ('more or less another [copy of oneself]'). The criteria of praise for both are their ingenuity (*lepide atque argute reperta* 13.10.3; *non minus arguto subtilique* 13.10.4). In sum, Labeo the legal scholar in his commentary on the Praetorian Edict produced something for more general intellectual consumption. This, then, adds a second dimension to Gellius' interest in Labeo (and by extension to other jurists and their texts as well). Not only does Labeo command authority because of his wide learning and the ways in which he deploys his vast knowledge in analysing and solving legal questions, but his discussions of legal problems, and the thought that has gone into them, are also so rich and full of astute insights that they are worth reading by intellectuals far beyond the narrow confines of jurisprudence.

Gellius offers an ideal of encyclopaedic learning for the elite Roman reader, which includes at a fundamental level familiarity with legal knowledge and writing.[24] How much there is at stake in his own days emerges from several vignettes in which jurists are drawn, at times disastrously, into intellectual discussions for which legal expertise might provide essential input. A well-known case is that of chapter 16.10, where a recitation of Ennius' *Annales* gives rise to a debate over the meaning of the word *proletarius*. All eyes turn towards an unnamed expert in the *ius ciuile*, who refuses to engage by arguing that this is a matter for grammarians, not jurists. Gellius, who appears as a dramatic character in this scene, reprimands him by pointing out that Ennius borrowed the term from the Twelve Tables and the question may hence very well be directed to a lawyer. Clearly caught out for his ignorance, the jurist in question denies rather aggressively that he has any business with matters of outdated law. After saying that the *antiquitas* of the Twelve Tables has long been put to bed by the *lex Aebutia* (*consopita*, 16.10.8), he quickly extracts himself from what is about to become a harsh public shaming. Gellius' question is eventually solved by a poet who happens to walk by. The jurist comes off very poorly in this scene. He evidently does not live up to the expectations that Gellius has of jurists. Even though the much-admired Labeo may be a larger-than-life figure in Gellius' work, this jurist is not even able to explain the meaning of a term in the Twelve Tables. The scene thus sets up a paradox problematizing the boundaries between law and literature: whereas the poet's familiarity with literature has equipped him to tackle any hermeneutical question, including legal ones, the lawyer's narrowly specialized legal expertise does not even enable him to solve what is arguably a legal problem.

The jurist Sextus Caecilius, whom Gellius presents as a contemporary as well, clearly fits Gellius' ideal much better. This emerges in particular from the long legal discussion in *Attic Nights* 20.1. This chapter stages a debate between Caecilius and the philosopher-orator Favorinus about the value of the Twelve Tables for their second-century present. Favorinus attacks several provisions in the Twelve Tables as harsh (e.g. *talio*), incomprehensible (e.g. the *quaestio lance et licio*), or as punishable by a ludicrously light penalty (e.g. a fine of 25 *asses* for *iniuria*). In the case of this last provision, Favorinus cites Labeo's commentary on the Twelve Tables in order to make the point that the Twelve Tables have not had any meaningful bearing on the life of Romans for a long time. Labeo in his commentary brought up the case of a certain Lucius Veratius, who was in the habit of beating random people in the face on his walks around Rome and asked the slave accompanying him to hand them the trivial sum of 25 *asses* on the spot. In response, Caecilius claims at two points that Favorinus is reading the ancient statutes in an unproductive way:[25]

> (5) 'obscuritates,' inquit Sex. Caecilius, 'non adsignemus culpae scribentium, sed inscitiae non adsequentium, quamquam hi quoque ipsi, qui quae scripta sunt minus percipiunt, culpa uacant. nam longa aetas uerba atque mores ueteres oblitterauit, quibus uerbis moribusque sententia legum conprehensa est. (...)
>
> (22) non enim profecto ignoras legum oportunitates et medellas pro temporum moribus et pro rerum publicarum generibus ac pro utilitatum praesentium rationibus proque uitiorum quibus medendum est feruoribus mutari atque flecti neque uno statu consistere, quin, ut facies caeli et maris, ita rerum atque fortunae tempestatibus uarientur.'
>
> 'The obscurities', Sextus Caecilius said, 'let us not ascribe them to the fault of those who wrote them, but to the ignorance of those who do not understand them, although also those are free from blame who grasp less well what has been written. For a long stretch of time has consigned words and old customs to oblivion; and through those words and customs the meaning of the law is understood. (...)
>
> For you surely are not unaware that according to the manners of the times, the conditions of governments, considerations of immediate utility, and the vehemence of the vices which are to be remedied, the advantages and remedies offered by the laws are often changed and modified, and do not remain in the same condition; on the contrary, like the face of heaven and the sea, they vary according to the seasons of circumstances and of fortune'.

Caecilius argues that a lack of proper understanding in the present does not imply that the laws were not beneficial in the past and that they have nothing useful to offer to the present. Rather, by placing them in their historical context, we might appreciate what the laws aimed to do, and this may benefit our own legal thinking. The discussion takes up many more pages, but in the end all present appear to agree that Caecilius made an excellent point. Even the ever-critical Favorinus seems to be content, as is indicated by his praising of Caecilius at the very end of the chapter. Once again, I suggest, we can see how Gellius is promoting his ideal of the legal scholar, and once more it becomes clear that for Gellius law, legal scholarship, and writing on law are part of a much wider world of knowledge. Only by considering law in the context of Roman cultural history in a broad sense can we properly appreciate its significance and value. In the rest of the *Attic Nights*, Labeo appears to serve as an embodiment of this ideal. His role in this chapter might at first sight seem somewhat paradoxical, as he comes across as a stubborn and narrow-minded jurist in the hands of Favorinus. But the point may be precisely that: Favorinus' handling of Labeo's commentary tells us something about the challenges narrow-minded jurists face when they read him. Labeo's writings contain invaluable intellectual work, but that does not mean that his readers do not need to be competent as well. Proper engagement with Labeo presupposes an intellectual outlook and literary cultured-ness much like that of Caecilius and, by extension, Labeo himself. This is key to the protreptic agenda and the intellectual work envisioned by Gellius for his readers.

The two conflicts over what to do with the Twelve Tables hint at the existence of a different type of jurist, one who is little concerned with the legal tradition and with possessing the right expertise to solve legal questions authoritatively. Gellius' ideal type, embodied by a scholar active a century and half earlier, faces competition from a newer trend of intellectual lightweights but has not yet been completely displaced by them in Gellius' days – or so Gellius wants us to believe. Moreover, Gellius' claim that Labeo in his work was oriented strongly towards *antiquitates* and *mores maiorum* fortifies the impression of a traditional scholar who found himself engulfed by the Principate. But the contrast between Labeo's broad intellectual outlook and the narrow-minded (and stiff-necked) lawyers points to different and changing conceptions of law, and the nature of legal discourse, as well. For Gellius and his Labeo, law is closely connected to other forms of literary production and scholarship. Labeo's contributions to law were so exceptional because of his vast learning, and because he kept in dialogue with an entire universe of letters and learning. On the other hand, the jurists of Gellius' day are presented as retreating ever further within the confines of a technical-legal here and now. They are inward looking, and they avoid debate except among themselves. For Gellius, the tendency of increased specialization is not necessarily a blessing. While the specialists have Labeo's work to rely on, Gellius suggests that they are very poor readers. When read with the right kind of education, however, Labeo has so much to offer, also to those whose interests lie beyond the law.

Labeo's reception among the jurists and the emergence of a juristic canon

Labeo was an equally exceptional mind for the jurists of the first centuries CE. In line with what we have seen for Gellius' *Attic Nights*, the jurists turn to Labeo's work as a source for valuable ideas on many occasions. But other than Gellius' nostalgic admiration for Labeo as an all-round intellectual and author, the jurists focus more narrowly on his conceptual contributions to the law, often treating him as a point of departure for their discussions. The juristic texts have of course been transmitted mostly in fragmented state, which allows for a less granular analysis than in the case of Gellius. Yet the *Institutes* of Gaius, which feature Labeo repeatedly, have survived largely complete and provide a valuable insight.

The *Institutes* are an introductory textbook of Roman private law that is almost exactly contemporary to Gellius. The text provides a discussion of the major institutions of Roman law, and it often includes a succinct description of the historical development of specific pieces of legal doctrine. In doing so, Gaius usually sets out from the Laws of the Twelve Tables and traces changes up to his present. An example is his discussion of theft at book 3.183–209. Without mentioning the Twelve Tables explicitly yet, Gaius begins his discussion by debating how many types of theft there should be distinguished (*furtorum genera*, 3.183). He reviews the position of Servius Sulpicius Rufus (consul 51 BCE) and Masurius Sabinus, who claimed that there are four types, namely 'manifest, non-manifest, found through a search, and theft by planting' (*manifestum et nec manifestum, conceptum et oblatum*, 3.183). No immediate assessment is given, but Gaius follows on with Labeo's view that there are only two types of theft (manifest and non-manifest). This is said to be 'certainly more correct' (*sane uerius*). Gaius then takes some time to discuss the meaning and characteristics of these various types of theft before moving on to the subject of penalties for theft at 3.189. We should note that Gaius begins his discussion of the penalty for each type of theft with the penalty provided by the Twelve Tables, which indicates clearly that the types of theft already discussed also occurred in this codification. For manifest theft, we hear that the Twelve Tables set capital punishment but that the praetor in his edict changed this to fourfold damages. Thus, even though the provision in the Twelve Tables had been supplanted by legal innovations made long before Gaius wrote, the *Institutes* nonetheless find it important to mention the development of the law of theft from the earliest beginnings up to their present. What is more, we are told in a short sentence that Labeo had a part in the development of the law, and Gaius offers brief (and rare) praise of his contribution by means of two adverbs (*sane uerius*).

Several cases can be added in which Labeo played a defining role in the development of the law current in Gaius' days. In Gaius' treatment of the law of sale, we hear that for an agreement to qualify as a sale (and not barter) the exchange needs to have a price (3.139). Moreover, Gaius adds, the price needs to be fixed (*certum*). If the parties agree that the price will be set later, for example after a valuation, the agreement does not constitute a sale. This point, we hear, was established by Labeo, and it was accepted by the later jurist Cassius Longinus as well. We also hear that Ofilius and Proculus thought an un-set price might still amount to a sale (3.140). Gaius does not add any further comment, but his introductory statement about fixed prices indicates that Labeo established the doctrine here. Along the same lines, Labeo seems to have settled the point that in the case of legal action concerning two jointly bought slaves two formulas, one concerning each slave, might be used, since 'it is correct that the person who bought two slaves also bought each slave individually' (*quia uerum est eum qui duos emerit singulos quoque emisse*, 4.59).

In the cases just discussed, Labeo emerges as a crucial chapter in the history of Roman private law, not unlike what we have seen for Gellius. While on the topic of theft he made a valuable contribution, narrowing down earlier debates about the nature and types of theft, the discussion continued and crystallized further until it reached the status quo of Gaius' days. In the case of the law of sale and the law of actions, Labeo established the doctrine that was still current in Gaius' time. While Labeo in this way undoubtedly formed the endpoint of long existing discussions, Gaius suppresses this perspective here and frames Labeo instead as the founder of contemporary practice.

It is crucial to note that Labeo is not simply the conceptual starting-point of later legal doctrine, but that he is also a foundation stone of the canon of legal authorities that Gaius cites.[26] These authorities are all writers of texts on private law, and many of the names we find in Gaius also populate the works of other jurists, including the long excerpt from Pomponius' *Encheiridion* on the history of jurisprudence in Rome (*Dig.* 1.2.2). Here, we should keep in mind that the formation of canons plays a fundamental role in the emergence and development of intellectual traditions. Rather than being a neutral process, the listing of authorities that are somehow 'worth citing' is a highly selective endeavour that almost invariably has a rhetorical function: this type of list is often used by authors to create or recreate (in their own image) a tradition and to shore up their own authority by inscribing themselves in that tradition. At the same time, we should note that the selection process is not free and unconstrained. In order for a canonical list to do its persuasive work effectively, it will need to find common ground with readers' beliefs, and it will need to appeal to widely held notions about what and/or who counts as an authority. Thus, while their precise make-up may differ from one author to the next, canons tend to be characterized by a stable, steadily perpetuated set of names that forms the core of the intellectual discipline in question. If this is indeed a fair assessment, the presence of a set of canonical legal authors in the work of Gaius and other lawyers is a strong indication that they saw themselves as working in a specifically legal-juristic tradition of writing. Moreover, the absence of any references to authors on Roman customs and traditions who do not focus strictly on the institutions of private law suggests that the jurists considered law an exclusive, specialist, technical discourse separate from wider normative and/or literary discourse.[27] For Gaius, Labeo is a crucial figure at the base of this specialist discourse;[28] Gellius, on the other hand, is interested in Labeo and the wider world of literature.

Gaius provides us with a view of the place of Labeo's work in Roman legal history. This view is echoed to some extent in the work of other jurists, most notably in Pomponius' survey of jurists. In the passage in which Pomponius offers a *synkrisis* of Labeo and Capito, Labeo's legal work is characterized in terms of 'making a great many innovations' (*plurima innouare*, Ench. l.s. = Dig. 1.2.2.47). More explicitly than Gaius ever articulates it, Pomponius states that Labeo broke new ground in his legal work. But it is also interesting to see that Pomponius does not specify in any way what the innovations entailed. Rather, he seems primarily concerned with pitting the two rivals as forward looking and tradition-oriented archetypes. If we want to get a better impression of how Labeo was used in legal argumentation and the development of legal doctrine, and to what extent Gaius' approach is representative for the larger juristic world, we will have to scour the more fragmentary material.

A convenient first port of call is the passage of Ulpian on the Augustan legislation that we have seen above. In this excerpt, Ulpian uses Labeo as an authority on Augustus' law and as an authority on whom he can build his own critique. In more general terms, engaging with Labeo as a starting-point for doctrinal discussions is something we encounter with considerable regularity in Ulpian, Paul, and several other jurists. We should also note that these jurists on occasion cite Republican authorities predating Labeo, but these cases are in fact quite rare. Lenel's *Palingenesia* contains 392 (indirect) fragments of Labeo from juristic sources, of which (ca.) 214 are from Ulpian and 99 from Paul.[29] The fragments make it abundantly clear that Ulpian based his commentary on the Praetorian Edict on that of Labeo, as he often opens his lemmas with the words *Labeo scribit*. In comparison, the Republican jurists Quintus Mucius Scaevola and Servius Sulpicius Rufus, to take two authoritative examples, have 56 and 97 fragments in Lenel, of which respectively 47 and 82 are citations in imperial jurists. Considering all this, we have good reason to agree with Pomponius that Labeo set the stage for future jurisprudence.[30]

Conclusions

I hope to have shown in this chapter that Labeo's legacy offered authors at various points under the Principate the opportunity to explore big-picture questions about the nature of law, literary production, and political power. While Labeo's rich reception profile may seem to take us in various directions, many of the engagements discussed above ultimately revolve around the nature and ownership of legal discourse.

The two most extensive surviving interactions with Labeo, those of Gellius and Gaius (the latter as a representative of the jurists), both communicate that by their time jurisprudence had grown into a discrete technical discourse. Both also place Labeo at a critical juncture in legal and literary history. In his intellectual protreptic for the literary elite, Gellius presents Labeo as a link between an older world of law and letters, in which law was integral to the study of Roman culture, history, and morals;[31] as opposed to the modern world populated by more narrowly focused, technical jurists who may not even know much about the Twelve Tables. Labeo was firmly grounded in this older world. But by introducing conceptual innovations informed by his wide learning, he changed Roman civil law in an irreversible way. The jurists similarly cast Labeo as a patriarch of their discursive space inhabited by canonical legal authorities. In the light of the rise of a juristic canon, it is striking that Gellius recommends reading Labeo but not contemporary legal works. For Gellius, Labeo's work is worth reading for its perceptive insights and its general knowledge that are valuable also beyond the narrow confines of the law. On the other hand, it appears that contemporary works were mostly not the kind of reading that Gellius would recommend, presumably since he considers them as technical and narrow-minded as the average jurists who wrote them. Gellius' relative silence, then, can also be taken to point to the existence of legal literature of a technical and specialist character. We should also note that Gellius' agenda of encouraging his readers to take law seriously suggests that even the writings of Labeo and other jurists were increasingly the preserve of specialists, avoided by a more general readership. But according to Gellius, Labeo was clearly worth wresting from the experts and reclaiming for a wider readership of *litterati*.

If these texts invite us to think about the nature and evolution of legal discourse, Labeo's biographical tradition in turn draws attention to the question as to who is or should be in control of the law. The episodes that we have encountered above all feature a confrontation between Labeo and Augustus that raises the question of the authority to formulate the law in a context of large structural changes to how power, including the power to set binding norms, was held. In most of the surviving scenes, Labeo comes across as a staunch defender against the assertiveness and encroachments of the princeps. The interest of authors such as Suetonius, Tacitus, and Pomponius indicates that these issues played out over a long time and were still very much alive in the Antonine Age.

Finally, this may also go some way towards explaining why, across the panorama of his reception, Labeo and his lifetime are presented as a turning point in legal history, which resonates clearly with the assessments of the Augustan age as opening a new era that we find across the literary spectrum. The civil wars and the emergence of the princeps were an enormous shock to the system, creating waves that rippled out over many decades. Labeo was there at a crucial moment and aggressively negotiated the position of jurists within the new balance of power. The Augustan age was, and was memorialized as a time of profound changes, also to the legal landscape. Labeo, who may have been the first jurist to devote himself full-time to law and allegedly wrote 400 books (Pomp. *Ench. l.s.* = *Dig.* 1.2.2.47), saw a chance to make a massive contribution. And despite the clashes and the drama, Augustus may have been content to let Labeo do his thing to some extent,[32] perhaps in order not to come across as too tyrannical.[33] Later authors, as we have seen, remembered Labeo not simply as a great scholar but as an author after whom literature and legal literature would never be the same again.

Notes

1. I would like to thank Erica Bexley and Ioannis Ziogas for bringing such wonderful participants together at the conference in Durham in September 2019. I am also grateful for their feedback and patience as we all had to deal with the impact of the Covid-19 pandemic on our lives. Due to limitations of space, I have kept referencing and engagement with the scholarship to a minimum. Translations are mine unless indicated otherwise.
2. Frier (1985); see also Harries (2006). Schiavone (2012) is an attempt in very broad strokes at placing the same development in the framework of the history of the entire Western legal tradition.

3 See e.g. Cic. *Top.* 28, with the discussion of Harries (2002).
4 See e.g. *RGDA* 8; Suet. *Vesp.* 10; Crook (1955) 56–9 (on Hadrian). On the slow but steady rise of the emperor as supreme judge, see Tuori (2016a).
5 Sometimes called the Roman 'cultural revolution'; see Habinek and Schiesaro (1997); Wallace-Hadrill (1997) and (2008). This 'revolution' is often seen as embedded in a long-term historical process starting with Rome's imperialist expansion in the Mid Republic, with the Principate forming one (but an important) chapter.
6 See Ziogas (2021), especially the introduction and chapter 6. For thoughtful approaches to Ovid and the Principate, see also Hardie (1997) and Barchiesi (1997).
7 On this, see Mantovani (2017) as a starting-point.
8 For a prosopographical study, though with a highly problematic evidential basis, see Bauman (1989) 25–55.
9 On the procedure and the dating of this episode, see Pettinger (2019) 47–51.
10 See Wallace-Hadrill (1982) for a classic discussion of *ciuilitas* and imperial virtue.
11 The commentator Helenius Acro was active around 200 CE. His commentary survives in two recensions dating not earlier than the fifth century. Information at Zetzel (2018) 149–50 (with warnings that the commentary has been much abridged and interpolated in late antiquity).
12 Not all modern commentators agree that the Labeo mentioned by Horace should be identified with Marcus Antistius Labeo the jurist. See e.g., recently, Courtney (2013) 84, tracing the name to Lucilius and suggesting identification with C. Atinius Labeo (tribune of the plebs 131 BCE).
13 Note that Porphyrio qualifies the term *libertas* with *in qua natus erat* ('in which he was born'). This might at first glance simply refer to the period before the Principate (Labeo's father died at Philippi in 42 BCE). However, if we consider that the Roman biographical imagination tended to conceive of individuals as part of families, often assigning character traits to whole family lines, the characterization of Labeo's father as a key conspirator against Caesar and a fighter on the side of the liberators gives Labeo a strong anti-authoritarian pedigree. On Pacuvius Labeo, see Plut. *Brut.* 12, 51; App. *BC* 4.135.
14 Discussion about legal details at Nörr (1974) 104–5. Eck (2019) discusses wider ('popular') resistance against Augustus' legislative initiatives.
15 Note that, if we accept the letter as genuine, Labeo was already branded as a lover of *libertas* between Augustus' death (*diuo*) and Capito's in 22 CE.
16 On this, see Howley (2013), specifically about Gellius and the jurists. For general studies on Gellius' intellectual outlook, see Holford-Strevens (2003), Keulen (2008), Gunderson (2009), and Howley (2018). Cf. also Nörr (1976).
17 On the ways in which Gellius sets up his chapters, see Howley (2018) 7–14.
18 The immediately following chapter, 13.13, features the same question in a rather different dramatization.

19 The first half of the translation is adapted from Wibier (2016) 120.
20 Although not essential to my argument, Gellius' formulation *de iure publice responsitauit* has raised questions about the nature of Labeo's activity: did he merely offer *responsa* 'in a public place' or did he possess the so-called *ius respondendi* (*ex auctoritate principis*)? The latter is only known from Pomponius (*Ench. l.s.* = *Dig.* 1.2.2.49), but its details and existence remain an unsolvable problem; see Tuori (2004). Given Pomponius' claim that Masurius Sabinus was its first holder, and given Labeo's open criticism of Augustus and his laws, it is not straightforward to suggest that Labeo received this *ius respondendi*, not even as a backhanded way to co-opt his authority; see Novkirishka-Stoyanova (2015).
21 See Lenel (1889) vol. 1, coll. 534–6 (for Labeo's *Posteriores*); coll. 299–315 (for Iavolenus' *Ex Posterioribus Labeonis libri X*). For further discussion, see below.
22 This is also the main attraction of Labeo for Festus.
23 See also Gell. 4.20; cf. 11.18.6, 20.1.
24 Howley (2013).
25 The translation of the two passages is Rolfe's in the Loeb edition.
26 Examples of debates in which Labeo was less decisive though still worth citing (according to Gaius) at *Inst.* 1.135, 1.188, 2.231.
27 Striking absences are Varro and Ateius Capito.
28 For Servius Sulpicius Rufus, see Harries (2016); for Masurius Sabinus, see Mantovani (2017).
29 While reporting a much higher number of Labeonic fragments, the proportions in Bremer (1898) are roughly the same. The higher number is due primarily to Bremer's editorial choice to separate excerpts from the *Digest* (and other sources) into several fragments where meaningful.
30 It is important to keep in mind that Labeo was not the only jurist credited with a foundational role. Based on an extensive analysis of whom the jurists tend to designate as *uetus/ueteres*, Mantovani (2017) points out that Masurius Sabinus is the earliest jurist never considered *uetus*, indicating his foundational role for imperial jurisprudence.
31 Cf. Zetzel (2018) 57–8.
32 While I agree with Pettinger (2019) that the antagonism between Labeo and Augustus does not preclude that the two found each other useful for pushing their own ideas and agendas, I am sceptical about his suggestion that Labeo was a key mastermind behind the purge of the Senate of 18 BCE simply on the basis of a sense of nostalgia for a Senate of Republican size (pp. 55, 58).
33 It is interesting to note that the legal 'revolution' continued under Tiberius on a rather different model, at least in the version of Pomponius. By promoting Masurius Sabinus to the rank of Equestrian and by granting him the *ius respondendi*, Tiberius appears to have moved to claim greater control of legal discourse.

Part Three

Literature and Property Law

8

Poetry, Prosecution and the Author Function

Nora Goldschmidt

In 1969, partly in response to Roland Barthes' declaration of the death of the author, Michel Foucault addressed the issue of how we talk and think about authors.[1] Attempts to abolish the author, Foucault observed, will inevitably have limited success, because the concept has such a powerful cultural function – and one that seems all pervasive. '[W]hen we reconstruct the history of a concept, literary genre, or school of philosophy', Foucault noted, 'the author and the work', in contrast to almost all other interpretive filters, take on an inordinately powerful role in how we interpret texts (141). To understand why this is the case, Foucault set about addressing not the construction of the 'individual author' but what he called the 'author function', that is, in Foucault's words, 'the relationship between text and author and ... the manner in which the text points to this "figure" that, at least in appearance, is outside it and antecedes it' (141).

From this apparent promise of an analysis of the dynamics of literary texts, Foucault moved outwards to what reads, and has been read, much more like a socio-historical aetiology of the construction of authorship. How and why did texts come to be associated with authors, and what were the social, cultural and legal contexts that made the author function possible? These are all fundamental questions, and – whether in agreement or dissent – Foucault's essay, and its socio-historical dimension in particular, has long featured prominently as 'an obligatory reference' in discussions of modern authorship.[2] The idea of the author function has come to play a part in the law and literature movement, too, where issues of authorship and copyright constitute an important intersection of the two fields.[3] Yet the concept rarely features either in work on Greek and Roman authorship or on Roman law.[4] Foucault's author function and its later evolutions, however, are worth interrogating, not least because the concept has important implications both for how we think about ancient authorship and for how we might consequently think differently about the narrative of the emergence of authorship that we tell more broadly across disciplines. At the heart of the issue are the interactions between literature and the law. The juridical construction of the author is central to Foucault's argument and – in one way or another – central, too, to the cultural emergence of poetic authorship in Rome.

This chapter revisits Foucault's author function and the relationships that it exposes between law and literature in the context of the emergence of poetic authorship in Republican Rome. Where Foucault located the author function in the late eighteenth century and the beginning of the nineteenth, and where several others have since projected it back in time, primarily to the early modern period, this chapter shifts the discussion much further back to the Roman context and specifically to the creation of a written literature in Latin in the third century BCE. Latin literature appeared surprisingly late, long after other cultural institutions – including the institution of the law – had been established in Rome.[5] The particular conditions surrounding the beginnings of literature in Rome, therefore, offer a powerful type-case for the author function and its relationship to juridical culture. While revisions of the author function generally follow Foucault's original essay by dealing with the hypothetical 'emergence' of the author in periods when literature was already well established, the Roman example enables us to put the Foucauldian author function to work in circumstances where the emergence of the author is a much more palpable cultural fact, disclosing with particular clarity the relationships between law and the creation of literary authorship.

This chapter takes Foucault's insights to the Roman context by looking at how Roman poetic authorship emerged from, and was imagined through, juridical culture. Beginning in Section 1 by interrogating Foucault's paradigm and its later developments, I move on to consider the implications of the author function and its juridical conditions specifically for Roman Republican contexts. Section 2 ('Fescennine Licence and Literary *furta*') looks at the dynamic interactions between poetry and the law in the pre-literary and so-called 'archaic' periods of Latin literature and the ways in which they were imagined by later readers. Penal responsibility (an essential precondition for Foucault's author function) was written into the literary history of Rome, while a concept of literary property, couched in the quasi-legal language of theft imported from Alexandria and adapted to Roman juridical language, was central to the creation of the early canon of Roman poets. The final section focuses on one of Rome's earliest poets, Gnaeus Naevius, as a case study in how poetic authorship can emerge in dialogue with the law.

Locating the author

For Foucault, the author function comes about through a confluence of two principal socio-cultural conditions, both of them broadly juridical in nature. The first involves the establishment of a system governing the ownership of texts, which he links with the modern system of copyright law and its related networks:

> Once a system of ownership for texts came into being, once strict rules concerning author's rights, author–publisher relations, rights of reproduction, and related matters were enacted ... the possibility of transgression attached to the act of writing took on, more and more, the form of an imperative peculiar to literature (148).

For Foucault, 'the imperative peculiar to literature' which created the author concept as we understand it, is tied in decisively with modern copyright law, 'the moment when a system of strict copyright rules were established': that is, towards the end of the eighteenth century and the beginning of the nineteenth, when 'the social order of propriety which governs our culture' was codified.

The second condition necessary for the author function is what, Foucault says, 'one might call penal appropriation':

> Texts, books, and discourses really began to have authors (other than mythical, 'sacralized' and 'sacralizing' figures) to the extent that authors became subject to punishment, that is, to the extent that discourses could be transgressive (148).

'Penal appropriation' can precede ownership of texts. But it is when the two conditions pertain together that, for Foucault, the 'author function' proper arises:

> It is as if the author, beginning with the moment at which he was placed in the system of property that characterizes our society, compensated for the status that he thus acquired by rediscovering the old bipolar field of discourse, systematically practicing transgression and thereby restoring danger to a writing which was now guaranteed the benefits of ownership (148–9).

Foucault thus tries to tie together the 'transgressive' potential of texts with modern ideas about private property, and, in doing so, locates the emergence of the author function at the point when law and literature were closely bound together: that is, when penal appropriation and copyright law created a combination of juridical and social pressures that enabled particular discourses to be classified as literature and associated with a named author.

Where Foucault located this moment in the late eighteenth century and at the beginning of the nineteenth century, a whole raft of scholars have since nudged his aetiology of the author function back in time.[6] Notably, in Britain, where the Copyright Act was passed in 1710 (about eighty years before similar laws were passed in France), the dynamics of censorship, literary property and print culture have been systematically shown to have allowed for the emergence of an author function at least a hundred years earlier than Foucault's.[7] Rome has had a walk-on part in the story. As Brian Vickers importantly argued, the relationship between poetry and the law voiced in the canonical texts of Augustan poetry – particularly those of Horace and Ovid which interrogate or instantiate relationships between law, poetry, patronage and power – offered parallels through which early modern writers, deeply steeped in the Augustan classical canon, negotiated discourses of authorship.[8] Yet while Augustan and imperial figurations of the poet's role may have set important later paradigms for the emergence of the author function in the modern world, the productive relationship between law and literature was established long before that.

In what follows, I contend that a version of the author function can be located much earlier than Foucault and others have located it, in the interactions between law and the emergence of literature – and especially of poetry – in third-century-BCE Rome. I am not aiming primarily to expose historical weaknesses in Foucault's argument, though, as others have pointed out, they do exist.[9] Instead, I want to utilize Foucault's theoretical insights to explore the relationship between law and literature at a moment when professional poetic authorship in Latin became a cultural fact in Rome. Foucault himself expressed unhappiness with the ways in which he tended to rely on clichés when talking about antiquity.[10] It is hardly surprising, and probably would not have surprised Foucault much either, that the ancient evidence is significantly more vital than he acknowledged. While Homer receives a mention in the essay (along with Hippocrates and Hermes Trismegistus, said to be the author of the Hermetic corpus) as part of the demonstration of the idea that you do not need a flesh-and-blood figure to have an author function, Foucault essentially elides Rome in his account of the prehistory of authorship.[11] This is a crucial omission. Arguably, it changes the whole story, because Roman culture provided a microclimate in which the rise and codification of authorship in just the kinds of social and juridical contexts that Foucault influentially identified as germane to 'our culture' (159) was closely approximated much earlier than his aetiology of authorship and its later developments have allowed.

Literature in Rome began notoriously late. As Denis Feeney has observed, there was in some ways no need for it.[12] One of the consequences of that late arrival is that when Roman literature did emerge, there was already a long-established legal culture and legal vocabulary within which it unfolded and in dialogue with which it developed. It is striking that the Twelve Tables were already two centuries old when what we identify as 'archaic' Roman poetry began to be written and performed. Literature came to adopt the language and even part of the literary function of the law. Historical works like Ennius' *Annales* and Cato's *Origines* presented themselves as compendia of the *moribus antiquis* (*Annales* 156 Skutsch) on which the legal foundations of Rome were based.[13] We find linguistic echoes of the Twelve Tables in Ennius' *Annales*,[14] juridical language in Plautus,[15] legal dodges in the prologues of Terence,[16] and references to contemporary law in Roman *togata*.[17]

As I argue here, in important ways, poetic authorship itself also emerged in and through dialogue with the law. The issue is complicated by the fact that early Roman poetry, like early Roman law, is riddled with problems of fragmentary evidence. There are almost no hard facts for the preliterary period, and even for the period when literature was written down, what we have is unavoidably mediated by later sources.[18] Real juridical culpability is hard to prove, as are details of the biographies of authors (which are often projected from the texts themselves), or even in some cases the authenticity and interpretation of lines ascribed to them. Yet though it is hard to say many positivistic things about the early period of Latin literature, the material we have points to elements of a prehistory of the conditions for Foucauldian authorship and its dialogue with the law that are worth taking seriously. Moreover, if early Roman poetry is subject more than most evidence to the distortions of reception, what we can see with more certainty is that Roman readers retrospectively understood Latin literature as emerging in a socio-cultural – and indeed juridical – context that is very close to the modern author function. In doing so, they strikingly anticipated later ideas about the conditions conducive to poetic authorship and the creative interactions between penal appropriation and ownership of texts.

Fescennine licence and literary *furta*

In its earliest phase, the author function could only begin to emerge, for Foucault, when literature became 'subject to punishment, that is, to the extent that discourses could be transgressive' (148). The idea of a primitive phase of authorship rooted in transgressive discourse and its eventual punishment by law has a striking analogue in the ways in which Roman poets themselves imagined their own literary prehistory and the rise of literary authorship in Rome. Transgression – a key condition of the modern author function – was identified as a foundational moment in the emergence of Latin literature.[19] Virgil imagined the early Italians singing unrefined verses imported from Troy in a Bacchic state of 'unchecked laughter' (*risu ... soluto*, Geo. 2.385–6). As his contemporary Horace recounted it, the primitive rural inhabitants of Italy had their own native traditions of pre-literary *carmina* (trans. Rudd (2005)):

> agricolae prisci, fortes paruoque beati,
> condita post frumenta leuantes tempore festo
> corpus et ipsum animum spe finis dura ferentem,
> cum sociis operum et pueris et coniuge fida,
> Tellurem porco, Siluanum lacte piabant,
> floribus et uino Genium memorem breuis aeui
> Fescennina per hunc inuenta licentia morem
> uersibus alternis opprobria rustica fudit,
> libertasque recurrentis accepta per annos
> lusit amabiliter, donec iam saeuus apertam
> in rabiem coepit uerti iocus et per honestas
> ire domos impune minax. doluere cruento
> dente lacessiti; fuit intactis quoque cura
> condicione super communi; quin etiam lex
> poenaque lata, malo quae nollet carmine quemquam
> describi: uertere modum, formidine fustis
> ad bene dicendum delectandumque redacti.
>
> Horace, *Epistles* 2.1.139–55

Farmers of old – sturdy men, well off with a little –
when the crops were in, at holiday time relaxed the body
and the mind as well (which bears a lot when it has an end
in sight) with the sons and loyal wives who had shared the work.
They used to placate Silvanus with milk and Earth with a pig,
and the Genius who knows the shortness of life with wine and flowers
These occasions saw the beginning of wild Fescennines –
verses in which they exchanged volleys of rustic abuse.
Freedom was gladly given a place in the year's cycle,
and people enjoyed the fun, until the joking began
to get vicious and turned into sheer madness, becoming a menace

and running unchecked through decent houses; its tooth drew blood,
and the victims smarted; even those who escaped were worried
about the state of society. At last a law was enacted
involving penalties; no one, it said, should be traduced
in scurrilous verse. They changed their tune, and in fear of the cudgel
returned to decent language and the business of giving pleasure.

Like Virgil, Horace imagines native proto-literature emerging from a state of contained free speech associated with the carnival licence of religious festivities, when, historically, legal proceedings were suspended.[20] Horace links the carnivalesque freedom specifically with the *licentia* (145) of Fescennine verses, pre-literary abusive songs that were alternately sung (*uersibus alternis*, 146; cf. Livy 7.2.5). In time, the social licence granted to Fescennine songs grew out of hand, spilling over the boundaries of designated yearly religious festivals (148–51). The jokes became serious, broke the confined limits of the previously controlled holiday transgression and started to turn to frenzy (*in rabiem coepit uerti*, 149). Without the threat of punishment (*impune*) the impromptu compositions began to run wild, threatening the 'decent houses' (*honestas ... domos* 149–50) of the community. Worse still, pre-literary song morphed into a threat to the institution of the law itself. As Susanna Braund points out,[21] Horace's mutant Fescennines, verbally attacking Roman homes, look a lot like the *Volksjustiz* of *flagitatio*, the practice of hurling abuse at a thief in order to demand back property (like Catullus in poem 42),[22] or the associated practice of *occentatio*, both of which seem to have been associated with an attack on the offender's house door (*honestas ... domos* 149–50) and sometimes took the form of alternate chants (*uersibus alternis*, 146).[23] Over time, a move to curb this activity was made on the part of the community, including those untouched (*intactis*, 151) by the attacks who were worried for the state of society (*condicione super communi*, 152, or, as Brink renders it, the 'state of order of the body politic').[24] At last, formal legal measures were taken to check the transgression, when 'a law involving a punishment was brought in' (*lex/poenaque lata*, 152–3). Under the real and present threat of penal retribution (*formidine fustis*, 154), discourse (*dicendum*, 155) reverted to the bounds of juridically licensed decency, and the quasi-legal power inherent in the Fescennines – whose injurious speech had begun to take on the force of law itself – was reappropriated by the real juridical power of the state.

Horace's literary history in *Epistles* 2.1 is notoriously tendentious. Fescennine verse did not completely die out: along with the often subversive *uersus quadratus*, the genre continued to be practised and circulated in certain contexts (Octavian is even said to have written *Fescennini uersus* against Pollio, Macrob. *Sat.* 2.4.21), and it clearly fed into Roman satire, much as Horace liked to locate the origins of his favourite genre in the aristocratic Lucilius.[25] The accuracy of Horace's version of early Roman literary history, probably modelled on Greek paradigms taken over from Varro, remains open to question, not least since the earliest forms of Latin verse are shrouded in mystery, and already were for Horace and his contemporaries. Still, the penal appropriation of licentious song to which *Epistles* 2.1 gestures is grounded in a cultural and legal reality. In particular, the *lex* to which Horace refers has been linked directly by both legal historians and scholars of Latin literature to a law in the Twelve Tables (VIII.i):[26]

> qui malum carmen incantassit ... <quiue> occentassit carmen<ue> cond<issit>...
>
> Whoever cast a magic spell ... <or whoever> sing in enmity <or> compose a song...

Dating from the fifth century BCE, this was probably a single law, dealing with two types of *carmen*: magic spells (*qui malum carmen incantassit*) and the composition of libellous songs or poems (*<quiue> occentassit carmen<ue> cond<issit>*).[27] Like Horace's out-of-control *Fescennina licentia*, the language seems to echo the culture of *occentatio* and *flagitatio* (a longer section in Cicero's *De republica* qualifies the *carmen* as *quod infamiam faceret flagitiumue alteri*, *Rep.* IV.12 = Aug. *de Civ. Dei* 2.9), which the law might have been partly designed to quell.[28] Moreover, like Horace's prehistory of Latin literature, it suggests a Foucauldian alignment of the possibility of legal transgression with the dawn of authorship: while the law prohibits spells from being chanted (*incantare*), it outlaws not only the singing of songs (*cantare*) but their authored composition (*condere*).

Most commentators think it unlikely that anyone was ever put to death for composing or singing libellous verses, and the law probably fell into desuetude in the later Republic, when defamation was thought of as a kind of *iniuria*.[29] Physical *iniuria* was covered under the Twelve Tables (VIII iv) and modified by the praetorian *edictum de iniuriis aestumandis* (and eventually by the *actio iniuriarum*), and this came to cover non-physical forms of injury as well.[30] In two recorded cases, Roman poets themselves pursued litigation for *iniuria* on stage: Accius (170–*c.* 86 BCE) is said to have won a prosecution on those grounds against a *mimus* who attacked him by name, and Lucilius (180–103/2 BCE) pursued (and lost) a prosecution for literary *iniuria* against someone who defamed him on the stage (*Auct. ad Her.* 1.24; 2.19). The interpretation of the law to include verbal injury was probably relatively recent for Accius and Lucilius around the mid-second century BCE,[31] but even before that, the existence of a legal provision against transgressive composition in the Twelve Tables – *fons omnis publici priuatique iuris* (Livy 3.34.6) – provided a broad-brush cultural sanction for the possibility, at least, of associating the act of transgression with the act of composing *carmina*. Even if it was rarely or never implemented, its existence institutionalized literary composition as, in Foucault's terms, 'a gesture fraught with risks' (148), underwriting social constraints on the practice of writing and codifying the conditions of penal appropriation necessary for the author function to emerge.[32]

All this suggests some kind of productive dynamics (in various degrees of actual danger to the author) between literature, libel and prosecution not all that different from the entanglements that have been seen to lead to the modern author function. On its own, however, penal appropriation is not necessarily an indication that Rome had a workable version of the modern author function, which could only pertain with the introduction of a system of ownership of texts that would bind a named 'author' to the work. Roman law granted no statutory rights to authors about the circulation and use of their work. There was no official copyright law in the Roman legal system.[33] The only clear law dealing with textual ownership related to the text as material and moveable object, not to its content.[34] But there were other ways in which ownership could be established and contested. Even if they faced no legal redress for their misuse, Roman poets, far from producing the kinds of authorless 'sacralizing' texts Foucault envisaged, mirrored Greek practices of writing and reading to inscribe authorial ownership into their works through autobiographical references and other forms of signature right from the beginning.[35]

More broadly, a quasi-legal discourse of ownership of texts was embedded in the ways in which literature was interpreted and received. As Scott McGill has shown, plagiarism, the presentation of another's work under the new author's name – and the consequent discourse of literary ownership it brought with it – was clearly 'a legible item in the cultural vocabulary' of Rome, even if it was not strictly codified in legal terms.[36] When a written literature in Latin arrived on the scene and its audiences began to discuss and disseminate it, literary plagiarism became couched in the existing Roman vocabulary of legal transgression. In Greek literary criticism, reuse of material from another author was commonly called a 'theft' (κλοπή) and its practitioners 'thieves' (κλέπται) in the context of a broader literary critical vocabulary that encompassed property violations as well as more neutral language of assumption and transference.[37] At some point in the second century BCE Greek exegetical practices were exported to Rome, effectively, in Sander Goldberg's formulation, constructing literature in Republican Rome, and the concept of literary theft and the violation of literary ownership that it implied became naturalized on Roman soil.[38] Modelling their methods on Greek practices, a growing cohort of professional *critici* adapted Alexandrian modes of exegesis and applied them to the emerging body of literary writing in Latin. Like their Greek colleagues, Roman literary critics adopted the practice of making comprehensive lists of literary 'thefts', and the identification of purloined lines, characters or scenes became a key part of the dynamics of literary discourse.[39] Terence self-consciously dramatized accusations of theft against him by theatrical rivals (*Eun.* 19b–26), and even before that, Caecilius (*c.* 230/20–168/7 BCE), who was purportedly Ennius' housemate (Jer. *Ab Abr.* 1838, 179 BCE), was making charges of literary purloinment, probably because he, too, had faced them himself from professional *critici* and rival playwrights.[40]

The language which the new *critici* used to approximate Greek terms naturally overlapped with the already developed professional discourses of Roman law. There was no official term for plagiarism or what we would understand as copyright infringement; the term *plagiarius*, 'kidnapper', was only later used by Martial (1.52.9) to describe literary filching, from which the English word derives. But transgression was clearly apparent in the quasi-legal valency of the terminology. The literary critical language of authorial ownership could encompass a whole spectrum of possibilities from the relatively neutral to the technically legal: Macrobius, who was probably working from an older list of *furta Virgilii* himself,[41] used the term *alieni usurpatio* (*Sat.* 6.1.2) – a legal term denoting the act of taking hold of property without a legal right – to describe what audiences, accustomed to the practice of listing literary parallels, might think of the list of Virgil's literary transgressions he offered.[42] Generally, the most common noun Roman authors employed to describe the use of another author's intellectual property was *furtum* ('theft') and the verb usually *surripere* 'to steal' or 'to filch'.[43] *Furtum*, like the English 'theft' overlapped with the technical term for a wrong punishable by law.[44] In early law, the delict of *furtum*, legislated for in the Twelve Tables, may have encompassed specifically the asportation of someone else's movable property (the word was etymologically derived from *ferre*, 'to carry' in antiquity), though this point is debated by modern legal scholars.[45] When the *Lex Aquilia* codified *damnum iniuria datum* around 286

BCE, *furtum* came increasingly to encompass several kinds of 'theft' or unlicensed borrowing, including some types of fraud, and became an elastic catch-all *crimen omnium generalissimum*,[46] which made it particularly prone to adaptation.

Though textual *furtum* had no real-world legal valency, then, its juridical connotations helped to create a literary-critical system in which the author function could flourish. As the available juridically inflected language of theft was absorbed into literary critical terminology, a strong concept of ownership of texts became essential to the discourses surrounding the creation of a canon of early Latin literature in the first century BCE. This might not be modern copyright law, but it does imply 'a system of ownership of texts' that mirrors Roman poets' own proprietorial claims to authorship which they had inscribed into their works. Combined with 'the possibility of transgression', early Roman poetic production could, more and more, take on 'the form of an imperative peculiar to literature'.[47] That imperative – and the role of textual ownership and penal appropriation in its formation – play a central role in the case of one of the earliest Roman poets, Gnaeus Naevius, whose career is marked by the perceived infringement of copyright and a notorious brush with the law.

Naevius and the Metelli

Naevius, whose first stage production is dated to 235 BCE, is known for several works, none of which survives intact: a series of *fabulae praetextae* (plays on Roman themes), comedies, tragedies, and an epic on the First Punic War written in Saturnians, known as the *Bellum Punicum*. Along with Livius Andronicus (his precursor) and Quintus Ennius (his successor), Naevius is seen as a key player in the emergence of Roman literary authorship. Together, they helped to create a poetic canon which was still substantially in place in Horace's lifetime, and whose emergence need not have been taken for granted. It involved an effort of socio-political self-positioning as well as poetic self-fashioning – and the dynamics of that process anticipate Foucault's author function in important ways.

When Cicero – who was crucial to forming the canon of early Roman poetry retrospectively – looked back at the history of Roman epic, he identified the *Bellum Punicum* as an object of quasi-copyright infringement in the hands of Naevius' epic successor Ennius through the discourse of petty theft:

> sit Ennius sane, ut est certe, perfectior; qui si illum, ut simulat, contemneret, non omnia bella persequens primum illud Punicum acerrimum bellum reliquisset.

"scripsere," inquit, "alii rem uorsibus" – et luculente quidem scripserunt, etiam si minus quam tu polite. nec uero tibi aliter uideri debet, qui a Naeuio uel sumpsisti multa, si fateris, uel, si negas, surripuisti.

Brutus 75–6

Let Ennius be more polished, as he surely is. But if he really disdained Naevius, as he pretends, he would not, in undertaking to go through all our wars, have passed over the sharply contested first Punic War. 'Others have treated the subject in verses,' he says. And indeed, they have written excellently, even if they did so in a less refined way than you. Nor should it seem any different to you, since you have borrowed (*sumpsisti*) much from Naevius, if you admit it (*si fateris*), or have stolen (*surripuisti*) much from him, if you deny it (*si negas*).

The boundaries between theft and imitation were already blurred in the language of Roman literary criticism, and Cicero, a lawyer himself, couches his accusations as a forensic drama. *Brutus* is set up as a dialogue between Cicero and M. Iunius Brutus, and Cicero opens by giving a third-person account of the beginnings of Roman literature and the development of judicial and political speech in Rome (an elision that itself reflects the wider co-dependence of literature and law in Latin culture). In this passage, he suddenly switches to the second person, calling on Ennius as if he were a living courtroom witness to admit (*fateri*) or deny (*negare*) the allegations he levels against him.

As Scott McGill points out, for Cicero, the crucial issue in question is not *imitatio*, 'intending not to steal but to borrow openly, so that it would be noticed' (*non subripiendi causa, sed palam mutuandi, hoc animo ut uellet agnosci*, Sen. *Suas.* 3.7), but an intentional assumption by one author of the intellectual property of another. Cicero accuses Ennius of what McGill calls 'the intent to deceive readers' to the effect that substantial material (*multa*) belonging to Naevius, and known under the author's name, in fact belongs to Ennius.[48] Despite Cicero's assertion that Ennius 'passed over' the First Punic War, there are a number of fragments that suggest he covered at least parts of it.[49] As Ennius himself was probably aware when he dismissed his rival as a preliterary *uates* before entering his quasi-copyrighted territory (*scripsere alii rem /uorsibus quos olim Faunei uatesque canebant*, 'others have written on the topic in verses which once the Fauns and seers used to sing', *Ann.* 206–7), this is not just a question of poetic imitation, but a contest about literary property and the ownership of texts.[50]

Foucault's second condition, penal appropriation, also contextualises Naevius' career. Several fragments suggest that Naevius' work was, in one way or another, concerned with the limits of authorial rights and literary and political transgression. Like Horace's *Fescennina licentia* or Virgil's prehistory of drama in the *Georgics* discussed above, one of Naevius' most well-known dramatic fragments links the carnival licence of the theatre with the festival of Liber, the Roman equivalent of Bacchus: *libera lingua loquemur ludis Liberalibus*, 'with a free tongue (*libera lingua*) we will speak at the games held in honour of *Liber*' (113 Ribbeck). Another fragment, from the *Tarentilla* (72–4 Ribbeck), probably part of a metatheatrical comment spoken by a slave, seems to pit the freedom of a *rex* against the superior *libertas* of the stage.[51] Just how 'outspoken' Naevius actually was is debatable, but the *frisson* between the possibility of transgression (however abstract) and the authorial act seems to lie behind parts of his output. Gellius (7.8.5) refers to a moment 'in the historical record' (*ex historia*) that 'may or may not be true' (*uerone an falso incertum*) in which Naevius criticised the future Scipio Africanus on stage. According to Gellius, Naevius subversively reminded the audience that while Scipio may have been a man 'who often performed glorious deeds by his hand ... [and] whose reputation stands supreme among the people' (*qui res magnas manu saepe gessit gloriose ... qui apud gentes solus praestat*, 108–9 Ribbeck), he was dragged away in shame from his lover's arms by his father, bundled up in the Greek *pallium* which he wore as an affectation (*eum pater cum pallio unod ab amica abduxit*, 110 Ribbeck; cf. Livy 29.19.13).[52] The episode could be read as a stock scene in a comic plot, but as H. D. Jocelyn points out, it would also have had a particular resonance in the political landscape of Rome: '[a] Roman audience aware of the political camp of the magistrate who had commissioned the play and of current gossip could not have failed to identify the person referred to as a contemporary statesman.'[53] There was no way of proving who was meant, but the dramatic fragment clearly tapped into political hearsay in a way that allowed its author to dance the line of transgression while managing to give 'no indisputable legal cause for police action' against him.[54]

The crucial event in Naevius' career (at least as it was constructed retrospectively in reception) concerns an encounter with the Caecilii Metelli which led to a much mythologised brush with the law. At some point, whether in a literary work or independently, Naevius wrote the riddling line:[55]

Fato Metelli Romae fiunt consules

The words tend to be translated as 'by chance the Metelli are elected consuls at Rome'.

But *fato* is difficult to pin down: it could be innocuous ('by divine will') or it could be a lot less innocuous: 'the Metelli become consuls to the ruin of Rome'.[56] In response, the consul Metellus is said to have reacted by writing the following reply:[57]

> Dabunt malum Metelli Naeuio poetae
>
> The Metelli will make trouble for the poet Naevius

What exactly went on is inextricable from the constructions of later sources, but that construction is itself instructive in terms of how Roman readers understood the emergence of authorship in relation to the discourses of legal or quasi-legal constraints. Naevius' line was clearly well-known in first-century BCE Rome. Cicero alludes to it in *Ad Verrem* 1.10.29 at the expense of Verres' ally Q. Metellus Creticus, who was consul designate at the time of Verres' trial, and he does so before a senatorial jury in a way that expects them to know the un-named source: 'The story went that Verres used to say that you were elected consul not by fate (*fato*), as the rest of your family were, but through his influence'.[58] A fifth-century commentator on Cicero, who was probably drawing on Asconius Pedianus (first century CE), explains this as follows:[59]

> An old saying of Naevius was directed wittily and insultingly at the Metelli ... The consul Metellus became angry at this, and replied in a hypercatalectic iambic verse, which is called Saturnian: *Dabunt malum Metelli Naeuio poetae.*

Caesius Bassus (first century CE, too) also knew about the exchange, and insists that the Metelli were 'wounded' by the verse (*Metelli ... ab eo lacessiti*, GLK 6.266).

If we accept the historical reality of the exchange, it is not clear what the import of Metellus' response would have been. According to Caesius Bassus, it was put up 'in a public place' like an edict or official promulgation, which suggests that it was intended as a threat that came dangerously close to mimicking the force of law.[60] At the same time – as both Naevius and Metellus would have been aware – the line could also be construed as an exercise in urbane literary banter. The Ciceronian commentator explicitly identified Metellus' line as *parodia* (Ps.-Asconius I.29, p. 215 Stangl): it is metrical, apparently in Saturnians, Naevius' favoured epic metre, and it is couched as a deliberate structural parallel to the poet's initial attack. As Robert Germany points out, *poetae* can be read not just with *Naeuio* but with *Metelli*, in a 'syntactical equivocation that would echo Naevius' case-play on *Romae*', suggesting implicitly that the Metelli were not only powerful politicians, but could play at being poets, too.⁶¹ The phrase *malum dabo* is a common idiom of comedy, and the line would have evoked just the kind of set-up – a clever slave who is threatened for his impudence (but, as the audience knows, always gets away with it in the end) – that might have been found in one of Naevius' own plays.⁶²

Whether Naevius was actually prosecuted through the implementation of the law against offensive *carmina* in Table VIII.i of the XII Tables is a more serious point of contention, and one which is deeply implicated in later sources. Modern scholars are divided about whether and to what extent to accept the historical reality of the story, though the pendulum has more recently swung in the direction of cautious acceptance.⁶³ The story of Naevius' prosecution is attractive: if true, the poet would have been prosecuted for his *carmen* around 206 BCE (the year of Caecilius Metellus' consulship), a time when poets in Rome had just started to attain a cultural foothold,⁶⁴ making penal appropriation a key ingredient in the rise of Roman poetic authorship. Virtually all the information is filtered by several layers of reception, however, and the problem is compounded by the fact that stories about the lives of ancient poets are essentially 'creative', regularly extracted from the works themselves and those of others writing in parallel genres.⁶⁵

Whatever really happened to Naevius aside, it is instructive that the narrative of penal appropriation was so important for later readers looking back on the beginnings of Latin literature. So much so that a full-blown biofictional story of prosecution and exile takes centre stage in the biographical tradition about the poet. Gellius (3.3.15), probably drawing on Varro, tells the tale that Naevius was thrown into prison by the *triumuiri capitales* because of the 'constant abuse and insults he aimed at the leading men of the city' (*ob assiduam maledicentiam et probra in principes ciuitatis*), only to redeem himself by writing two further plays in his prison cell, thereby atoning for his transgressions.⁶⁶ The narrative is then completed by Jerome (again probably based ultimately on Varro),⁶⁷ who has Naevius die in exile, driven out of Rome by the *nobiles*, with the Metelli at the vanguard, and ending his days in Utica in North Africa in 201 BCE.⁶⁸

With or without the writing of the plays in prison, it looks like some ancient audiences connected the story with a work of Plautus, and probably specifically a cryptic passage in *Miles Gloriosus* (209–12). The scene concerns the slave Palaestrio, who, observed by Periplectomenus, strikes a comic sequence of pantomime poses as he desperately tries to think up a plan. At last, Palaestrio adopts a thinking pose, with his chin propped on his arm like a column:

> ecce autem aedificat: columnam mento suffigit suo.
> apage, non placet profecto mihi illaec aedificatio;
> nam os columnatum poetae esse indaudiui barbaro,
> quoi bini custodes semper totis horis occubant.
>
> Plautus Mil. 209–12

> Look, he's building! He's got a column propped under his chin.
> No thanks! I don't like that kind of building work at all:
> for I've heard there's a barbarian poet with a columned mouth
> and two guards each watching him all the time.

The image of an imprisoned poet evokes a clear moment of penal appropriation in which literature is subject to punishment: the *barbarus poeta* has paid for his transgressions with the ultimate sanction against an author: the 'columning' of his outspoken mouth.[69] As Erich Gruen puts it, the lines are 'obscure and nearly impenetrable',[70] though the obscurity is not surprising if they were meant to be understood by the original audience as a reference to an imprisoned contemporary *poeta* who had been prosecuted specifically for the act of writing.[71] Whether Naevius himself would have been read into the passage by Plautus' audience is a subject of contention, but, again, recent work has moved in the direction of cautious acceptance.[72] The identification goes back to antiquity, though the trail is pretty cold: Festus' epitome (known through Paulus' own epitome) of the first-century BCE scholar Verrius Flaccus, who himself may have been drawing on earlier lexicographers, tells us that Plautus called the poet Naevius a *barbarus* (i.e. Latin-speaking) *poeta*.[73] Verrius would probably have been aware of more than the twenty-one known plays of Plautus, so (if the reading does go back to him) it is not necessarily the passage in the *Miles* in particular he was thinking of, though the linguistic coincidences make it likely. It is still possible that Plautus was pointing to another poet, or to none at all.[74] But the interpretation of the imprisoned poet, bound in chains as a punishment for his *os*, may well have been possible for the play's immediate audience, and (whether as fact or as biofiction) it was certainly an interpretation available to readers in the first century BCE, who, like Cicero and his audience, knew the story of the famous exchange between the Metelli and Naevius, and who, like Verrius, could well have recognised Naevius in Plautus' *poeta*.

In the end, all we really have that dates securely to Naevius' lifetime is the text of the fragments themselves, and even that is subject to the filters and distortions of reception. Later readers writing in different political contexts may well have read more transgressive possibilities into Naevius' encounter with the Metelli than there may originally have been, mingling the life of the author with his work, and if the work was not available to them, reading his life from and into the works of others. Yet even if Naevius did not fall foul of the Metelli and was neither prosecuted nor punished by law, the *possibility* of transgression powerfully invested the act of writing with just the kind of *frisson* Foucault sees as an essential characteristic of the later stages of the development of the author function. Like the modern author identified by Foucault, Naevius – whether in earnest or in jest – was dicing with the discourse of the law. For later readers, implicated in a conceptual system which saw Roman poets as authors of their works and filchers of the intellectual property of others, Naevius provided an ideal paradigm for the Roman author function. It is just as he is penally accountable for his work that he became a fully-fledged, culturally central native version of a *poeta* – ready for his rivals to steal from him. In constructing the canon of Roman poetry *post hoc*, Roman readers tied penal appropriation with poetic ownership into the narratives which they told about the emergence of Latin literature, and, in doing so, they helped to create an author function that predates the phenomenon identified in modern author criticism by almost two millennia.

The Foucauldian author function is not the only way in which we can account for the emergence of authorship in Rome. There are several other methods by which Roman writers turned themselves and each other into authors, and other ways in which Roman culture facilitated the growth of its own literature. But the Foucauldian idea of an author function co-dependent on the law, 'linked to the juridical and institutional system that encompasses, determines, and articulates the universe of discourses' (153), helps to explain the ways in which the emergence of literature was constructed and understood by Roman writers themselves. The paradigm retrospectively set by Naevius would continue to be negotiated much more explicitly under Augustus and Nero: Ovid would claim he had been exiled for a transgressive *carmen*; Lucan (according to the *Lives* at any rate) would be banned by Nero from publishing in his lifetime;[75] Horace would position himself *vis-à-vis* the constraints of Roman libel law 'with Caesar as judge' (*iudice ... Caesare*, 2.1.84) in his conversation with the jurist Trebatius in *Satires* 2.1.[76] Those interactions between poetry, authorship, and the possibilities of prosecution, however, were already powerfully implicated in the emergence of literature in Republican Rome.[77]

Notes

1. Foucault (1969). The English text is from Joseph Harari's translation (= Foucault (1979)), to which all page numbers cited in this chapter refer.
2. Chartier (1992) 29.
3. Woodmansee and Jaszi (1994); Ward (1995) 28–42; Wharton (2018). On Foucault and law more broadly, see Goulder (2013).
4. Martelli (2013) esp. 146, and 231–2, and Peirano (2013) 252 mention Foucault's essay in the context of issues of the author's voice and authorial signatures in Roman poetry, though neither deal with issues of law and literature. See also the brief mention in Lowrie (2009) 283 with Goldschmidt (2019) 83–4; 180.
5. On the complex cultural processes underlying the emergence of literature in Rome, see Rüpke (2000); Gildenhard (2003); Goldberg (2005); Feeney (2016); Biggs (2020).
6. Woodmansee (1984); Rose (1988); Rose (1993); Chartier (1992); Greene (2005). In *Before the Law* (originally composed in 1982) Derrida similarly located the cultural moment when 'law regulates the problems of the ownership of creative works' which he saw as beginning '[i]n broad terms ... between the end of the seventeenth century and the beginning of the nineteenth century in Europe' (Derrida (2018) 69). Cf. Wharton (2018) for modern copyright law and broader definitions of creative production.
7. Sinfield (1996) 10–12; Loewenstein (2002); Greene (2005) esp. 10–15.
8. Vickers (2002) 511–18. See also Goldschmidt (2019) esp. 83–4 on the staging of Augustan poets in Ben Jonson's *Poetaster* and issues of the Foucauldian author.
9. Vickers (2002) 510 is particularly vituperative on this point ('his claim to be taken seriously as a historian seems increasingly slight').
10. Elden (2016) 134; cf. Porter (2006), 159 ('Foucault's grasp of Greece and Rome is not direct or immediate by any stretch of the imagination'). On Foucault and antiquity more broadly, see Detel (1998), Porter (2006), and Alston and Bhatt (2017).
11. Foucault makes an exception for Jerome, who comes up at 150–1 as part of the discussion of assigning authorial names to texts.
12. Feeney (2016).
13. Cf. Lowrie (in this volume).
14. Goldschmidt (2013) 44–5.
15. Gaertner and McGinn (in this volume).
16. Introduction to this volume.
17. Manuwald (2011) 165 (on Afranius' *Vopiscus*).
18. For the distortions involved in the sources of early Latin poetry, see esp. Elliott (2013).
19. Roman prehistories of poetry, and especially of drama, probably go back to a passage in Varro's *De poetis*, itself based on Alexandrian narratives about Greece: Rudd (1989) 28–32.

20 Cf. Introduction to this volume.
21 Braund (2004) 416.
22 Richlin (2017) 172.
23 On the dynamics of *occentatio* and *flagitatio* with particular reference to Plautus, see Richlin (2017) 171–84; on *flagitatio* and *occentatio* as a challenge to the official law of the state, see Usener (1900), and on the history of the practices, see Lintott (1999b) 9; 10. For *flagitatio* see also Kelly (1966) 22–3 and for *occentatio*, see Rives (2002) 283–4.
24 Brink (1982) 195.
25 For Fescennines and satire, see Braund (2004).
26 Crawford (1996) Vol. II, 677–80; Brink (1982) 196 on *lex*: 'the present reference can only be to the Twelve Tables'; Rudd (1989) 100 on 152–4. The reconstructed text and translation are taken from Crawford (1996) Vol. II, 677.
27 Crawford (1996) Vol. II, 679; Rives (2002) 282 (two clauses in the same law).
28 Richlin (2017) 179 reads the passage in Cicero specifically as a reference to *flagitatio* and *occentatio*.
29 Crawford (1996), Vol. II, 679; Momigliano (1942b) 122–3; Frier (1989), 177–200.
30 Zimmermann (1996) 1050–9.
31 Frank (1927) 109, following Huvelin (1903), puts the incident in the post-Gracchan period, arguing that the inclusion of verbal abuse under the scope of *iniuria* was then relatively recent: cf. also Smith (1951) 171.
32 On social constraints (rather than official laws) curbing the potential transgressions of dramatic poetry in the Republican period, see Manuwald (2011) 293–4.
33 McGill (2012) 10.
34 Gaius 2.77; McGill (2012) 10 n.34.
35 Suerbaum (1968); Goldschmidt (2019) 11–13; Biggs (2020) 54–8 on 'Naevius' as a historical character in the *Bellum Punicum*.
36 McGill (2012) 30. While McGill mentions Foucault in a footnote (30 n. 102), he makes no connection between his own findings and the light they might shed on the author function.
37 McGill (2012) 6; Stemplinger (1912); Ziegler (1950).
38 The moment is commonly dated (following Suetonius *Gram.* 2.1) to the extended visit of the Pergamene scholar Crates of Mallos to Rome: Goldberg (2005), 27. It may be, as McGill (2012) 7 argues, that comic poets like Terence were partly responsible for the importation of the practice, but it was embedded much more widely through the broader culture of literary professionalism at Rome, not least because many of the new literary critics were also teachers.
39 Goldberg (2005) 49. The *critici* were aware of their own author function, too: M. Pomponius Andronicus wrote an *elenchi Annalium Enni* (probably a list of 'thefts', though this may also have included other forms of criticism) which Orbilius,

finding out of circulation, took care to publish specifically 'under the author's name' (*uulgandos curasse nomine auctoris*): Suet. *Gram.* 8.1; Kaster (1995) 124.

40 Porph. ap. Euseb. *Praep. evang.* 465d: Goldberg (2005) 49; Manuwald (2011) 237.

41 Skutsch (1985) 31.

42 McGill (2012) 182-3. McGill discusses a whole range of vocabulary used by Roman authors, much of it legally inflected, to equate literary borrowing with criminal wrongdoing.

43 Derrida's 1977 essay 'Limited Inc a b c' points up a fundamental paranoia about theft underlying modern copyright claims: cf. Greene (2005), 12-15, and for an application of Derrida's ideas to 'copyright' understood as 'the kinds of authenticating expectation that we find attached (with varying degrees of credibility) to the authorial name' in the *Res Gestae* and Ovid's exile poetry (24 n.8), see Martelli (2010).

44 The use of *surripere* for stealing a commodity is common in Plautus (e.g. *Asin.* 929; *Aul.* 39; *Curc.* 581) and appears three times in Cato *Agr.* The participle *subruptum* seems to have appeared in the Twelve Tables or the Lex Atinia of 197 BCE: Crawford (1996) 620. Cf. Zimmermann (1996) 929 n. 58 on the 'older terms', *subripere, tollere,* and *amouere*.

45 Twelve Tables, 1.17-22 Crawford. For *furtum* in early law, see Zimmerman (1996) 927-8.

46 Zimmermann (1996) 922.

47 Foucault (1979) 148.

48 McGill (2012) 2-3.

49 *Ann.* 216-19 Skutsch, with Goldberg and Manuwald (2018) 221-3.

50 Ennius stops short of explicitly naming Naevius, though the anonymous plural *alii*, common in polemical texts, can only be a reference to him: Skutsch (1985) 371.

51 For discussion of the fragment (quoted by the grammarian Charisus, *GLK* I.216.10) and its presumed speaker, see Leo (1913) 77; Jocelyn (1969) and Goldberg (2005) 169. On the *Tarentilla*, see esp. M. Barchiesi (1978) 2-66.

52 Gellius' ultimate source was probably the Augustan critic Julius Hygius whom he mentions elsewhere: Jocelyn (1969) 39-40. The lover referred to in the fragment may have been male: Cornell (2013) II. 570 adopts the variant reading *amico* ('boyfriend') for *amica*.

53 Jocelyn (1969) 40. For stock comic themes in the fragment, see Goldberg (1995) 37.

54 Jocelyn (1969) 40. The fragment and the story have also been linked with Cicero's report (which may ultimately be based on Cato) at *De or.* 2.249 of a pun on the name Naevius made *seuere* by Scipio (*Quid hoc Naeuio ingnauius*, 'Is there anyone lazier (*ignauius*) than Naevius'): Jocelyn (1969) 38-9. Cf. Marmorale (1950) 91-104. For speculations about the transgressive role of other Naevian fragments, see Marmorale (1950) and Beta (2014).

55 Ps.-Asconius I.29, p. 215 Stangl. Boyle (2006) 52 tentatively assigns the line to the *Clastidium* (cf. Mattingly (1960) 415), but there is no particularly strong evidence for this: cf. Goldberg (1995) 35 for a note of caution, with Jocelyn (1969) 43–4.
56 For the multiple meanings of *fato*, see Frank (1927) 105–6 and Gruen (1990) 98. Jocelyn (1969) 47 suggests 'with predictable disaster' among a spectrum of possible translations.
57 Caesius Bassus *GLK* 6.266; Ps.-Asconius p. 215 Stangl.
58 *Nam hoc Verrem dicere aiebant, te non fato, ut ceteros ex uestra familia, sed opera sua consulem factum.*
59 Ps.-Asconius I.29, p. 215 Stangl: *dictum facete et contumeliose in Metellos antiquum Naeuii est "fato Metelli Romae fiunt consules", cui tunc Metellus consul iratus uersu responderat senario hypercatalecto, qui et Saturnius dicitur: "dabunt malum Metelli Naeuio poetae".*
60 *proposuerunt*: Caesius Bassus *GLK* 6.266 with Fraenkel (1935) 624. For the inscriptional context 'blending official edict and personal lampoon', see Mattingly (1960) 420 with Boyle (2006) 54.
61 Germany (2019) 71.
62 Goldberg (1995) 35. Beta (2014) 205 reads another double entendre in Metellus' line (*malum* = apple).
63 Notably Wiseman (1998) 39; Boyle (2006) 54–5; Beta (2014); Germany (2019); Gallia (2020). Crawford (1996) 40, citing Momigliano (1942b), sees the story of Naevius' prosecution at the hands of the Metelli as 'still the best explanation' for the connection between the legal possibility enshrined in the XII Tables and the story of Naevius spending time 'in detention awaiting trial' and dying in exile, though, he argues, the death penalty would not have been implemented.
64 Gallia (2020) 723.
65 See esp. Graziosi (2002); Lefkowitz (2012); Fletcher and Hanink (2016); Goldschmidt (2019). On Naevius in particular, see Goldschmidt (2019) 11 and Biggs (2020) 56. As Jocelyn (1969) 34 puts it, the basic outline of the anecdotes (that Naevius criticised Scipio and the Metelli), at the very least, seems unlikely to have been completely invented by later sources, who tended to date the beginnings of serious dramatic poetry at Rome after the second Punic War.
66 The detail of the poet composing some of his plays in prison in order to redeem himself may be based on Naevius' own plays: Jocelyn (1969) 38. The story also echoes the similarly constructed biography of Plautus (said to have ended his days chained to a mill, where he wrote three comedies), also told by Varro, an important source for Naevius' life: Goldberg (1995) 35–6. On the ancient Lives of Plautus and Terence as creative readings of their works, see Goldschmidt (2015a) and (2015b).
67 Rostagni (1944) vi.

68 As Jocelyn (1969) 42 points out, the exile story may be 'a post-Varronian guess based on the story of the exchange of verses'.
69 The word *os* signals outspokenness in Plautus at *Mil.* 189: see also Ter. *Eun.* 597, 807, 838 with Jocelyn (1969) 36.
70 Gruen (1990) 104.
71 Plautus' *columna*, in particular, has been interpreted in several ways: a figurative description of Naevius' actual pose; a suggestion of sexual abuse (Lambinus (1576) 669); an architectural allusion referring to the vertical roof supports in the poet's cell (Jocelyn (1969) 36); the *columna Maenia* which stood near the *carcer Mamertinus* (Jocelyn (1969) 36), or even a (speculative) column crowned with a comic mask, hubristically erected by the poet himself (Gallia (2020)).
72 Jocelyn (1969); Rochette (1998); Moore (1998) 62; Leigh (2004b) 20 n.95; Germany (2019) 71, and Gallia (2020) all find the link credible. Gallia (2020) 722 n. 3 points out that much of the scepticism has been based on a rigidly schematic understanding of the differences between Old and New Comedy.
73 Paulus *Exc. Fest.* 32. For Verrius' sources, see Jocelyn (1969) 35. On Festus' dictionary, see Cornell (2013) I. 67–8. For *barbarus* as Roman or 'Latin speaking', see Gallia (2020) 723 with Plaut. *Asin.* 11; *Trin.* 19; *Capt.* 884.
74 Fontaine (2020) (Sotades).
75 *interdictum est ei poetica*, *Vita Vaccae* 46: Rostagni (1944) 183; cf. Tacitus, *Ann.* 15.49; Dio 62.29: Goldschmidt (2019) 91.
76 Lowrie (2009a) 327–48.
77 I am very grateful to the original audience of the conference paper on which this chapter is based, and especially to stimulating comments from Matthew Leigh, Michèle Lowrie, John Oskanish and Alexander Schwennicke, as well as to the volume editors for their astute remarks.

9

The Sea Common to All in Plautus, *Rudens*: Social Norms and Legal Rules

Thomas A. J. McGinn

The category of property in Roman law known as 'things common to all' (*res communes omnium*),[1] though destined to enjoy a long afterlife, arose somewhat belatedly in antiquity, far along in what modern legal historians conventionally label the late classical period (*c*. 190 – *c*. 235 CE).[2] The Severan jurist Ulpian populates the classification with only three items, the sea, the seashore and the air.[3] To this list his colleague Marcian adds a fourth, flowing water.[4]

Our earliest relevant Roman evidence is Plautus, who identifies one of these items, the sea, as common to all. A central question to consider is whether we are to understand this claim simply as representing a social norm or an actual legal rule. The matter is almost bound to pose a challenge when, as here, it does not originate in a canonical legal context, the *Digest* of Justinian serving as a familiar example. In any case, a claim is truly 'legal' if and only if it offers a basis for adjudication before a court with jurisdiction under a relevant cause of action. Does Plautus' assertion, or any of those similar to his own made by his Greek predecessors, withstand such scrutiny? The answer has interesting implications not just for the historical development of a fascinating aspect of Roman property law, but also for the broader questions of whether and to what extent Latin literature can offer reliable evidence for Roman law in the absence of sources that are strictly legal in nature.

It might be useful for this purpose to invoke a counterfactual question. If we were not in possession of the bulk of our legal sources for the classical period of Roman law (*c*. 31 BCE – *c*. 235 CE), how would we go about reconstructing this from the literary and documentary sources? The point is that for the age of Plautus this question is not so counterfactual. We find ourselves in a position for much of this 'pre-classical' period very much like that of students of ancient Greek law in terms of the types of evidence we have at our disposal.

Our focus in what follows falls on an important chapter of the pre-history of the classification of the *res communes omnium*, examining in particular how Plautus in his *Rudens* treats one of what later emerged as its four canonical elements, the sea. This he famously identifies as 'common to all'. Before coming to grips with this key source, however, we are obliged first to examine the evidence of a Greek tradition, in comedy and beyond, that also views the sea as common to all. Tracing this as far back as possible, to the fifth century BCE, helps shed light on the meaning of such an assertion when it appears in an early Roman source such as Plautus.

The idea that the sea was common to all, meaning all humankind, enjoyed great currency with the Greeks in their classical period (meaning not just for law) and later. Our earliest witness appears to be the fifth-century tragedian Sophocles, in an undated fragment consisting of two words from his *Water Carriers* (*ΥΔΡΟΦΟΡΟΙ*): πολύκοινον Ἀμφιτρίταν ('the sea common to many/ all').⁵ The double entendre – including an allegation of Amphitrite's sexual availability – guarantees this meaning, in my view. She becomes a resource accessible to all, not entirely unlike a fish. It also suggests a point that, though rarely stated outright, seems to be broadly assumed by the Greek sources. The sea is common not to all living creatures, nor just to all Greeks (or Athenians), but to all humans, certainly males.

Just as later with Phoenicides and Plautus, the appearance of this principle in a literary genre – this time tragedy – that was performed publicly before, notionally, the entire city, suggests a broad acceptance. Some evidence indicates that it was in fact a widely held ethical value. For example, Plato in his *Laws*, composed in the middle of the fourth century, postulates regulations allowing, *inter alia*, bird-catchers broad access to untilled land and fishermen to the sea, as well as to other bodies of water that are not either ports or sacred in nature.⁶ None of this evidence suggests that violations of the norm in question could be addressed though a court of law.

Another source suggests that at Athens the principle that the sea is common to all did enjoy the status of a legal rule, meaning that it stood as the basis for claims that were susceptible of judicial adjudication. Athenaeus cites the early third-century comic playwright Phoenicides to the effect that the sea is common (to all) but the fish in it become the property of their purchasers:⁷

Φοινικίδης . . . τὴν μὲν θάλασσαν ἔλεγε κοινὴν εἶναι, τοὺς δ'ἐν αὐτῇ ἰχθῦς τῶν ὠνησαμένων.

Phoenicides ... used to say that while the sea is common (to all), the fish in it belong to those who have bought them.
                                            Athenaeus *Deipnosophistae* 8.345E

This observation, delivered upon serving fish to diners who had made financial contributions for a common meal, implicitly excludes the claims of those who had failed to pay up. They had no standing to petition or to sue for fish that did not belong to them. The sea is common to all but its fish belong only to those individuals who have a legally recognized right to them, meaning that they could assert this right at law, if need be.[8] The second part of Phoenicides' assertion reflects what must have been a legal principle, namely, that buyers of fish acquired ownership through market purchase.[9] This point depends in turn on an unstated assumption holding that fishermen were by law able to own and therefore to dispose of their catch by sale, either to retailers or directly to consumers.[10] The clear result is that seizure of fish at sea conveys (original) ownership, much as happens in Roman law. Such a right the courts in both societies were obliged to protect.

While one might argue that the conclusion does not inevitably follow that the first part of Phoenicides' statement also stands as legal principle, and instead that it simply reflects a situation of fact, this line is impossible to draw, in my view. Given the obvious link between the sea's status as common and a fisherman's acquisition of legal ownership of his catch, it seems unlikely that only one of the two principles has the force of law. We do not know precisely how the Athenians protected the right of access of fishermen to the sea, but a possible candidate for an applicable cause of action is the *graphē hybreōs*.[11]

The idea of a common sea also emerges in this context as the product of a diffuse cultural and political consensus, the fruit of an ideology that held well beyond the law.[12] At the same time it possesses a demonstrable legal heft. The point serves as the premise for a joke in the genre of comedy, where it is presented to a broad sector of the population as though it is received wisdom. A fragment of Antiphanes, the fourth-century writer of comedies, makes a similar point, if less directly.[13] A character complains, with comic exaggeration, that certain wealthy individuals are so successful in purchasing the supply of fish before they arrive on the market that they are effectively buying up the sea, conveying the sense that the latter act is both a moral outrage and a legal impossibility.

The concept of a common sea translated into a generalized ideology recognizing a diffusely held right to free navigation and trade.[14] Over time, some Stoics developed an interest in it, though it is a mistake to attribute the principle's origin to them, since it is demonstrably earlier, as we have seen, dating as far back as the fifth century.[15] Plautus may have taken it from his Athenian model, a lost play by the fourth-century Diphilus whose precise identification remains unknown.[16] The point is moot for our purposes, however. Though the status of the sea as common to all forms part of a cultural patrimony shared by Greeks and Romans, whether it manifests itself as a social norm, philosophical ideal, or legal rule for the former can hardly predict how the matter stood with the latter.

Recent scholarship has recognized the importance of Plautus' evidence in the *Rudens* (or *Rope*) for our understanding of the *res communes omnium*, specifically as applied to the sea and its contents.[17] The play, of uncertain date, falling between 218 and 184 BCE, sets the crucial scene on the shore near the town of ancient Cyrene.[18] Its name derives from the instrument employed in a physical and verbal tug-of-war between two slaves vying for control of a trunk that one of them, Gripus, has fished out of the sea. He had taken hold of the rope and was using it to drag the trunk away when he is interrupted by the other slave, Trachalio, who also grabs the rope, thereby asserting a counter-claim to the trunk and its contents.

Gripus is the slave of Daemones, an impecunious Athenian exile who, together with his wife, migrated to this spot after their daughter, Palaestra, was kidnapped. The young woman is later sold to a pimp, Labrax, who takes her, without her father's knowledge, to Cyrene. There Trachalio's master, Plesidippus, himself an Athenian, falls passionately in love with Palaestra. He contracts with Labrax for her sale, making what is in effect a down payment. Labrax instead attempts to flee with Palaestra to Sicily in order to sell her a second time and at a higher price. He is stopped when his ship is wrecked by a storm off the coast of Cyrene near the place where Daemones resides. Labrax, along with Palaestra and her friend and fellow-slave Ampelisca, survives this catastrophe, though at the cost of separation from the trunk that contains his belongings, including the bulk of his wealth, consisting of a hoard of gold and silver. The trunk also holds a small box with items that belonged to Palaestra before her abduction, two of which are pieces of jewellery identifying Daemones and his wife as her parents. This is the trunk around which the dispute between Gripus and Trachalio revolves. Its recovery is indispensable for Palaestra to establish her rightful identity and status.

Modern scholars have for some time recognized that the debate between Gripus and Trachalio is strongly coloured by legal ideas and legal language. We find reference to the status of items found in the sea and on the shore as the property of no one, or *res nullius* in the much later attested technical term,[19] whose ownership can for that reason be acquired by private individuals through seizure. Seizure (*occupatio*) is perhaps the oldest manner of acquiring ownership of property under Roman law, and was all but certainly recognized as such a means by this time.[20] There is also what appears to be a mention of *conserere manu(m)*, an element in the contemporary legal procedure known as *legis actio sacramento*, meaning a ritual that was employed in the initial phase of a civil trial, *in iure*, that is, before the Praetor, in which the litigants contested the ownership of an item through making physical contact with it.[21] This shows incidentally how a fisherman or anyone else legally entitled to the ownership of fish would be able to pursue their rights at law.

What Gripus asserts is that no one but himself has any claim at law over the fish he catches. With far less legal justification he analogizes to those fish the trunk he has recovered from the sea. Most importantly, there appears to be at least a sideways glance at the *res communes omnium*. Here is the passage that directly concerns us:[22]

> TR: non ferat si dominus ueniat? GR: dominus huic, ne frustra sis,
> nisi ego nemo natust, hunc qui cepi in uenatu meo.
>
> TR: itane uero? GR: ecquem esse dices in mari piscem meum?
> quos quom capio, siquidem cepi, mei sunt; habeo pro meis,
> nec manu asseruntur neque illinc partem quisquam postulat.
> in foro palam omnis uendo pro meis uenalibus.
> mare quidem commune certo est omnibus. TR: assentio.
>
> TR: Wouldn't the owner take (the trunk) if he showed up? GR: Its owner, don't kid yourself, has never been born, unless it's me, since I seized hold of it in my hunt.
>
> TR: Is that so? GR: Is there any fish in the sea that you will concede belongs to me?
> When I catch them, since I've caught them, they are mine. I keep hold of them as my property.
> They are neither formally claimed by another at law nor does anyone make a legal request for a part of them.
> In the main square I sell them all as my merchandise.
> The sea is certainly common to all, that's for sure. TR: Agreed.
>
> <div align="right">Plautus <i>Rudens</i> 969-75</div>

The same juxtaposition asserts itself as with the fragment of Phoenicides: the sea is common but its fish belong exclusively to those who catch them or who buy from fishermen.[23] Gripus simply assumes that fish are the property of no one, ownership of which can be acquired by seizure,[24] and, crucially, that the sea is common to all. The link between the two assumptions might not seem inevitable, in the sense that in classical law it is the effective seizure of a wild animal not in the control of another, rather than the venue, that counts, so that such seizure can occur even on private property, whether it is accomplished by the landowner himself or a third party.[25] So the clear reference to a Roman legal institution for acquiring ownership over wild animals, including fish, would not at first glance seem to guarantee by itself the status of the first point as law.[26] Worth conceding is that the successful recovery of a number of aspects of Roman law from the text of the play does not prove anything about the principle under discussion.[27]

A complication immediately ensues. Trachalio agrees with Gripus, but it turns out that he appears to have a somewhat different conception of what 'common to all' means:

> TR: qui minus hunc communem quaeso mi esse oportet uidulum?
> in mari inuentust communi.
>
> How, please, should this trunk not be 'common' with me?
> It was found in the 'common' sea.
>
> Plautus *Rudens* 976–7

Trachalio asserts a right to a half-share of the trunk, as emerges over the course of his debate with Gripus.[28] The latter responds forcefully that such a rule would bankrupt all fishermen. Trachalio clarifies that his view of 'common' implying shared property applies not to fish but specifically to the trunk. Because Gripus found this in the common sea, it belongs to both of them.[29] At first glance, this argument for sharing such property appears to carry some weight, and it is worth observing that the notion of sharing, meaning to split an asset in half, forms an important aspect of the solution discovered by Daemones in the end that allows for the manumission of Gripus and Ampelisca in the context of a settlement with Labrax.[30] Caution is enjoined however in that Plautus is almost certainly satirizing the claim in this context.[31] The satire would have operated not just on a verbal but also on a visual level through the on-stage manipulation of key objects. These include not just the trunk but the fishing net that encloses it and the famous rope that Gripus uses to drag it from the sea, just like a catch of fish.[32] The scene suggests that the two are somehow both the same and not the same, in a manner that communicates the absurdity of the first assumption.

In a similar way, Gripus' assertion that the sea is common to all is made to look ridiculous as a justification for his retaining the trunk.[33] Both he and

Trachalio talk nonsense about the trunk, but are Solons on the subject of fish. As spokesmen for grand notions concerning the fundamentals of the law of property, neither of these two antagonists can inspire unqualified confidence. Although the complication in their debate discussed here is clearly comic in nature, it is not without some serious implications.[34]

The outcome of this wrangling is, to be sure, that a different logic operates for fish and trunks in the sea. In fact, the absurdity of the assertions advanced concerning the latter do not conflict with, but seem to sustain and be sustained by the assumptions which spectators are expected to share about the former.[35] That much is not open to debate, it seems. Once again, we find the status of fish in the sea confirmed as an item of property belonging to no one, what our legal sources later call a *res nullius*, but capable of being acquired by anyone through seizure (*occupatio*). As in Athens, fishermen, as owners of their catch, are fully entitled to dispose of their property in the marketplace. There is no need to choose between Plautus as a source for Attic or Roman law in this instance; he testifies to both.[36] His conception of the status of the sea itself under the rules of the law of property remains a bit more ambiguous. It is common to all, but some uncertainty attends the exact meaning of this attribute, at least for the Romans.

To be crystal clear, the point of contention between Gripus and Trachalio, a vital issue in the economy of the play, is not over the status of fish, but whether the trunk found in the sea counts as one.[37] Daemones as arbitrator decides the case against the claim of the fisherman.[38] This verdict is shown to be just, especially insofar as in effect he rules, as the master of Gripus, whose property would automatically accrue to himself, against his own interest.[39]

Worth observing is that the outcome is consistent with the juristic rule, attested much later, that property retrieved from the sea does not belong to the person who recovers it until the owner considers it abandoned.[40] Classical jurists allow the finders of chattels washed up on the shore with no identifiable owner to obtain their immediate ownership under 'natural law', even where this property was of great value, as with gems and other precious stones.[41] Obviously, if these items were recovered in a container whose ownership could be traced, the outcome would be a different one. The upshot is that neither Trachalio nor Gripus are entitled to a share of the trunk, as are not, of course, their respective masters. While the decision vindicates the principle that the sea is common to all, it implicitly subjects its interpretation to the authority of the courts, which will adjudicate any disputes over its precise meaning.[42] This is the legal position, at least as Plautus presents it. But is this more than a simulacrum of law, a Roman fantasy of the *ius ciuile* that supposedly held in Cyrene?

Two matters must give us pause. One is that the *Rudens* represents on a plausible interpretation *the* Plautine play about law and justice.[43] Here law serves not merely as the set-up for a joke, material for parody, or a plot device, though it without doubt fulfils all of those functions, but stands at the centre of the play. Its crucial role weighs against viewing the premise of a key legal argument as itself somehow constituting something extra-legal beyond the compass of the work. Second, the objection raised above about the unimportance of the venue for the operation of the civil mode of acquisition known as *occupatio* may not be thought to hold in the case of fish. Simply put, unlike an ostrich or a bear, which can be seized on public or private property, they apparently, to judge from the *Rudens*, can be acquired in their wild state only in the sea. Should this not matter in our reconstruction of the law?

In fact, refutation of this second point helps underscore the validity of the first. In classical law, the venue of the capture of fish, apart from one immaterial exception, did not matter for the acquisition of original ownership by seizure, *occupatio*.[44] Whether fish were caught in the sea or in a privately owned lake or pond, they accrued to the fisherman, even though the owner in the latter pair of scenarios might forbid entry to his property.[45] It is the same rule, as postulated above, that holds for other wild animals. Was it contemporary to Plautus? If we refuse to regard this rule as dating back to the playwright's day, then it seems we must accept the special status of the sea as a legally defined one: common to all, as the only legitimate source of fish in the wild. But if, as arguably more likely, the rule was contemporary to the author, that same legal status would appear all the more guaranteed, precisely by the contrast, namely, the fact that some smaller bodies of water could be privately owned. Fishing therein might be legally proscribed by the owner, but violators could still acquire ownership to fish they caught in his lake, pond, lagoon, or river. The point holds *a fortiori* for the sea, which could not be privately owned. The link between acquisition of original ownership of fish in the sea and the status of the latter as common to all seems firmer than ever as a matter of law.[46]

If the sea is indeed common to all, what of the shore? David Konstan argues that '[t]he shore is the boundary between two domains',[47] meaning the sea, where items are common to all, and the land, where laws protect private property. But this is far from clearly the case, especially if we fully credit the fact that the venue where Trachalio stakes his claim to the trunk is precisely the shore, upon which the same norms would seem to operate as for the sea itself.[48] Though he (eventually) argues that the trunk is not an ownerless item of property, like a fish in the sea, the setting gives him an opening to assert his claim to a share, just as by grabbing the famous rope he threatens to compromise the control exercised by Gripus over his prey, and so the very legal foundation of his *occupatio*, or seizure, of this object.[49]

The assertion of ownership through the placing of the characters' hands on trunk or rope in performance adds another dimension of 'reality' to this legal act, which secures the acquisition of ownership.[50] Plautus also sets up a neat parallel between action in court, meaning the formal assertion of ownership, and action on stage. This brings out law's performative element, suggesting how law may resemble theatre as much as theatre may resemble law.

Scholars have long discussed the problem of whether the content, and specifically the legal content, of Roman comedies is in fact Roman or reflects the substance of the Attic models that lie behind these plays. There is no magic formula to help us decide and the question must be evaluated on a case-by-case basis, meaning not just between plays, but within them.[51] Even so, we can expect no guarantee that scrutiny of the evidence will yield a neat division of rules into Attic and Roman law, or even that a more complex classification will do the trick.[52] It is perhaps more useful in many instances to examine what Plautus does with the law than to attempt to trace the origins of the rules he postulates.

The results are almost bound to be complicated, and not just for law. Plautus' use of legal material, typically pragmatic, flexible, and instrumental, makes it tempting to view law in his work as something ontologically distinct from 'actual' law; insofar as it is distorted for dramatic effect, 'his' law, understood in terms of the material he represents as such, seems to comprise something apart, a 'law of literature', or perhaps a 'law of comedy'.[53] We have seen enough so far however in order to recognize that this conclusion is hardly inevitable, either for his own plays or for those of his Athenian precursors. The challenge remains, and not just for legal historians, to identify that Plautine content which is genuine Roman law when contemporary legal sources are lacking for confrontation, let alone corroboration.

As suggested above, the principle that the sea is common to all is a part of a cultural patrimony shared by Greeks and Romans. For the Athenians it also appears to have constituted a point of law, a conclusion that our play itself supports. This does not inevitably mean of course that the Romans recognize the concept as a legal one. Instead for them the assertion might be understood to rely not on law but on general considerations of equity and an ideal of justice that looks past their system of legal rules. What this would mean is that, although we are close to law in this matter, we find ourselves not in its shadow but beyond it.

Presented by Plautus as values that are universal in nature, natural in origin, and shared among all humans, law and justice are themselves *res communes omnium* of a sort. Their status as such is linked to that of the sea and shore as things common to all. Do these reflections help establish that the play also communicates an anticipation of the juristic conception behind this category?

One scholar who has expressed scepticism over drawing such a conclusion is Martin Schermaier, who, while tracing the idea back to Greek, especially Stoic, philosophy, argues that it remains for a long time a vague and undefined notion, a condition that persists, in his view, even after its entry into Roman law.[54] Schermaier levels a trenchant point of criticism:[55]

> Legal concepts must be clearly defined, must be 'sharp', otherwise it is difficult to use them as arguments, but the topos 'there are things belonging to all' is not sharp at all. First of all: who are these 'all': the Romans, all mankind or all living creatures? Secondly: what is the genetivus possessivus *(omnium)* supposed to imply – ownership in the technical legal sense or rather a common right to simply use things for all who want to use them and are in the position to do so? Both questions could be answered quite differently, and even the Roman law itself does not seem to have given consistent answers to these questions.

One might respond that Schermaier's general argument for distinguishing law from non-law depends on an idealized conception of the former, which is not always so clearly-defined or 'sharp'. Experts disagree, change occurs over time, and some rules can seem downright counter-intuitive.

In fact, the exceptions to these postulated criteria are so numerous as to threaten their foundation. Justinian's *Digest* abounds in inconcinnities of the first two types, meaning both juristic disagreement and change over time, despite the charge he gave his compilers to weed them out. The third kind is perhaps even more interesting. For example, a legal rule may seem clear enough, while both its application and the rationale behind this remain hotly contested.[56] The post-Roman history of the category of the *res communes omnium* witnessed a robust and long-running debate among legal experts, centring not least on the key question of the precise relationship between the concepts of 'public' and 'common' in the law of property.[57]

The point is not just that a great deal of what one can reasonably consider to be 'law' is contested, ambiguous, or uncertain. Another possible objection is that Schermaier's conception of law subscribes to what is perhaps an overly strict model of formal realizability. This approach to legal rules, tracing back to Rudolf von Jehring,[58] contrasts with another, that of the standard, which refers directly to one of the 'substantive objectives of the legal order'.[59] The standard was of course perfectly familiar to the Roman jurists, in whose works examples abound, such as *bona fides* and *culpa*.

Rather than becoming embroiled, however, in a discussion of whether Plautus means to suggest law as rule or law as standard, I think it preferable to recognize that, despite these objections, Schermaier's position retains considerable force. One important reason for respecting the strength of his view is that we possess no contemporary evidence for a remedy by means of which a Roman could assert the kind of 'right' adumbrated by Plautus.[60] Another is that, even in a play dedicated to exploring the themes of law and justice, we cannot assume an interest on the playwright's part in presenting the substance of the former.[61]

There is thus potentially more to be gained from attempting an examination of the question through rigorous application precisely of the criteria of sharpness and clarity Schermaier sets forth than by trying to work around these. It is fair to say that, first, the answers to his queries the *Rope* offers are far from pellucid, and, second, this is arguably so by design. The challenge goes to the heart of the project of trying to extract Roman law from Latin literature.

The setting of the play is ostensibly a 'not-Rome', or rather some Hellenized Neverland populated by 'Greeks', and yet shot through with a remarkable number of Roman motifs. In other words, it is a world portrayed by the playwright in a manner consistent with the demands and expectations of the genre known as the *fabula palliata*, 'Roman comedy in Greek dress'.[62] But in the *Rudens* the point of dislocation is pursued more aggressively than is usually the case, as we find ourselves transported to a wilderness situated on the margins – at best – of the Greek world.[63]

Something close to a state of nature prevails here, which is far removed from the typical *polis*, i.e., city-state, or any identifiable political community, and its norms.[64] This sets the stage for the articulation of a universalizing message that at first glance appears at odds with the possibility of offering any concrete answers to Schermaier's two questions.[65] All the same, the unusual setting in which the action plays out offers a clue for the resolution of the mystery of the status of the sea as 'common to all'. We may begin by offering a tentative response to his first interrogative. The 'all' to whom the sea pertains cannot be regarded in this context as Roman citizens, and there is no sign that they are imagined as embracing all living creatures,[66] leaving the human race as the logical alternative.[67]

Important recent research on the relationship of the playwright to his audience suggests that this 'universalizing' message did in fact resonate at all social levels in the capital, at minimum, among citizens and non-citizens alike. First, those who attended public performances of Roman comedies were in fact broadly diverse in terms of their backgrounds.[68] Plautus however succeeds in addressing these very disparate individuals as a unity, even as he tailors various comic elements in his plays to suit their diverse sensibilities.[69] His true talent perhaps lies in his ability to craft a message that different members of the audience heard in different ways.[70] For example, the phrase 'the sea is common to all' might strike some as a high-sounding statement of moral principle, while others felt they were being offered a business opportunity. This is important, because it suggests how this slogan functioned as a widely and firmly held social norm at this point in time, and later.[71]

In the *Rudens*, only the sea is described as 'common to all'. Not even the shore is clearly identified in this way, even if its status as such seems taken for granted. The result is that we lack even the semblance of a classification.[72] Another impediment is that the play offers no contrasting categories to help define *res communes* by opposition. Instead, the somewhat amorphous notion of the sea is set against the equally vaguely defined one of the land. Given the setting, we might expect to see Plautus invoke 'natural law' as a justification for the status of the sea, but here too we are disappointed, at least in terms of receiving any direct, literal information on this score. Yet the strikingly unusual setting remains crucial, especially as a backdrop against which the words and actions of the god Arcturus, that avatar of justice, are placed.[73]

At minimum we are left with one legal rule that justifies the acquisition of ownership by a fisherman of his catch through seizure, a rule that is recognized, moreover, in both Attic and Roman law. This principle is grounded in yet another that holds that the sea is common to all, meaning that it is notionally open to anyone to obtain ownership of fish in this venue. This norm too was apparently the law in Athens, to judge from the evidence examined above. Here we have a tentative answer to the second question posed above: the rule protects a right of access, or use, not of ownership, to the sea itself.[74] But at Rome, in the time of Plautus, did this principle count as something more than a widely, perhaps universally held, social norm?

Worth emphasizing is that the notion of the sea common to all forms part of a chain of assumptions about law shared by the characters in the play. It is firmly and unambiguously presented to the public precisely as law, indissolubly linked to the regime of the acquisition of original ownership of wild animals through seizure. As with the fragment of Phoenicides, it seems unlikely that only one of these two principles had legal force.[75]

Partly through this linkage, the norm is embedded in the deep structure of the work, written, as noted, to be performed before a broad and sizeable slice of the capital's population. The play offers solid evidence that the fundamental cultural and ethical matrix productive, eventually, of explicit recognition of this fact in the legal sources, was in place long before we can be certain that the juristic engagement with 'things common to all' made its mark in this regard.

It is easier, after all, to accept the status of this norm as law exactly as articulated by the playwright than to reject this, insisting instead that both in terms of ownership and access/use the sea was in some way 'closed'. That would suggest a situation of significantly greater normative ambiguity than Plautus' audience seems likely to have accepted. This result also emerges as all but certainly less 'rule-ish' under Martin Schermaier's severe criteria than the alternative.

Yet, for the reasons explored above, we cannot simply regard as Roman all of the 'law' presented in their theatre.[76] To be blunt, the spectators congregated there for the purpose of a public festival, not a legislative assembly.[77] Moreover, even if we accept that the idea of 'the sea is common to all' in the *Rudens* offers a true statement of the law, it must be conceded to be in an important respect incomplete. Plautus does not, and perhaps cannot, account for a possible role played in this connection by the state. More specifically, how does the designation of 'common' for the sea intersect with its potential identification as 'public'? In other words, can we reconcile the principle adumbrated by Plautus with the recognition of the sea at law as a *res publica*, whenever this happened? Regrettably, this important aspect must be left for consideration at a future date.

In sum, we are left with a statement, the sea is common to all, that is consistent with what we know of later Roman law, and that possibly, or even likely, represents a legal rule of theirs at the time of writing, even as certainty eludes us. Further investigation may move the question further in that direction, albeit with no guarantee of achieving complete assurance. At the fraught intersection of Roman law and Latin literature, one often finds qualified conjecture reigning over absolute conviction.[78]

Notes

1   Another acceptable translation is 'things belonging to all'. Neither rendering by itself resolves the question of whether ownership or a right of access/use is in play, a matter taken up in the discussion that follows.

2 On the ascription of the category to the late classical period of Roman law, see the discussion in Dursi (2017) 5–16; Frier (2019) 643; Ruhl and McGinn (2020) 166–7.
3 Pomp.-Ulp. (57 *ad edictum*) D. 47.10.13.7.
4 Marcian (3 *inst.*) D. 1.8.2.1. This version of the category exercised a great influence on Justinian (*Inst.* 2.1.1) and through him later legal history.
5 Soph. fr. 612 Nauck = *TrGF* 4.673. Virtually nothing is known about the content of this play: Wright (2019) 2.127.
6 Plato *Leges* 7.824B-C. Bresson (2016) 181–4 argues that Plato limits access to citizens of a political community and this only in coastal waters, though there is no evidence for either restriction in this text or elsewhere, limitations that are more consistent with modern theory than ancient practice. In fact, a passage that immediately precedes this one explicitly and firmly discourages citizens from pursuing such activities: Plato *Leges* 7.823D-E. Even apart from this consideration, it made little practical sense to bar members of certain resident non-citizen groups, such as slaves and metics. Nor was the prospect of incursions from poachers across the border sufficiently likely to prompt an attempt to exclude them, in my view.
7 Phoenicides fr. 5 K-A: the author parodies a line of Aeschylus.
8 On the procedural protections available to property-owners in classical Athenian law, see Harrison (1998) 1.206–27.
9 The power to dispose of property especially through alienation was for the Athenians a true sign of ownership: Harrison (1998) 1.202.
10 Aristotle *Pol.* 1.3.4 suggests, but does not prove, that recognition of the acquisition of original ownership through hunting and fishing was a widespread rule of law in classical Greece. This uncertainty has led modern scholars to debate whether a part of the passage from the *Rudens* (971–5) discussed below guarantees the existence of the rule at Athens: Harrison (1998) 1.244–5 with n. 1. My argument is that to establish this point one need look no further than this fragment of Phoenicides. The fact that he makes two assumptions in this regard, one stated and one not, offers persuasive evidence in the affirmative. This conclusion only buttresses the claim, advanced by Wolff (1964) 335 n. 5 (and others), that the Plautus passage serves as evidence of Attic law, which in this instance does not exclude the possibility that it reflects Roman law as well: see the discussion below.
11 The *graphē hybreōs*, the suit on aggravated assault, appears to have enjoyed a broad sphere of application, and punished offences even against slaves: see Fisher (1992) esp. 36–85; Phillips (2013) esp. 85–7, 91–101. Acts of piracy likely elicited a more robust, especially extrajudicial, response.
12 See the considerations of Purpura (2004) esp. 172–4.
13 This is fr. 188 K-A = Athenaeus 8.342F; see Lytle (2016) 108.
14 See Andocides 3.19 (likely early in 391); Aeschines 2.71 (343). Unlike the assertions made by Phoenicides, these declarations are vague and difficult to relate to a clear

legal rule, instead representing what are better characterized as political, military and/or ideological claims. While such concerns expressed over freedom of navigation and trade on the 'common sea' might appear to echo modern usage regarding the 'High Seas', it is worth emphasizing that the ancients did not share our (legal) conception of territorial waters: Lytle (2016) 109–10; Arcaria (2017) 642. What might appear to be an exception to this principle, a term of the agreement framed by the belligerents during the Peloponnesian War regarding the armistice of 423, does no more than regulate the use by Sparta and its allies of certain vessels in waters along their coasts: Thuc. 4.118.5.

15 Frier (2019) 643–4 argues that the principle is not, in any legally significant sense, Stoic, insofar as members of this philosophical school were decided advocates of 'private property and appropriation' (644 n. 16).

16 Marx (1959) [1928] 274 identifies this model as the *Epitropē* (*Arbitration*) but the matter remains uncertain.

17 Dursi (2017) 141–6, who tentatively raises the possibility that Plautus articulates the common status of the sea as a legal rule, so anticipating the juristic category of the *res communes omnium* (he does not consider whether the norm represents Athenian law). See also Charbonnel (1995) 315–16, 321–2; Ducos (2011) 163–4; Lambrini (2019) [2016] 10; Arcaria (2017) 648–9, 655–6; Frier (2019) 643.

18 An uncertain reference to the *lex Laetoria* does not help narrow the range, unfortunately: Plautus *Rudens* 1380–2.

19 See Gaius 2.9, 11; Gaius (2 *inst.*) D. 1.8.1 pr.; *Inst.* 2.1.12.

20 Gaius clearly implies the antiquity of the rule: Gaius (2 *rerum cott. sive aur.*) D. 41.1.1 (the jurist uses the same verb as does Gripus to describe the action of acquiring: *capere*). See Kaser (1971) 1.138.

21 See Santoro (2009) [1971] 152–8.

22 I follow the text here and below almost without exception as in De Melo (2012) 504.

23 On the contrast in Plautus, see Henderson (2009) 105.

24 See, for example, Gaius (2 *rerum cottid. sive aur.*) D. 41.1.1, 3, 5 pr.–2, and above.

25 Gaius (2 *rerum cottid. sive aur.*) D. 41.1.3.1, 5.3.

26 For a different view, see Charbonnel (1995) 315–16, 321–2; Ducos (2011) 163–4; Dursi (2017) 141–6, and below.

27 For discussion of such legal details, see Charbonnel (1995) 311–15, 319; Ducos (2011) 160, 163–4; Pellecchi (2013) 110, 133, 134, 135 n. 97, 137, 144, 153, 155; Pennitz (2013), and the discussion below.

28 Plautus *Rudens* 958–60, 1011, 1017–18.

29 Charbonnel (1995) 319 n. 93; Ducos (2011) 164.

30 Plautus *Rudens* 1405–10.

31 See Pellecchi (2013) 131, 134, 136, 141 n. 110, 146, 152 (on Trachalio's dubious character, see also 140, 144 n. 118).

32 See the observations of Calabretta (2015) 82.
33 Charbonnel (1995) 317; Pellecchi (2013) 131.
34 Legal satire is not inevitably a victimless exercise, as the tale of the Canadian 'pony-bird' suggests: https://law.stackexchange.com/questions/4116/r-v-ojibway-impact-of-the-pony-bird-on-case-law. I thank Bruce Frier for this reference.
35 The analogy that links trunk with fish is itself a parody of legal reasoning: Pellecchi (2013) 134.
36 The fact that it is more obviously a Roman legal rule does not automatically exclude the possibility that it can be a Greek one as well, despite the hesitations of Kränzlein (1963) 72, who comes around in the end however to acknowledging the strong probability that it is both. Kränzlein does not mention the key fragment of Phoenicides discussed above.
37 Konstan (1983) 74–5.
38 As the scene shifts from a dispute limited to the two slaves to an arbitration where they argue before Daemones, Trachalio turns his focus to the status of the box containing Palaestra's recognition tokens, while conceding ownership of the trunk to Labrax: Plautus *Rudens* 1065–6, 1077–9.
39 Konstan (1983) 82–3 argues that Labrax, despite the dubious nature of his claim, must lose title to Palaestra, meaning in a lawful and equitable manner, so that she can be restored to her rightful status (see also 84, 86 for discussion of the play's presentation of the morality of property ownership). Trachalio, like Gripus, is no paragon of virtue: see above in the notes.
40 Iav. (11 *ex Cassio*) D. 41.1.58; cf. Iav. (7 *ex Cassio*) D. 41.2.21.1-2; Sab.-Cassius-Celsus-Ulp. (41 *ad Sabinum*) D. 47.2.43.5–11. There is disagreement among scholars over whether Gripus actually invokes this argument, i.e., that the prior owner had abandoned the trunk. See the discussion in Charbonnel (1995) 313–15 and Pellecchi (2013) 134 n. 94.
41 Florent. (6 *inst.*) D. 1.8.3; Nerva *filius*-Paul. (54 *ad edictum*) D. 41.2.1.1, with Dursi (2017) 62–3.
42 On the role of the courts in 'Cyrene', see Pellecchi (2013) 117, 138, 152; Pennitz (2013). There are in fact three representations of judicial procedures in *Rudens*, not counting, of course, the pre-trial altercation of Gripus and Trachalio described above. The first, an arbitration before Daemones, concludes by establishing the freeborn status of Palaestra (1045–183). The second is an actual trial, held offstage, before a panel of *recuperatores*, in which Plesidippus formally and conclusively secures the denial of Labrax's claim to Palaestra (1281–3). The third is another arbitration conducted by Daemones, where he resolves a dispute between Labrax and Gripus over the trunk by recognizing the pimp's claim in principle while securing from him funds to underwrite the manumissions of Gripus and Ampelisca

(1357–423). The playwright's interest in presenting so many indications of judicial activity may in part be intended as an ironic comment on the suspension of public business during the festival when the play was originally presented to the public: below.

43 Pellecchi (2013) 104, 125, 150–3, 157–62; Pennitz (2013) 583.
44 One might conclude that a similar point held for birds, meaning that it was not necessary to seize them in the air. For a different view, see Arcaria (2017) 644.
45 Paul. (54 *ad edictum*) D. 41.2.3.14 (evidently quoting Nerva *filius*), makes an exception for fish kept in (artificial) fishponds (*piscinae*), which are also privately owned. On the implications of forbidding entry, which created liability for the trespasser under the delict of affront (*iniuria*), see Pomp.-Ulp. (57 *ad edictum*) D. 47.10.13.7, with Ofil.-Paul. (4 *ad edictum*) D. 47.10.23; see also Gaius (2 *rerum cottid. sive aur.*) D. 41.1.3.1, 5.3.
46 It is not impossible that, long before it crystallizes in our extant legal sources, a jurist transformed the idea of the sea common to all into law: see Scherillo (1945) 72.
47 Konstan (1983) 77; see also the essay by Dugan in this volume.
48 That the sea and shore enjoyed the same status at law, certainly in the earliest period, is the majority opinion among legal scholars: see Gutierrez-Masson (1993) 300. Some caution is required in that the jurists did not arrive at a definition of the landward boundary of the shore until Aquilius Gallus limited it to the highest water mark in the mid-first century BCE: see Cic. *Topica* 32, with Dursi (2017) 37–40. This would seem to suggest a certain lack of interest in the shore on the part of legal experts prior to this point in time.
49 It was not necessary for a fisherman to acquire, by *occupatio*, ownership of fish through beaching them, since securing fish in a boat, for example, would have sufficed. So also Melville, *Moby-Dick* ch. 89 ('Fast-Fish and Loose-Fish'), despite Konstan (1983) 77–80.
50 For on-stage physical interaction with both trunk and rope, see Calabretta (2015) 174–6, 179–80.
51 The scholarship published in the field of Roman law, as well as in those of ancient history and Latin literature, on the question of the cultural identity of legal detail in Plautus is well-nigh endless. See the recent discussions in Gaertner (2014); Bartholomä (2019). Of particular interest is Labruna (1995) [1968], who, after a critical survey of previous approaches, concludes that the playwright, motivated by dramatic considerations, meaning his sense of what worked before an audience, offers a jumble of culturally diverse influences difficult for the modern reader to disentangle. On the importance of examining each passage on its own terms, without preconceptions as to the source(s) of its legal content, see Paoli (1962) 68.
52 A well-known example is the three-fold division of the legal material by Paoli (1962) 46 into elements that are Athenian, those that are Roman, and those that he

describes as 'Romanized Athenian' (*attici romanizzati*). Paoli was reacting to trends in the scholarship that viewed Plautus as a mine exclusively for either Attic or Roman legal material. Cf. Ortu (2017) 165, who identifies the Plautine articulation of the principle that 'the sea is common to all' as an example of Paoli's third category of 'Romanized Athenian' law.

53 See the reflections of Lotito (1996) 187, 201, 206–8; cf. the Intoduction to this volume. On the sometimes porous, at other times impermeable, borders between the two distinct fields of law and literature, see Dolin (2007) especially 8–9.

54 We depend mostly on Roman sources, chiefly Cicero and Seneca, for our knowledge of Stoic doctrine in this area: see Schermaier (2009) esp. 38–42 (he mentions the evidence of the *Rudens* at 41 n. 126). The idea of the *res communes omnium* cannot have been Stoic in origin: above. For a more nuanced view, see Schermaier (2012) 781.

55 Schermaier (2009) 21.

56 There are a number of instances one might cite, such as the rule from Roman property law excluding the identification of a slave-woman's offspring as a fruit, whose precise rationale both ancient jurists and modern scholars have debated at length: see the recent contribution by Di Nisio (2017), with abundant discussion of both traditions.

57 See the discussion in Fiorentini (2003) 1–58; Ruhl and McGinn (2020) 145–62.

58 von Jehring (1852) 1.42–7.

59 See the well-known discussion by Kennedy (1976) esp. 1687–8 (quotation on 1688). A further objection might be that formal legal rules do not exist in a pure state: see the considerations of Fish (1991).

60 The most likely, if not the only possible, candidate is a suit on the delict of affront (*iniuria*). Scholars disagree on some key aspects of its early development: see, for example, Hagemann (1998) 49–61; Milazzo (2011). Though evidence is lacking, it seems possible that as early as Plautus' day the Praetor might grant this remedy in case of interference with one's use of a public facility such as a bath or a theatre, conducting business, or just sitting and talking, as we know held much later thanks to the jurist Ulpian: Pomp.-Ulp. (57 *ad edictum*) D. 47.10.13.7 (an important proviso is that any remedy for obstruction of access would not be dependent on assertions of either public or common ownership). An equally plausible source of social friction that might have prompted such action is denial of access to the sea, albeit this very passage can be read to suggest that this occurred only with the Antonine jurist Pomponius. An interdict, even one protecting publicly-leased fishing rights, also mentioned by Ulpian, is a more remote possibility at this early date. Lack of space forbids adequate discussion of the problem.

61 See the essay by Gaertner in this volume: 'Plautus and Terence rarely position themselves directly with regard to legal norms'. The explanation may lie at least in

part in their acceptance of the traditional Roman position that privileged social and ethical values over law. If so, general customary acceptance of a rule would be preferable in their view to enforcement of a legal norm.

62 See the recent essays by Gruen (2014); Manuwald (2019a).
63 The *Rudens* is the only play in all of New Comedy as it survives whose setting is not urban, with 'Athens' serving as the overwhelming preference: Konstan (1983) 86; Faure-Ribreau (2009) esp. 19–22; Dumont (2010) 9–10.
64 See Dumont (2010) 12, who argues that the setting of the sea, and its connection with the sky, lends the play 'une dimension cosmique et une couleur tragique'.
65 On the universalizing morality of the *Rudens*, see Konstan (1983) 86–7, 93–5; Dumont (2010) 13–14.
66 In a subsequent discussion Schermaier (2012) 781 offers for the classical juristic concept of *res communes omnium* an interpretation that allows for the inclusion of all living creatures in this category of 'all', citing as an authority Behrends (2004) [1992]. Most modern scholars writing on the *res communes omnium* reject this idea: see, for example, Lambrini (2019) [2016] 1, 4, 7–8; Arcaria (2017) 639; Casola (2017) 5, and next note.
67 From a Roman legal perspective there are in fact only two alternatives, realistically speaking. Their law was in ideological terms markedly anthropocentric, leaving little space for the recognition of the interests of living creatures who were not humans: see Corbino (2019) 26.
68 Marshall (2006) 75–6; Manuwald (2019a) 28. For a different view, holding that the audience was more elite and highly educated than most scholars suppose, see Fontaine (2010) esp. 149–200.
69 Marshall (2006) 77–8: '[h]eterogeneous appreciation characterizes the audience's engagement and arises directly from its diversity' (on 79 the author is careful to note that the spectators did not comprise a cross-section of the population); Dressler (2016) 49; Manuwald (2019a) 28.
70 One does not have to accept that these plays were created exclusively or even primarily by and for slaves and/or other members of the lower orders of Roman society in order to recognize that a great deal of the content had appeal for them: see the recent investigation by Richlin (2017). On their interest to women, see especially Peppe (2002).
71 See the observations of Cangelosi (2014) 64.
72 In other words, Plautus does not, strictly speaking, offer an anticipation of the juristic *category* of the *res communes omnium*. For a different view, see Dursi (2017) 146.
73 On the role of Arcturus, see Lotito (1996) 192–3; Pellecchi (2013) 154–5; Gruen (2014) 606.
74 This is the interpretation Schermaier himself later gives for the classical juristic concept of *res communes omnium*, an attribute that he appears to extend back in

time to Plautus: Schermaier (2012) 781. Plautus' use of the dative, *omnibus*, in his formulation *mare quidem commune certo est omnibus* supports, if it does not prove, this conclusion. At any rate, it is important not to elide the dative into the genitive (*omnium*), as some scholars appear to do. There is disagreement over whether the legal regime in the classical period comprises ownership and/or use: besides Schermaier, see recently Lambrini (2019) [2016] 1, 4, 7–8; Arcaria (2017) 641; Dursi (2017) 11–12, 17–19, 71, 139; Casola (2017) 5; Corbino (2019); Frier (2019) 646. To underscore: my concern in this paper is with Plautus.

75 Those wrongfully denied access to fish in the sea could in classical law launch a suit under the delict of affront (*iniuria*): Pomp.-Ulp. (57 *ad edictum*) D. 47.10.13.7. It is possible that this was also available in Plautus' day: see above in the notes. As at Athens, acts of piracy presumably provoked a more robust, especially extrajudicial, response. The same might very well hold in more banal cases where a thwarted fisherman appealed to a public official to exercise *coercitio*, but we lack evidence.

76 No more can we merely assume that what Plautus reliably presents as Roman law is their classical law, as the discussion above repeatedly emphasizes.

77 I refer of course to the original presentation of the plays to the public: Manuwald (2019a) 28. The suspension of not only legislative, but judicial activity during the festival is worth stressing, since Plautus and other comic playwrights may exploit the public's awareness of this in, for example, their many direct and indirect presentations of trials. Cicero, in his famous riff on this subject in the *Caeliana*, certainly does so, and to great effect, but perhaps in a manner suggesting that he is an even greater student of the genre than some have supposed: see Leigh (2004a) especially 325 for comic evidence for the suspension of public business. On Cicero's use of Roman comedy in his oratory, see now the survey in Hanses (2020), esp. 123–200.

78 My thanks to Bruce Frier and Ioannis Ziogas for their valuable suggestions.

10

Intellectual 'Property': Ownership, Possession and Judgment among Civic *Artes*

John Oksanish

According to Cicero's dialogue *De oratore*, in 91 BCE a handful of elite statesmen met in the garden of the orator L. Licinius Crassus to discuss the status and role of oratory and orators in the maintenance of the republic.[1] Although the discussion can hardly have occurred as Cicero imagines it,[2] the dialogue conveys much about Cicero's philosophy of political oratory, central to which is the notion that the ideal orator-statesman will wield authoritative influence in virtually all areas of public life. Though such claims were hardly unprecedented, the discourse around them had long been characterized by controversy. Most famously, Plato's Socrates in *Gorgias* had dismantled similar claims made on behalf of rhetoric on grounds that the latter had no business meddling in the subject matter of other disciplines: if political virtue and ethical reliability were found only in disciplines grounded in a delimited sphere of teachable knowledge (*technai*; L. *artes*), then rhetoric – a mere 'knack and habitude' (ἐμπειρία καὶ τριβή) – was effectively barred from political involvement.[3]

In *De oratore* Cicero drew on an Isocratean model of *paideia* in an attempt to satisfy these Socratic misgivings about the 'technicity' of oratory (i.e., its status as *techne* or *ars*) by insisting that the ideal orator-statesman be widely educated.[4] Since the 'power of the orator' and the very claim of being able to speak well seem to imply a definite promise to speak distinctively and abundantly about whatever subject is put forward', the ideal orator – though not omniscient – will have gained 'a knowledge of all major subjects and arts', Cic. *De or.* 1.21 *uis oratoris professioque ipsa bene dicendi hoc suscipere ac polliceri uidetur, ut omni de re, quaecumque sit proposita, ornate ab eo copioseque dicatur*; 1.20 *omni laude cumulatus ... orator ... erit omnium rerum magnarum atque artium scientiam consecutus.*

For all its innovation, however, Cicero's prefatory salvo in the battle over oratory's technicity ultimately fails to achieve parity between what the orator learns (i.e., a mere selection of subjects and arts, albeit major ones) and what he is authorized to treat (any subject put forward). Cicero understood this deficiency well, and he therefore allowed the dialogue's interlocutors – particularly Crassus – to argue the point more fully.[6] Even Crassus, however, fails to meet the Socratic criterion that true arts require particular training in a discrete and peculiar subject (medicine, physics, law).[7] From the strict perspective of rational argument, at least, it would seem that neither Cicero nor his mouthpiece Crassus 'solve' the problems associated with the orator's untenable claims to broad influence.

Fortunately for Cicero, protestations voiced in a fourth-century BCE Greek philosophical context do not doom his ambitious Roman project three centuries later. For, as this paper suggests, *De oratore* succeeds in legitimating Cicero's ambitions for his ideal orator by adopting the theoretical and terminological frameworks provided by Roman law. Those frameworks, somewhat ironically, are first introduced in an *objection* to Crassus early in book 1 of the dialogue. Specifically, the great jurist Scaevola accuses Crassus' orator of 'rashly trespassing on 'possessions' belonging to other [disciplines]', thereby invoking the distinctive language of Roman law on property (1.41 *in alienas **possessiones** tam temere inruisses*). In my analysis, the language and indigenous categories of Roman property law offer Crassus (and thus Cicero) a distinctly Roman path by which to authorize the orator's power over all intellectual and political domains without damaging the orator's political or intellectual *bona fides*. In sum, whereas the ideal orator's influence over all 'fields' of knowledge would seem farcical by any philosophical standard, Roman property law will recognize and accept him as a *uir bonus* who is legally 'entititled' to the whole estate of civic knowledge.

If, however, the law provides the means by which to authorize the orator's broad claims in *De oratore*, what remains for those disciplines over which oratory claimed precedence? I address aspects of this question in the second part of this paper, which considers how Cicero's unprecedented approach to the orator's authority may have influenced writers seeking to articulate comparable (and, often, *competing*) claims of universal authority for their own disciplines, such as architecture.[8] For example, Vitruvius in *De architectura* (mid-20s BCE) addresses analogous problems of knowledge and influence in the formation of his ideal *architectus*, and he addresses these problems in the language of law and property, echoing his putative Ciceronian model. For either author, these questions are not just professional but also political. At the core of both texts is a practitioner whom the author deems essential to the *respublica* – whether that *respublica* is managed by consuls and the senate or the *princeps*. Also present is a clear sense that the law, even when used metaphorically, is able and perhaps even necessary to make the arbitrary boundaries of civic and professional authority sensible.[9]

No trespassing

As I have noted, Cicero in the preface to *De oratore* stipulates that the authoritative civic orator, although he is not omniscient, will be adequately educated in 'the great subjects and arts'; this training will allow him to speak with distinction on any topic presented. In the dialogue proper it is Crassus who comes closest to representing this view, claiming early in book 1 that the orator is a witty and omnicompetent speaker in whom resides, inter alia, the very safety of the entire republic. Such a figure is able 'to engage in elegant conversation and show oneself a stranger to no subject', and his 'leadership and wisdom ... provide the chief basis ... for the safety of countless individuals and of the state at large' (1.32 *sermo facetus ac nulla in re rudis*; 1.34 *perfecti oratoris moderatione et sapientia ... et priuatorum plurimorum et uniuersae rei publicae salutem maxime contineri*). Near the conclusion of the dialogue in book 3, Crassus asserts this view more forcefully, closely linking the orator's authority with his broad learning: 'if we are looking for the one thing that surpasses all others, the palm must go to the learned orator', in whom 'all knowledge [sc. of the philosophers, etc.] is present' (3.143 *in oratore perfecto inest illorum* [sc., e.g., *philosophorum*] *omnis scientia*').[10] In Crassus' view, eloquence 'sets a capstone' (*cumulum adferre*) on the arts of other thinkers and specialists.

The first speaker to notice that these grand assertions are undermined by a mismatch between oratorical training and influence is the jurist Q. Mucius Scaevola [Augur]. Scaevola, appropriate to his field, frames his objection in legal terms (1.41–4).[11] To Scaevola Crassus is a thief of (or trespasser on) subjects properly held by philosophers – whose authority to pronounce on general questions Scaevola implicitly endorses – and by experts in other *artes* (maths, music, grammar etc.). Scaevola grants that Crassus *himself* may demonstrate certain 'proprietary qualities' (*propria*) in common with the imaginary ideal *orator*, but he balks at the notion that they are 'shared among all orators'. And so, as if contemplating a legal action, Scaevola enumerates all the fictive plaintiffs wronged by Crassus in a lengthy peroration, a rhetorical tour de force that underscores the gravity of Crassus' error through various modes of rhetorical emphasis (amplificatio, anaphora [*nihil ... nihil ...*], praeteritio, etc.).

Scaevola's assertions of professional legal expertise surely constitute more than a clever nod to the speaker's juridical fame. For, apart from its formal, rhetorical fireworks, Scaevola's peroration also performs several important thematic functions. For example, his defence of philosophers and specialists – on whose turf Crassus has evidently tread – clearly evokes the sorts of philosophical arguments levied against rhetoric's technicity in *Gorgias*.[12] Yet in *De oratore* Cicero (through Scaevola) complements these theoretical concerns for technical integrity by introducing the interests of practicing legal professionals. That is, the jurist Scaevola applies his own, discrete specialist knowledge – that of Roman law – to aid the parties allegedly wronged by Crassus and his ideal, omnicompetent orator.[13] Accordingly, Scaevola's demonstration of his professional expertise introduces a thematic tension between the power of oratory and the power of Roman law, both of which have clear roles to play in the civic sphere. On the one hand, the ideal orator's claims will benefit from, or perhaps even require, the legitimating power of the law (even as Scaevola's legalistic reply relies also on the formal tools of the orator). On the other, the law itself may be insufficiently wide-ranging to suit the many civic needs of the republic.

Property and possession / *proprietas* and *possessio*

Let us now turn to the particular legal procedures that Scaevola invokes, as these are crucial to Cicero's larger efforts to legitimate tendentious claims about the relationship among oratorical training, knowledge and influence. One might expect these fictional invocations of the law to prioritize 'spirit' over 'letter', but insofar as Roman law was broadly speaking 'procedural' (i.e., consisting less in abstract rights than in the provision of legal remedies), attention to such particulars is likely to adumbrate the most salient features of property law in Cicero's Roman imagination. Indeed, although Scaevola initially characterizes Crassus' claim to oratory's wide scope in somewhat general legal terms, viz., as misprising the rights of others (1.41 *quasi tuo iure sumpsisti*, 'you took them as if by your own right'), he soon invokes specific remedies available only in Roman law.

For example, Scaevola notes that, were the speakers not in Crassus' domain, he would have come to the aid of the aggrieved by 'dictating for them the relevant legal formula' (*praeissem*[14]), by which they would either challenge Crassus with an interdict *or* 'summon him from court to engage in a struggle for ownership, because he had encroached so recklessly upon the possessions of others' (*aut interdicto tecum contenderent aut te ex iure manum consertum uocarent, quod in alienas possessiones tam temere inruisses*). The Pythagoreans would 'initiate a legal action' (*agerent . . . tecum lege*), whilst 'the followers of Democritus and the rest of natural philosophers would initiate a *uindicatio* to recover their property' (*Democritii ceterique in iure sua physici uindicarent*); according to Scaevola, Crassus would lose these contests soundly, and would 'not be allowed the standard action at law [known as] *iusto sacramento contendere*' (1.42 *quibuscum tibi iusto sacramento contendere non liceret*).[15] Still others, following Socrates, would prove (*conuincerent*) that Crassus knew nothing about important moral questions, and the 'individual schools would initiate actions of their own' (*singulae familiae litem tibi intenderent*). Among these, the 'Peripatetics would force Crassus to seek from *them* the very things that he claimed to be the supporting embellishments of speaking and [thus also according to Crassus] the orator's exclusive property' (1.43 *Peripatetici autem etiam haec ipsa quae propria oratorum putas esse adiumenta atque ornamenta dicendi a se peti uincerent oportere*.[16])

Roman law was distinctive for its definition of and distinction between claims of ownership/title on the one hand and possession on the other (*proprietas* or *dominium* and *possessio*, respectively); the remedies invoked by Scaevola are meant to protect precisely these rights.[17] In simplest terms, the titular owner of a property held the comprehensive right to its use and disposal (*proprietas*); that right, if violated, was recoverable by *uindicatio*, on which more below. In many cases, the titular owner might also hold physical control of that same property (*possessio*); this too, was a protected category, albeit hierarchically subordinate to *proprietas*. Conversely, in certain forms of property transfer, the owner might yield *possessio* of said property to another while still retaining title.[18] (Perhaps surprisingly, even *de facto* possession of a property taken by a party against the owner's wishes was still legally recognized, at least insofar as it gave the possessor recourse to the relevant possessory interdicts.[19]) In short, both *proprietas* and *possessio* were recoverable by distinctive procedures, and neither presumed nor prohibited the possession of the other, as illustrated by a pithy remark from Ulpian: 'Ownership has nothing in common with possession; hence, a man who institutes a *uindicatio* for land will not be refused the [praetor's] interdict *uti possidetis* ('as you possess'); for he is not deemed to have renounced possession by asserting ownership.'[20]

Having identified Scaevola's appeal to specific rights and remedies, we may wonder what bearing they have on both his argument and that of the dialogue overall. First, it is significant that Scaevola imagines Crassus as having taken possession (at least in the physical, *de facto* sense; 1.41 'because he had encroached so recklessly upon the *possessiones* of others'), and that he further characterizes Crassus as claiming ownership of anything that could be construed as embellishments supporting speaking (*haec ipsa quae propria oratorum putas*).[21] Mere *possessio* placed the holder thereof in a better position to claim title, since, as Capogrosso Colognesi notes, 'disputes over possession were preliminary to the *vindicatio* of ownership [and] their outcome often conditioned future developments'. Without possession, it was often difficult for the dispossessed claimant of title to give strong evidence of his property right.[22]

To be sure, the abstract nature of the 'intellectual' property at issue – i.e., general and specialist knowledge, and the right to treat either – stymies thorough contemplation of the various real-world remedies that might resolve the situation in favour of either party. Not only do the 'fields' in question not exist physically, but they do not really resemble what is meant by 'intellectual property' in the now common sense (e.g., a literary work).[23] Many of the remedies in question required tangible evidence, for instance, and it is hard to know what abstractions could stand in as proxy for them. Further difficulties are presented by the timescale implied by the quarrel (associated with philosophical schools active across many centuries) and the fact that most of the original claimants and their 'schools' were not in Rome. In other words, we are in doubly speculative 'territory'.

At the same time, to suspend disbelief regarding these impracticabilities illuminates the characteristics, boundaries and possibilities of the law's authorizing power in general. For example, the various legal means of transferring of Roman property (in which questions of owership and possession were paramount) typically required that said transfer be made in good faith: thus, certain possessory interdicts offered restitution for property taken 'by force or stealth' (*ui aut clam*).[24] In this context we may consider Crassus' *narratio* in *De oratore* book 1, in which he explains the cultural and chronological priority of the orator over philosophers and legal professionals. Elaborating on the 'archaeology' of Cicero's youthful *De inuentione*,[25] Crassus asserts that no force *other than that of the orator* 'could have gathered the scattered members of the human race into one place, or could have led them away from a savage existence in the wilderness to this truly human, communal way of life, or, once communities had been founded, could have established laws, judicial procedures and legal arrangements' (1.33). The simple but important legal implication of which is that, if the orator was there first, no one who came later could claim authority on a topic unless the orator had willingly 'transferred' that notional property. As we will see, Crassus denies that any such willing transfer ever took place.

Now, as the Mucii Scaevolae had been prominent in law for generations, it is natural that our Scaevola takes special umbrage at any notion that oratory preceded it in any sense (1.39–40).²⁶ Nevertheless, Crassus takes up a variation on this theme when the interlocutors of book 3 finally conclude their debate over oratorical knowledge and influence, where the question of oratorical knowledge is broached via discussion of *ornatus* ('distinction' in speaking).²⁷ According to Crassus, 'distinction' required real knowledge of particular subjects and it was, by implication, the bedrock of the earliest orators. This was the status quo until Socrates and his followers fractured the original (and, it is implied, natural) unity of speech and knowledge (3.63–8). At that point, the orators 'were forcefully dispossesed of what was [theirs], and were left with a paltry piece of land (and even that contested)', 3.108 *de nostra possessione depulsi in paruo et eo litigioso praediolo relicti sumus.*²⁸ 'Most disgraceful', Crassus continues, is that the orators, albeit natural protectors of others (cf. 1.34), 'have now been forced to borrow from those who invaded the orator's inherited property', viz., from philosophers or technical rhetoricians (*ab eis, quod indignissimum est, qui in nostrum patrimonium inruperunt, quod opus est nobis mutuemur*).

Before proceeding to the implications of Crassus' 'concession' that the orators now must procure their former territory from those who dispossessed them, we should note that, despite Crassus' consistent use of legal language in the passage, the jurist Scaevola had long since left Crassus' estate by this point in the dialogue. (He departs after the first day of discussion, i.e., after book 1.) Such terminological and thematic continuity – despite the break of a book and Scaevola's departure – demonstrates not only the subtle brilliance of *De oratore*'s persuasive design, but also the signal importance of legal language to its argument.

As for the implications of the aforementioned legal procedures for that argument, Elaine Fantham argued in *Comparative Studies in Republican Latin Imagery* that Crassus here admits that orators had lost their right to their extensive estate through negligence because of their commitment to the public good. On Fantham's view, interlopers from philosophy and technical rhetoric were able, via the mechanism of *usucapio*, to gain legal ownership of the vast estate of knowledge in question. In simplest terms, *usucapio* allowed a property's owner to yield *possessio* to another party, the 'good faith *possessor*', who immediately occupied the relevant property.²⁹ After an uninterrupted period of two years, the good-faith *possessor* became the new owner, i.e., a *dominus* with *proprietas*. Crucially, however, usucapion was not without its conditions. The second-century BCE *Lex Atinia* clearly affirmed what the Twelve Tables probably also asserted: there could be no *usucapio* of stolen property, a qualification not considered by Fantham.³⁰

Admittedly Crassus invokes neither the law nor the table, but his subsequent assertions rest firmly on the principle underlying both of them. That is, he soon abandons notions that the orator will *borrow* from others; instead, they must outright reclaim the extensive stolen property that they had once rightfully inhabited. At 3.122 Crassus forcefully asserts the orator's claim to the 'complete possession of understanding and learning', which people 'with far too much leisure have invaded while we orators were occupied, as if it had been property unclaimed and uninhabited' (*nostra est ... omnis ista prudentiae doctrinaeque* **possessio**, *in quam homines quasi caducam atque uacuam abundantes otio, nobis occupatis, inuolauerunt*).[31] At 3.123 the orators are enjoined to take back their knowledge 'about ... the whole of the conduct of life, and yes, even about the explanation of nature' from the very people who plundered *them* (*sumenda sunt nobis ab eis ipsis, a quibus expilati sumus*). The final, triumphant image in the sequence is one in which the orator wanders freely on the estate that he has reclaimed for himself as well as enjoying its fruits, undergirding his legal status as titular owner and *dominus*: 3.124 'since the orator may range freely in this enormous, immense field, and ... he is on his own ground wherever he chooses to stand, all the elaborate provisions for speaking with distinction will be readily at his disposal' (*hoc igitur tanto tam immensoque campo cum liceat oratori uagari libere atque ubicumque constiterit, consistere in suo, facile suppeditat omnis apparatus ornatusque dicendi*).[32] Indeed, the arresting image gilds the legal lily: to take possession of a property did not require a person to wander its every corner, but merely to set foot in a part of it.

All of this rests on a cultural framework that had been unavailable to Socrates and Gorgias in Plato's dialogues. The quarrel between philosophy and oratory – when decided in a Roman court – could find resolution in its laws. At the same time, this position accommodates another key element in Cicero's cultural programme, namely, his interest in a philosophically informed (rather than merely technical) oratory. When the orators are allowed to retain secure title qua *domini* with *proprietas*, there is no need to fear philosophers' incursions. If the latter are granted tenancy as *possessores*, such figures remain in the picture, albeit always subject to the authority of the oratorical owner.

Building on Cicero : Knowledge and power in Quintilian and *De architectura*

In *Gorgias* Socrates dismantled the sophist's claim that rhetoric's purview was universal on grounds that rhetoric was a knack, that is, a sort of pseudo-knowledge that lacked a discrete subject matter. In the language of Roman law, however, and in particular its concepts of *dominium* or *proprietas*, Cicero found a culturally specific solution to Gorgias' problem: the ideal Roman orator could hold title and mastery of a field (whether literal or figurative) without cultivating its every corner, as did the specialists and philosophers that Crassus scorned.

Remarkably little attention has been given to how much Cicero's application of legal thinking to the question of disciplinary boundaries may have influenced later texts in the Roman intellectual and professional traditions. Any conclusions must be qualified, as usual, because of the loss of other relevant works (e.g., Cato's *Libri ad filium* or Varro's *Disciplinae*). Still, key facts remain: Cicero is the first extant author to refer to disciplines and their subject matter (e.g., *ars*, *materia*, etc.) as *propria* and its cognates (or as *possessiones*), and these references clearly occur in a context in which the legal sense of these terms is activated[33]; when disciplinary boundary disputes arise in subsequent works, similar juridical language prevails to clarify stakes and desired outcomes.

Unsurprisingly Quintilian gives the most direct testimony for Cicero's influence on the matters at hand.[34] In book 2 of *Institutio Oratoria*, he revisits the issue of the subject matter and influence appropriate to oratory and orators, clearly adopting and expanding the legal language of *De oratore* specifically.[35] At *Inst.* 2.1.4, for example, Quintilian asserts that the *grammatici* must 'observe their own boundaries', which their art has overstepped (2.1.4 *fines suos norit*). In the same passage, he reiterates Crassus' aetiology of oratory's territorial troubles, noting that the orator 'should neither neglect his duties nor take pleasure because the toils that belong to him are being taken up by others [i.e., the *grammatici*], since, when the orator abandons his art, his work has already nearly been taken from his possession by force' (2.1.5 *officia sua non detrectet nec occupari gaudeat pertinentem ad se laborem: quae, dum opere cedit, iam **paene possessione depulsa est***; cf. Cic. *De or.* 3.108 *de nostra **possessione depulsi***). Later in the same book Quintilian clearly follows Cicero in using *proprius* in several instances to object to those who said that oratory was not an art. Quintilian acknowledges that all arts have a subject, but he denies those who say that 'rhetoric does not have its own' (2.17 *rhetorices nullam esse propriam*), a view that Quintilian, now adopting a different sort of juridical language, claims he shall prove false (*falsum ... probabo*).[36]

Cicero's influence on Quintilian's argument for the technicity of oratory and the 'proprietary' nature of the subject matter to which it is entitled is obvious. But Quintilian's multi-pronged argument to defend oratory qua art with 'its own subject' (*propria materia*) also develops the Ciceronian position somewhat further, leading us (topically, not chronologically) to Vitruvius, whose own discourse on professional and civic expertise likely bears the Ciceronian stamp. At 2.21.8 Quintilian points the reader to 'minor arts', such as architecture, which, like oratory, has a 'multifarious material' that is still its own, and which 'deals in everything useful for building', *multiplicem materiam ... namque ea in omnibus quae sunt aedificio utilia uersatur*. Although comparisons of oratorical and architectural subject matter had already appeared in both *Gorgias* and *De oratore*, the aim in those works was to glorify the all-embracing power of speech at the expense of the lesser expertise of architects.[37] Enter Vitruvius, the first-century BCE author of *De architectura*, who spends a significant portion of that treatise's first book to defining the scope of the discipline and the comprehensive influence of his practitioner. Vitruvius, it is commonly held, relied on Cicero's formation of the polymathic *orator* for his definition of the ideal *architectus*[38]. That Vitruvius frames his discussion of the *architectus*' training and influence with recourse to the language of property law, specifically *propria* (and congeners) and *possessio*, is therefore significant. Indeed Vitruvius' use of *proprius* etc. to mark out intellectual domains is the earliest extant example thereof after that of Cicero himself.

Vitruvius, too, is able to solve architecture's 'technicity' problem in ways that his Greek forebears (we may suppose) were unable to do. He also deploys legal language for this purpose, though his manner in doing so differs somewhat from Cicero's own in several important aspects. The majority of *De architectura* broadly encompasses principles of design and application within the three, main 'parts' (*partes*) of *architectura*, viz., building, gnomonics and mechanics.[39] Yet, the opening sentence of the treatise directs our attention to the ideal practitioner who embodies the art. There, Vitruvius highlights the architect's constitutive knowledge (*scientia*) and the impressive authority (*iudicium*) that derives from it, Vitr. 1.1.1:

> Architecti est scientia pluribus disciplinis et uariis eruditionibus ornata cuius iudicio probantur omnia quae ab ceteris artibus perficiuntur opera.
>
> To the architect belongs a domain of knowledge adorned by many different areas of learning and instruction; every product of the other arts is put to proof by his authority.

Both of these ideas – *scientia* and *iudicium* – extend well beyond architecture when construed as the sum of its parts, an illogicality that should recall Ciceronian discourse on oratorical training and influence. The former, *scientia*, is introduced somewhat paradoxically by a reference to its disciplinary embellishments (*pluribus disciplinis et uariis eruditionibus ornata*; see n. 40 on Ciceronian *ornatus*) rather than by a proprietary architectural subject matter (e.g., a *res architectonica*).[40] The required curriculum ranges widely, and it includes an emphasis on law. Although Vitruvius' recommendation that the ideal *architectus* 'should be acquainted with the *responsa* of the jurists' and 'ought to take note of rights, too' (1.1.3 *responsa iurisconsultorum nouerit*; cf. 1.1.10 *iura quoque nota habeat oportet*) may initially surprise readers, knowledge of the law – and property law in particular – was evidently necessary when considering interests of contiguous buildings. For example, the *seruitus stillicidii* ('rainwater servitude') granted the right to allow rainwater to drip from one property onto another, as Vitruvius suggests.[41] In the end, the architect's authority (*iudicium*, another term with legal resonance) is so expansive that all arts (or at least the works that they produce) are subject to the architect's approval.

One of the ways in which Ciceronian influence is most perceptible is in Vitruvius's hand-wringing over the appropriate scope of the ideal architect's knowledge, with *De architectura* enacting in miniature (though not in dialogue form) a struggle over the very issues raised in *De oratore*.[42] The affinity is most clear in Vitruvius' repeated recourse to the language of ownership (*proprius, proprietas*) early in first book of *De architectura*. Of course, these terms are common outside the law, and Vitruvius has not populated his treatise with Roman jurists to point up their legal valence. But even if we discount the various throughlines linking *De oratore* to *De architectura*, it is worth emphasizing that both of these literary works – like the law itself – are particularly self-conscious about their efforts to accommodate (and police) even irrational disciplinary boundaries, provided that those disciplines are tied closely to civic goods such as the political institutions or buildings of the republic.[43] The mere invocation of concepts such as 'ownership' and 'property' within the cultural products of a society that has laws to protect those categories cannot but invite legalistic thinking of a sort, even when they appear outside an overtly legal context. Such thinking is encouraged when *De architectura*, as a taxonomic and stipulative technical text, is in its own way a text on the 'laws' of architecture, much as *De inuentione* or the *Rhetorica ad Herennium* have been seen as resembling textbooks on law as much as on rhetoric.[44]

This is not to say that disputes over intellectual property of this sort were easy to solve. Vitruvius actually offers competing visions of the depth and influence of architectural knowledge, just as Crassus in *De oratore* occasionally softens his strongest claims on oratorical knowledge to mollify the reader (temporarily, at least). For instance, shortly after his initial assertion (above) that the architect's authority can judge all other arts, he revises his position at 1.1.14, noting that the 'execution of a work', *operis effectus*, remains 'the exclusive property of those trained in the individual subjects' (*unum **proprium** esse eorum, qui singulis rebus sunt exercitati*), while the work's *ratio* (in this case, 'logic' or 'intellectual basis') is held in 'common with all men of learning' (*commune cum omnibus doctis*).⁴⁵ Similarly at 1.1.12–17 Vitruvius attacks the views of Pytheos of Priene, a Greek architect of the fourth century who declared 'that an architect must be able to do more in every art and pursuit (*plus oportere posse facere*) than those who have brought individual subjects (*singulas res*) to distinctive splendour through diligent practice'.⁴⁶ Such a view corresponds, somewhat, to the most extreme versions of what Crassus claims for oratory.

Like Scaevola Vitruvius rejects Pytheos' view as impracticable, specifying instead a moderate position that initially posits the architect's mere sufficiency in the contributing disciplines without yielding its broad authority.⁴⁷ Thus, Vitruvius adds that, since even those 'who hold an individual art's exclusive property as their own' are not universally capable of receiving the highest praise (*qui priuatim **proprietates** tenent artium*), the *architectus* (1.1.16) need only be 'moderately familiar with the parts and principles' (*partes et rationes . . . mediocriter*) of the disciplines necessary for architecture, 'in case he needs to judge and approve anything on these subjects and arts' (*si quid de his rebus et artibus **iudicare et probare** opus fuerit, ne deficiatur*; cf. 1.1.1 *cuius **iudicio probantur** omnia quae ab ceteris artibus perficiuntur opera*). In general for Vitruvius tasks completed and refined by hand or by special procedures 'belong to those who have been trained to accomplish things in their art exclusively (*proprie*)', and in example of this he considers the differing place of musical knowledge in the mental toolkit of doctors and musicians, again invoking ownership and property. Although musicians and *medici* all know something about musical theory (of rhythm and pumping blood, respectively), the treatment of wounds – i.e., the actual *practice* of medicine – is exclusive to the physician, 1.1.15 'if a wound needs to be healed, or a sick person kept from peril, the musician will not be summoned; rather, this work is the property of the doctor' (*id opus **proprium** erit medici*).

Two things may be noted. First, albeit broadly resembling Cicero's Crassus in his final claim for universal authority (and a related relegation of excessive specialism within lesser arts to their expert practitioners), Vitruvius differs from Crassus by relinquishing title to those areas of knowledge qua property (*proprietates*). What matters is the authority to judge, and by abandoning 'title' altogether, Vitruvius avoids many of the controversies created by Crassus' treatment of oratorical knowledge.⁴⁸ Second, when it comes to disciplinary ownership and possession, Vitruvius nearly denies the importance of 'title' altogether, with one important exception. Reflecting on his own 'well-rounded training in literature and all of the liberal arts' at the start of his treatise's second half (6.pr.4), he thanks his parents for encouraging him to pursue 'the acquisition of such **possessions** for his soul, the **chief fruit** of which is [the knowledge that] '**ownership**' is, above all, not to long for riches' (6.pr.4 *eas possessiones animo paraui, e quibus haec est fructuum summa: nullas plus habendi esse necessitates eamque esse proprietatem, diuitiarum maxime nihil desiderare*).[49]

Commentators have overlooked Vitruvius' clear use of legal language in his description of the fruits (*fructuum*) yielded by his '*possessio*', a wide-ranging education.[50] (Even his characterization of 'mental possession' has a technical legal flavour, since 'mental' rather than physical possession, i.e., an intent to possess, *animo possessio*, was occasionally dispositive of possession itself.)[51] Most striking, however, is Vitruvius' representation of *proprietas* as an ethical stance that condemns personal greed and ambition. Claims of humility are common in professional and technical works, but this one seems particularly unusual, given Vitruvius' rather haughty claims early in the treatise to possess a quasi-juridical authority (*iudicare et probare*) over the products of all other arts without extensive training in them.[52] To understand this, we may consider why Crassus in *De oratore*, unlike Vitruvius, never relinquished claims of universal 'title'. One cannot say for certain, but this seems likely to have to do with the realtively privileged status of oratory and orators at Rome, versus that of architecture and architects. Vitruvius throughout his text often presents himself as a man devoid of ambition and a hater of corruption in contrast with his peers, many of whom were *scribae* and distrusted as untrustworthy social upstarts: one thinks, mutatis mutandis, of the Horatian pest of *S.* 1.9.[53] Yet since Vitruvius wields a powerful technology (e.g., of aesthetic judgment, so crucial to imperial representation in architecture), the field of architecture must reflect this same duality. No mere architect, unlike an orator of Crassus' stripe, could claim title to the whole civic estate without seeming to outstep social and cultural bounds; he could only enjoy its possessions and the benefits accruing to their humble caretaker.

* * *

To be sure, the evaluative language of judgment and approval are well attested within the authoritative texts of rhetoric, philosophy, and literary criticism, even in the Greek tradition.[54] In a Roman context, one is reminded of the closing of Cicero's *Orator*, Cic. *Orat.* 237: 'Brutus, you have my judgment on the orator (*de oratore ... iudicium*) ... Pursue it, if you approve it (*sequere, si probaueris*), or persevere in your own, if different.' Yet in conjunction with Cicero's innovation in framing disciplinary debates over intellectual property, possession, and encroachment in *legal* terms, the notion that Vitruvius would fashion his ideal architect as the source of judgment and proof in all *other* domains strongly suggests not only that some sort of legal thinking undergirds his work, but that such thinking is a source of architecture's viability as an authoritative form of Roman aesthetic and political discourse. That discourse, like the discourse of Ciceronian oratory, is notable both for the ways in which it legislates, so to speak, a broad scope for the ideal practitioner of an art with universalizing ambitions, and for the way it conversely relegates the specializing and narrow practitioner – the philosophizing Greek – well outside the realm of a Roman *ciuilis scientia*. The civic arts of Rome, which included its law, protected their own borders as vigorously as they maintained that they had no borders at all, a civic and intellectual *imperium sine fine*.

Notes

1 The author would like to thank the organizers of the conference, panel moderators and other discussants for their valuable input and expertise. Translations of *De oratore* generally follow May and Wisse (2001), with occasional alterations for emphasis; translations of *De architectura* are my own. Other authors follow the Loeb editions.
2 For the setting of the dialogue and its dramatic date, May and Wisse (2001) 13–18 and Mankin (2011) 23–35 are clear and concise. Though much of what follows examines Cicero's involvement in *De oratore* with Plato's *Gorgias*, Zetzel (2003) rightly notes the importance of *Phaedrus* for the setting. Fantham (2004) studies the dialogue and its contributions from a variety of perspectives.
3 Pl. *Grg.* 463b. A key moment in the so-called 'quarrel' or 'schism' between rhetoric and philosophy. For this and adjacent issues, see May and Wisse (2001) 20–6 and Mankin (2011) 35–41.
4 On the importance of the orator's cultural education, see especially Narducci (1997), Dugan (2005) and Connolly (2007).
5 My translation of *uis oratoris* as 'the power of the orator' departs from May and Wisse to reflect my prioritization of Cicero's direct response to Plato's *Gorgias*; cf. Pl. *Grg.* 455e [GORG.] Well, I will try, Socrates, to reveal to you clearly the whole power (δύναμιν ἅπασαν) of rhetoric; cf. 456a [ΣΩ.] ἡ δύναμις . . . τῆς ῥητορικῆς. Especially important is 456b [GORG.] Ah yes, if you knew all, Socrates, how it comprises in

itself practically all powers at once! (ὡς ἔπος εἰπεῖν ἁπάσας τὰς δυνάμεις συλλαβοῦσα ὑφ' αὑτῇ ἔχει).

6   *De or.* 1.22–3.
7   Though this does not stop him from doubling down on his assertions of oratory's comprehensive reach; May and Wisse (2001) 13–19.
8   Fantham (1972) 148 speaking of *De or.* 1.41, 'The legal and gladitorial imagery is purely Roman.'
9   For the law's role in boundary making and breaking, see Gunderson (in this volume).
10 3.143 *sin quaerimus quid unum excellat ex omnibus, docto oratori palma danda est.*
11 Fantham (1972) 148.
12 See above on Pl. *Grg.*
13 At *De or.* 1.39, e.g., Scaevola casts the powerful and pro-social influence of civil law as wholly distinct from what is produced by eloquence.
14 Preferred by many editors to *praeessem.*
15 The *sacramentum* (*tibi iusto sacramento contendere non liceret*) was a standard 'action-at-law' in the early Republic. This was an oath-cum-wager saying that the party who brought the *uindicatio* procedure to assert ownership would stake a monetary deposit (as would the party who had been challenged before the magistrate). The notion was to avoid frivolous lawsuits.
16 My interpretation of the text, by taking *propria* as the complement to *adiumenta atque ornamenta dicendi,* differs from that of May and Wisse, who limit Crassus' claim of ownership (*proprietas*) to 'the tools and ornaments of speaking'.
17 The concepts are neither simple nor static, and the literature on either is vast. Book 2 of Gaius' *Instutiones* (second century CE) embraces 'the law relating to things' (*ius quod ad res pertinet*). Relevant and accessible overviews of property law in recent scholarship include Baldus (2016), Colognesi (2016) and Riggsby (2010) 135–71; 135–51 are especially relevant to this discussion. Also useful are the expositions in Borkowski (1994) (esp. chapter 6), Nicholas (1962) 98–157. The *Casebook* of Hausmaninger and Gamauf (2012) explores a variety of real-world contingencies alongside theoretical discussion; Watson (1968) focuses on the laws of property in the later Republic. Fantham (2004) 102–30 examines the place of oratory and the law in *De or.*, albeit focusing on jurists and trials mentioned in the dialogue (rather than its legal metaphors, which are briefly broached at Fantham (1972) 148–9 and 162–3; it is curious, and possibly signficant, that a good many of the trials mentioned by Fantham pertain to property law. Although both Roman and Athenian law are broadly conceived of as procedural (see above), property rights in Athenian law were limited to acting on (*krátēsis*) and to disposing of (*kyrieía*) property; damages done to property were covered by criminal law. At Rome in the Classical period *proprietas* and *dominium* were not strictly synonymous, since the former was

most closely associated with the allocation aspect of the *uindicatio* formula (see below) rather than notions of control, though the two terms were regularly used together.

18 See below on *usucapio*.
19 To quote the necessarily circular definition of *possessio* at Borkowski (1994) 153, 'it is perhaps safest to describe Roman [interdictory] possession as such *physical* control over property as was protected by possessory interdicts', but see preceding note and especially Baldus (2016) for a breadth of approaches to the topic.
20 *Dig.* 41.2.12.1 *Nihil commune habet proprietas cum possessione: et ideo non denegatur ei interdictum uti possidetis, qui coepit rem uindicare: non enim uidetur possessioni renuntiasse, qui rem uindicavit.* (Note the pun on *commune*, 'common'.)
21 See n. 16.
22 Scaevola's use of *aut . . . aut*, which (so *Lewis and Short*) indicates 'an actual and positive alternative' (cf. *vel*) may conceal doubts about the ultimate standing of his 'clients'. We may note that, were this a real-world dispute, even if the praetor should issue an interdict *uti possidetis* (in this case stipulating that the philosophers and specialists *were* the rightful possessors of their knowledge and should have possession), Crassus – if he believed his claim to possession was legitimate – could simply ignore the order, forcing the plaintiffs to initiate a *uindicatio* to establish title definitively. The aggrieved parties, however, would have a legal right to eject Crassus from their possessions via self-help, even with force.
23 For an exploration of authorship and 'intellectual property' in antiquity in the latter sense, see Goldschmidt (in this volume).
24 See also below on the *lex Atinia*.
25 *Inu.* 1.2.
26 There is no scope to discuss this here, but Scaevola's suggestion that Socrates was the 'source' (*fons*) for later schools of moral philosophy (1.42) may evoke legal rights pertaining to access to and the drawing of water, servitudes pertaining to *aquae haustus* and of *iter*. For other passages treating the right to draw on literary 'sources' in legal terms, see Volk (2010).
27 'Distinction' is one of four aspects of style; the three others are Latinity, clarity, and appropriateness. For the importance of *ornatus* in Cicero's oratorical and cultural programs, see Dugan (2005).
28 The 'paltry piece' suggests a narrower view of the orator as a professional speaker in the courts and forum.
29 This was a less formal (and therefore more efficient) means of transferring property than traditional mechanisms that required the presence of the *praetor* and other formal encumbrances.
30 An alternative interpretation of the provision of the Twelve Tables is that 'they simply prohibited *usucapio* by the *fur* but did not generally prohibit the *usucapio* of *res furtivae*', Watson (1968) 27.

31 May and Wisse (2001) follow the *OLD* s.v. 'caducus' 10 ('like property unclaimed'), another legal term; but cf. the additional possibilities raised by *Lewis and Short* II B 2, as properties 'which did not fall to the heir mentioned in a will, because he was childless, but passed to other heirs (in default of such, to the exchequer)'.

32 I note here only briefly that 3.123 may allude to an orator's right to draw water (*ius aquae haustus*) from the property that he owned; see n. 25 above with Volk (2010) for similar imagery in Manilius and Vitruvius.

33 Cicero also uses *proprius* in related sense in a letter to Atticus, *Att.* 2.9.3 (59 BCE), at *Rep.* 1.28 (54–51 BCE) and *Nat. D.* 2.57.5 (45 BCE).

34 The example least securely attributible to Ciceronian influence comes from the encyclopedist Celsus ('the Cicero of medicine'), who in the prooemium to *De Medicina* notes that many things 'not properly belonging to particular arts' (*ad ipsas artes proprie non pertinentia*) are still helpful for stimulating the minds of those who do practise them, using *proprie* to denote the purview of individual arts. One imagines that a preface to his *Artes*, which comprised twenty-six books on (inter alia) rhetoric, philosophy, and jurisprudence might have addressed the question of disciplinary boundaries directly. That Celsus' argument somewhat recalls the Hippocratic *On the Art* – in which the author, like Cicero in *De oratore*, aimed to rebuff Socratic misgivings about technicity of the medical art ('*techne iatrike*') – may add to the possibility of Ciceronian influence. See Hippoc. *Peri Technes* (esp. 1–7) with Mann (2012).

35 See the comments of Reinhardt and Winterbottom (2006) ad loc.

36 See Quint. *Inst.* 2.21 for comparable uses of *proprius*. '*Probo*' appears with some regularity in similar senses in Ciceronian *rhetorica*; see below.

37 Pl. *Grg.* 456e, Cic. *De or.* 1.62

38 Vitruvius mentions Cicero among his Latin literary and cultural heroes (*auctores*) in an important passage, Vitr. 9. pr. 17. Ciceronian influence on Vitruvius is fleshed out more fully with further references in Oksanish (2019).

39 1.3.1 *Partes ipsius architecturae sunt tres: aedificatio, gnomonice, machinatio*; cf. 1.2.1–9 *ordinatio, dispositio, eurythmia, symmetria, decor*, etc. For the 'fragility' of the terminology of *diuisio* (including '*partes*'), see Moatti (1997) 234.

40 The notion of essential supplement/embellishment is paradoxical and invites comparison with oratory. Hence at *De or.* 3.96, Cicero labours to define *ornatus* as a concept inhering in speech rather than supplemental to it. Elliott (2013) 35–6, 326–7. For extension of *ornatus* into other domains of Roman culture, see Dugan (2005) and especially 48 n. 79. NB Caye (2011) 79 'L'architecture est en réalité un art, non pas de l'édification, mais de la surédification.'

41 1.1.10

42 Oksanish (2019).

43 Some more boundary language in *De architectura*: at 2.pr.5, Vitruvius describes the work of the previous book of his treatise (i.e., the first, from which most passages

discussed here derive) as an effort to set the *terminationes* ('limits') of the art; much the same claim is made at 3.pr.4, where Vitruvius says that he has 'delimited its [paradoxically expansive] boundaries' (*finitionibus terminaui*).

44 Harries (2006) 93.

45 Translations of these terms vary in accordance with the views of the translators. See especially the distinct approaches of Fleury (1990), Gros, Corso and Romano (1997), Ferri (2002) at 1.1.1.

46 1.1.12.10–15, *ait in suis commentariis architectum omnibus artibus et doctrinis plus oportere posse facere quam qui singulas res suis industriis et exercitationibus ad summam claritatem perduxerunt*. According to tradition Pytheos designed the Mausoleum at Halicarnassus and, according to Vitruvius, the temple of Athena in Priene. At Vitr. 1.1.15 he appears to have been among the first Greek architectural theorists to speak systematically about the architect's knowledge, but Vitruvius' attribution of these ideas to Pytheos may simply reflect a Vitruvian interpretation (and, indeed, a systematization) of offhand remarks made in Pytheos' commentaries.

47 Vitruvius' moderated view finds the architect striving neither to be 'uniquely outstanding in the other areas nor unskilled' (1.1.13 *nec in ceteris doctrinis singulariter excellens, sed in is non inperitus*), neither illiterate nor a literary critic (*grammaticus*; cf. Quint. *Inst.* 2.1.4), nor a specialist in musical theory (*musicus*) yet not unmusical, etc.

48 That he creates others in the process is beyond the scope of this paper to investigate.

49 For the sense of *encyclios disciplina* and discussion of the distinctions between Vitruvius' own education and that of his ideal *architectus*, see Oksanish (2019) 128–9 with further references.

50 For the fruits of *bona fide* possession, see Borkowski (1994) 183–4.

51 Baldus (2016, esp. 539 ff.) addresses the difficulty of distinguishing these abstract components given the lack of a unified Roman concept of *possessio*; for a basic distinction, see Borkowski (1994) 152–3 with *Dig.* 41.2.3.1.

52 On which question Nichols (2017) is essential; see also Oksanish (2019) chapter 5.

53 See Nichols (2007, esp. chapter 2).

54 E.g., Pl. *Plt.* 260c ἡ κριτική [τέχνη]; see Lausberg 1998 §10.3(b)

11

Seneca's Debt: Property, Self-Possession and the Economy of Philosophical Exchange in the *Epistulae Morales*

Erik Gunderson

Man, pursuant to his immediate existence within himself, is something natural, external to his concept. It is only through the development of his own body and mind, essentially through his self-consciousness's apprehension of itself as free, that he takes possession of himself and becomes his own property and no one else's.[1]

Law and literature are odd partners at Rome. Their relationship is, in practice, dialectical. And my case study for this claim will come from Seneca's *Moral Letters*. But what Seneca does with and to the law is not distinct from the practice of others. A first thesis: Law is abstract, fixed, binding, and authoritative for the subject.[2] Law is likewise the authoritative discourse of boundaries. The antithesis: Law does not bind. It is instead mere metaphor and as such it is freely appropriable by the subject. The literary subject is free to play with his imagination as he sees fit, and transferring legalisms out from a narrowly bounded discourse of law and redeploying them is emblematic of this freedom.[3] The synthesis: the act of appropriation modifies the law such that it is no longer fixed while nevertheless remaining authoritative. Meanwhile the appropriated law nevertheless constrains that which had been free. There is self-binding to the spirit of law even as the letter of the law is violated. And this dialectical process that renders the law literary and the literary legal has always already happened.[4] Seneca's text only registers the outlines of the dialectic, it does not invent it.

An irreverence for the law is strikingly manifest in our elite sources. At Rome there are many alternate fonts of authority that would determine our acts as per their dictates: *mos maiorum*, *imperium*, *ratio*. The law is often presented as being consonant with these hegemonic categories rather than guiding or governing them. Meanwhile legal knowledge is generally possessed only by specialists, and these specialists do not reside at the peak of the cultural scale.[5] Instead we often see orators and philosophers jockey for position as the supreme cultural authorities. The jurists are largely forgotten. Rebarbative legal questions are the domain of pedants, not leading citizens.[6] Orators tend not to know the law, even as they are the public face of the legal system.[7] Meanwhile Philosophers are content to found their own Republics and to fill them with laws of their own invention.[8]

Quintilian's discussion of law in the *Instiutio Oratoria* at 7.5–8 is symptomatic and ominous. Quintilian teaches the student how to massage legal questions. He offers no instruction about the law itself. The discussion of law comes as a sequel to the section on *qualitas*, that is, the instructions one receives on redefining an act: 'The act was not base, it was in fact noble.'[9] We are slipping around and out from under legal categories. The first piece of advice in 7.5 is that if you can not deny the deed, then you fight the legitimacy of the proceeding against you. This is strategic and legalistic behaviour. It does not reflect of a pious love of the law as such. In 7.6 we meditate on the spirit as against the letter of the law. Again, the orientation is strategic: if the one is against you, turn to another. In 7.7 we explore a corollary: sometimes two laws clash, how can you use this to your advantage?

Most dire of all, virtually every example of a law that Quintilian adduces throughout his discussion is derived from declamation. But he is not alone. That is, it comes from a fake legal world.[10] Quintilian has erred on the side of fiction. Declaimers endlessly play around with their indigenous discourse of law. Roman law proper is left to one side. And, as would be expected of any elite gentleman, Seneca's appreciation of the law is assuredly mediated by rhetorical training in general and declamation in particular. In fact Seneca's own father had written up a collection of reminiscences of declamation and dedicated it to his sons.

The intelligentsia feel free to appropriate the law as they see fit. But what of 'the law itself', how fixed and solid is it? The letter of the law comes folded up in a variety of conventions, rituals and mystifications.[11] The law possesses more than one logic. People have varied relationships to these logics. For the most part they are *ad hoc* and strategic.[12] Consider the question of *manus* and marriage. Since a man can acquire property by use, a wife who does not want to fall into her husband's *manus* needs to absent herself from his house for at least three days every year.[13] The tensions between the law of property and of persons are evident here. Evident as well is a willingness to accept social fictions and symbolic gestures as a valid means of intervening into a legal situation. People play around with the law, they do not blindly accede to it.

As an example of the ritualized quality of the law, I would like to adduce *uindicatio*. It is a word that will crop up more than once in our discussion. Buckland's *Text-Book of Roman Law* presents *uindicta* as follows:

> Vindicta: In form a fictitious claim of liberty, a formal application of the machinery by which a man who alleged that he was wrongly held in slavery claimed his freedom (*causa liberalis*), modelled on the ancient process for recovery of property (*vindicatio*), by *sacramentum*. Some person seems to have claimed on his behalf (*adsertor libertatis*), he being present. The formal words were modeled on those in *sacramentum*. The *adsertor* touched the slave with a rod (*festuca, vindicta*) as he would if the claim was a real one, from which act the process draws its name. The master did the same, but otherwise made no reply. The magistrate declared the man free.[14]

While it is certainly important to have a means of claiming one's own liberty, the process described here does not center around documents, oaths and witnesses. Such would be necessary and entirely sufficient within a modern legal framework. The Roman situation is saturated with legal fictions and legal dramas. And when we look at the *adsertor* and his *festuca*, we note that the drama includes actors and props. Observers of the legal drama will see something filled with the products of the literary imagination: tensions, ambiguities, metaphors, plots and resolutions.

But one need not see *uindicatio* as a mere game. In fact, few likely did. It really mattered. It was a life and death affair for those concerned.[15] Indeed Seneca's *Moral Letters* begins with an earnest evocation of *uindicatio*. One of the first words of the first letter puts us on notice: the law matters; and the law can be a positive resource for a student of philosophy:

> Ita fac, mi Lucili: uindica te tibi, et tempus quod adhuc aut auferebatur aut subripiebatur aut excidebat collige et serua.
>
> Yes, just so. Make a claim upon yourself. All that time that hitherto was snatched away or pilfered or fell by the wayside gather it up and preserve it.
>
> *EM* 1.1

Seneca has taken the already complex legal situation that surrounds *uidicatio* and extended it.[16] Seneca plays with the situation by complicating both the question of agency and the question of property.[17] One is to lay claim to oneself for oneself.[18] The self is here on the one hand a mere object, but, on the other hand, we are also playing with the situation Buckland describes. Moreover this self-appropriation is also self-liberation. One emancipates oneself by treating oneself as a special kind of object. And, interestingly, one acquires the self-as-object by means of attending to a special kind of property, namely time. Plunder, theft, and negligence have damaged one's supply of time. And only when one has worried over the matter of time will one be able to lay claim to oneself.

Seneca leverages our sense of rights and privileges and the legal status of subjects and objects in order to orient us towards his new project. Law becomes propaedeutic for the ethical enterprise. One can use the old categories provided a few terms are shifted around. Instead of *res* one worries about *tempus*, instead of *mancipia* one worries about taking oneself in hand, instead of *bona* one worries about the *summum bonum*.[19]

As the project opens, the universe of literary-philosophical metaphors grounds itself in a pre-existing domain of concepts.[20] While many of the metaphors and conceits on offer might be familiar to us, this familiarity should not lead us to scorn the significance of what is transpiring. This letter sets a price and value on time and stresses by repetition that an economic calculus is the appropriate method of attending to time. And then we take these metaphors and run with them. They are not 'dead metaphors' but rather the ones that will get us our lives back.

One is asked to 'seize the day', but the metaphor for this is derived from law: 'lay claim to it', *manum inicere*.[21] Time, says the letter, is the only possession that is truly ours.[22] The narrator of the letter says that his own account books square when it comes to the use of his time (*ratio mihi constat inpensae*). But, he says with an ironic twist, they are the ledgers of a wastrel: he is able to give an exact reckoning of his impoverishment (*EM* 1.4).

Amidst all of the emphasis on 'possession' and the invocation of property law, then, we see a collection of displacements that can be grouped under the heading of 'dispossession'. They alienate language from its limited, technical use and extend it out towards moral philosophy. This gets us to the manifold irony of the letters: there is an affable roguery afoot. A wastrel confesses and even as he makes his confession he picks our own pockets, consumes our time, and both dispossesses time of its properties and misappropriates legal idioms so as to shift them over into an alien discourse.

Strategic reappropriation is the name of the game in the early portion of the *Moral Letters*. The narrator continually talks about property, possession, and debt. But he is constantly challenging our relationship to these categories. And he does so via a constant tug against the law as letter or literal. Throughout the epistles law is turned into a question of the human spirit more generally. Earthly law is forced to make a metaphorical ascent from the law of the human world and towards cosmic law. The literary emplotment of the letters themselves induces this transition. Law and literature is here a programmatic moment: literature moves us from one notion of the law and towards a still higher conception of the law. The sublation of the law – that is, the fulfilment of law's own dialectical destiny – requires literary intervention. And the constant literary play with the language of property within this philosophical context primes us to make this transition for ourselves.

The epistles in the first books of the *Moral Letters* have as one of their literary conceits the notion of philosophical debt. The theme is worked through with some regularity. At the tail ends of letters Seneca will adduce a piece of philosophy that he has appropriated from elsewhere and he will distribute it to Lucilius and then offer some commentary on it.[23] That is, mixed into the principal project of self-appropriation we have a subsidiary theme of intellectual appropriation.

There is a certain amount of 'value added' on display when we realize that the quotes are always attended by commentary as well. That is, philosophical labour is yielding surplus value, but the narrative voice of the letters disingenuously pretends that little is going on beyond a case of moving material from one place to another, drawing, that is, from one account and registering it in another. Each of the metaphors in my description of the situation is native to Seneca's own project.

The extremely imperfect fit between the metaphorical register and a full accounting of the issues at hand reveals a narrator who is running roughshod over the familiar concepts of property law. And this seems to be one of the points of the exercise. For example, the calculus of intellectual debt is revealed to converge with but ultimately remain heterogenous from the way the things of the world circulate. The careful student of this new set of property relations comes to appreciate that laying claim to oneself involves a radical abrogation of the standard ways of talking about 'mine' and 'yours'. It also means recalibrating one's sense of 'legality' more generally.

But such a student is in fact the careful, attentive reader, the reader who lets literature unfold over time and across letters. The philosophical thesis about property and self-appropriation evolves as a quiet counterpoint to the main melodies of the letters. The claims are ostentatiously relegated to seemingly incidental closing remarks that can and will break with the main topics of any given letter. And, further, one is never flat out told that the law is being systematically rewritten for us. Instead it happens before our eyes with some winks and smiles that give the whole matter a seemingly unserious air.

In the first two books of letters Seneca is constantly talking about Epicurean philosophy with Lucilius. It is only in the first letter of the third book that we make a pivot more obviously to Stoicism in its own right.[24] Much as property law is presented as a means of getting started with philosophy, so is Epicureanism a means of approaching Stoicism. In fact these two themes intersect in as much as the Epicurean content is constantly being referred to as something stolen, borrowed, or owed.[25]

For the first three books of letters we are frequently presented with a situation where Lucilius is said to be eager to hear a philosophical *sententia* and Seneca's comments on it. Seneca obliges him. The act of gratification is figured as the payment of a debt or as some other sort of economically-inflected gesture. The fifth and sixth letters offer bits of the Stoic philosopher Hecato to Lucilius. In the former case the offering is a *lucellum* (*EM* 5.7). In the latter it is a *mercedula* (*EM* 6.7). Seneca is happy to share some slight profits. Lucilius is owed a bit of cash as his wages. The debt is interpersonal. The terms of the arrangement are affable but obscure and imprecise. The work is done by writer and reader. And payment is made with other men's words.

All of this money banter is presented as a self-aware closural device for a variety of letters. The joking around is all supposed to be entered into the literary ledger under the heading of irony. But the commentary on property rights is more than a mere joke. We are notified of this presently. The eighth letter announces the arrival of its ending segment by declaring that a payment needs to be made (*pro hac epistula dependendum*). Then the narrator announces that the debt will be paid from another's stock: *id non de meo fiet*. As if that were not suspect enough, Seneca then declares that the payment does not come from a gift or a loan but from some more plunder: 'I'm still pillaging Epicurus.'[26]

Then a question is put in Lucilius' mouth: 'Perhaps you wonder why I put so many fine sayings of Epicurus in my letters rather than those of the Stocics [*nostrorum*].'[27] The answer represents a truly radical case of wilful appropriation: if a thing is well said, then it is common property, not private property. Imperialistic plunder tramples on particular rights in the name of building a domain of 'the true' where the truth itself is not a private thing but a universal matter. Seneca is asking us to think about the inner logic of ideas: what does it really mean to have them, to own them, to borrow them, to exchange them, to owe them to one another? Those verbs are all metaphors, metaphors about transfer, in fact. So the part where property law was 'just a metaphor' only leads us to a problem of metaphor more generally: can wisdom be shifted from one place to another?[28]

The letter closes both with a set of reflections on these headings and a collection of verses that run in parallel to the letter's commentary. But there is not so much a conclusion here as an accumulation of issues and then a declaration that Seneca's debt to Lucilius has been paid and the letter can close. But even as a payment has been made more questions arise and the reader perhaps feels that he or she is owed still more by way of explanation. What is the real *ratio* of all of these *rationes*? What is the logic behind the accountancy?

The passages all concern property and possession. Their aggregation indirectly proves Seneca's point about Epicurus' maxim: many people have said similar things, so it is hard to say that the conceit is peculiar to any one of them. But Seneca does not push that point, instead he is acting as a literary critic of places where people talk about 'that which is truly ours'.

Books are full of things that are 'really mine' to the extent that they are true. Reading is a species of appropriation. Citation and reuse are disjoint from anything like plagiarism provided one's aim is a service to the truth.[29] But the letter does not argue any of this quite so directly. Instead it elects to perform its thesis while also offering a wry commentary about property relations to one side of the central issue. The abrupt close of the letter comes after Lucilius has been handed his own words as appropriated by a Seneca who is defending himself against a charge of lifting similar words from Epicurus. Seneca says that the gift of Lucilian verse made to Lucilius will not be calculated against Seneca's balance sheet because the man is being paid from his own purse: *de tuo tibi*.

This null transaction in fact gives the formula for ultimate enlightenment. When one realizes that we are already in possession of the truth and that we only need to truly lay hold of it as our truth, then we will, as the opening of the first letter put it, lay claim to ourselves. We need to be able to hear our own words echoed back to us and at that moment to realize that these are not Epicurus' words or Seneca's words or Publilius' words or even words that came from a book with our name on it but that instead these words are our truth and that our truth has converged with the truth. At that moment we will be free. But until that moment arrives Seneca will close his epistles with his irony-laced game of ledgers and debts.

Seneca has staged a dialectical situation that, unsurprisingly, closely resembles my own portrait of the dialectics of literature and law above. First step: the truth is alien. Second step: the truth is seized, appropriated, and transferred. Third step: one realizes that the truth was not alien to begin with. The movement was on the side of the subject, not the truth. The subject opened out to the truth. And the truth authentically became 'the subject's truth' without for that losing its own autonomous, objective status.

Legal categories, philosophical categories, social categories and the language of property are circling madly in these passages. And the very roiling of the metaphorical situation offers an index to the major theme of the letters as announced from the start: how can we be free; what do we owe one another; what do we owe ourselves? The last letter of the first book, namely *Epistulae Morales* 12, ends with a series of nasty jabs against the hunt for allusions and intertexts. As in letter 8, there is a problem of the proper name, of literary proprietorship, and of property itself: scrupulous attention to the rights and privileges of *nomina* only serves to steer us away from the real substance of the affair, namely substance itself. If we stress the economic force of a verb like *aestimare*, then we hear in the closing of the letter a return to the calculus of profits, losses and debts more generally. But we are simultaneously warned against our desire to put things in these same terms: 'If a thing is true it is mine. I will keep on heaping you up with Epicurus, and so those who swear on the words of another and take no stock of what is said but only who says it might hereby come to know that the best things are in fact common property.'[30]

The problem of debt and proprietorship haunts the endings of these letters. And it appears vividly at the end of the first book.[31] A bright communist future awaits us as soon as we can redeem ourselves from slavery. We will pay some sort of abstract debt to the truth by circulating coins of the philosophical realm that have on their faces the busts of famous individuals. But the value of the currency comes from the truth that each maxim embodies, not from the name inscribed on its surface. This is a very interesting pose to strike given that Seneca is a very wealthy man, has never been a slave, and would likely be horrified if one presented him with a copy of *The Communist Manifesto* or even of *The Social Contract*: 'Man is born free, and everywhere he is in chains.' 'The history of all hitherto existing society is the history of class struggles.' 'Working Men of All Countries, Unite!' How many of these *sententiae* would he embrace? Perhaps lingering a bit more with the political economy of philosophical debt will help us to make some sort of reply to this question. We need to figure out why it is that a dialectic of enlightenment does not suspend the evils of empirical law. That is, we never really set aside property law and the class relations that the law (re)produces and sustains. And this is true even though Seneca is consistently mocking property rights in these letters.[32]

The next book of letters continues this play of mixing and matching social and economic terminology. The end of the second letter of the book is full of puns on the idea of 'gold'. We flag the close of the letter yet again with the portrait of an all too lowly Lucilius. Look at him as he stretches out his hand for his daily alms (*ad cotidianam stipem manum porrigis*; *EM* 14.17). He's had enough talk about fear earlier in the letter, he just wants the pay-out that has been deferred. But the transition also scolds him in the name of the letter's opening. There the letter talked about our relationship to the body. The narrator even used legal terminology to refine his sense of this relationship: we exercise a custodial capacity relative to it (*gerere tutelam*; *EM* 14.1).

The *tutela* of Seneca has yet to convert Lucilius from a subordinate person into a peer in his own right. And one of the obstacles is a perverse hunger for philosophy as shiny, golden, and precious. After talking about the outstretched hand Seneca continues: 'I will satiate you with a golden gift. And seeing as talk of gold is afoot, here's how the use and enjoyment of it can be the more agreeable to you'.[33] The golden gift is a word about gold which happens to be something akin to one of Epictetus' Golden Sayings. Taking it to heart would allow the beneficiary of Seneca's hand-out to become his own person, to learn to be something other than a filthy beggar and instead to stand forth as a Roman gentleman who knows *usufructus* inside and out and, more importantly, knows that the real uses and the real fruits are abstract and ethical rather than commercial.

But Lucilius is conjured as uninterested in the golden coin itself. He just wants the name of the man who said it. Thus the words, 'He most enjoys riches who least needs them' flow in one ear and out the other if Lucilius' response to them is, 'Tell me who said it'. Seneca says he'll say but then refuses to say: 'Some Epicurean or other' is the answer Seneca provides. He focuses in on a familiar issue instead: 'What difference does it make who said it? He was speaking to everybody.'[34] If you need riches you worry about them. You spend your time trying to increase them. A portrait of the daily economic woes of a Roman gentleman ensues. We hear about *rationes* again, and again they are not a matter of logic and proof and philosophy but instead merely economic. And this economism in and of itself keeps us from appreciating the value of golden philosophical *ratio*. Instead we are too busy heaping up and poring over entries in our fiscal *rationes*. Meanwhile both the man of money and the man of citations loses his own status: he lapses from the condition of a dominus and becomes instead a mere procurator, bogged down in the daily grind and worried about accounting for every penny (*EM* 14.18).

Seneca will not stop badgering Lucilius about this issue. Two letters later he confronts Lucilius again with an aggressive tainted gift that closes the letter, a *pharmakon* of knowledge that the narrator suggests might be more likely to kill than to cure. As Letter 16 closes Seneca says, 'If I know you, from the very beginning you will be looking around wondering about what little gift this letter has brought with it.'[35] The narrator is being teasing, but the same joke made over and over starts to look serious: perhaps all that really matters to Lucilius are the memorable quotes at the end rather than the bodies of the letters.

By now we should also appreciate that the theme of 'appropriation' as inserted into the ends of these letters is a much more durable and regular issue than are the ostensible list of topics of these letters.[36] That is, if the letters have had as their various topics friendship, the fear of death, crowds, old age and so forth, the economic and quasi-legal issue of the status of wisdom as a possession has been consistently with us throughout these miscellaneous discussions.[37]

The shape of an implicitly defined zone of natural law has been emerging in the course of these letters.[38] There is an open space in which true things are held in common. And one ought not to go beyond this space for to do so is to fall into the world of mine-and-yours, names-and-debts – *nomina* means both things, of course – and unbounded desires. One reaches this communal space by freeing oneself from the very desires and appetites that necessitate a law against thievery and laws that govern debts contracted and repaid.[39]

A man lays claim to himself as his own when he finds that the metaphorical golden coins of the philosophical realm will let him buy his freedom. Lucilius is told this in hinting terms over and over again, but the process of ascending to the domain of that higher law is oblique, asymptotic and profoundly literary. In fact Lucilius' desire for wisdom-as-thing means that he remains stuck in the opening dialectical moment while merely fantasizing about the sequel to the same: wisdom is a thing; it is alien; and, ideally, I would like to get my hands on it.

Debt can poison friendship. Letter 19 gives us this grim news in the course of the debt-payment that arrives at its end. In 19.10 Seneca first claims that he does not need to make a payment as this letter ends because he has already furnished a quote in the body of the letter. Nevertheless he imagines a litigious Lucilius who will dispute this point. And so, given such circumstances, Seneca declares he will need to take a loan from Epicurus. A debt is being paid off by means of contracting a new debt, it would seem. The quote concerns friendship: dining without friends is bestial. Seneca's rhetorical expansion of this idea leads him to discuss friends more generally. And in so doing he mentions the problem of rich men who are surrounded by false friends at their tables. Heavy debts turn these companions into enemies. The quotable quote here is: 'The more they owe, the more they hate' (*EM* 19.11).

Given the constant talk about debt in these letters and the constant posturing about the manner in which Lucilius' demands for payment cause Seneca to chafe, we have here an ever stronger warning that friendship – one of the supreme goods in the universe of the letters and for philosophers more generally – is being imperiled by all of this talk about debt and credit, mine and yours. Seneca backs away from this suggestion by instead assuring Lucilius that gifts sensibly given to good people will prevent problems from arising. But in so doing he also reminds Lucilius of the very thing that the letters began with, namely that Lucilius is not really his own man yet, that, specifically he is not yet *mentis suae*. A stickler for property law, Lucilius is clamouring for handouts and payments. And there is a profound primary alienation that leads him to behave this way.

The debt games will not abate until the end of the third book. But we have enough material in front of us to draw some conclusions and then to transition over to an alternative model. One notes throughout that the presentation of credit and debt and obligation is quite muddled. We are not supposed to produce a simple allegorical reading here. Instead the tangle itself is the point: there are all sorts of available metaphors for what is going on, too many of them in fact. And they tend to trip us up. We are getting something on the one hand, but we are also losing something on the other. Credit-and-debt reproduce themselves simultaneously. Infinite longing and boundless debt propel us forward through the letters. But as any given letter ends we still want something more and something different in addition to what had just been given to us. There is a constant desire that some big name with some memorable saying do the hard work for us. Or, rather, we ask them to do a pseudo-work that is all too easy. One only needs to remember and rehearse words rather than to actually do the hard work of living well and so freeing oneself.

Set against this boundary-transgressing jumble of debt metaphors and property disputes is a different, higher law, the law of nature. A substantial number of the uses of the word *lex* in the *Epistulae Morales* are in passages where we are specifically talking about the *lex naturae*, a law that is strongly differentiated from the derisively labelled 'laws of human bondage', the *leges seruitutis humanae* (65.20). The here and now of empirical law is a tangle, and its very confusion is a symptom of our want of freedom and need for self-emancipation. But natural law is something quite different.

The very first time we hear of the *lex naturae* it is in a passage that has been pilfered from another's garden, that is, we see it in one of the quotes that closes the fourth letter. And here the law of nature is specifically defined as a matter of limits (*fines*) themselves.[40] Natural law is a determination that is premised on negation: non-hunger, non-thirst, non-cold is all we need (*EM* 4.10).[41]

Note, however, that natural law is not a question of the universal rights of man. Instead natural law is an inverted double for human law. *Termini* and *fines* play a very strong part in the figuration of natural law. The (owed/obligated) maxim on offer says, 'A poverty adjusted to the law of nature, this is true wealth.'[42] When we finally 'get it', we learn that a lesson in not-having is the thing most worth appropriating. And then we will live in accordance with nature and so have the happiness that we long for.[43] Seneca pays his debt to our greed for golden riches, but even as he smashes the same lesson into us yet again, he knows that we will have trouble hearing it.

We are making headway towards a destination, but we do not in fact 'possess' anything other than the formal idea of philosophy. We love it, long for it, think ourselves owed it, swap it with one another, and engage in any number of activities. But we are all also guilty in the eyes of the law, guilty of yearning to usurp wisdom, to lay hands upon it, to seize it for ourselves and to make it our own without doing so legitimately. And the irony here is that there is nothing to own and nothing to grab. All that wisdom requires of us is that we do the first deed from the first line of the first letter. Lay hold of yourself as the free man that you are and you will have enacted wisdom rather than talked about it and harried another to pay up some sort of imagined verbal debt.

Only an overdetermined set of poetic gestures allows one to make these metaphorical journeys towards wisdom financed via a collection of loans, promissory notes, and outright thefts. The letters are a literary experiment that is supposed to help to transport us towards wisdom. They will also transport us away from one set of metaphors about property and put us in possession of a new collection of metaphors about property. We will rise and break out of the narrow bonds of particularity. But in so rising and in so breaking bonds, we are violating boundaries in multiple senses. Some of this is, obviously, for the good: those boundaries needed violation. But there is a paradox folded into the situation: philosophy knows boundaries and it also enjoins us to violate them. We can only stay within the real *termini* and *fines* after we have violated the old ones.[44] We can only appropriate ourselves for ourselves when we have abandoned our particularity and become part of a communistic cosmic community.

As a legal case study, this makes for a fascinating read. But there is an important caveat: one needs to attend to the spirit of the law rather than its letter. That is, the reader needs to read the whole performance as a rhetorical and literary performance. Anyone who is overly particular about the details of the contract laid out in front of us can be expected to object to its terms. The philosopher will claim that this detractor makes mere trivial objections. But they are the complaints of a sort of person who is very attentive to boundaries in his or her own right. It is just that Seneca is mooting boundaries as otherwise understood. Instead only the philosopher is going to be allowed to say which boundaries are the really real ones and which are the irrelevant ones.

Perhaps the ends justify the means: we are seeking to liberate ourselves, after all. But a resistant reader might look at the legal and ethical question of philosophical self-arrogation and offer a more lawyerly reply. Has law been stolen from itself by philosophical literature?

Or, to use the idiom of McGinn's essay in this volume, has a usurper fished the law itself from the semiotic sea and pretended that it was just one of the things in there that are 'common to all'? And, in accordance with the angling angler's self-serving interests, he presently claims that the law is his to dispose of as he see fits in the present circumstances despite other, competing (legal) claims as well as objections that a law-fish is not quite like all the other fish? In any case, does the alleged recompense of a higher law, a natural law, justify this act of appropriation? And is the higher law really just the lower law relabelled and then put on sale at an exorbitant price? Perhaps we should ask someone other than a philosopher to be the judge in such a case.

Let us return to the dialectical issue flagged at the opening. First, law was never as fixed as pretended. Nor was it autonomous. Nor was it necessarily binding. Law has always needed interpretation, even if one were simply to confine the interpretation to self-declared monopolists over interpretation, namely the jurisconsults. Further, the law has always borrowed at least some of its authority from domains like religion and ritual. And law has always been the object of evasions, work-arounds and rewrites in concrete practice.

The free appropriation of the law, of course, is itself constrained. Not everyone gets to interpret. Not everyone gets a hearing when they rewrite the legal system. Some gestures meet resistance and they are received as if they went too far. And so, in practice, only certain authoritative appropriations are efficacious. And the authority underwriting the appropriation of Roman law tends to ground itself by a notional appeal to the law as something fixed, autonomous, and binding.

This at once gives us the socially mediated dialectical synthesis of the question of the subject and the law: the appropriator is not wholly free, he only acts as if he were free. Further, the thing appropriated is not quite what was pretended. And the thoroughly practical quality of Roman law re-emerges here. Usufruct and *usucapio* matter.[45] Using the law changes the law. The law itself has to admit as much the moment it lets itself 'get used'. And we have just seen that the *usucapio* matters not just materially, but so too immaterially. When property law becomes subjected to the law of use-and-possession, it is transformed. It becomes both more abstract and more intimate. This transformation of the law activates a metaphorical pathway that leads both upwards and inwards. 'Mere empirical law' is replaced by a version of the law that is both 'higher' and one that is also 'mine' in as much as I feel in myself owing-*cum*-obligated relative to it. In fact, throughout the letters Seneca will play on the tension between ought and owe in *debere*.[46] Empirical debt is sublimated into moral obligation: *debere* is transformed into *debere*, something it always was, and yet only incompletely so. In the end, the law is not something that one confronts as alien and exterior. Seneca's path of metaphors connects the concrete individual to the abstract ideal. The literary path unfolds the discursive articulation of the law as both discursive and discursively mobile.[47] And we 'owe it to ourselves' to take up the ethical debt of claiming self-possession.

Seneca may at times seem to 'trick the law' and to move along a disparate path from that of a jurist, but the detour is nevertheless the path, the *Umweg* is also the *Weg*.[48] In transferring wisdom about the law to us, Seneca moves along this road and moves us with him. Meanwhile, as Lucilius strives to lay claim to himself, the law becomes both more itself in its abstract universality and loses itself in its concrete particularity: the mere law of things yields to the laws that govern the human condition. And so Seneca's letters perform a law-and-literature thesis that stages the discursive articulation of a 'free' philosophical subject who emerges in the process/*procès* of putting his own relationship to property law on trial.

Notes

1 Hegel (1942) §57.
2 Do not trust this thesis: the law's foundation is a performative gesture of interpretive violence. See Derrida (1992a) 13. Derrida is also offering a critique of 'natural law' and so would set himself athwart the foundation of the philosophy of law that Seneca eventually offers.

3 But does one have a perfectly free choice? 'Les réalités juridique peuvent server de 'modèle', au sens que l'épistémologie donne à ce terme, c'est-à-dire d'analogie aidant à se représenter et à penser une réalité pour laquelle on manque d'instruments d'investigation propres.' (Armisen-Marchetti (1989) 232.) 'La métaphore est d'abord un moyen de corriger l'*inopia linguae*, en complétant les insuffisances du lexique par le biais de catachrèses.' (Armisen-Marchetti (1989) 24).
4 See Derrida (2018) 46 on the conjoint origins of both literature and law at the site of a non-event.
5 See the sixth chapter of Riggsby (2010) on legal education and social status.
6 Compare Aulus Gellius, *NA* 20.1 which attempts to legitimate legal hermeneutics (in the eyes of the bibliomaniacal). See Gunderson (2009) 79–84.
7 See Quintilian, *Inst.* 12.3 – i.e., the peroration to the whole work – where Quintilian has to plead with his readers to bother to learn the laws of Rome.
8 In his *De Legibus* one of Cicero's very first agenda items is to draw a hard line between the traditional Roman study of law and his own 'philosophical' approach to it. See *Leg.* 1.14 and Dyck (2004) 4.
9 See Quintilian, *Inst.* 7.4.4.
10 Nevertheless see again Derrida (2018): the conditions of the law and of literature are one and the same (Derrida (2018) 35). So Quintilian's 'abuse' in fact touches upon something about 'the law proper'. The same will be true of Seneca. See also the Introduction to this volume for further reflections about 'law and literature' more generally, including Derridean ones.
11 Compare Cover (1995) 95–6: 'No set of legal institutions or prescriptions exists apart from the narratives that locate it and give it meaning.'
12 See all of the talk about 'my rights' on Plautus' stage. In multiple scenes across a number of plays characters show how 'seizing what's mine' is, effectively, at the heart of their legal thinking. In the phrase *ius meum*, the word that really matters is *meum*. See Gunderson (2015a) 91, which owes a great deal to Batstone (2009). For more on Plautus, see also McGinn (in this volume).
13 Buckland and Stein (2007) 120–2: *trinoctium abesse*.
14 Buckland and Stein (2007) 73.
15 The *uindicatio* ceremony can be compared to Austin's account of the wedding as his *locus classicus* of a 'performative utterance'. See Austin (1976). But see again Derrida (1992a) and compare the remarks of Derrida (1988) on Austin.
16 *Lewis and Short sv vindicare*: 'A: To lay claim to as one's own, to make a claim upon, to demand, claim, arrogate, assume, appropriate a thing'; 'B: To place a thing in a free condition.' Maruotti (2019) notes a disjunction between Seneca's philosophical project and the master-student template of much philosophical education. And this disjunction is present even here at the very start.
17 Throughout I am ploughing under important narratological questions: Seneca the man can and should be distinguished from The Letter Writer, i.e., the character who

is addressing Lucilius-and-us. See the warnings against this conflation at Wildberger (2014) 431–2. Compare Schönegg (1999) 160–1.
18 Edwards (2009) explores *uindica te tibi* and 'self-possession' in detail. She includes the remark, 'Seneca's deployment of legal metaphors such as *sui iuris* suggest we also need to look at his discussion of *libertas* in a more specifically Roman context.' (Edwards (2009) 154). Here one could emphasize that this is a 'Roman legal context'.
19 Readers who linger long enough with the *Moral Letters* will discover that this beginning really was just a beginning. In *Letter* 34 we completely invert the opening lines of the first letter. At the end of the third book the narrator says, 'I claim you for myself. You are my handiwork' (*EM* 34.2: *Adsero te mihi; meum opus es*). The man who was asked to appropriate himself as a full free subject has been converted into a mere piece of property, a produced product, signed by the hand of the master and also asserted to be his by right of law. Throughout the letters, then, legal fictions are revised, extended and expanded. 'En effet, avec la fin du troisième livre, le premier niveau de la formation de Lucilius est terminé, comme Sénèque le remarque dans la lettre 34.' (Maruotti (2019)).
20 Do note Inwood's crucial observation that Seneca is a Roman philosopher and not a Greek one and that '[Seneca] prefers to work his ideas out in Latin terms, because that is the language he thinks in.' (Inwood (2005) 21).
21 *EM* 1.2: *si hodierno manum inieceris*. Lewis and Short sv *injectio*: 'II A laying on: *manus*, a laying on of the hand, an act by which one takes possession of a thing belonging to him without a judicial decision.'
22 *EM* 1.3: *Omnia, Lucili, aliena sunt, tempus tantum nostrum est; in huius rei unius fugacis ac lubricae possessionem natura nos misit.*
23 The 'Spruchepilog' is a notable feature of the early letters. It is something that fades after the first three books. See Hachmann (1995) 13 and 220.
24 Schiesaro (2015) 241: 'While almost all of the twenty-nine letters in Books I to III quote Epicurus regularly, in *Ep.* 30 to 97 he is mentioned much less frequently (eleven times in total), while neither quotations nor even his name appear from Letter 98 to the end.'
25 The ostentatious (mis)appropriation is part of a broader strategy of transforming Epicurean thought and so symptomatic of Senecan *usus* more generally. 'In privileging Epicurus' teachings on ethics while silencing or criticizing his physics, Seneca tames the disruptive potential of [Epicurus'] doctrine' (Schiesaro (2015) 240). Epicurus is disappropriated from himself even as we talk about 'borrowing' from him. 'Die meisten Zitate dienen, wie es auch bei den Dicta der Fall ist, der Stützung und Bestätigung von Senecas eigener Lehrmeinung' (Hachmann (1995) 222). Compare Wildberger (2014) 440.
26 *EM* 8.7: *Id non de meo fiet: adhuc Epicurum compilamus*

27 *EM* 8.8: *Potest fieri ut me interroges quare ab Epicuro tam multa bene dicta referam potius quam nostrorum*
28 Compare Gunderson (2015b) 40–1.
29 See also Goldshmidt's remarks about literary appropriation and plagiarism in this volume.
30 *EM* 12.10: *Quod uerum est meum est; perseuerabo Epicurum tibi ingerere, ut isti qui in uerba iurant nec quid dicatur aestimant, sed a quo, sciant quae optima sunt esse communia. Vale.* Compare the imperiousness of Hegelian Spirit relative to property: 'A person has as his substantive end the right of putting his will into any and every thing and thereby making it his, because it has no such end in itself and derives its destiny and soul from his will. This is the absolute right of appropriation which man has over all "things"' (Hegel (1942) §44).
31 Henderson (2004) 27: 'To repeat, for Book 1 + for what follows. One last time, for now: what counts is *"what* is said, not *who* said it" (12.11).'
32 The whole rhetorical performance of indifference to concrete economic law is of itself an enactment of symbolic privilege. And, it should be stressed, the symbolic capital accrued at such a moment is always itself connected to structures of economic domination. See Bourdieu (1990) 119.
33 *EM* 14.17: *Aurea te stipe implebo, et quia facta est auri mentio, accipe quemadmodum usus fructusque eius tibi esse gratior possit.*
34 *EM* 14.18: *Et quid interest quis dixerit? omnibus dixit.*
35 *EM* 16.7: *Iam ab initio, si te bene noui, circumspicies quid haec epistula munusculi adtulerit*
36 Nevertheless, as is widely appreciated, the letters of the first book do consist of a cycle. See Richardson-Hay, 2006 which is participating in while also updating a mode of reading that goes back to Maurach (1970). Note that for Maurach letter-cycles do not tidily overlap with book endings.
37 Richardson-Hay (2006) 43: 'letter endings are where we find the unity of Book 1.'
38 Inwood (2005) 226: 'We will find, as we consider Seneca's conceptions of natural law … that natural law in Seneca's works invokes a variety of different associations. And the only way to sort through this variety is to get down to particular applications.' One will note that Inwood's examples from the *Epistulae Morales* are drawn from later in the work: letters 45, 65, 70, 98, 101, and 117.
39 This posture is adopted, I presume, in full awareness of the whole discourse of literary *furtum* that Goldschmidt describes in this volume.
40 It is merely hypothetical, but note the structure of *EM* 16.5: *siue nos inexorabili lege fata constringunt* 'whether fate binds us by an inexorable law'. Similar is *EM* 117.19: *an et haec quae fortuita dicuntur certa lege constricta sint* 'and whether even these events which we call fortuitous are bound by strict law'. See also the 'boundedness' issue in *EM* 40.8: *Vix oratori permiserim talem dicendi uelocitatem inreuocabilem ac*

sine lege uadentem 'I would barely allow an orator such an irrevocable speed of speaking, which proceeds without a law.'

41 The next use of the phase 'law of nature' in 25.4 has a nearly identical context: *Ad legem naturae reuertamur; diuitiae paratae sunt. Aut gratuitum est quo egemus, aut uile: panem et aquam natura desiderat.* 'Let us return to the law of nature; riches are ready and waiting. What we need is either free or cheap: nature wants only bread and water.'

42 *EM* 27.9: 'But take what I owe you and then farewell: "Wealth is a poverty adjusted to the law of nature"' (*'Sed accipe iam quod debeo et uale. 'Diuitiae sunt ad legem naturae composita paupertas.'*)

43 Living according to natural law is, in effect, a stronger way of articulating the end of living in accordance with nature (*EM* 45.9) See the eighth chapter of Inwood (2005) on the interplay between 'law of nature' and 'law of life' in Seneca.

44 See Früh (2015) on poverty, paradox and philosophical progress in the *Epistulae Morales*. Her piece is in oblique contact with the current one with its investment in disappropriation, dialectics and philosophical movement.

45 Buckland and Stein (2007) 269: '*Usufructus* was the right to enjoy the property of another and to take the fruits, but not to destroy it, or fundamentally alter its character.' Buckland and Stein (2007) 241: '*Usucapio* was acquisition of dominium by possession for a certain time.'

46 In *Epistulae Morales* 81.26 concrete and moral debt-and-obligation are forced together strongly.

47 See the third chapter of Sjöblad (2015) on the interplay between the metaphors of *iter uitae* and *iter ad sapientiam* in the *Epistulae Morales*.

48 On tricking the law see Derrida (2018) 70–1. On the (de)tour, see Derrida (1987) 354.

Part Four

Literature and Justice

12

Law in Disguise in the *Metamorphoses*: The Ambiguous *Ecphraseis* of Minerva and Arachne

Stella Alekou

Introduction

Ancient legal and literary texts are inescapably bound to historical developments and may generate, if studied in parallel, new meanings of legal concepts as well as offer alternative approaches to well-established interpretations of Latin literature. The fluidity of the boundaries between Roman law and Latin literature is particularly evident in Ovid's poetry, a *corpus* which is pervaded by legal vocabulary. What distinguishes Ovid's literary appropriation of legal concepts from that of other Roman poets is his professional participation in the administration of the law, which seems to have significantly marked his poetical creations with legal nuances.[1] Ovid studied rhetoric and law as part of his formal education, under Arellius Fuscus and Porcius Latro, and embarked upon a career that largely involved legal training, to serve on the board of the judicial panel of *tresuiri capitales*.[2] Notwithstanding the poet's expressed choice in his *Tristia* to abandon his legal career and to follow the creative path of poetry (4.10.17–20),[3] his practical experience of legal matters appears to be attested in his literary treatment of the Graeco-Roman myth, suggesting that Ovid's legal thought never stopped being present in his poetical creations.

At a time of significant legal reforms, which included Augustus' moral legislation, with all the turbulence it caused,[4] Ovid writes poetry to revisit myths and, as will be shown in the following pages, to discuss the power of art as a tool of resistance, often by placing women in the role of the art-maker. Interestingly, even though scholars seem to agree that Ovidian poetry often alludes to specific historical accounts,[5] most Ovidian scholars choose not to focus on the role women play in Ovid's creative reflection of Roman history, in which law appears as a cornerstone. As argued in this chapter, the study of Ovid's women within a legal context is crucial for our understanding of the poet's legal mind as well as for our understanding of the role women were expected to play in Roman law and society. As I will demonstrate, the re-examination of the *femina ovidiana* through a legal lens may suggest that Ovid's literary exploration of women's myths (and myths on women) acts as a veiled critique of Roman law.

The *ecphrasis* of Arachne and Minerva in the *Metamorphoses* is an excellent case in point,[6] because it concerns a female storytelling which is rife with courtroom rhetoric. The double ecphrastic interlude explores two contrasting attitudes towards law, by further reflecting the spider's double nature already attested in Homer, that of the peaceful artist and of the dangerous animal.[7] This double perspective forms the foundation of my chapter's argumentation, which unwinds across two readings of the episode in question: Sections 1–3 focus on the legal vocabulary employed in the description of the weaving competition – namely vocabulary that also bears legal meanings and is attested in legal texts – to disclose the ambiguous employment and the potentially conflictual perspectives of law. Sections 4–6 address the ambivalent resolution of the ecphrastic 'trial' within the perspective of the Augustan legal landscape. Placed against the poet's era, the episode is examined as a court-like spectacle through a historical reading of the Ovidian myth. This study will eventually show that the spider's conflictual duality participates in Ovid's mythographical spectacle as an ecphrastic platform for legal criticism, to serve a specific agenda: to expose the elusive ambiguities of the law.

1

The legal vocabulary in the 'Arachne and Minerva' episode transforms the *ecphrasis* into a *lis*, a legal action.[8] The narrative itself encourages a legal reading of the text, as it does not only concern the story of a talented weaver (*non illa loco nec origine gentis / clara, sed arte fuit*, 'Neither for place of birth nor birth itself had the girl fame, but only for her skill' 7–8),[9] but also that of a competition between the goddess of weaving and a mortal transgressor, boastful enough to refuse that Minerva taught her 'the art' (*scires a Pallade doctam* 'you could know that Pallas had taught her' 23). As the narrator informs us at the very beginning of the episode, Arachne's skills were so graceful that despite her unprivileged background, her reputation was spread throughout the Lydian towns: the nymphs would leave their own vineyards, and the water-nymphs would leave their waters, for the pleasure not only to see her finished work but to watch her as she worked (14–18). The talented weaver's reputation intrigues Minerva, who first appears to the young girl as an old wise lady to provide advice (*Pallas anum simulat* 'Then Pallas assumed the form of an old woman' 26), but as soon as the competition is completed, she ends up tearing Arachne's tapestry and hitting her with a shuttle:

> doluit successu flaua uirago
> et rupit pictas, caelestia crimina, uestes,
> utque Cytoriaco radium de monte tenebat,
> ter quater Idmoniae frontem percussit Arachnes.
>
> The golden-haired goddess was indignant at her success, and rent the embroidered web with its heavenly crimes; and, as she held a shuttle of Cytorian boxwood, thrice and again she struck Idmonian Arachne's head.
>
> *Met.* 6. 130–3

The episode gradually takes on the qualities of a commentary on the ambivalent meanings of 'crime' and 'punishment': The mortal woman's attempt to end her life (134–5) proves to be an unsuccessful one, as in her final appearance Minerva as *dea ex machina* (135) transforms the unfortunate creature into a spider (*de quo tamen illa remittit / stamen et antiquas exercet aranea telas.* 'Still from this she ever spins a thread; and now, as a spider, she exercises her old-time weaver-art' 144–5). This twist invites the reader to further examine the legal ambiguities of suicide and *clementia*, in a narrative that is evocative of language (also) used in court.

The very opening of the narrative, marked by terms such as *iustam* (2) and *poena* (4), situates the story within the context of juridical literature,[10] while the narrator's descriptive wording in his presentation of the goddess' disguised appearance and the mortal woman's reaction, namely *Non cedere* (6) and *offensa magistra* (24), translates Arachne's refusal to 'withdraw her action' (*cedere actione lite*),[11] and foreshadows her conviction:

> PRAEBVERAT dictis Tritonia talibus aures
> carminaque Aonidum iustamque probauerat iram;
> tum secum: 'laudare parum est, laudemur et ipsae
> numina nec sperni sine poena nostra sinamus.'
> Maeoniaque animum fatis intendit Arachnes,
> quam sibi lanificae non cedere laudibus artis
> audierat.

TRITONIA had listened to this tale, and had approved of the muses' song and their just resentment. And then to herself she said: 'To praise is not enough; let me be praised myself and not allow my divinity to be scouted without punishment.' So saying, she turned her mind to the fate of Maeonian Arachne, who she had heard would not yield to her the palm in the art of spinning and weaving wool.

Met. 6.1–7

quod tamen ipsa negat tantaque offensa magistra
'certet' ait 'mecum: nihil est, quod uicta recusem!'

Yet she denied it, and, offended at the suggestions of a teacher ever so great, she said: 'Let her but strive with me; and if I lose there is nothing which I would not forfeit.'

Met. 6.24–5

An offence (*offensa*) committed against the master was punishable, and Minerva was after all, unlike Arachne, a *magistra*.[12] *Magister* may be interpreted as 'teacher', and as noted in Berger, teachers 'enjoyed exemption from certain public charges'.[13] The term's etymological roots additionally allude to the Roman magisterial power, based on two fundamental conceptions, *imperium* and *potestas*, that non-citizens were not eligible for,[14] and Arachne was a non-citizen – in fact, Arachne's origins are particularly accentuated in the Ovidian narrative.[15] Furthermore, two verbs, *certet* and *recusem* (25) act as a supporting vehicle for the heroines' legal investment. *Certo*, also attested in legal texts, particularly of judicial disputations, *to contend at law*,[16] reveals the nature of the debate as a *certamen* which turns readers into judges, in the way the Euripidean *agon*, a verbal and distinctly judicial conflict between two main contestants, occasionally included a third party, a judge, influenced by real court debates.[17] The alliteration of 'c' at line 25 is emphasized by the strong position of the terms *certet*, at the beginning of the verse, and *recusem*, at the very end of the same verse, that engages the reader in a *recusatio* which is not limited to the literal 'rejection' of epic poetry on aesthetic grounds.[18] In juridical language, *recusare* means to object, plead in defence.[19] *Recusatio* additionally alludes to the *recusatio imperii*, the strategy employed by Augustus for establishing his sovereignty,[20] whereas the use of the term may also point to the poets' refusal to participate in Roman imperialism, a refusal that is a potent device which is informed by acts of denial performed as political art by the emperor himself.[21] These are the terms in which the competition is introduced, a competition that is foreshadowed to bear many interpretative layers as both a *certamen* and a *recusatio*.

2

The description of the competition places Minerva's tapestry first in a court-like spectacle in which six judging gods stand on each side of Jupiter and the disputants on opposite sides (*bis sex caelestes medio Ioue sedibus altis / augusta grauitate sedent* 'There sit twelve heavenly gods on lofty thrones in august majesty, Jove in their midst' 72–3). The legal verisimilitude is misleading in Minerva's work, as the scene alludes to a pre-existing contest depicted in Phidias' sculptural work; this is where Athena and Poseidon appear in the centre, separated by the olive tree, namely the goddess' signature.[22] As a reprise, a *mise en scène*, the staged trial is, in fact, a *simulatio*, and may reveal the very nature of literary narrative: the Ovidian work, as a poetic construction and therefore a form of art, may be seen as an act of *simulatio* because it imitates reality, the process of simulation being 'the primary means by which one can gain any type of subjective knowledge from a literary narrative'.[23] A second layer of simulation emerges to further invalidate Minerva's testimony, as the value of the first simulation, that of the tapestry itself as a work of art that reflects 'reality', is enriched by another one that concerns Minerva's disguise. The term *simulat* marks Minerva's first appearance as an old lady (26) and is echoed at line 80, to seal her calculated presentation, as a peaceful weaver:

> Pallas anum simulat: falsosque in tempora canos
> addit et infirmos, baculo quos sustinet, artus.
> Then Pallas presents herself an old woman, put false locks of grey upon her head,
> took a staff in her hand to sustain her tottering limbs,
>
> *Met.* 6.26–7

> percussamque sua simulat de cuspide terram
> edere cum bacis fetum canentis oliuae
> and she represents the earth, smitten by her spear's point, bringing forth the
> pale-green olive-tree hanging thick with fruit
>
> *Met.* 6.80–1

Specific key terms suggest the falsity of Minerva's transformation: *falsum*, that which in reality does not exist, and is only asserted as true,[24] includes, in the field of penal law, any kind of forgery.[25] In a paronomasia of some sort, the use of the term *mentis* ('*mentis inops longaque uenis confecta senecta, / et nimium uixisse diu nocet*'. 'Doting in mind, you come to me and spent with old age; and it is too long a life that is your bane' 37–8), which principally illustrates the mind,[26] calls attention to the actual nature of deception, as *mentior* would sketch the act of asserting falsely, thus deceiving.[27] The use of the term *simulat* by the Ovidian narrator twice with regard to only one of the two disputants is of significance. *Simulare*, which means 'to pretend', is also used in legal texts to describe simulated acts, which were not valid: 'more valid is what is being done than what is being expressed in simulated terms'.[28] What matters is the 'truth of the matter' (*ueritas rei*) and not what had been feigned in a written deed.[29] We are thus to assume that Minerva's testimony was not legally valid because she chose to deliver it in disguise.

The performative nature of Minerva's appearance as well as the ecphrastic arrangement of characters and scenes, expressed in legal terminology, embodies the qualities of theatre in the law-court, in which orators instead of actors used techniques or performance to manipulate their audience and to elicit specific emotional reactions.[30] That oratorical performance abides by the same rules of the theatrical performance has already been demonstrated by scholars.[31] However, while Minerva employs rhetorical strategies in order to persuade her opponent to withdraw and admit defeat, in a rhetorical triangulation of some sort, the audience is asked to decode her strategic means of deception and to question the legal validity of her arguments.[32]

3

Law in disguise is exposed in Arachne's tapestry, which acts as a response to the Minervan *simulatio*. As opposed to the goddess' orderly and classical work, this is a visually charged martial field in which gods attack, abduct and rape mortal women *incognito*.[33] The contradictory nature of the subject that the *ecphrasis* narrates becomes evident from the beginning of the description: a pair of antithetical concepts, that of illusion and of reality (*uera putares* 104), introduces an invoked measure of artistic value, suggested in the illustration of the *elusa Europa* (103–4) and of the *uerus taurus* (104):[34]

> Maeonis elusam designat imagine tauri
> Europam: uerum taurum, freta uera putares;
> ipsa uidebatur terras spectare relictas
>
> Arachne pictures Europa cheated by the disguise of the bull: a real bull and real waves you would think them. The maid seems to be looking back upon the land she has left
>
> *Met.* 6.103–5

This mélange, employed in the literary text, may translate the narrator's allusion to legal matters and poetic imagery. In fact, the introduction of Arachne's tapestry emerges as a programmatic disclaimer, pointing to a testimony delivered in court that touches on its truthfulness, already attested in Hesiod's *Works and Days*, a work in which the poet attempts to settle his dispute with his brother Perses out of court.[35] What is interesting in the punning fashion in which the *ecphrasis* is introduced is the fact that, instead of Hesiod's invocation of Zeus to straighten verdicts with justice,[36] the Ovidian Zeus appears in the form of a bull (104). This is a subversive twist that may refer to the Roman laws on an animal's aggressive behaviour, according to which, if the use of an instinctive self-defence mechanism is consistent with the animal's nature, no one is to be held liable for the damage. As a matter of fact, as Roman law developed, owners were held liable only in the event that the animal had acted 'contrary to its nature'.[37] Zeus as a bull would have not acted contrary to his nature, had the bull not been unreal, but it was, both because it was actually Zeus who appeared transformed into a bull and because the image of the bull constitutes an artistic representation embedded in a fictional narrative. It seems therefore worth examining whether underneath the Arachnean veil lies 'the truth of the matter', one that may unmask the immorality of staged justice.

The legal reading of this passage is further encouraged through a comparison with Ovid's account of the myth of Europa in Books 2 and 3.[38] While Europa gazes backward (*ipsa uidebatur terras spectare relictas* 'The maid seems to be looking back upon the land she has left', 105), the reader looks back on Ovid's textual field which was perhaps to be seen, as implied in the use of the term *simulatio*, as 'feigned in a written deed', whereas the truth of the matter would lie in Arachne's 'oral-like' tale.[39] If the mortal woman's illustrations revealed 'the truth of the matter' with regard to previously narrated stories, the negatively painted transformations and their intent, characterized in Book 6 as *caelestia crimina* ('divine crimes', 72), add a legal layer to the mythological accounts in question. It is notable that, as opposed to the Minervan narrative, which mainly treats myths that are not explicitly addressed in the *Metamorphoses*, the stories employed in Arachne's work had already been explored by Ovid in that same *epos*. It seems thus reasonable to examine whether the Arachnean and Ovidian tapestries coincide in the way, perhaps, 'allusion' interferes with reality as 'illusion' does, or better yet, in the way performative law interacts with poetic imagery.

The heroine explores the blurry boundaries between literary text and legal context, by playfully redefining art as a legal weapon. The ring composition between *antiquam litem* (71), that introduces Minerva's tapestry, and *antiquas telas* (145), which comments on Arachne's transformation, may confirm the hypothesis that the spider's web acts as a *lis*, a lawsuit, an action or process at law:[40]

> Cecropia Pallas scopulum Mauortis in arce
> pingit et antiquam de terrae nomine litem.
>
> Pallas pictures the hills of Mars on the citadel of Cecrops and that old dispute over the naming of the land.
>
> Met. 6.70-1

> cetera uenter habet, de quo tamen illa remittit
> stamen et antiquas exercet aranea telas.
>
> Still from this she ever spins a thread; and now, as a spider, she exerises her old-time weaver-art.
>
> Met. 6.144-5

The association between the legal value of *lis* and the military interpretation of *tela*, a web, acoustically alluding to *telum*, a weapon, employed for fighting at a distance,[41] further reveals the potentially aggressive character of law illustrated through art. More importantly, the acoustical similarity between the terms in question may suggest that Arachne's legally empowered story introduces the Ovidian reader to a new era, in which the art of narrative in the *Metamorphoses* becomes a legal tool of resistance. This shift is not the result of an abrupt change of perspectives in Ovid's *epos* and in the episode in question. Despite the common view that Arachne's tapestry is asymmetrical and unfinished,[42] the arrangement of the gods' transformations (103-14) reveals a gradual decrescendo from eight (Jupiter's transformations, 103-15) to six (Neptune's transformations, 115-22), then four (Apollo's disguises, 122-4) and, finally, two (Liber's and Saturn's attacks, 125-6). This textual chart suggests that Arachne's *ecphrasis* not only *is* orderly but also completed, as what is to follow (from two to zero) can be interpreted as the end of the passive victimisation of women in Ovid's textual tapestry, confirming the gradual, yet consistent empowerment of the voice of those who once seemed powerless or were muted by authority.

4

The integration of legal vocabulary and legal images in Ovid's treatment of the 'Arachne and Minerva' episode points to the juridical character of Latin literature and is proof that legal discourse is neither culturally nor historically isolated. The mortal woman's refusal to surrender to Minerva's tutelage[43] activates a series of incidents that encourage a historical reading of Ovid's *epos*, in which the literary technique of *ecphrasis* may be explored as a juridical tool by which the heroine reevaluates the multiple shapes and forms of what appears as legal dependence. In the following pages, emphasis will be laid on the presentation of illustrative analogies between the mythological account in question and the Ovidian reader's contemporary history, to show that the gap between speech act theory and the performativity of law is a gap that literature addresses not by acting as a passive recipient of established laws but by claiming its power to subject legal concepts to reassessment.

The Ovidian reader is called to review the illusory nature of Augustus' two-sided legal programme, by also acknowledging the ambiguities of *tutelage*: *tutela* may as well be presented as Minervan 'pedagogy', but is in fact a form of legal authority that concerns the art's legal dependence on official myth-making.[44] While the audience attests to the artist's claim for independence, it is also called to make a judgment on the legality of the punishment to come, one that not only reflects on the conflictual interaction between Minerva and Arachne, but further extends to that between Augustus and, among others, Ovid who is to be exiled, in light of Augustus' social legislation reforms and the provocative nature of the poet's work.[45] More specifically, the employment of the word *oliuae* (81) and *oleis* (101) may be interpreted as an allusion to Augustus' *pax Romana*, also treated in Book 15:[46]

> percussamque sua simulat de cuspide terram
> edere cum bacis fetum canentis oliuae

> and from the earth smitten by her spear's point upsprings a pale-green olive-tree hanging thick with fruit
>
> *Met.* 6.80–1

> circuit extremas oleis pacalibus oras
> (is modus est) operisque sua facit arbore finem.

> The goddess then wove around her work a border of peaceful olive-wreath. This was the end; and so, with her own tree, her task was done.
>
> *Met.* 6.101–2

> Pace data terris animum ad ciuilia uertet
> iura suum legesque feret iustissimus auctor
> exemploque suo mores reget inque futuri

temporis aetatem uenturorumque nepotum
prospiciens prolem sancta de coniuge natam
ferre simul nomenque suum curasque iubebit

When peace has been bestowed upon all lands he shall turn his mind to the rights of citizens, and as a most righteous jurist promote the laws. By his own good example shall he direct to future time and coming generations, he shall bid the son, born of his chaste wife, to bear his name and the burden of his cares.

Met. 15.832–7

Augustus' programme on universal peace and the laws on marriage, discussed in the final book of the *Metamorphoses*, in the passage cited above, resembles the emperor's *Res Gestae* (Augustus, *Res Gestae* 8.5).[47] However, it is not only Augustus' legal programme that seems to be presented as two-sided. The proximity between the terms *simulat* (80) and *oliuae* (81), the peaceful olive leaves, confirms that Minerva's initial appearance as a wise and kind old woman, as opposed to her authoritarian one that follows, is a simulated one. After all, the Ovidian audience might in fact recall that Minerva is previously portrayed as a Roman patron-figure with respect to the Muses (5.269 ff.) and thus endowed with a Roman sort of *auctoritas*, and is to confirm, by the end of the 'Arachne and Minerva' episode, that passion, whether jealousy or vengeance, is what initiates and guides the goddess' actions. As the Ovidian readers move forward (and backward) in the *epos* to filter, revisit and review both the 'Arachne and Minerva' myth and the Ovidian and Augustan reality on peace, love and law, they are also asked to identify the ambiguous causes of divine *ira* and its consequences, in book 15 (*Iouis ira*, 'the wrath of Jove', 871) as well as in book 6 (*doluit successu flaua uirago* 'The golden-haired goddess was indignant at her success', 130). The Arachnean depiction of the rulers' behaviour as contrary to the principles they themselves promulgate suggests that law is *not* a mind without desire, as defined in Aristotle, *Politics* 3.11.4. Passion might as well be a regression to the primitive rules of the *lex talionis*, as subjective emotions undermine the rationality of the law,[48] however, as Ziogas puts it, '[t]he legal system does not replace passions with reason, but creates an elaborate apparatus that conceals the very source of justice, which is none other than the will of the legislator [...]. [O]nce we strip law of all layers of referentiality, we are left with the arbitrary choices of the legislator or the will of a god. [L]aw is the division of passions into legitimate and illegitimate'.[49]

What is provocative in Arachne's tapestry is not the 'perfect illusion' it creates as a flawless artefact (129–30), but its realism, one that is perceived as offensive to the 'legislator' and is judged, for this reason, illegitimate – the term *Liuor* (129) is crucial particularly in this context for its moral and political nuances:

> Non illud Pallas, non illud carpere Liuor
> possit opus: doluit successu flaua uirago
> et rupit pictas, caelestia crimina, uestes
>
> Not Pallas, nor Envy himself, could find a flaw in that work. The golden-haired goddess was indignant at her success, and rent the embroidered web with its heavenly crimes
>
> *Met.* 6.129–31

The term *liuor* appears in *Amores* 1.15 in the context of poetic immortality as a self-defence against *Liuor edax* (1.15.1ff.) and associated with the standards of social morality (1–6), whereas in *Remedia amoris* (316–98) it is employed within the province of literary criticism.[50] *Liuor* then reappears in Ovid's *Tristia* 4.10.123. The use of this poetic convention, namely the reference to the power of poetry to survive, while Ovid is banished from Rome and suffers an exilic death, acquires a new meaning: By alluding to earlier works in his exile poetry, Ovid shows that his poetic power surpasses that of the emperor's by which he banished him, as he continues to be read. An additional, clearly political meaning is added in the employment of the term in *Ex Ponto* 4.16, when Ovid exhorts *Liuor* to stop the cruelty against the exiled poet, the persecuted artist, showing, just like in Arachne's case, whose work reaches the Callimachean standards of perfection (*Epigr.* 21.4), that literary criticism and moralism may, in fact, be indistinguishable. As stated by Barchiesi in *The Poet and the Prince*, '[a]rtistic rivalry and repressive power seem to be inseparable here'.[51]

5

Art and power appear as interwoven in Arachne's account. The young woman's tapestry grows to become a dramatized visualization of rape, redefined, from 'legitimate passion' to 'crime' (131: *caelestia crimina*). Her *ecphrasis* acts as a drama which, although conveyed by the written word, is acted by the figures which are represented and can therefore be seen as a dramatic script as well as 'a miniature drama', an outcropping of the dramatic impulse.[52] However, endorsed with legal vocabulary, the Arachnean drama of repeated illustrations of rape, presented as divine crimes,[53] eventually takes the form of a commentary on the legal implications of 'passion'. Even though, according to the legal sources, charges of seduction, attempted seduction, adultery, abduction and ravishment covered rape, scholars state clearly that there were no legal charges exclusively for rape.[54] However, the series of laws that the authorities passed in the Augustan period affected women significantly: As stated in scholarship on gender and law, 'originally, rape was indictable because "the rapist had committed *stuprum* or *adulterium*"'[55] with the woman, and the victim herself was deemed to have committed adultery with the rapist due to her suspected consent. As noted by scholars, a claim of consent could be a defence of rape, but this defence lost its strength after the enactments of the Augustan laws,[56] a shift that seems to act as the foundation of Arachne's argument, as suggested in her focus on deception in the description of divine disguise (103-28). Arachne's tapestry acts, thus, as an indictment. Her artefact brings charges against the Olympian gods and exposes the hypocrisy of Minerva, a virgin goddess and staunch supporter of patriarchal violence against women. The emphasis on accusations (*crimina*: 131) confirms the fundamentally juridical character of Arachne's work, as the mortal woman grows to resemble a prosecutor who displays shocking images in a courtroom to highlight heinous crimes.

The mortal woman does not only catch the gods *in flagrante delicto*, but also forces the advocate of virgins to participate as a spectator in a quick-shifting series of scenes in which her father is depicted as the 'arch-rapist'[57] who attacks Mnemosyne, amongst others (*Mnemosynen pastor, uarius Deoida serpens*. 'Mnemosyne, as a shepherd; Deo's daughter, as a spotted snake', 114). The proximity of this particular scene to the sexual assault against Persephone acts as a mnemonic trigger: Persephone's story, previously treated in the *Metamorphoses* (5.533-71), is remembered and narrated as a rape-story in Arachne's tapestry, allusively commenting on the legal relationship between daughter and father. *Tutela* which was not all that different from the relationship between wife and husband (*tutela mulierum perpetua*),[58] assured the perpetual guardianship and control of women, all the while acting both as a safeguard for feminine weakness and a shield from exploitation.[59] The ambivalent and often inappropriate perspectives of *tutela* become part of the Arachnean argument on divine crimes. Arachne's tapestry revisits previously narrated myths not only to rectify the narratives but also to expose what had been violently silenced or intentionally hidden. The reference to Mnemosyne just before Persephone's rape in the Arachnean tapestry alludes to Book V which presents the poetic contest, narrated to Minerva, between the Muses, the divine patronesses of the arts and sciences who are also the daughters of Jupiter and Mnemosyne, and the nine daughters of Pieros, the Emathides (5.294-331). Calliope's song describes the wandering of Demeter, who, while in search of Persephone, is told by Jupiter that their daughter married well (5.523–32). The reference to Mnemosyne before Persephone's rape triggers a memory of what has not been reported, about Demeter and Triptolemus. The story in Calliope's song does not follow the traditional ending, according to which Demeter sent Triptolemus to teach the Greeks the art of growing grain and to bring civilization through its cultivation.[60] The replacement of the traditional ending by a description of Triptolemus' adventures (5.642–78)[61] pleases Minerva, but also reveals the art's patronage, once again (*Praebuerat dictis Tritonia talibus aures / carminaque Aonidum iustamque probauerat iram*; 'Tritonia had listened to this tale, and had approved of the muses' song and their just resentment' 6.1–2).

Similarly in Arachne's account, the tearing of the *uestes* reveals Minerva's attempt to destroy evidence that was judged as offensive and to obliterate the crimes (*et rupit pictas, caelestia crimina, uestes*, 'and rent the embroidered web with its heavenly crimes' 131).[62] Politically informed, Arachne's story mediates on the conditions of the artists' performance and the severe penalties of daring creative expression, censored by tyrannical and often abusive power.[63] The goddess' reaction is not a testament to the artist's defeat but part of the poet's strategically calculated rhetoric; it aims to serve the Arachnean agenda, as it reveals the illegitimate actions taken for the regulation of art and the intellectual suppression, which the mortal artist resists, by attempting to commit suicide (*non tulit infelix laqueoque animosa ligauit / guttura* 'The wretched girl could not endure it, and put a noose about her bold neck' 134–5). Artistic expression in Arachne's case is violently suppressed by the hitting of her forehead with a shuttle, an action that may be viewed as a reflection of the main theme of the mortal woman's tapestry, namely a divine rape (*utque Cytoriaco radium de monte tenebat, / ter quater Idmoniae frontem percussit Arachnes*. 'and as she held a shuttle of Cytorian boxwood, thrice and again she struck Idmonian Arachne's head' 132–3). Does Arachne identify herself with the rape victims and does she punish herself out of shame, in her choice to commit suicide? Is this an act of weakness and, if so, is it a legitimate or an illegitimate one? To answer these questions, we need to examine the ambivalent illustration of suicide in Latin literature, which is undeniably prolific in images of self-killing.

The Roman culture of self-inflicted death is more often than not correlated with status: it indicates an upper-class man's choice for a glorious ending of his life, as an act of political resistance,[64] one that is governed by honour and courage. Could Arachne's attempt to commit suicide fall within such a category, or was this practice exclusively reserved for men? What constitutes a 'good', honourable, virtuous suicide from a 'bad', dishonourable and shameful act leading to self-death in Roman culture is a question that remains to be answered, but the political consequences of the choice of female practitioners – such as the famous Lucretia, as well as Cleopatra, particularly in Horace's *Ode* 1.37, and Pliny's Arria (3.16) – to cause their own death suggest that the discourse expressed through the decision to pre-empt execution and to escape humiliation by committing suicide is a statement of political rebellion, a sort of 'noble death' that may be outlawed, but acts at the same time as a crime without a sanction, in line with modern Anglo-American laws on suicide.[65] If suicide is killing that evades the juridical order then it cannot be included in it. It is thus a declaration of sovereignty and is often viewed, in its stoic conception, as a road to freedom.[66] Be that as it may, Arachne's attempt, whether a rebellious escape from punishment or a virtuous shame,[67] is interrupted.

6

The image of art as a weapon, allusively illustrated in the ring composition already discussed (*antiquam litem*: 71 – *antiquas telas*: 127), eventually takes form in a literary epitaph, as Arachne's woollen noose becomes her sword,[68] a duality to be further echoed in the epitaphic text engraved on Ovid's tomb in his *Tristia* (3.3.74). Within his own epitaphic inscription, that serves the poetic plea for remembrance and acts as a marker of permanence,[69] it is clearly stated that poetic wit has become the cause of the poet's death. This word-play reflects the narrator's description of *telas/tela* at lines 54–5 in the 'Minerva and Arachne episode', with respect to the equal ground on which the two disputants are being judged:

> quosque legat uersus oculo properante uiator,
> grandibus in tumuli marmore caede notis:
> HIC ·EGO · QVI · IACEO · TENERORVM · LVSOR · AMORVM
> INGENIO · PERII · NASO · POETA · MEO
> AT · TIBI · QVI · TRANSIS · NE · SIT · GRAVE · QVISQVIS · AMASTI
> DICERE · NASONIS · MOLLITER · OSSA · CVBENT

and on the marble tomb carve lines for the wayfarer to read with hasty eye, lines in large characters:
I, WHO LIE HERE, WITH TENDER LOVES ONCE PLAYED, NASO, THE BARD, WHOSE LIFE HIS WIT BETRAYED. GRUDGE NOT, O LOVER, AS THOU PASSEST BY, A PRAYER: "SOFT MAY THE BONES OF NASO LIE!".

Tr. 3.3.71–6

> et gracili geminas intendunt stamine telas:
> tela iugo uincta est, stamen secernit harundo
>
> And they stretch the fine warp upon them. The web is bound upon the beam, the reed separates the threads of the warp
>
> Met. 6.54–5

As Wheeler mentions, the word *lis* echoes the original 'dispute' of chaos settled by the demiurge in Ovid's *Met.* 1.21 (*Hanc deus et melior litem natura diremit.* 'God – or kindlier Nature – composed this strife'),[70] and Arachne acts here, even after her transformation, as a demiurge. The epitaphic text is undeniably powerful, as it claims the capacity to transform a poetic plea into a petrified form of expression in which the 'I' is both the author of the main text as well as of the epitaphic composition.[71] Literary death is another form of art, and as expected, art survives the artist. Arachne's quasi-epitaphic inscription of suicide becomes a powerful, public indictment.[72] The goddess' cruel attack on Arachne is not (only) the result of a profound embarrassment nor of shame for being defeated by a mortal. Minerva's transformation of Arachne reveals her refusal to allow the mortal woman to expose publicly the illegitimate actions taken by the *magistra*.

The *lex Iulia de ui* also covered the abuse of public office as a crime committed by magistrates.[73] Abuse of power is particularly, albeit implicitly, evident in Minerva's appearance as *dea ex machina* (*pendentem Pallas miserata leuauit* 'As she hung, Pallas lifted her in pity', 135). The goddess's intervention as she prevents Arachne from committing suicide by transforming her into a spider is ironically presented by the narrator as an act of pity. Clemency, an extra-judicial action, occupies a consistent position in Roman ethics and law as the privilege and power of a single individual. The definition of 'the virtue of a superior to an inferior' derives from *De clementia* (2.3), in which Seneca suggests a number of definitions for a concept that he clearly regards as a complex one.[74] Augustan *clementia* is echoed in many literary works as a legal tool of concealed censorship,[75] the law's attempt to regulate literature, but the paradox is that this very attempt to regulate art highlights the power of literature as art to challenge legal norms and to trigger legal reforms. *Clementia* is important in establishing the sovereignty of the prince, because it signals the suspension of the law (due punishment) in the name of justice. Both suicide and *clementia* are acts that aim to establish one's sovereignty by being excluded from the juridical order.[76] The magisterial *clementia* is what destroys Arachne, as it places her in the position of the person who deserves to be convicted, whereas it forces her to a regulated and censored intellectual expression, doomed to mere repetition (*cetera uenter habet, de quo tamen illa remittit/ stamen et antiquas exercet aranea telas*. 'Still from this she ever spins a thread; and now, as a spider, she exercises her 'old-time weaver-art' 144–5). Arachne incorporates the traits of the poet destroyed by power,[77] perhaps to reflect the ending of the elegiac poet Gallus, who was led to commit suicide and who, according to Ovid, 'could not hold his tongue' (Ovid *Tr.* 2.446), an ending which was forced by the 'merciful' emperor who had presumably wept over his death nonetheless.[78]

Ovid's project of constructing 'his poetic career as a constant pain in Augustus' neck'[79] is foreshadowed as one to follow the same path. The abuse of tyrannical power in Ovid's sentence to come may in fact be prophetically insinuated in the Arachnean quasi-epitaphic illustration of attempted self-death and survival, conditional to restrictions of artistic expression. As in Arachne's case, this kind of *clementia* is ambiguously both a forgiveness and a punishment, driven by emotions and passions that appear as legitimate.[80] The criminalization of adultery (18–17 BCE), which is one of the principle themes in the mortal woman's tapestry, is to lead to Augustus' conviction of Julia in 2 BCE, that appears to be relevant to Ovid's *relegatio*.[81] One may thus justly assume that, in implicitly endorsing criticism on the pretentious nature of Augustan moral conservativism, Ovid seems to be paving the way towards an exile with no return.[82] Scholars are right to note that '[t]here is discernible movement in Ovid's writing, from praise and gentle mockery of Augustus in the *Fasti* to the more naked assaults in the poems from exile', as 'Ovid grew increasingly bitter about the injustice of the harsh punishment that his judge persistently called clemency'.[83] Notwithstanding his obvious bitterness, as Lowrie points out, 'Ovid gets his revenge on Augustus via poetry. The power of representation remains his and Augustus goes down for all time as an emperor who refused clemency to a harmless and entertaining poet'.[84] But how harmless and entertaining is Ovid's poetry?

The criminalization of rape and adultery in Arachne's artistic web alludes to the rearrangement of boundaries between public and private spheres:[85] Prominent in Arachne's revelation of scenes otherwise unseen, it reflects the unprecedented invasion in private life of a series of radical legal measures on marriage[86], an intrusion which Arachne's legal *narratio* (short, clear and plausible, in line with Cicero's definition in *De Inuentione*)[87] may point to. Despite the authorities' effort to protect, control and regulate matters of marriage, the gap between the legislation of the 'iron hand' disciplining or punishing the Senate[88] and the performativity of the laws in question is undeniable. In reality, the Romans continued fully to explore the politics of arranged matrimonial settlements – such is the case of Caesar's marriage arrangements for Julia[89] – based on calculated synergies and in absolute disregard for the *affectio maritalis*.[90] Furthermore, a *simulatio* occurred in cases of contractual relations, that is 'when the parties with mutual understanding concluded a transaction while their intention was to conclude another or none at all', to feign that the legal situation of an imaginary marriage, known as *nuptiae simulatae*, existed which in fact did not exist, 'in order to avoid the disadvantages imposed on unmarried persons by the Augustan legislation on marriages'.[91] Just as this social legislation invaded the private sphere, the Arachnean tapestry intruded into the emperor's concealed life, to disclose his well-known extramarital relationships as well as quite inappropriate parties with politicians dressed up as gods, echoed, perhaps, in the transformations of divinities into animals.[92]

The incriminating evidence is registered, covered with many layers, intratextual and intervisual. Arachne's tapestry is not only a successful stratagem but can also be interpreted as a *flagitatio*, a primitive form of extra-legal self-help whereby a wronged man could, as an alternative to instituting legal proceedings, find the wrong-doer, surround him in a public place and give a loud and abusive account of the crime.[93] If this is the cause of Arachne's punishment, even then, her body is transformed and she is no longer a person, recalling the writ of *habeas corpus*:[94]

> et extemplo tristi medicamine tactae
> defluxere comae, cum quis et naris et aures,
> fitque caput minimum; toto quoque corpore parua est
>
> and forthwith her hair, touched by the poison, fell off, and with it both nose and ears; and the head shrank up; her whole body also was small
>
> Met. 6.140–2

What remains of her exposes the invasive practices of courtroom procedures, an aspect of the law that demonstrates exactly how sovereign power penetrates the subjects' bodies and forms of life.[95] Arachne's quite ambiguous transformation acts as a violent submission to the force of law, the supreme power, but renders her wounded body an indisputable piece of evidence in favour of her legal claims, all the while depriving her of any legal rights, as she is no longer a legal person. The veil of the law in disguise is removed to reveal this disturbingly unquestionable ambiguity in the double nature of the woman-transformed-into-a-spider.

Concluding remarks

The mythological *exemplum* becomes an exemplary case study for Ovid's legal and literary appeal to come. Empowered with a legal voice in the weaving competition, Arachne resembles an 'informer' (*delator*), an *index* giving and *indicium*, who denounces the Olympian gods' sexual crimes and is punished for it.[96] Interestingly, Ovid's courtroom setting has two female contenders in this particular account, even though women were both formally and informally barred from participation in Roman legal institutions, and could not actually bring lawsuits in Augustan Rome.[97] By employing legal language in a narrative about female lives and activities, Ovid's story of Minerva and Arachne not only becomes discursively transgressive; indeed, Arachne's tapestry exposes to public scrutiny private crimes in a way that resonates with Augustus' moral legislation, which made family matters the business of the state by establishing a standing criminal court. However, the female artist serves also to unfold, as an 'inside informer', what is hidden about the public image of the regime. If art becomes the vehicle for women to exit the private sphere by giving voice to legally powerless persons, literature enables the reader to have a glance at what is concealed, about their lives, from the public eye.[98]

Literature proves to be the appropriate form of art both to reflect the injustice of the Augustan legal system and serve as an indictment. By shedding light on the concealment mechanisms of the Augustan propaganda, Arachne raises one important legal question that lies at the heart of this regime: Is the sovereign master subject to the law or does he lie outside it? The Arachnean *exemplum* proves, in a distinctly Ovidian touch, that the sovereign cannot be inscribed in the juridical order, as the extrajuridical actions of punishment-without-trial and clemency suggest. However, even though Arachne-the-artist dies after all, the Ovidian text becomes her own epitaphic registration of dying, one that condenses her defence into a lasting, replicable indictment. Her epitaphic *telae* are not to be prevented from weaving a story to be endured in the *Metamorphoses* by other rebellious women, like Philomela (6.438–619), ideal veils for the poet's criticism of established laws. The literary appropriation of juridical and extrajuridical concepts, such as *crimen* and *clementia*, shows that, inescapably bound to historical developments, the legal matters revisited in the Ovidian 'Minerva and Arachne' account attest to the dynamic character of the law in Latin literature. By stressing the polysemy of legal notions and images, the Ovidian women will have continued to speak in silence – an ecphrastic quality, indeed – of the elusive ambiguities of the law, exposing in its divine foundations its inhumanity.

Notes

1   Ziogas (2021); Alekou (2018); Sabot (1976).

2   Spencer (1996) 13 n. 3; On Ovid's familiarity with Roman law see Versteeg and Barclay (2003) 396. Against this notion, see Gebhardt (2009) 86-8.
3   See Ziogas (2016a) 214.
4   See McGinn (1998) 140-215; Edwards (1993) 34-42; Treggiari (1991).
5   Ahl (1984) 174-208; Curran (1972); Williams (2009) 155.
6   On *ecphrasis* in antiquity see Squire (2015); Graf (1995) 143-55; Boehm and Pfotenhauer (1995); Heffernan (1993).
7   On the spider's double nature see Hom. *Od.* 8.272-81 and 16.33-5 and a discussion in Aeppli (1986) 190-1 and Ballestra-Puech (2006) 25. On the episode's double perspective with focus on cultural and political ambiguities see Alekou (2021).
8   See Gebhardt (2009) 305 ff. who argues that trial-type situations occur repeatedly in Ovid's *epos* and mentions that the creator god is depicted as settling a cosmic *lis* when separating the elements (1.21).
9   For the Latin text and its translation, I follow the Loeb edition, occasionally modified.
10 On *ius*, the Latin word for 'law' or 'right', in Ovid's *Metamorphoses*, see Versteeg and Barclay (2003) 404.
11 This term can also indicate, as *cessio bonorum*, that 'a debtor who became insolvent without his fault might voluntarily surrender his property to the creditors in order to avoid an execution by a compulsory sale thereof which involved infamy': Berger (1953) 387.
12 The wording may be alluding to a mention in Quintilian on both *Minerua* and *magistra*. See Maltby (1991) 385 s.v. Minerva: Quint. *Inst.* 1.4.17.
13 Berger (1953) 570.
14 Berger (1953) 488.
15 Dufallo (2013) 165-70.
16 Cf. Hor. *Sat.* 2.1.49.
17 See Lloyd (1992) on Euripidean *agones*.
18 See the use of the term in Hor. *Sat.* 2.1; Prop. 3.3. See Schmitzer (2013).
19 Cf. Cic. *Caecin.* 28.8; Dig. 17.1.48.
20 See a discussion in Ziogas (2021), particularly chapter 2.
21 Freudenburg (2014).
22 On Ovidian geography with regard to this hypothesis see Vincent (1994) 364-5 and n. 10.
23 On simulation in literary narrative see Stroud (2008) 20.
24 Paul. *Coll.* 8.6.1.
25 The fundamental statute on *falsum* was the *Lex Cornelia de falsis* by Sulla (81 BCE) which was also called the *Lex Cornelia testamentaria* or *nummaria*. See Robinson (1995); Berger (1953) 467.
26 *OLD* s.v. *mens* 1.b. 6.

27 OLD s.v. *mentior*.
28 Berger (1953) 708.
29 See Berger (1953) 708 s.v. *simulare*; G. Pugliese (1938).
30 On theatre in law-court see Papaioannou, Serafim and Da Vela (2017) 1. On the complex relations between legal process and performances see Read (2016) who refers to 'actor lawyers' in discussing the ways in which theatre and law are related.
31 Fantham (1982) and (2002); Papaioannou, Serafim and Da Vela (2017) 2.
32 On triangulation in theatrical justice see Papaioannou, Serafim and Da Vela (2017) 1.
33 On Ovidian rape see Richlin (1992) 158–79; Murgatroyd (2000) 75–92; Murgatroyd (2005); Keramida (2019).
34 On 'the perfect illusion' created at the specific line see Vincent (1994) 374 n. 23. Hardie (2002) 174 refers to Ovid's pictorial illusionism and verbal fictionality in the *Metamorphoses*.
35 Hesiod, *Works and Days* 10. See a discussion in Ziogas (2016b) 32.
36 Hesiod's *Works and Days* is, as a didactic poem, a very important intertext for Ovid's *Art of Love*. On intertextuality between Ovid and Hesiod see Ziogas (2013); Ziogas (2021) 204-26.
37 Versteeg and Barclay (2003) 404; Nicholas (1962). See also Gebhardt (2009) 309 ff., on Ovid's allusion to contemporary discussions on the concept of natural law. Gebhardt refers to the monologues of Myrrha and Byblis, who present an argumentation with appeal to animal behaviour, as justification for their wish for sex with father and brother, respectively.
38 Dufallo (2013) 169 and n. 111: Arachne's tapestry offers various images of Greek maidens who are subjected to lustful gods, with the exception of the Phoenician princess, Europa, but also one man (Admetus).
39 On the orality of Arachne's tapestry see Vincent (1994).
40 OLD s.v. *lis* 1. The term can additionally be employed with regard to a judge who pronounces an unjust sentence, out of favour or through bribery: *L&S* II. b.
41 OLD s.v. *telum* 1 and 2.
42 Anderson (1972) 151–71 and Leach (1974) 102.
43 On *tutela* see Gaius 1.145, 194. On women being subject to *tutela* see Cic. *Mur.* 27. See a discussion in Treggiari (1991) 60–80.
44 On the laws on guardianship see Ng (2008) 681–5.
45 On Ovid's exile see Johnson (2008) 3–21 and 74–95.
46 On the use of olives in this context see Salzman-Mitchell (2005) 131.
47 *Legibus noui[s] m[e auctore l]atis m[ulta e]xempla maiorum exolescentia iam ex nostro [saecul]o red[uxi et ipse] multarum rer[um exe]mpla imitanda pos[teris tradidi.]* 'By new laws passed on my initiative I brought back into use many exemplary practices of our ancestors which were disappearing in our time, and in many ways I myself handed down to later generations many exemplary practices for

them to imitate.' For the translation see Cooley (2009). See a discussion in Ziogas (2021) 308–15.
48 See a discussion in Ziogas (2021), chapter 1.
49 Ibid.
50 Barchiesi (1997) 41.
51 Barchiesi (1997) 42.
52 Kurman (1974) 13. On *ecphrasis* and drama see also Norton (2013) 106.
53 On kidnapping as a crime see Robinson (1995) 32 n. 121 and 33 n. 135 where it is stated that '[t]he man who took away for sexual purposes a female slave who was not a prostitute was liable for theft, unless he concealed her, when he fell under the penalty of the *lex Fabia*.'
54 Nguyen (2006) 76. See also Fantham (1991) 267: Augustus' *lex Iulia de adulteriis coercendis* was, with its *quaestio perpetua*, the first law to subject the extramarital sexual activity of women to public prosecution, an issue which was previously reserved for the family court.
55 Bauman (1993) 558.
56 Nguyen (2006) 98; Gardner (1986) 119.
57 The term is employed by Ziogas (2011) 26.
58 Ziogas (2016b) 38 n. 76: 'Ovid refers to this older form of marriage [marriage *cum manu*], in order to stress that according to Roman law's legal fictions a daughter is indistinguishable from a wife.' See also Gardner (1986) 118: under the *lex Iulia de ui*, a raped *sui iuris* woman could bring a prosecution in criminal court on her own behalf.
59 Nguyen (2006) 78.
60 Matheson (1994).
61 Hinds (1987) 3–50. See also Johnson (2008).
62 Ziogas (2011) 30.
63 See a discussion on the abuse of power in Ovid's time in Syme (1979) 487.
64 On Roman suicide see Hill (2004); Shelton (2013) 28.
65 Manson (1899) 319.
66 Seidler (1983) 434 and n. 20.
67 Van Hooff (1990) 24.
68 Ziogas (2013) 32.
69 Ramsby (2005) 366.
70 Wheeler (1999) 30–2.
71 Ramsby (2005) 365.
72 See Hejduk (2012) 767, who argues that Arachne's words 'carry an unintentionally prophetic second meaning more poignant than "if I lose".' See also Feeney (1991) 193. See Kurman (1974) 6 on prophecy and *ecphrasis*.
73 Berger (1953) 554.

74 Konstan (2005) 339. On *clementia* see Dowling (2006); Tuori (2016a); Könczöl (2008b), 61–9.
75 On Augustan *clementia* see De Lachapelle (2011) 121–70. On clemency in Ovidian poetry see Lowrie (2009a), particularly chapters 11 and 16.
76 On sovereign power in the Roman world see Bexley (in this volume).
77 Harries (1990).
78 Suet. *Aug.* 66. See Ziogas (2013) 34.
79 Casali (2006) 219.
80 On recent scholarship on the recurring motif of art and punishment in the *Metamorphoses* and the fate of Ovid himself see Ziogas (2011) 30, who states (p. 35), this is '[a]n outburst of anger disguised as a touch of pity'. Also see Ziogas (2013) 35 and Ahl (1984) 203.
81 See Michalopoulos (2014) 17. Tac. *Ann.* 4.71.
82 On criticism on Augustan law see Wibier (in this volume).
83 See Dowling (2006) 106 who notes, 'Ovid offers a concept of clemency that incorporates both the traditional Roman reluctance to embrace mercy or to offer it and the necessity in the new age to recognize that the changed structure of the Roman state requires a new ethic of *clementia* in order to negotiate affairs between *princeps* and subject. The discomfort of Ovid with his status as subject, as perpetual suppliant, reflects the distaste of many for the new era. His continued appeals for further clemency and his attacks on the clemency already extended him reveal that Ovid is wrestling with his subordination.'
84 See Lowrie (2009a) 371.
85 On the rearrangement of boundaries between public and private spheres in the age of Augustus see Milnor (2005).
86 See a discussion on the 'social legislation' in Levick (2010) 94.
87 See a discussion of Cicero's definition in Versteeg and Barclay (2003) 412.
88 Levick (2010) 94.
89 See Tac. *Ann.* 1.53. Cf. Antony's wedding to Octavia in Plut. *Ant.* 31.1–5.
90 On the *maritalis honor et affectio* see *Digest* 24.1.32.13; 39.5.31. See also Fayer (2005) 352; Orestano (1951) 79.
91 See Berger (1953) 708 s.v. *simulare*.
92 Suet. *Aug.* 68–70. See Ziogas (2013) 36.
93 On *flagitatio* see Versteeg and Barclay (2003) 408; Williams (1968) 197.
94 On the writ of *habeas corpus* see Haverkamp and Vismann (1997).
95 On the invasive practices of courtroom procedures see Ziogas (2018) 87.
96 Cf. the all-seeing Sun in *Met.* 4.169 ff. who reveals Venus' adultery.
97 See Hemelrijk (2015).
98 On the rearrangement of boundaries between public and private spheres in the age of Augustus see Milnor (2005).

13

What the Roman Constitution Means to Me: Staging Encounters between US and Roman Law on Equality and Proportionality

Nandini Pandey

Act I: Prologue

In thinking through law's ability to inspire literature, and literature's to critique law, my road to Rome begins with Heidi Schreck's acclaimed 2017 play *What the Constitution Means to Me*. This (mostly) one-woman show explores Schreck's changing relationship with the US Constitution. As a teenager, she delivered dewy-eyed orations about it to win college scholarships. As an older woman, after grappling with personal and familial gender-based violence, Schreck understands the Constitution's failure to provide true equality. Her ambivalence manifests in a debate toward the end of the play, as Schreck and an African-American high school student[1] toss coins to determine who will argue to keep or abolish the Constitution. Though the audience are told we get to vote for the winner, one person is selected at random to judge for the whole. Activating questions of representation, equality, arbitrariness and synecdoche that animate this volume, this twist reminds us that juridical fairness comes down in the end to the individual minds of judges who are also audiences and interpreters.

The night I went, on 30 July 2019, the randomly selected audience member chose 'abolish'. And Schreck happened to have voiced the winning argument: that the Constitution is a document that has continually failed women and minorities, written to protect the property interests of dead, rich white men. Why should we, the living, be 'ruled by zombies'? Her point is that even in its purportedly objective and egalitarian language, the Constitution allows now-defunct interests and value systems to govern and prey upon present-day people.[2] Equally important is *how* Schreck argues, finding drama not only in the text of the Constitution but in her relationship with its living consequences. The law too often feels abstract and distant, the province of highly trained specialists rather than a possession for all. Schreck's personal vignettes – though avowedly selective, specific, meant to drive home points – render palpable the law's impact on real lives and generated the strongest sense of community I have ever felt in a theatre.

Could we set a play like Schreck's in or around Rome? Rome, of course, had no single written constitution to fetishize as in the United States. There are attempts to codify prior practices or statutes, from the Twelve Tables to Gaius' *Institutes* to the Theodosian and Justinian codes and the *Digest*. But what Rome had, more loosely, was a *con*-stitution: a way of standing together. As Michèle Lowrie notes in Chapter 2 of this book, Roman history, precedents, even stories play important roles in forming the law. Legal precedent was already vividly built into social and civic lives, even the material and ritual landscape of the city. And literature gives us special insight into law's consequences for Roman lives both personal and civic. From Plautus to Polybius, from Livy to Aulus Gellius, Romans were constantly talking about what their constitution meant to them.

This paper offers some thoughts on what the Roman constitution means to *me*, as a classicist combining intersectional 'minority' identities (female, non-white, first-generation immigrant), in ten 'acts' that each offer an interpretive challenge to readers of this volume. It is a tenet of Critical Race Theory that even legal systems that seem to be colourblind can perpetuate racism. American and for that matter Roman literature can tell us stories that law cannot about what happens while Justice is blind. To me, there's a double yield from comparing Rome and America's legal and literary practices aroud freedom, opportunity and (in)equality. On most, Rome was no model society; it did far worse than the US by quantitative measures. But from my perspective, Rome clarifies where and how the US fails minorities, immigrants and the descendants of former slaves – those people we lump under that hard, lump-in-your throat term 'race'.[3]

Principle: Pierre Bourdieu has analysed the law's implicit claim to impart 'universal and eternal values, transcending any individual interest'.[4] Here, and in many other cases, we could easily substitute 'classics' for 'law'. **What would happen if we interpreters of law and literature refused to maintain our disciplines' modes of authority and investment in systems of power that have harmed minorities? Could we break the cycle by letting go our disciplinary pose as objective/expert/comprehensive and instead, taking a cue from**

Schreck, embracing the idiosyncrasy of our individual perspectives and the arbitrary fortunes that called us forward from the collective audience?

To reprise Lowrie's quotation of Bonnie Honig: 'How we tell the story matters a great deal. It also matters what stories we tell.' This is mine.

Act II: Reparational reading

If today's juridical systems, nation-states, and field of classics all struggle with equity, it's because all were invented to enshrine inequality.

The first written law codes, even in articulating a *lex talionis* or law of equivalence, are equally concerned with *non*-equivalency. 'If a man put out the eye of another man,' states the Code of Hammurabi, 'his eye shall be put out' (196). Yet if he put out the eye of a freed man, he need pay one gold mina (198); if the eye belonged to a slave, he owed half the slave's value (199).[5] The honour of free men who suffer injury can be made whole only by similarly harming and thus diminishing others. Harming a slave, on the other hand, requires only financial reparation; his lesser intrinsic worth makes his body fungible with other forms of property.

Far from being confined to an archaic past, this type of logic persists even in legal documents still in force over modern lives, including the US Constitution.[6] This document and the new nation were created with an eye toward Greece and Rome by elites who justified their monopolization of the means of production via forms of cultural capital to which only they had access, including classical educations.[7] They used that education to protect their own privileges and properties, including their claims to superiority, colonial rights, and ownership over other humans.

This is only one of many foundational crimes with which classics is coming to reckon.[8] This growing awareness of classics' role in propping up racist and colonialist endeavours, parallel and indebted to Critical Race Theory, means that it is no longer enough simply to express shock when we see white supremacy raise its head in Graeco-Roman form.[9] Instead, we need to start dismantling systems of oppression that have masqueraded with help from classics as virtuous, just, traditional. We can begin by giving up the illusion that the classical past and the present bear natural, continuous, or value-neutral relationships with one another. These connections were constructed by and for elites to keep others in their place. Moreover, strive as classics scholars might for 'objectivity', we are always interpreting the past selectively – both because we are working with incomplete evidence, and because as humans we are always choosing which evidence to fit into what framework, informed by our different and unequal experiences of the world, following a disciplinary rulebook and *habitus* shaped by systems of power and privilege.

One solution, I suggest, is to practise a reparative but disruptive method of reading that rejects classics' traditional interest in lineage, *Quellenforschung*, patriarchal and archival authorization. Varro famously defined slaves as 'speaking tools' (*DRR* 1.17). Laws, literature, and citations, too, have served as 'speaking tools' of the powerful, hands that fed the belly of privilege. It's time to break their chains.

Principle: In honour of fellow-citizens whose ancestors were dislocated to the Americas against their will, this paper seeks to practice a new kind of classical reception that resuscitates the violent and gainful act of *captio* behind this implicitly passive term. Rather than drawing lines of continuity, tracing educational pedigrees and transfers of bibliographic wealth that will always continue to enshrine the dominant system, I kidnap classical texts across the millennia and across the Atlantic. I am not concerned with cataloguing classical allusions or credentialling authorial intentions. Instead, I will violently juxtapose Latin law and literature on slavery with the United States' treatment of the Black and brown people who built its wealth. **My hope is to make (intellectual) dislocation and disruption a force for good, as one reparation for classics' past service as a tool of oppression. This is the way the law works, after all: ripping name from history, sentence from story, someone else's trauma into precedent for all.**

Act III: 'We the people'?

'Are we Rome?' Commentators regularly ask this question in thinking through the end of the American empire.[10] But cracks were there from its foundation. While land-owning white men set up the new nation's political and legal systems, their human property was thanklessly constructing their infrastructure, feeding their communities and tending their families. A quarter of a millennium later, simply talking about those enslaved people's role in creating American prosperity has been banned in several states.[11]

The US and Rome may most closely resemble one another in our fraught first-person plural, troubled by the dissonance between soaring rhetoric of republican equality and still underacknowledged realities of exploitation and exclusion. Roman elites like Seneca saw no contradiction in owning people but declaring that all humans, regardless of accidents of birth, shared citizenship in a universal commonwealth (e.g. at *De Otio* 4.1). Stoic ideals of equality informed Kant's declaration, despite racist and sexist views, that humans have an intrinsic worth or 'dignity' which makes us valuable beyond price, to be treated 'always as an end and never as a means only'.[12] Around the same time, across the Atlantic, other classically educated elites declared, 'We hold these Truths to be self-evident, that all Men are created equal.'

What many Americans do not realize – particularly those who do not have to take a citizenship test – is that these stirring words are not in the Constitution. And of the 56 men who signed the document, 41 owned slaves. Rather, this radically egalitarian language was aimed at uniting colonists to shrug off British rule, which Jefferson unironically compared to 'slavery'. The biggest beneficiaries, of course, were the property-owners who took Britain's place as overlords of the new nation's people, resources and legal structures. From the beginning, then, the United States was not founded on equality so much as elites' manipulation of that ideal to grab a bigger share of the pie.

Principle: Philology and jurisprudence's shared fixation on the written word can create closed worlds that do not answer to reality. 'As the quintessential form of legitimized discourse,' writes Bourdieu, the law (like classics?) 'can exercise its specific power only to the extent that it attains recognition, that is, to the extent that the element of arbitrariness at the heart of its functioning (which may vary from case to case) remains unrecognized. The tacit grant of faith in the juridical order must be ceaselessly reproduced.'[13] **Forcing law and literature into dialogue with social realities, across cultures and ages, can break this self-authorizing cycle.** As Derrida says in his own deconstruction of what Pascal called the 'mystical foundation of authority': 'Can what we are doing here resemble a general strike or a revolution, with regard to models, structures but also modes of readability of political action? Is that what deconstruction is? Is it a general strike or a strategy of rupture? Yes and no.'[14]

Act IV: Listening for the silences

Only a decade after declaring human (read: their own) equality, the 'Founding Fathers' wrote the Constitution as a legal and political basis for their new nation.

If we could trust entirely to close reading, and had as fragmentary access to America's documents as to Rome's, we might be forgiven for believing that the Constitution really did confer equality on all Americans. As Schreck points out, the Constitution did not specifically exclude women from citizenship until Section 2 of the Fourteenth Amendment, immediately after the Equal Protections Clause. And the Constitution as first issued is deliberately, deafeningly silent on the matter of slaves. James Madison, for one, 'thought it wrong to admit in the Constitution the idea that there could be property in men'.[15] So slaves are mentioned only in the negative, as persons 'other' than free men and Indians. In other words, the framers were ashamed to acknowledge the very existence of an entire group of people whose continued oppression it tacitly endorsed. Contrast the huge body of Roman law concerned with owning, selling, treating and manumitting enslaved people. Romans at least owned up to the division between enslaved and free people that formed the basis of their society.[16]

Where the Constitution does refer implicitly to enslaved people, it is to draw and quarter them numerically. As the Constitutional Convention debated how to redraft the failed Articles of Confederation, slave-holding states had hoped to count each enslaved person fully for representational purposes even while classing them as property. One thing even northern states could agree on was giving them no vote. After long debate, the very first Article of the Constitution, right beneath the famous preamble, sets forth the Three-Fifths Compromise:

> Representatives and direct Taxes shall be apportioned among the several States which may be included within this Union, according to their respective Numbers, which shall be determined by adding to the whole Number of free Persons, including those bound to Service for a Term of Years, and excluding Indians not taxed, three fifths of all other Persons.
>
> US Constitution, Article 1, Section 2, Clause 3

This article privileges white people with voting rights even when 'bound to Service for a Term' and denies 'Indians' political membership altogether. 'All other Persons,' mostly enslaved Africans and their descendants, are assigned only an arbitrary fractional value. This makes racial inequality one of our constitutive values and consigns Black Americans to an ontologically impossible status, three-fifths of the way between property and humans. Black people began their history in the newly United States not as 'speaking tools' but as *non*-speaking tools for political use by both sides. In slave-holding states, they enhanced enslavers' property interests by giving them voting power disproportionate to their number. But even moralizing northerners were not above using them as a bargaining chip.

I often wonder how the descendants of 'all other Persons' feel about their fellow Americans' fetishization of the document that surgically excluded them. The Constitution sits enshrined in the Rotunda of the National Archives as our most sacred national text. 'Originalism', the legal principle of seeking and obeying the writers' original intentions, is one of two major interpretive veins. All federal employees, including elected leaders and legislators, police officers, and justices, swear an oath to 'support and defend the Constitution'.[17] This loyalty not to people but to a document that denies some of us full humanity makes sickening sense of today's police shootings and other racial violence. After all, the Constitution's very first page declares that some humans are less equal than others: are not entitled, in fact, to be political animals. Agamben's idea of the *homo sacer*, the person who has biological but not political life and whose killing is therefore outside of the law, is surely relevant here.[18] That Black Americans continue to be killed with impunity by the hands of the state is no mere accident, or historical aberration, but inscribed deep into a national document that has for generations classed them between humans and property.

Principle: Silences and circumlocutions speak as loudly as words. And documents' histories, uses, and receptions matter as much as their language. We classicists know that texts are 'pliable and sticky artifacts gripped, moulded and stamped with new meanings by every generation of readers and they come to us irreversibly altered by their experiences' (Gaisser (2002) 387). Surely laws, statutes, constitutions are subject to the same processes. **How then, as modern citizens, can we grapple with the foundational miasma that clings to them – words as fallible and biased as their makers that nevertheless retain real power over us? Is America, like Rome, founded on fratricide: the legal drawing and quartering of Black people in order to sustain the privileges of the body politic that stands on their shoulders?**

Act V: Roman manumission

For all their reliance on enslaved labour, Romans practised a remarkable policy: they regularly manumitted enslaved individuals without constraint by race or colour.[19] Even more remarkably, someone freed by a Roman citizen would himself become a citizen, with no fractional humanity along the way. Literary texts like Petronius' *Satyricon* and Juvenal's third satire attest the social scorn, but also the enviable wealth, that could attach to people whose backs had once borne the whip.[20] Over generations, though, freedpeople's descendants became indistinguishable from other citizens – and upheld 'Roman' values just as staunchly, as we see in the 'Roman odes' of Horace, only one generation removed from servitude.

America's continuing failure to render equal rights and protections to the descendants of former slaves stands in striking comparison. Alan Watson noted that his book on Roman slave law is 'about the Dred Scott case without his name being mentioned' (Watson (1987) xvii); this piece sketches a few of the comparisons that he leaves readers to draw for themselves (Treggiari (1988) 434). Why were Romans more willing than Americans to share power with the people they enslaved? Literature, history, and self-interest all shed light on this question. For one, Roman slavery likely began close to home and ad hoc, as a product of local warfare, rather than as a mass system of exploiting whole peoples. Romans were familiar with the people they enslaved and subject to reciprocal enslavement. Early postliminium laws developed allowing Romans to reassume their civic rights and properties after capture as slaves.[21] Patterson (1982) famously suggested that war captivity, and by extension slavery, were initially understood as a kind of reversible social death that could happen to anyone.[22]

This sense that free and enslaved people could easily trade places, through accidents of fortune or birth, threads through classical Latin literature – from the plays of Plautus to the philosophical works of Seneca.[23] This provides cultural context for the legal view, often expressed by jurists, that slavery is contrary to natural law even if it is common to nations (G. *Inst.* 1.3.2; Flor. *Dig.* 1.5.4, Ulp. *Dig.* 1.1.4, 50.17.32).[24] So manumission was envisioned as a reversion to natural law, wherein all men are born free (Ulp. *Dig.* 1.1.4; Marcian. *Dig.* 40.11.2). It is difficult to overemphasize the contrast with American chattel slavery and its accompanying ideologies of hereditary racial inferiority. Would US lawmakers have clad racialized hierarchies in iron if they felt themselves as vulnerable as classical authors to arbitrary enslavement?

The Roman *res publica* also gained enormous pragmatic advantage from its open model of citizenship. Even enemies like Philip V of Macedon linked Rome's growth and success with its enfranchisement of former slaves:[25]

> The Romans ... receive into the state even slaves, when they have freed them, giving them a share in the magistracies, and in such a way not only have they

augmented their own fatherland, but they have also sent out colonies to almost seventy places.

On a more individualized scale, the hope of manumission, though unevenly distributed, offered buy-in to people at the bottom of the social ladder and incentivized behaviours that benefitted the state and elites alike. It was more efficient for slaveowners to extract labour and obedience using the carrot of manumission than the sticks of surveillance and punishment.[26]

Principle: Law will always serve the self-interests of its makers; it is fairest when its makers must imagine it working against as well as for them. Literature plays a role in stretching citizens' imaginations to envision how they can benefit from advancing others' interests.

Case in point: Gardner (1993: 11) argues that the three types of manumission – by census, rod (*uindicta*) and testament – were based first on the actual, then symbolic ritual consent of the community. Indeed, we can read the associated legal rituals as miniature morality plays. Manumission by *uindicta*, for instance, is a variation of the *mancipatio* and *uindicatio* rituals: the formal claiming of movable property, *res mancipi*, through a transaction or dispute witnessed by a magistrate. To free a slave, an owner would initiate but refuse to make such a claim in the presence of a praetor. A third party touched the slave with a rod and asserted him to be free. This rite makes a presumption of *freedom* in the collusive silence of all parties. It is as an actor in a legal ceremony, capable of coordinating with citizens to withhold truth, that the slave attains personhood and natural law is restored.

Livy is less concerned with the specifics of the ritual than with offering a backstory for Rome's remarkable practice of granting citizenship along with freedom. At the beginning of Book 2, Livy observes that the Roman people were not yet ready for liberty immediately after Brutus' overthrow of the Tarquins. As shepherds and immigrants, they needed 'sufficient time [to] elapse for either family ties or a growing love for the very soil to effect a union of hearts' (2.1, trans. Roberts). This leaves room for enslaved people to prove themselves worthy, and well-born people to prove themselves unworthy, of membership in the new republic. When Brutus' own sons conspire with the expelled Tarquins, Brutus must let go of fatherly affection to administer "the nation's retribution." The sons are stripped, scourged with rods, and beheaded for treason: the first degradations worthy of slaves, the last, of the attempt to overthrow heads of state.

When the guilty had suffered, that the example might be in both respects a notable deterrent from crime (*ut in utramque partem arcendis sceleribus exemplum nobile esset*), the informer was rewarded with money from the treasury, emancipation, and citizenship. He is said to have been the first to be freed by the *uindicta*. Some think that even the word *uindicta* was derived from his name, which they suppose to have been Vindicius. From his time onwards it was customary to regard those who had been freed by this form as admitted to citizenship.

2.5.9–10, trans. Foster

The phrase *in utramque partem* marks the carrot and stick within this exemplum. It sends the message that even a slave can save the state; that civic responsibility will be rewarded and treachery will be punished across classes, with a concomitant adjustment of social standing.[27] This slave's elevation to legal equality with citizens is a reprimand to the aristocratic traitors and reduction of their relative honour. They had betrayed country for property, so their human property becomes their equal, even their replacement within the citizen body. By granting the slave legal personhood in exchange for his loyalty, the state enters into a paternal relationship with him that may prove more powerful than Brutus'. Livy's story thus enters into Rome's unwritten constitution by illustrating enslaved people's worthiness of political entry into the state, even as it contains seeds of the zero-sum resentment that would flourish in American soil.

Act VI: Naturalizing inequality in the body politic

Counterbalancing citizens' theoretical equality under the law was the highly stratified inequality of their votes, in keeping with their division into classes based on their means. The system of voting by tribe in descending class order meant that the poorest citizens' votes rarely played any determining role and were diluted in any case by their greater numbers. The effect was not unlike modern gerrymandering, if more transparent procedurally, and the Romans were more willing than we are to talk about the resultant inequalities.

In a scene toward the beginning of the conflict of orders, Livy offers a powerful allegory for the differentiated nature of the supposedly unified body politic. Senatorial spokesman Agrippa Menenius compares the plebs to parts of the body that rebel against feeding the stomach. However, when the belly starves, they do too, as they are mutually dependent on the same body. Livy calls this an ancient and horrid mode of expression (*prisco illo dicendi et horrido modo*, 2.32.8) that predates the current cooperation of man's members (2.32.9). But this allegory naturalizes the body politic's constitutive inequality and succeeds in persuading the *plebs* who listen – enlisting them in their own self-subordination. This of course is not dissimilar from the law, which Bourdieu (1987: 844) notes manages to extract even 'the complicity of those who are dominated by it.'[28] We have 'con-stitutions' not because we already see eye to eye, but because, like bones and muscles, we could not stand together without them.[29]

Though our figures of speech have evolved, some fundamental inequalities have not.[30] In a speech to the all-white Atlanta Cotton States and International Exposition (1895), Booker T. Washington deploys body politic imagery to the stomach on behalf of the *membra*, the 'masses' of Black folk who 'are to live by the productions of our hands'. 'In all things that are purely social we can be as separate as the fingers,' he promises, 'yet one as the hand in all things essential to mutual progress.' In effect, Washington was offering Black labour toward white prosperity in return for 'separate but equal' standing.[31] But he undergirds this accommodationist proposal with a reminder of Black hands' power to undo the body:

> Nearly sixteen millions of hands will aid you in pulling the load upward, or they will pull against you the load downward. We shall constitute one-third and more of the ignorance and crime of the South, or one-third its intelligence and progress; we shall contribute one-third to the business and industrial prosperity of the South, or we shall prove a veritable body of death, stagnating, depressing, retarding every effort to advance the body politic.

In what could almost be a retort to Agrippa Menenius, the limbs here threaten to rot the whole body unless they receive nominal equality. And Washington values their contributions not at a lesser rate but as integral and proportionally equal to whites'.

Principle: Literature provides images that rationalize what the law cannot: how and why citizens can simultaneously be equal and unequal, unified and differentiated. But it also provides tools for reenvisioning and challenging one's place within the system.

Act VII: The ethnic indifference of Augustan manumission legislation

The parable of the belly explains why extra hands help the body politic; the *uindicta* aetiology endorses the inclusion of newcomers loyal to the state. Both messages go unheard by modern hate groups afraid that white people will be 'replaced' by immigrants. One website quotes the emperor Augustus, in Cassius Dio's much later account, as an anti-immigrant exemplar:[32]

> How otherwise shall families continue? How can the commonwealth be preserved if we neither marry nor produce children? ... It is neither pleasing to Heaven nor creditable that our race should cease and the name of Romans meet extinguishment in us, and the city be given up to foreigners, Greek or even barbarians. We liberate slaves chiefly for the purpose of making out of them as many citizens as possible; we give our allies a share in the government that our numbers may increase: yet you, Romans of the original stock, ... are eager that your families shall perish with you.
>
> Roman History 56.7.4–6, trans. Cary

Even in Dio's historically dubious dramatization, this is not an anti-immigrant speech. Its driving concern is for population decline. High mortality rates, particularly in urban centres, necessitated birth, immigration, and enslavement/manumission.[33] Dio's Augustus singles out Rome's oldest families for failing to do their part through low birth rates.[34] But he also endorses the freeing of slaves (who included many foreigners) as one means of expanding the citizen body.

Far from keeping immigrants out, Augustan-era marriage and manumission legislation (summarized below) incentivizes citizens of all classes and ethnicities – including the newly minted freedpeople who were one important conduit of genetic diversity – to marry and have children. This legislation simply imposes nominal state control over the extraordinary power thus far wielded by private individuals to enter their own clients into the citizen body.[35]

> **lex Iulia de maritandis ordinibus** (18 BCE) encourages marriage, but not across class
>
> **lex Fufia Caninia** (2 BCE) limits testamentary manumissions by household size
>
> **lex Aelia Sentia** (4 CE) sets age minimums for manumission (20 years for owner, 30 for slave)
>
> **lex Papia Poppaea** (9 CE) punishes celibacy, childlessness, marriage between senators and freed slaves
>
> **lex Iunia Norbana** (19 CE?) confers Junian Latin rights on informally manumitted freedmen; full citizenship on those who are married with a one-year-old child

None of these laws are remotely concerned with race or foreign origin – only class. The *leges Juliae* and the *lex Papia Poppaea* encouraged population growth by incentivizing marriage and children, except between senators and emancipated slaves.³⁶ The *lex Papia Poppaea* forced people to marry in order to receive inheritances; released freedmen who bore certain numbers of children from the duties they normally owed their former masters; and released freedwomen from guardianship after bearing four children.³⁷ The law also stipulated that when a freedman died, his patron would receive the equivalent of one child's share of his inheritance, unless he had three or more children (Gaius, *Inst.* 3.42) – a clear incentive to reproduce (Gardner 1993: 40).

Other laws limited slaveowners' ability to flood their communities with new freedmen without blocking other routes to citizenship – and again, without discriminating by colour or origin. The *lex Fufia Caninia* (2 BCE) limited manumissions by testament on a sliding scale dependent on household size (one-half, one-third, etc.), up to a maximum of 100 – a testament to the large scale of the practice. The *lex Aelia Sentia* of 4 CE sets a minimum age limit of 20 for a manumitting owner, and 30 for the person being freed. Again, there was an easy legal bypass if conditions were not met: a tribunal could determine good cause, including exceptional service or intention to marry. The *lex Junia* assigns Junian Latin rights to people whose manumissions did not meet these full qualifications. But again, they could bypass this rule and obtain full citizenship if they married and had a child reach one year of age.

Far from keeping people out, these laws (as argued by Gardner 1993: 39–41) integrated newcomers into the citizen body while maintaining social stability. They had the added benefit of regulating the mass inflow of new citizens loyal to men other than the emperor. Rather than confining freedslaves to a separate and subequal category of citizenship, these laws encouraged them to marry, have children, and conduct economic activity that helped the whole state. Such legislation, combined with Rome's grudging but gradual expansion of citizenship, suggests that Roman citizenship was no less meaningful for being open.

Roman citizenship would remain the gold standard of equality and protection under the law through John F. Kennedy's famous 1963 speech: 'Two thousand years ago, the proudest boast was *civis Romanus sum*. Today, in the world of freedom, the proudest boast is "Ich bin ein Berliner."' He also declared: 'Freedom is indivisible, and when one man is enslaved, all are not free.' Yet the US had to wait four more years for *Loving v. Virginia* (1967), the Supreme Court decision that struck down state bans on interracial marriage as violations of the Fourteenth Amendment. Here, again, Roman law dramatizes just how regressive the US has been in its reluctance to share the rights and liberties that supposedly belong to all.

Act VIII: The un-erasability of intention

American students are taught that Lincoln 'freed the slaves' with his Emancipation Proclamation effective 1 January 1863. But Eric Foner reminds us this was a war measure designed to undermine the South. It did not apply to enslaved people in states loyal to the Union, and it was not put into law until the Thirteenth Amendment was ratified on 6 December 1865.[38] 'Juneteenth', a federal holiday as of 2021, marks the day that federal troops finally informed Texas of 'an absolute equality of personal rights and rights of property between former masters and slaves', over two years after the proclamation and months after Robert E. Lee's surrender.[39]

These events did exactly what Augustus feared: create a mass influx of former slaves into society. But in Rome, former slaves retained strong legal, economic and social ties with patrons, who were responsible for their entrée into society and benefitted from their success.[40] In the US, the formerly enslaved got no seed money, education or social connections to accompany or protect their newfound freedom, simply the vague prospect of being kept on as hired labour. So their 'equality' was inequitable from day one. The results of the intervening century and a half are visible in today's police shootings, voter suppression, mass incarceration, and disparate health and financial outcomes of the Covid-19 pandemic. No wonder Malcolm X argued in a 29 March 1964 speech that true racial equality was impossible:

> We are Africans, and we happen to be in America. We are not Americans. We are a people who formerly were Africans who were kidnapped and brought to America. Our forefathers weren't the Pilgrims. We didn't land on Plymouth Rock; the rock was landed on us. We were brought here against our will; we were not brought here to be made citizens. We were not brought here to enjoy the constitutional gifts that they speak so beautifully about today.

Contrast the imaginary that Roman literature constructs around slavery and freedom. Dio's Augustus suggests that Romans liberated slaves *for the purpose of* making them citizens (56.7.4–6). Petronius has a freedman character, Hermeros, assert that he sold himself into slavery because he he preferred to be a citizen rather than a tributary subject of Rome (*quia ipse me dedi in seruitutem et malui ciuis Romanus esse quam tributarius, Satyricon* 57).[41] It is impossible to imagine anyone similarly volunteering for the transatlantic slave trade. Malcolm X reminds us that the original intentions behind Black presence in America – to possess, to dominate, to use – can never fully be erased by egalitarian rhetoric. His view combines a kind of originalism with a reception scholar's awareness that the past continually sticks to the present.

Principle: The meaning(s) of laws, as of literature, can never be detached from the original contexts, purposes, and problems behind their production no matter how often they are revised. Communities must keep these revision histories alive in shared memory to offset the idealizing tendency of foundation narratives.

Act IX: When comedy becomes tragedy

'Government of the people, by the people, for the people.' Much like 'all Men are created equal', these words are nowhere in the US Constitution. But Lincoln's 19 November 1963 address at Gettysburg sought in only 272 words to redefine America's unwritten constitution. Slave-owners had been able to cite the 1787 Constitution as proof that they upheld America's founding ideals. Lincoln's address recast the Civil War as a struggle not just for unity but for human equality, in keeping with the Declaration of Independence signed 'four score and seven years ago' to found 'a new nation, conceived in Liberty, and dedicated to the proposition that all men are created equal'. With this speech and emancipation, Lincoln was attempting a radical and arguably ongoing expansion of the 'we the people' whom the law is expected to protect and serve.

It was easier, of course, to revise this relationship verbally than to change social practice. Roman comedy and US history offer contrastive, anecdotal measures of the law's perceived operation 'of, by and for' even marginalized people. In Plautus' *Poenulus*, a cross-class, cross-cultural alliance makes effective use of Roman law to extract the young woman whom Agorastocles loves from her pimp, Lycus.[42] In a scheme devised by Agorastocles' clever slave Milphio, they render Lycus legally responsible for harbouring a slave of Agorastocles', then plan for the Carthaginian Hanno to claim the girl as his own freeborn child, rendering Lycus liable for another crime. The claim turns out to be true, justice is served, and a happy ending ensues for all but Lycus. These characters successfully collude to use the law as a tool or script for obtaining what the play represents as justice.

Plessy v. Ferguson, the 1896 US Supreme Court case that enshrined 'separate but equal', began like a Roman comedy before going horribly wrong. After federal troops withdrew from the South to end Reconstruction (1865–77),

Democrat-controlled state legislatures began passing the precursors to Jim Crow laws. In New Orleans, a multiracial citizens' group wanted to challenge a law mandating segregated railroad cars. Homer Adolph Plessy – a light-skinned 'octoroon' who was legally classed as Black under Louisiana's one-drop rule – agreed to help. On 7 June 1892, he bought a ticket on a train from New Orleans bound for Covington, Louisiana. The railroad company, feeling that the 1890 requirement of 'equal, but separate' cars posed an undue hardship, was in on the game. They trusted in the law and their ability to use it.

But what began as a comedy ended up tragically endorsing a half century of 'separate but equal'. The court voted 7–1 that there was no inherent inequality in separation, only the 'construction' that 'the colored race chooses to put ... upon it' (Justice Henry Brown, voicing the majority opinion). Justice John Marshall Harlan, a former slaveholder who reversed his opposition to civil rights after witnessing the horrors of the KKK, argued that 'the arbitrary separation of citizens on the basis of race while they are on a public highway is a badge of servitude wholly inconsistent with the civil freedom and the equality before the law established by the Constitution. It cannot be justified upon any legal grounds.'

There is a direct line between this failed comedy and modern America's strategies for keeping some citizens less equal than others, including legal and extralegal violence, juridical injustice, poll taxes, intimidation, discriminatory lending and employment practices, residential segregation and the open suppression of the Black vote. In an eerie recollection of the Three-Fifths Compromise, Black people in the penal system enhance their incarcerators' electoral power without getting a political voice. In Wisconsin, for instance, 13% or 1 in 8 Black men are imprisoned – double the national rate – yet have no vote, even as their captivity in prisons often distant from their homes is used to increase those areas' electoral weight. As one told an NPR reporter, 'Forgive me for not being able to articulate this the way I want to, but it's almost like your body being used.'[43]

Even 'affirmative action' policies to correct discrimination often end up reducing minorities to parts of a whole, ironically, because of Supreme Court rulings based on the Equal Protections Clause of the Fourteenth Amendment. Regents of the *University of California v. Bakke* (1978), for instance, ruled against quotas of seats set aside for minority students at the UC Davis School of Medicine. *Gratz v. Bollinger* and *Grutter v. Bollinger* (both 2003) similarly struck down the University of Michigan's allocation of a 20-point bonus to underrepresented minorities. These and other cases affirm that race should be taken into account only if it serves a compelling majority interest – i.e., diversity measures must benefit the university as a whole, rather than correct for the historical injustices that create racial inequities in the first place.[44] Denise Ferreira da Silva (2016: 185) offers complementary insights on how affirmative action in Brazil serves compelling state interest in 'meeting the needs of global capital'. Diversity laws and practices that use minorities instrumentally, to benefit the majority, fail to honour their personal dignity and worth – to treat them, in Kant's terms, 'always as an end and never as a means only'. Affirmative action law also endorses a kind of tokenism or metonymic thinking that the Romans knew was a legal fiction. They brought a clod of earth into court so they didn't have to move the whole field; we admit a few minorities into our universities so we don't have to face the underlying unevenness of the playing field.[45]

Act X: Slaying the zombies

Schreck's play made me contemplate all the rituals the US has constructed, from the Pledge of Allegiance to jury duty, designed to reassure us that laws made by a few (often long ago, for reasons we'd abjure) reflect our own will and interests. Such ceremonies sustain the State's 'monopoly of legitimized symbolic violence' and the wedge the juridical system places between 'judgments based upon the law and naive intuitions of fairness'.[46] These rituals help transubstantiate laws from textual objects into speaking subjects – in Schreck's phrase, 'zombies' – capable of objectifying, enslaving, even executing us. Who's responsible, then, when they commit or abet crimes? Their authors, their interpreters, or us, for standing by and watching the tragedy?

Firing squads use one blank bullet, randomly assigned, so no one has to feel responsible for execution. The mystification and multiplicity of laws' authorship, too, protects any one person from bearing guilt. A reflexive reverence for the past, shared by many Americans, Romans, and classicists alike, is another means of dodging moral responsibility toward the present. It's easier to show *pietas* toward deified 'Founding Fathers', toward words printed in black and white, than toward the mixed, modern, multiethnic humans who live within their power. It's hard, as philologists, not to feel professionally complicit with this fetishization of 'heritage' as embedded within the written word. But what we can give our unequal and divided America is an ability to negotiate multiplicity and contradiction; an interest in authorship, intertextuality, and the stickiness of texts; and an awareness that the same people who make justice also make 'truth'.

We also have authoritative texts that upset authority. In book 20 of the *Attic Nights*, Aulus Gellius recounts a debate between the jurist Sextus Caecilius and the philosopher Favorinus. Favorinus notes that the Twelve Tables cannot be taken literally; some are obscure, cruel, or lapsed by popular consent. Caecilius attributes some of the interpretive difficulty to the ignorance of readers and the long elapse of time and custom. This debate is fascinating in the ways it does *not* map on to the debate between US Constitutional originalists and 'loose constructionists'. Neither Favorinus nor Caecilius advocates taking the words of old laws literally; both acknowledge that their original cultural context is different from their own and concede that laws and interpretations should 'vary according to the seasons of circumstances and of fortune' (*Attic Nights* 20.1, trans. Rolfe). Their argument ends in an embrace, and the message that we need to be humane and generous readers, of one another and the laws that hold such force over our lives.

This is what the Roman constitution, and the literature in which it lives, mean to me. Both help us think of truth and justice as an ever-changing discursive universe, where 'we the people' are constantly interpreting, negotiating, and reconstructing ourselves with and through one another. *What the Constitution Means to Me* ends by creating just such a space. At its close, the debate opponents shake hands, sit down back-to-back, and answer personal questions the previous night's audience has left behind. We watch the actors shift out of the constructed world of the play to become equal individuals interacting honestly. If only we, too, could wipe the slate clean, and start from the premise of integral worth. If only we too could stop litigating who owns what proportion of that foundational lie, 'we the people', and reimagined ourselves simply as 'you and I'.

Notes

I thank interlocutors at Durham (2019) and NYU (2019) for enriching this piece, but especially Ioannis Ziogas and Erica Bexley for including and supporting even newcomers like myself to Roman law, and Patrice Rankine for inspiration. All errors that remain are mine alone. I regret I was unable to include many bibliographical items that came to my attention after I drafted this piece in 2020, but I am hopeful they will fuel future scholarship.

1 Played alternately by freshman Rosdely Ciprian and senior Thursday Williams.
2 As I revise this essay in June 2021, I am struck by the parallels with the recent 'discourse' about racism and colonialism in classics.
3 For the modern term 'race' in the study of classics, see McCoskey (2012). Roman law makes no recognition of race or ethnicity, but is concerned instead with class differentials.

4 Bourdieu (1987) 841. At the editors' suggestion, I overlayer conceptual frameworks from Bourdieu and Derrida over what began as a personal piece.
5 In King's translation (1900). Laws 196–223 well illustrate the differential worths of men and women, enslaved and free people. Schmid (2017) discusses other ancient near eastern and Biblical law codes as evolving out of economic considerations.
6 Law scholars have long pointed out that the Constitution is not colourblind, e.g. Sealing (1998); Greene (2011).
7 Richard (1995) and others argue that Graeco-Roman texts were formative of the founders' thought rather than mere window-dressing.
8 This movement is often led 'from below' by younger scholars, e.g. in the August 2020 open letter to Cambridge faculty of Classics on anti-racism (https://docs.google.com/document/d/1SmCCvM4Psmk25lWnx1WHTpzbZZ-hxwQnRgkNHoOTyW8/edit?usp=sharing).
9 With Donald Trump's attempted mandate of classical federal architecture, for instance, or his supporters' appropriation of Spartan imagery in storming the Capitol.
10 Most famously, Murphy (2007).
11 On 10 June 2021, the teaching of Critical Race Theory (defined as 'the theory that racism is not merely the product of prejudice, but that racism is embedded in American society and its legal systems in order to uphold the supremacy of white persons') and the use of the 1619 Project were banned by the Florida State Board of Education. For this and other state bans, see Dutton (2021).
12 In Kant's second formulation of the categorical imperative. Nussbaum (1997) discusses the idea in relation to Stoicism. See Allais (2016) on Kant's racism.
13 Bourdieu (1987) 844.
14 Derrida (1992a) 38.
15 According to the transcript of the Madison debates, 25 August 1787, edited by G. Hund and J. Scott (1920), Oxford, online at https://avalon.law.yale.edu/18th_century/debates_825.asp.
16 Among the copious bibliography, Gardner's overview treats slaves' ability to serve as masters' agents and the law's 'uneasiness' in treating them entirely as *res* (2011: 423).
17 According to 5 US Code § 3331. The language for the President is slightly different and is the only text spelled out by the Constitution (Article 2, Section One, Clause 8).
18 See Agamben (1998). I thank the editors for this productive comparison.
19 The number, proportion, average age, and term of service of the manumitted are much debated, with Scheidel (1997) particularly valuable. Wiedemann (1985) lays out some of the central issues, focusing on epigraphical and literary evidence, though note the well-known inscriptional overrepresentation of freedmen.

Household workers who interacted closely with owners (doctors, tutors, nurses) were most likely to be freed.
20 Further discussion in Pandey (2020).
21 Cf. especially Ando (2015c).
22 Patterson (1982); cf. also Treggiari (1969); Gamauf (2016); MacLean (2018).
23 Leigh (2004b) 88–90 discusses this very question in the *Captivi* with relation to Aristotle's idea of natural slavery.
24 For the concept of natural law, see Humfress (2021).
25 *IG* IX.2.517 = *Sylloge Inscriptionum Graecarum*, 3rd edition, 543.
26 See, e.g., Gardner (2011) 436 for this point, memorably made by Keith Hopkins.
27 Kleijwegt (2009) further notes that Livy diminishes Vindicius' betrayal of his *familia*.
28 Bourdieu (1987) 835–6 also discusses the creation of new juridical needs among marginalized groups.
29 As Lowrie (in this volume) points out in her discussion of *constituere*.
30 As the Covid pandemic makes clear with the disproportionate toll borne by society's 'hands'.
31 If Black people are given 'education of head, hand, and heart,' Washington offers, 'you will find that they will buy your surplus land, make blossom the waste places in your fields, and run your factories.'
32 The website, entitled 'The Great Replacement' (https://www.great-replacement.com/), features quotations from Renaud Camus.
33 I simplify complex demographic dynamics well discussed by Morley (2003) 150 and Jongman (2003).
34 Not dissimilar to falling fertility rates today among wealthy nations and educated women.
35 Gardner (2011) 431–2 also documents some slight additional protections under the Augustan principate, though Gamauf (2016) 396 rightly cautions against attempts to locate concern for slaves' dignity and humanity in Roman law.
36 The prohibition suggests that the practice was not uncommon.
37 *Dig.* 38 tit.1. Free women enjoyed the same privilege after three children.
38 See Foner (2019).
39 General Order Number 3, relayed in Galveston, 19 June 1865.
40 Tacoma (2016) discusses evidence that freed slaves continued to live near and interact with their patrons.
41 Schmeling (2011) 233–5 compiles evidence on self-sale.
42 Gaertner (in this volume) analyzes Plautus' mash-up of Graeco-Roman law in the *Poenulus* and other plays more thoroughly than I can here.
43 In an episode of the NPR podcast *Code Switch* entitled 'Political Prisoners' (https://www.npr.org/templates/transcript/transcript.php?storyId=764809210). The film *13th* (2016) also treats imprisonment.

44 Cf. Pandey (2020), inspired by Sara Ahmed and Ellen Berry's writings on the paradoxes of diversity.
45 Cf. also da Silva's analysis (2016) 188–9 of the racial dialectic that translates white people's colonial debt to their Black labourers into a moral deficit that is rendered as the racial other's mental deficiency.
46 Bourdieu (1987) 838 and 817, respectively.

Bibliography

Aeppli, E. 1986 [1951]. *Der Traum*. Zurich.
Aftsomis, K. B. 2010. *The Performance of Justice in Imperial Latin Literature*. PhD Diss. Stanford.
Agamben, G. 1998. *Homo Sacer: Sovereign Power and Bare Life*. Trans. D. Heller-Roazen. Stanford.
Agamben, G. 2005a. *State of Exception*. Trans. K. Attell. Chicago.
Agamben, G. 2005b. 'The State of Exception' in A. Norris (ed.) *Politics, Metaphysics, and Death: Essays on Giorgio Agamben's Homo Sacer*. Trans. G. Agamben and K. Attell. Durham, NC: 284–98.
Agamben, G. 2017. *The Omnibus Homo Sacer*. Stanford.
Ahl, F. 1984. 'The Art of Safe Criticism in Greece and Rome', *American Journal of Philology* 105: 174–208.
Alekou, S. 2018. 'Medea's Legal Apology in Ovid's *Heroides* 12', *Latomus* 77: 311–34.
Alekou, S. 2021. 'Underneath the Arachnean and Minervan Veil of Ambiguity: Cultural and Political *Simulatio* in Ovidian Ecphrasis', in M. Vöhler, T. Fuhrer and S. Frangoulidis (eds) *Strategies of Ambiguity in Ancient Literature*. Berlin: 175–91.
Allais, L. 2016. 'Kant's Racism', *Philosophical Papers* 42.1–2: 1–36.
Allély, A. 2012. *La Déclaration d'hostis sous la République romaine*. Bordeaux.
Alston, R., and S. Bhatt (eds). 2017. 'Foucault and Roman Antiquity: Foucault's Rome', *Foucault Studies* 22.
Anderson, W. S. 1972. *Ovid's Metamorphoses: Books 6–10*. Norman, OH.
Ando, C. 2013. 'The Origins and Import of Republican Constitutionalism', *Cardozo Law Review* 34: 917–35.
Ando, C. 2015a. 'Fact, Fiction and Social Reality in Roman Law', in M. del Mar and W. Twining (eds), *Legal Fictions in Theory and Practice*. Cham and New York: 295–323.
Ando, C. 2015b. '*Exemplum*, Analogy, and Precedent in Roman Law', in M. Lowrie and S. Lüdemann (eds), *Exemplarity and Singularity: Thinking through Particulars in Philosophy, Literature, and Law*. London: 111–22.
Ando, C. 2015c. *Roman Social Imaginaries: Language and Thought in Contexts of Empire*. Toronto.
Anzinger, S. 2007. *Schweigen im römischen Epos*. Berlin.
Arcaria, F. 2017. '*Res communes omnium*', *Koinōnia* 41: 639–66.
Arena, V. 2012. *Libertas and the Practice of Politics in the Late Roman Republic*. Cambridge.
Aristodemou, M. 2000. *Law and Literature: Journeys from Her to Eternity*. Oxford.

Armisen-Marchetti, M. 1989. *Sapientiae Facies: Étude sur les Images de Sénèque*. Paris.
Armitage, D. 2017. *Civil Wars: A History in Ideas*. New Haven.
Arnott, W. G. 1970. '*Phormio parasitus*. A Study in Dramatic Methods of Characterization', *Greece & Rome* 17: 32–57.
Asmis, E. 2005. 'A New Kind of Model: Cicero's Roman Constitution in *De Republica*', *American Journal of Philology* 126: 377–427.
Austin, J. L. 1976. *How to Do Things with Words: the William James Lectures Delivered at Harvard University in 1955*. Oxford.
Badian, E. 1985. 'A Phantom Marriage Law', *Philologus* 129: 82–98.
Baldus, C. 2016. 'Possession in Roman Law', in P. Du Plessis, C. Ando, and K. Tuori (eds), *The Oxford Handbook of Roman Law and Society*. Oxford: 537–52.
Ballestra-Puech, S. 2006. *Métamorphoses D'Arachné: L'artiste en araignée dans la littérature occidentale*. Geneva.
Barchiesi, A. 1997. *The Poet and the Prince: Ovid and Augustan Discourse*. Berkeley.
Barchiesi, M. 1978. *La 'Tarentilla' rivisitata. Studi su Nevio comico*. Pisa.
Barratt, P. 1979. *M. Annaei Lucani Belli Civilis Liber V: A Commentary*. Amsterdam.
Barrière, F. 2016. *Lucain. La guerre civile: Chant II*. Paris.
Barsby, J. 1992. 'The Stage Movements of Demipho in the Greek Original of Terence, *Phormio* 311 ff', *Classica et Mediaevalia* 43: 141–5.
Barsby, J. 1999. *Terence: Eunuchus*. Cambridge.
Barsby, J. 2001. *Terence: Phormio, The Mother-in-law, The Brothers*. Cambridge, MA.
Bartholomä, A. 2019. 'Legal Laughter', in M. T. Dinter (ed.), *The Cambridge Companion to Roman Comedy*. Cambridge: 229–40.
Batstone, W. 2009. 'The Drama of Rhetoric at Rome', in E. Gunderson (ed.), *The Cambridge Companion to Ancient Rhetoric*. Cambridge: 212–37.
Bauman, R. A. 1983. *Lawyers in Roman Republican Politics: A Study of the Roman Jurists in their Political Setting, 316–82 BC*. Munich.
Bauman, R. A. 1989. *Lawyers and Politics in the Early Roman Empire: A Study of Relations between the Roman Jurists and the Emperors from Augustus to Hadrian*. Munich.
Bauman, R. A. 1993. 'The Rape of Lucretia, *Quod Metus Causa* and the Criminal Law', *Latomus* 52: 550–66.
Becker, A. H. 1896. *De facetiis iuridicis apud scriptores Latinos*. Paris.
Behrends, O. 2004 [1992]. 'Die allen Lebewesen gemeinsamen Sachen (*res communes omnium*) nach den Glossatoren und dem klassischen römischen Recht', in O. Behrends, M. Avenarius, R. Meyer-Pritzl, and C. Möller (eds), *Institut und Prinzip: Siedlungsgeschichtliche Grundlagen, philosophische Einflüsse und das Fortwirken der beiden republikanischen Konzeptionen in den kaiserzeitlichen Rechtsschulen*. Göttingen: 2.599–625.
Berger, A. 1953. *Encyclopedic Dictionary of Roman Law*. Philadelphia.
Bergson, H. 1995 [1899]. *Le Rire*. Paris.
Bergson, H. 2005 [1911]. *Laughter: An Essay on the Meaning of the Comic*. New York.

Beta, S. 2014. 'Libera lingua loquemur ludis Liberalibus: Gnaeus Naevius as a Latin Aristophanes?', in S. Douglas Olson (ed.), *Ancient Comedy and Reception: Essays in Honor of Jeffrey Henderson*. Berlin: 203–22.

Bhatt, S. 2017. 'The Augustan Principate and the Emergence of Biopolitics: A Comparative Historical Perspective', *Foucault Studies* 22: 72–93.

Bianco, M. M. 2009. 'Il *Phormio* e le intemperanze di Terenzio', *Aevum* 83: 69–88.

Biggs, T. 2020. *Poetics of the First Punic War*. Ann Arbor.

Binder, G. 1999. *L. Annaeus Seneca Apokolokyntosis*. Düsseldorf/ Zürich.

Blanchard, A. 1980. 'La composition du "Phormion" et l'originalité de Térence', *Revue des Études Latines* 58: 49–66.

Blaschka, K. 2014. 'Die Allegorie vom *funus Romae* in Lucans *Bellum Civile*', *Göttinger Forum für Altertumswissenschaft* 17: 181–207.

Boehm, G. and Pfotenhauer, H. (eds). 1995. *Beschreibungskunst – Kunstbeschreibung. Ekphrasis von der Antike bis zur Gegenwart*. Munich.

Bonner, S. F. 1949. *Roman Declamation in the Late Republic and Early Principate*. Liverpool.

Borkowski, J. A. 1994. *Textbook on Roman Law*. London.

Bourdieu, P. 1986. 'La force du droit: Éléments pour une sociologie du champ juridique', *Actes de la recherche en sciences sociales* 64: 3–19.

Bourdieu, P. 1987. 'The Force of Law: Toward a Sociology of the Juridical Field' Trans. R. Terdiman, *Hastings Law Journal* 38.5: 805–53.

Bourdieu, P. 1990. *The Logic of Practice*. Stanford.

Boyle, A. J. 2006. *An Introduction to Roman Tragedy*. London.

Brännstedt, L. 2016. *Femina Princeps: Livia's Position in the Roman State*. Lund.

Braun, L. 1999. '*Phormio* und *Epidikazomenos*. Mit einem Anhang zu *Mostellaria* und *Phasma*', *Hermes* 127: 33–46.

Braund, S. H. 1992. *Lucan. Civil War. Translated with introduction and notes by S. H. Braund*. Oxford.

Braund, S. M. 2004. '*Libertas* or *Licentia*? Freedom and Criticism in Roman Satire', in I. Sluiter and R. Rosen (eds), *Free Speech in Classical Antiquity*. Leiden: 409–28.

Braund, S. M. and James, P. 1998. '*Quasi Homo*: Distortion and Contortion in Seneca's *Apocolocyntosis*', *Arethusa* 31: 285–311.

Bremer, F. P. 1898. *Iurisprudentiae antehadrianae quae supersunt*. vol 2.1. Leipzig.

Bresson, A. 2016. *The Making of the Ancient Greek Economy: Institutions, Markets, and Growth in the City-States*. Trans. S. Rendall. Princeton.

Brink, C. O. (ed.). 1982. *Horace on Poetry: Epistles Book II: The Letters to Augustus and Florus*. Cambridge.

Brooks, P. and Gewirtz, P. 1996. *Law's Stories: Narrative and Rhetoric in the Law*. New Haven and London.

Brown, P. G. McC. 1995. Review of Lefèvre, Stärk, Vogt-Spira (1991), *Gnomon* 67: 676–83.

Brown, P. G. McC. 2002. 'Actors and Actor-Managers at Rome in the Time of Plautus and Terence', in P. E. Easterling and E. Hall (eds), *Greek and Roman Actors: Aspects of an Ancient Profession*. Cambridge: 225–37.

Büchner, K. 1957. 'Summum ius summa iniuria', in K. Büchner (ed.), *Humanitas Romana: Studien über Werke und Wesen der Römer*. Heidelberg: 80–105.
Büchner, K. 1974. *Das Theater des Terenz*. Heidelberg.
Buckland, W. W. and P. Stein, 2007. *A Text-Book of Roman Law from Augustus to Justinian*. Cambridge.
Buongiorno, P. (ed.). 2020. *Senatus consultum ultimum e stato di eccezione: Fenomeni in prospettiva*. Stuttgart.
Butler, J. 1997. *Excitable Speech: A Politics of the Performative*. New York/ London.
Butler, S. 2002. *The Hand of Cicero*. London.
Calabretta, M. 2015. *La Rudens di Plauto in teatro: Tra filologia e messa in scena*. Hildesheim.
Cangelosi, E. 2014. *Publica e communis: Acqua, mondo romano e beni comuni*. Rome.
Casali, S. 2006. 'The Art of Making Oneself Hated: Rethinking (Anti-)Augustanism in Ovid's *Ars Amatoria*', in R. Gibson, S. Green, and A. Sharrock (eds), *The Art of Love: Bimillennial Essays on Ovid's Ars Amatoria and Remedia Amoris*. Oxford: 216–34.
Casola, M. 2017. 'Il mare bene di tutti: Universalità del suo uso', *Ius Romanum* 2: 1–17.
Casson, L. 1971. *Ships and Seamanship in the Ancient World*. Princeton.
Caye, P. 2011. 'Architecture et rhétorique', in L. Pernot (ed.), *La rhétorique des arts: actes du colloque tenu au Collège de France sous la présidence de March Fumaroli, de l'Académie française*. Paris: 73–85.
Chaplin, J. D. 2000. *Livy's Exemplary History*. Oxford.
Charbonnel, N. 1995. 'Aux sources du droit maritime à Rome: Le *Rudens* de Plaute et le droit d'épaves', *Revue historique de droit français et étranger* 73.3: 303–22.
Chartier, R. 1992. *Order of Books: Readers, Authors, and Libraries in Europe between the Fourteenth and Eighteenth Centuries*. Stanford.
Chiarini, G. 1979. *La recita: Plauto, la farsa, la festa*. Bologna.
Coffey, M. 1961. 'Seneca, *Apocolocyntosis* 1922–1958', *Lustrum* 6: 239–311.
Coffey, M. 1976. *Roman Satire*. London.
Colognesi, L. C. 2016. 'Ownership and Power in Roman Law', in P. Du Plessis, C. Ando, and K. Tuori (eds), *The Oxford Handbook of Roman Law and Society*. Oxford: 524–36.
Connolly, J. 2007. *The State of Speech: Rhetoric and Political Thought in Ancient Rome*. Princeton.
Connolly, J. 2016. 'A Theory of Violence in Lucan's *Bellum Ciuile*', in P. Mitsis and I. Ziogas (eds), *Wordplay and Powerplay in Latin Poetry*. Berlin: 273–98.
Cooley, A. 2009. *Res Gestae Diui Augusti: Text, Translation, and Commentary*. Cambridge.
Copeland, R. 1991. *Rhetoric, Hermeneutics, and Translation in the Middle Ages: Academic Traditions and Vernacular Texts*. Cambridge.
Corbino, A. 2019. 'Cose e appartenenza: I "beni comuni" nel diritto romano', *Legal Roots* 8: 25–39.
Cornell, T. J. 1986. 'The Historical Tradition of Early Rome', in I. S. Moxon, S. D. Smart and A. J. Woodman (eds), *Past Perspectives: Studies in Greek and Roman Historical Writing*. Cambridge: 67–86.

Cornell, T. J. (ed.), 2013. *The Fragments of the Roman Historians*. 3 vols. Oxford.
Cornell, T. J. 2015. 'Crisis and Deformation in the Roman Republic: The Example of the Dictatorship', in V. Gouškin and P. J. Rhodes (eds), *Deformations and Crises of Ancient Civil Communities*. Stuttgart: 101–26.
Cornu Thénard, N. 2020. 'The Legal Construction of the Fact, between Rhetoric and Roman Law', in C. Ando and W. P. Sullivan (eds), *The Discovery of the Fact*. Ann Arbor: 39–71.
Cornwell, H. 2017. *Pax and the Politics of Peace: Republic to Principate*. Oxford.
Courtney, E. 2013. 'The Two Books of Satires', in H.-C. Günther (ed.), *Brill's Companion to Horace*. Leiden: 63–168.
Cover, R. M. 1986. 'Violence and the Word', *Yale Law Journal* 95: 1601–29.
Cover, R. M. 1995. *Narrative, Violence, and the Law: the Essays of Robert Cover*. Ann Arbor.
Crawford, M. H. (ed.), 1996. *Roman Statutes*. 2 vols. London.
Crook, J. 1955. *Consilium Principis*. Cambridge.
Curran, L. C. 1972. 'Transformation and Anti-Augustanism in Ovid's *Metamorphoses*', *Arethusa* 2: 71–91.
da Silva, D. F. 2016. 'The Racial Limits of Social Justice: The Ruse of Equality of Opportunity and the Global Affirmative Action Mandate', *Critical Ethnic Studies* 2.2: 184–209.
Davies, B. 2016. *Sex, Time, and Space in Contemporary Fiction: Exceptional Intercourse*. London.
Day, H. J. M. 2013. *Lucan and the Sublime: Power, Representation and Aesthetic Experience*. Cambridge.
De Lachapelle, G. F. 2011. *Clementia. Recherches sur la notion de clémence à Rome, du début du Ier siècle a. C. à la mort d'Auguste*. Paris.
De Melo, W. 2011. *Plautus II: Casina, The Casket Comedy, Curculio, Epidicus, The Two Menaechmuses*. Cambridge, MA.
De Melo, W. 2012. *Plautus IV: The Little Carthaginian, Pseudolus, The Rope*. Cambridge, MA.
Derrida, J. 1967. *De la grammatologie*. Paris.
Derrida, J. 1972. 'Signature, évenement, contexte', in *Marges de la philosophie*. Paris: 365–93.
Derrida, J. 1977. 'Limited Inc. a b c . . .'. *Glyph* 2: 162–254.
Derrida, J. 1987. *The Post Card: From Socrates to Freud and Beyond*. Chicago.
Derrida, J. 1988. *Limited inc*. Evanston.
Derrida, J. 1992a. 'Force of Law: The "Mystical Foundation of Authority"', in D. Cornell, M. Rosenfeld and D. Carlson (eds), *Deconstruction and the Possibility of Justice*. New York: 3–67.
Derrida, J. 1992b. *Jacques Derrida: Acts of Literature*. D. Attridge (ed). New York/London.
Derrida, J. 1992c. 'Before the Law', in D. Attridge (ed.), *Jacques Derrida: Acts of Literature*. New York/London: 181–220.
Derrida, J. 2018. *Before the Law: The Complete Text of the Préjugés*. Trans S. van Reenen and J. de Ville. Minneapolis/London.

Detel, W. 1998. *Foucault und die klassische Antike. Macht, Moral, Wisse*. Frankfurt am Main.
Di Nisio, V. 2017. *Partus vel fructus: Aspetti giuridici della filiazione ex ancilla*. Naples.
Dolin, K. 2007. *A Critical Introduction to Law and Literature*. Cambridge.
Dolin, K. (ed.). 2018. *Law and Literature*. Cambridge.
Dowling, M. 2006. *Clemency and Cruelty in the Roman World*. Ann Arbor.
Dressler, A. 2016. 'Plautus and the Poetics of Property: Reification, Recognition, and Utopia', *Materiali e Discussioni per l'analisi dei Testi Classici* 77: 9–56.
Duckworth, G. E. 1952. *The Nature of Roman Comedy*. Princeton.
Ducos, M. 2011. 'Justice et droit dans le *Rudens*', in B. Delignon, S. Luciani and P. Paré-Rey (eds), *Une journée à Cyrène: Lecture du Rudens de Plaute*. Montpellier: 157–68.
Dufallo, B. 2013. *The Captor's Image: Greek Culture in Roman Ecphrasis*. Oxford.
Dugan, J. 2005. *Making a New Man: Ciceronian Self-Fashioning in the Rhetorical Works*. Oxford.
Dugan, J. 2012. '*Scriptum* and *Voluntas* in Cicero's *Brutus*', in M. Citroni (ed.), *Letteratura e Civitas: Transizioni dalla Repubblica all'Impero. In ricordo di Emanuele Narducci*. Pisa: 119–28.
Dugan, J. 2013. 'Cicero and the Politics of Ambiguity: Interpreting the *Pro Marcello*' in C. Steel and H. van der Blom (eds), *Community and Communication: Oratory and Politics in Republican Rome*. Oxford: 211–25.
Dugan, J. 2018. 'Netting the Wolf-Fish: Caius Titius in Macrobius and Cicero', in A. Balbo, C. Gray, R. Marshall and C. Steel (eds), *Reading Republican Oratory: Reconstructions, Contexts, Reception*. Oxford: 135–48.
Dulckeit, G., F. Schwarz and W. Waldstein, 1989. *Römische Rechtsgeschichte: Ein Studienbuch*. 8th ed. Munich.
Dumont, J. C. 2010. 'Originalité du *Rudens*', *Vita Latina* 182: 9–19.
Dursi, D. 2017. *Res communes omnium: Dalle necessità economiche alla disciplina giuridica*. Naples.
Dutton, J. 2021. 'Critical Race Theory is banned in these states', *Newsweek* 11 June.
Dyck, A. 2004. *A Commentary on Cicero, De Legibus*. Ann Arbor.
Dyck, A. 2008. *Cicero: Catilinarians*. Cambridge.
Dyck, A. 2013. *Cicero: Pro Marco Caelio*. Cambridge.
Eck, W. 2019. 'At Magnus Caesar, and Yet!', in K. Morrell, J. Osgood, and K. Welch (eds), *The Alternative Augustan Age*. Oxford: 78–95.
Eden, K. 1987. 'Hermeneutics and the Ancient Rhetorical Tradition', *Rhetorica* 5: 59–86.
Eden, K. 1997. *Hermeneutics and the Rhetorical Tradition: Chapters in the Ancient Legacy & Its Humanist Reception*. New Haven and London.
Eden, P. T. 1984. *Seneca: Apocolocyntosis*. Cambridge.
Edwards, C. 1993. *The Politics of Immorality in Ancient Rome*. Cambridge.
Edwards, C. 2009. 'Free yourself! Slavery, Freedom and the Self in Seneca's *Letters*', in S. Bartsch and D. Wray (eds), *Seneca and the Self*. Cambridge: 139–59.

Edwards, C. 2019. *Seneca: Selected Letters*. Cambridge.
Elden, S. 2016. *Foucault's Last Decade*. Cambridge.
Elliott, J. 2013. *Ennius and the Architecture of the Annales*. Cambridge.
Elmer, D. F. 2013. *The Poetics of Consent: Collective Decision Making and the Iliad*. Baltimore.
Fantham, E. 1972. *Comparative Studies in Republican Latin Imagery*. Toronto.
Fantham, E. 1982. 'Quintilian on Performance: Traditional and Personal Elements in Institutio 11.3', *Phoenix* 36: 243–63.
Fantham, E. 1991. '*Stuprum*: Public Attitudes and Penalties for Sexual Offences in Republican Rome', *Échos du monde classique* 35: 267–91.
Fantham, E. 1992. *Lucan: De bello civili Book II*. Cambridge.
Fantham, E. 2002. 'Orator and/*et* actor', in P. Easterling and E. Hall (eds), *Greek and Roman Actors: Aspects of an Ancient Profession*. Cambridge: 362–76.
Fantham, E. 2004. *The Roman World of Cicero's De Oratore*. Oxford.
Faure-Ribreau, M. 2009. 'Les défis de l'*argumentum* du *Rudens*, ou comment jouer une comédie en bord de mer', *Vita Latina* 181: 18–28.
Fayer, C. 2005. *La familia romana: aspetti giuridici ed antiquari*. vol. 2. Rome.
Feeney, D. 1991. *The Gods in Epic*. Oxford.
Feeney, D. 2016. *Beyond Greek: The Beginnings of Latin Literature*. Cambridge, MA.
Ferri, S. 2002. *Architettura: (Dai Libri I-VII)*. Milan.
Fertik, H. 2018. 'Obligation and Devotion: Creating a New Community in Lucan's Bellum Civile', *Classical Philology* 113.4: 449–71.
Fiorentini, M. 2003. *Fiumi e mari nell'esperienza giuridica romana: Profili di tutela processuale e di inquadramento sistematico*. Milan.
Fiori, R. 1996. *Homo sacer: dinamica politico-constituzionale di una sanzione giuridico-religiosa*. Naples.
Fish, S. 1989. *Doing What Comes Naturally: Change, Rhetoric, and the Practice of Theory in Literary and Legal Studies*. Durham, NC/London.
Fish, S. 1991. 'The Law Wishes to Have a Formal Existence', in A. Sarat and T. R. Kearns (eds), *The Fate of Law*. Ann Arbor: 159–208.
Fisher, N. R. E. 1992. *Hybris: A Study in the Values of Honour and Shame in Ancient Greece*. Warminster.
Fletcher, R. and Hanink, J. (eds). 2016. *Creative Lives in Classical Antiquity: Poets, Artists and Biography*. Cambridge.
Fleury, P. (ed.). 1990. *De l'architecture. Livre I*. Paris.
Foner, E. 2019. *The Second Founding: How the Civil War and Reconstruction Remade the Constitution*. New York.
Fontaine, M. 2010. *Funny Words in Plautine Comedy*. New York.
Fontaine, M. 2020. 'Before Pussy Riot: Free Speech and Censorship in the Age of Plautus', in S. Papaioannou and C. Demetriou (eds), *Plautus' Erudite Comedy: New Insights into the Work of a doctus poeta*. Newcastle upon Tyne: 239–63.
Forehand, W. 1985. *Terence*. Boston.

Fortier, M. 2019. *Literature and Law*. London.
Foucault, M. 1969. 'Qu'est-ce qu'un auteur?', *Bulletin de la Société française de Philosophie* 63.3: 73–104.
Foucault, M. 1979 [1969]. 'What is an Author?', in J. V. Harari (ed.), *Textual Strategies: Perspectives in Post-structuralist Criticism*. Ithaca, NY: 141–60.
Foucault, M. 2007. *Security, Territory, Population: Lectures at the Collège de France, 1977–78*. Basingstoke.
Fraenkel, E. 1935. 'Naevius', *RE Suppl*. 5: 622–40.
Frangoulidis, S. A. 1996. '(Meta)theatre as Therapy in Terence's *Phormio*', *Classica et Mediaevalia* 47: 169–206.
Frangoulidis, S. A. 2013. '*Phormio*', in A. Augoustakis and A. Traill (eds), *A Companion to Terence*. Chichester: 281–94.
Frank, T. 1927. 'Naevius and Free Speech', *American Journal of Philology* 48.2: 105–10.
Fredershausen, O. 1906. *De Iure Plautino et Terentiano*. Göttingen.
Fredershausen, O. 1912. 'Weitere Studien über das Recht bei Plautus und Terenz', *Hermes* 47: 199–249.
Freud, S. 2009 [1927]. *Der Witz und seine Beziehung zum Unbewußten. Der Humor*. P. Gay (ed.). Frankfurt.
Freudenburg, K. 2014. '*Recusatio* as Political Theatre: Horace's Letter to Augustus', *Journal of Roman Studies* 104: 105–32.
Freudenburg, K. 2015. 'Seneca's *Apocolocyntosis*: Censors in the Afterworld', in S. Bartsch and A. Schiesaro (eds), *The Cambridge Companion to Seneca*. Cambridge: 93–105.
Frier, B. 1985. *The Rise of the Roman Jurists: Studies in Cicero's Pro Caecina*. Princeton.
Frier, B. 1989. *A Casebook on the Roman Law of Delict*. Atlanta.
Frier, B. 2019. 'The Roman Origins of the Public Trust Doctrine', *Journal of Roman Archaeology* 32: 641–7.
Früh, R. 2015. 'Verunsicherung im philosophischen Brief: Senecas *Epistulae Morales*', in R. Früh, T. Fuhrer, M. Humar, and M. Vöhler (eds), *Irritationen: rhetorische und poetische Verfahren der Verunsicherung*. Berlin/ Boston: 88–108.
Fuhrmann, M. 1971. 'Philologische Bemerkungen zur Sentenz "Summum ius summa iniuria"', in *Studi in onore di Edoardo Volterra*, vol. 2. Milan: 53–81.
Gadamer, H.- G. 1979. 'On the Scope and Function of Hermeneutical Reflection', in *Philosophical Hermeneutics* (trans. and ed. D. E. Linge). Berkeley and London: 18–43.
Gaertner, J. F. 2011. *Das antike Recht und die griechisch-römische Neue Komödie: Untersuchungen zu Plautus und seinen griechischen Vorbildern*. 2 vols. Habilitationsschrift Leipzig.
Gaertner, J. F. 2014. 'Law and Roman Comedy', in M. Fontaine and A. C. Scafuro (eds), *The Oxford Handbook of Greek and Roman Comedy*. New York: 615–33.
Gaiser, K. 1972. 'Zur Eigenart der römischen Komödie: Plautus und Terenz gegenüber ihren griechischen Vorbildern', *Aufstieg und Niedergang der römischen Welt* I.2: 1027–113.

Gaisser, J. H. 2002. 'The Reception of Classical Texts in the Renaissance', in A. J. Grieco, M. Rocke and F. Gioffredi Superbi (eds), *The Italian Renaissance in the Twentieth Century*. Florence: 387–400.

Gallagher, C. and S. Greenblatt. 2000. *Practicing New Historicism*. Chicago.

Gallia, A. 2020. '*Os columnatum* Again: Plautus *Miles Gloriosus* 211', *Classical Philology* 115.4: 722–6.

Gamauf, R. 2016. 'Slavery: Social Position and Legal Capacity', in P. du Plessis, J. Paul, C. Ando and K. Tuori (eds), *The Oxford Handbook of Roman Law and Society*. Oxford: 386–401.

Gardner, J. F. 1986. *Women in Roman Law and Society*. London.

Gardner, J. F. 1993. *Being a Roman Citizen*. London.

Gardner, J. F. 2011. 'Slavery and Roman Law', in K. Bradley and P. Cartledge (eds), *The Cambridge World History of Slavery*. Cambridge: 414–37.

Gebhardt, U. 2009. *Sermo Iuris: Rechtssprache und Recht in der augusteischen Dichtung*. Leiden.

Geffcken, K. A. 1973. *Comedy in the Pro Caelio*. Leiden.

Germany, R. 2019. 'The Politics of Roman Comedy', in M. Dinter (ed.), *The Cambridge Companion to Roman Comedy*. Cambridge: 66–84.

Gildenhard, I. 2003. 'The "Annalist" before the Annalists: Ennius and his *Annales*', in U. Eigler, U. Gotter, N. Luraghi and U. Walter (eds), *Formen römischer Geschichtsschreibung von den Anfängen bis Livius. Gattungen, Autoren, Kontexte*. Darmstadt: 93–114.

Gillespie, C. C. (forthcoming). 'Voiceless Grief: Domestic Disruption and the Failure of Fecundity in Lucan's *Bellum Civile*', in L. Fratantuono and C. Stark (eds), *Blackwell Companion to Latin Epic, 14–96 CE*. Malden, MA.

Godsey, E. R. 1928. 'Phormio the Magnificent', *The Classical Weekly* 22: 65–7.

Goldberg, S. M. 1978. 'Plautus' *Epidicus* and the Case of the Missing Original', *Transactions and Proceedings of the American Philological Association* 108: 81–91.

Goldberg, S. M. 1986. *Understanding Terence*. Princeton.

Goldberg, S. M. 1995. *Epic in Republican Rome*. Oxford.

Goldberg, S. M. 2005. *Constructing Literature in the Roman Republic*. Cambridge.

Goldberg, S. M., and G. Manuwald (eds). 2018. *Fragmentary Republican Latin: Ennius: Testimonia and Epic Fragments*. Cambridge, MA.

Golden, G. K. 2013. *Crisis Management During the Roman Republic*. Cambridge.

Goldschmidt, N. 2013. *Shaggy Crowns: Ennius' Annales and Virgil's Aeneid*. Oxford.

Goldschmidt, N. 2015a. 'Plautus: A Guide to Selected Sources', *Living Poets*, https://livingpoets.dur.ac.uk/w/ Plautus:_A_ Guide_ to_ Selected_ Sources.

Goldschmidt, N. 2015b. 'Terence: A Guide to Selected Sources', *Living Poets*, https://livingpoets.dur.ac.uk/w/ Terence:_A_ Guide_ to_ Selected_ Sources.

Goldschmidt, N. 2019. *Afterlives of the Roman Poets: Bioficiton and the Reception of Latin Poetry*. Cambridge.

Goodrich, P. 1990. *Languages of Law: From Logics of Memory to Nomadic Masks.* Oxford.

Goold, G. P. (ed.). 1984. *Ovid in Six Volumes. Metamorphoses. With an English Translation by F. J. Miller.* Cambridge, MA.

Goulder, B. (ed.). 2013. *Re-reading Foucault: On Law, Power and Rights.* Abingdon.

Gower, J. D. 2015. 'The Sovereign and the Exile: Archytas and Aristotle on the Living Law', *Epoché: A Journal for the History of Philosophy* 19.2: 311–28.

Gowers, E. 2019. 'Knight's Moves: The Son-in-Law in Cicero and Tacitus', *Classical Antiquity* 38: 2–35.

Gowing, A. M. 2005. *Empire and Memory: The Representation of the Roman Republic in Imperial Culture.* Cambridge.

Gradel, I. 2002. *Emperor Worship and Roman Religion.* Oxford.

Graf, F. 1995. 'Ekphrasis: Die Entstehung der Gattung in der Antike', in G. Boehm and H. Pfotenhauer (eds), *Beschreibungskunst—Kunstbeschreibung. Ekphrasis von der Antike bis zur Gegenwart.* Munich: 143–55.

Graf, F. 2005. 'Satire in a Ritual Context', in K. Freudenberg (ed.), *The Cambridge Companion to Roman Satire.* Cambridge: 192–206.

Granger, F. 1934. *Vitruvius: On Architecture.* Cambridge, MA.

Graziosi, B. 2002. *Inventing Homer: The Early Reception of Epic.* Cambridge.

Green, S. J. 2016. 'Recollections of a Heavenly Augustus: Memory and the *Res Gestae* in Seneca *Apocolocyntosis* 10.1–2', *Mnemosyne* 69: 685–90.

Greene, J. 2011. 'Originalism's Race Problem' 88 *Denver University Law Review*: 517–22.

Greene, J. 2005. *The Trouble with Ownership: Literary Property and Authorial Liability in England, 1660–1730.* Philadelphia.

Greenidge, A. H. J. 1901. *The Legal Procedure of Cicero's Time.* Oxford.

Griffin, M. T. 1976. *Seneca: A Philosopher in Politics.* Oxford.

Griffin, M. T. 1984. *Nero: The End of a Dynasty.* London.

Grimal, P. 1983. 'Le *Phormion* de Térence et l'histoire de la comédie', *Vita Latina* 91: 2–10.

Gros, P., A. Corso and E. Romano (eds). 1997. *De Architectura, Trad. e Commento.* 2 vols. Torino.

Gruen, E. 1990. *Studies in Greek Culture and Roman Policy.* Leiden.

Gruen, E. 2014. 'Roman Comedy and the Social Scene', in M. Fontaine and A. C. Scafuro (eds), *The Oxford Handbook of Greek and Roman Comedy.* New York: 601–14.

Gunderson, E. 2000. *Staging Masculinity: The Rhetoric of Performance in the Roman World.* Ann Arbor.

Gunderson, E. 2003. *Declamation, Paternity, and Roman Identity: Authority and the Rhetorical Self.* Cambridge.

Gunderson, E. 2009. *Nox Philologiae: Aulus Gellius and the Fantasy of the Roman Library.* Madison.

Gunderson, E. 2015a. *Laughing Awry. Plautus and Tragicomedy.* Oxford.

Gunderson, E. 2015b. *The Sublime Seneca: Ethics, Literature, Metaphysics.* Cambridge.
Gunderson, E. 2016. 'Declamatory Play', in R. Poignault and C. Schneider (eds), *Fabrique de la déclamation antique (controverses et suasoires).* Lyons: 179–95.
Gutierrez-Masson, L. 1993. '*Mare nostrum: Imperium* ou *dominium*?', *Revue internationale des droits de l'antiquité* 40: 293–315.
Habermas, J. 1992. *Faktizität und Geltung.* Frankfurt.
Habinek, T. 1998. *The Politics of Latin Literature: Writing, Identity, and Empire in Ancient Rome.* Princeton.
Habinek, T. 2005. *The World of Roman Song.* Baltimore.
Habinek, T. and A. Schiesaro (eds). 1997. *The Roman Cultural Revolution.* Cambridge.
Hachmann, E. 1995. *Die Führung des Lesers in Senecas Epistulae morales.* Münster.
Hagemann, M. 1998. *Iniuria: Von den XII-Tafeln bis zur Justinianischen Kodifikation.* Cologne.
Hammer, D. 2014. *Roman Political Thought.* Cambridge.
Hansen, M. H. 1991. *The Athenian Democracy in the Age of Demosthenes: Structure, Principles, and Ideology.* Oxford/Cambridge, MA.
Hanses, M. 2020. *The Life of Comedy after the Death of Plautus and Terence.* Ann Arbor.
Hardie, P. 1997. 'Questions of Authority. The Invention of Tradition in Ovid's *Metamorphoses* 15', in T. Habinek and A. Schiesaro (eds), 182–98.
Hardie, P. 2002. *Ovid's Poetics of Illusion.* Cambridge.
Harries, B. 1990. 'The Spinner and the Poet: Arachne in Ovid's *Metamorphoses*', *Proceedings of the Cambridge Philological Society* 36: 64–82.
Harries, J. 2002. 'Cicero and the Defining of the *Ius Civile*', in G. Clark and T. Rajak (eds), *Philosophy and Power in the Graeco-Roman World: Essays in Honour of Miriam Griffin.* Oxford: 51–68.
Harries, J. 2006. *Cicero and the Jurists: From Citizens' Law to the Lawful State.* London.
Harries, J. 2016. 'Servius, Cicero, and the *Res Publica* of Justinian', in P. du Plessis (ed.), *Cicero's Law: Rethinking Roman Law of the Late Republic.* Edinburgh: 123–41.
Harrison, A. R. W. 1968. *The Law of Athens.* vol. 1. Oxford.
Harrison, A. R. W. 1998. *The Law of Athens.* 2 vols, 2nd ed. Indianapolis.
Hausmaninger, H. and Gamauf, R. (eds). 2012. *A Casebook on Roman Property Law. Translated with Introduction, Supplementary Notes, and Glossary by George A. Sheets.* New York/Oxford.
Haverkamp, A. and Vismann, C. 1997. '*Habeas corpus*: the Law's Desire to Have the Body', in H. De Vries and S. Weber (eds), *Violence, Identity, and Self-Determination.* Stanford: 223–35.
Heffernan, J. 1993. *The Museum of Words: The Poetics of Ekphrasis from Homer to Ashberry.* Chicago.
Hegel, G. W. F. 1942. *Philosophy of Right.* Oxford.
Hejduk, J. D. 2012. 'Arachne's Attitude: *Metamorphoses* 6.25', *Mnemosyne* 65: 764–8.

Hemelrijk, E. A. 2015. *Hidden Lives, Public Personae: Women and Civic Life in the Roman West*. Oxford.
Henderson, G. 2015. *Creating Legal Worlds: Story and Style in a Culture of Argument*. Toronto/Buffalo/London.
Henderson, J. 1987. 'Lucan/The Word at War', *Ramus* 16: 122–64.
Henderson, J. 1989. 'Livy and the Invention of History', in A. Cameron (ed.), *History as Text*. London: 66–85.
Henderson, J. 2004. *Morals and Villas in Seneca's Letters: Places to Dwell*. Cambridge.
Henderson, J. 2009. *A Plautus Reader: Selections from Eleven Plays*. Mundelein, IL.
Hill, T. 2004. *Ambitiosa Mors: Suicide and Self in Roman Thought and Literature*. New York/London.
Hinds, S. 1987. *The Metamorphosis of Persephone: Ovid and the Self-conscious Muse*. Cambridge.
Holford-Strevens, L. 2003. *Aulus Gellius. An Antonine Scholar and his Achievement* (rev. ed.). Oxford.
Holmes, B. 2019. 'Bios', *Political Concepts: A Critical Lexicon*, https://www.politicalconcepts.org/bios-brooke-holmes/
Honig, B. 2009. *Emergency Politics: Paradox, Law, Democracy*. Princeton.
Howley, J. 2013. 'Why Read the Jurists? Aulus Gellius on Reading across Disciplines', in P. du Plessis (ed.), *New Frontiers. Law and Society in the Roman World*. Edinburgh: 9–20.
Howley, J. 2018. *Aulus Gellius and Roman Reading Culture: Text, Presence, and Imperial Knowledge in the Noctes Atticae*. Cambridge.
Humfress, C. 2021. 'Natural Law and Casuistic Reasoning in Roman Jurisprudence', in P. Adamson and C. Rapp (eds), *State and Nature*. Berlin: 247–66.
Hurka, F. 2010. *Die Asinaria des Plautus. Einleitung und Kommentar*. Munich.
Hurley, D. 2001. *Suetonius: Divus Claudius*. Cambridge.
Huvelin, P. 1903. 'La notion de l'*iniuria* dans le tres ancien droit romain', *Mélanges Appleton, Annales Univ. Lyon*, n.s. 2.3: 371–499.
Inwood, B. 2005. *Reading Seneca: Stoic Philosophy at Rome*. Oxford.
Jenkins, T. E. 2009. 'Livia the *Princeps*: Gender and Ideology in the *Consolatio ad Liviam*', *Helios* 36: 1–25.
Jocelyn, H. D. 1969. 'The Poet Cn. Naevius, P. Cornelius Scipio and R. Caecilius Metellus', *Antichthon* 3: 32–47.
Johnson, P. J. 2008. *Ovid before Exile: Art and Punishment in the Metamorphoses*. Madison.
Jongman, W. M. 2003. 'Slavery and the Growth of Rome', in C. Edwards and G. Woolf (eds), *Rome the Cosmopolis*. Cambridge: 100–22.
Jörs, P. 1888. *Römische Rechtswissenschaft zur Zeit der Republik. Erster Teil: Bis auf die Catonen*. Berlin.
Joshel, S. R. 1992. *Work, Identity, and Legal Status at Rome: A Study of the Occupational Inscriptions*. Norman, OK.

Kamini, D. 2015. 'The Contribution of the Law of *Epikleros* to the Comic Effect of *Phormio*', in J. Ngyllés (ed.), *Sapiens ubique civis. Proceedings of the International Conference on Classical Studies* (Szeged, Hungary, 2013). Budapest: 69–79.

Kaplan, S. G. 1991. *The Judicial Message in Seneca's Apocolocyntosis*. MA Diss. Portland State University.

Karakasis, E. 2014. 'Cicero *Comicus* – Catullus *Plautinus*: Irony and Praise in Cat. 49 Re-examined', in I. Perysinakis and E. Karakasis (eds), *Plautine Trends: Studies in Plautine Comedy and Its Reception*. Berlin: 197–223.

Kaser, M. 1955. Review of Kornhardt (1954), *Zeitschrift der Savigny-Stiftung für Rechtsgeschichte. Romanistische Abteilung* 72: 487–8.

Kaser, M. 1956. '*Infamia* und *ignominia* in den römischen Rechtsquellen', *Zeitschrift der Savigny-Stiftung für Rechtsgeschichte. Romanistische Abteilung* 73: 222–78.

Kaser, M. 1967. *Römische Rechtsgeschichte*. 2nd ed. Göttingen.

Kaser, M. 1971. *Das römische Privatrecht. Erster Abschnitt: Das altrömische, das vorklassische und klassische Recht*. 2nd ed. Munich.

Kastan, D. S. 1986. 'Proud Majesty Made a Subject: Shakespeare and the Spectacle of Rule', *Shakespeare Quarterly* 37: 459–75.

Kaster, R. (ed. and trans.). 1995. *Suetonius. De grammaticis et rhetoribus*. Oxford.

Keane, C. 2006. *Figuring Genre in Roman Satire*. Oxford.

Keith, A. 2008. 'Lament in Lucan's *Bellum Civile*', in A. Suter (ed.), *Lament: Studies in the Ancient Mediterranean and Beyond*. Oxford: 233–57.

Kelly, J. M. 1966. *Roman Litigation*. Oxford.

Kennedy, D. 1976. 'Form and Substance in Private Law Adjudication', *Harvard Law Review* 89: 1685–778.

Kenney, E. J. 1969. 'Ovid and the Law', *Yale Classical Studies* 21: 241–63.

Keramida, D. 2019. 'The Re-Imagination of a Letter-Writer and the De-Construction of an Ovidian Rape Narrative at *Ars Amatoria* 1.527–64', *Classica et Mediaevalia* 67: 153–87.

Keulen, W. 2008. *Gellius the Satirist: Roman Cultural Authority in Attic Nights*. Leiden.

King, L. W. (trans.). 1900. *The Letters and Inscriptions of Ḥammurabi, King of Babylon*. Vol. 3. London.

Kleijwegt, M. 2009. 'Creating New Citizens: Freed Slaves, the State and Citizenship in Early Rome and under Augustus', *European Review of History* 16: 319–30.

Klingmüller, F. 1914. '*Restitutio*', *Paulys Realencyclopädie der classischen Altertumswissenschaft*, 2. Reihe, 1: 676–85.

Knight, C. A. 1990. 'Imagination's Cerberus: Satire and the Metaphor of Genre', *Philological Quarterly* 69: 131–51.

Knoche, U. 1975. *Roman Satire*. 2nd ed. Trans. E. S. Ramage. Bloomington.

Könczöl, M. 2008a. 'Law, Fact and Narratives in Ancient Rhetoric: The Case of the *causa Curiana*', *International Journal for the Semiotics of Law* 21: 21–33.

Könczöl, M. 2008b. 'Clemency and Justice in the *De Clementia* of Seneca', *Iustum Aequum Salutare* 4: 61–9.

Koning, H. 2010. *Hesiod: The Other Poet. Ancient Reception of a Cultural Icon*. Leiden/Boston.

Konstan, D. 1983. *Roman Comedy*. Ithaca, NY.

Konstan, D. 2005. 'Clemency as a Virtue', *Classical Philology* 100.4: 337–46.

Kornhardt, H. 1953. 'Summum ius', *Hermes* 81: 77–85.

Kornhardt, H. 1954. '*Restitutio in integrum* bei Terenz', in O. Hiltbrunner, H. Kornhardt and F. Tietze (eds), *Thesaurismata: Festschrift für I. Kapp*. Munich: 65–78.

Kränzlein, A. 1963. *Eigentum und Besitz im griechischen Recht des fünften und vierten Jahrhunderts v. Chr.* Berlin.

Kraus, C. S. 1994. *Livy: Ab Vrbe Condita, Book VI*. Cambridge.

Kruschwitz, P. 1999. *P. Terentius Afer: Phormio. Lateinisch/Deutsch*. Stuttgart.

Kruschwitz, P. 2004. *Terenz*. Darmstadt.

Kuhn-Treichel, T. 2018. 'Das Epiklerat im *Phormio* des Terenz und im Ἐπιδικαζόμενος des Apollodor von Karystos', in H.-G. Nesselrath and J. Platschek (eds), *Menschen und Recht: Fallstudien zu Rechtsfragen und ihrer Bedeutung in der griechischen und römischen Komödie*. Tübingen: 111–35.

Kunkel, W. 2001. *Die römischen Juristen: Herkunft und soziale Stellung*. 2nd ed. Cologne.

Kupisch, B. 1974. *In integrum restitutio und vindicatio utilis bei Eigentumsübertragungen im römischen Recht*. Berlin/New York.

Kurman, G. 1974. 'Ecphrasis in Epic Poetry', *Comparative Literature* 26: 1–13.

Labruna, L. 1995 [1968]. 'Plauto, Manilio, Catone: Fonti per lo studio dell'*emptio consensuale*?', in L. Labruna, *Adminicula*. 3rd ed. Naples: 179–217.

La Bua, G. 2019. *Cicero and Roman Education: The Reception of the Speeches and Ancient Scholarship*. Cambridge.

Lambinus, D. 1576. *M. Accius Plautus ex fide atque auctoritate complurium librorum manuscriptorum opera emendatus*. Paris.

Lambrini, P. 2019 [2016]. *Strutture giuridiche romane e diritto privato europeo*. Naples.

Langlands, R. 2006. *Sexual Morality in Ancient Rome*. Cambridge.

Langlands, R. 2018. *Exemplary Ethics in Ancient Rome*. Cambridge.

Lape, S. 2004. *Reproducing Athens: Menander's Comedy, Democratic Culture, and the Hellenistic City*. Princeton.

Lausberg, H. 1998. *Handbook of Literary Rhetoric: A Foundation for Literary Study*. Leiden.

Leach, E. W. 1974. 'Ekphrasis and the Theme of Artistic Failure in Ovid's *Metamorphoses*', *Ramus* 3: 102–42.

Leach, E. W. 1989. 'The Implied Reader and the Political Argument in Seneca's *Apocolocyntosis* and *De Clementia*', *Arethusa* 22: 197–230.

Lebek, W. D. 1990. 'Standeswürde und Berufsverbot unter Tiberius: Das SC der Tabula Larinas', *Zeitschrift für Papyrologie und Epigraphik* 81: 37–96.

Leeman, A., H. Pinkster, H. L. W. Nelson, E. Rabbie and J. Wisse (eds). 1981–2008. *M. T. Cicero: De Oratore Libri III*. Heidelberg.

Lefèvre, E. 1978. *Der Phormio des Terenz und der Epidikazomenos des Apollodor von Karystos.* Munich.
Lefèvre, E. 1994. *Terenz' und Menanders Heautontimoroumenos.* Munich.
Lefèvre, E. 2008. *Terenz' und Menanders Andria.* Munich.
Lefèvre, E., E. Stärk and G. Vogt-Spira (eds). 1991. *Plautus barbarus: Sechs Kapitel zur Originalität des Plautus.* Tübingen.
Lefkowitz, M. 2012. *The Lives of the Greek Poets.* 2nd ed. London.
Lehne-Gstreinthaler, L. 2019. *Iurisperiti et oratores: Eine Studie zu den römischen Juristen der Republik.* Cologne.
Leigh, M. 1997. *Lucan: Spectacle and Engagement.* Oxford.
Leigh, M. 2004a. 'The *Pro Caelio* and Comedy', *Classical Philology* 99: 300–35.
Leigh, M. 2004b. *Comedy and the Rise of Rome.* Oxford.
Leigh, M. 2010. 'Forms of Exile in the *Rudens* of Plautus', *Classical Quarterly* 60: 110–17.
Lenel, O. 1889. *Palingenesia Iuris Civilis.* 2 vols. Berlin.
Leo, F. 1913. *Geschichte der römischen Literatur. Erster Band: Die archaische Literatur.* Berlin.
Leppin, H. 1992. *Histrionen: Untersuchungen zur sozialen Stellung von Bühnenkünstlern im Westen des Römischen Reiches zur Zeit der Republik und des Principats.* Bonn.
Levick, B. 2010. *Augustus: Image and Substance.* Harlow/London/New York.
Levick, B. 2012 [1990]. *Claudius.* London.
Liebs, D. 2006. 'Der ungeliebte Jurist in der römischen Welt', *Zeitschrift der Savigny-Stiftung für Rechtsgeschichte. Romanistische Abteilung* 123: 1–18.
Lintott, A. 1999a. *The Constitution of the Roman Republic.* Oxford.
Lintott, A. 1999b. *Violence in Republican Rome.* Oxford.
Lloyd, M. 1992. *The Agon in Euripides.* Oxford.
Loewenstein, J. 2002. *The Author's Due: Printing and the Prehistory of Copyright.* Chicago.
Lotito, G. 1996. 'Usi e funzioni del diritto: Qualche osservazione su Plauto e la Commedia Nuova', in D. Mantovani (ed.), *Per la storia del pensiero giuridico romano: Dall'età dei pontefici alla scuola di Servio – Atti del Seminario di S. Marino, 7–9 gennaio 1993.* Turin: 185–208.
Lott, J. B. 2012. *Death and Dynasty in Early Imperial Rome.* Cambridge.
Lowrie, M. 2007. 'Sovereignty before the Law: Agamben and the Roman Republic', *Law and Humanities* 1: 31–55.
Lowrie, M. 2009a. *Writing, Performance, and Authority in Augustan Rome.* Oxford.
Lowrie, M. (ed.). 2009b. *Oxford Readings in Classical Studies. Horace: Odes and Epodes.* Oxford.
Lowrie, M. 2010. 'Spurius Maelius: *Homo Sacer* and Dictatorship', in B. Breed, C. Damon, and A. Rossi (eds), *Citizens of Discord: Rome and its Civil Wars.* Oxford: 171–86.
Lowrie, M. 2016. 'Roman Law and Latin Literature', in P. du Plessis, C. Ando and K. Tuori (eds), *Oxford Handbook of Roman Law and Society.* Oxford: 70–81.

Lowrie, M. (forthcoming). 'Political Thought', in R. Gibson and C. Whitton (eds), *The Cambridge Critical Guide to Latin Literature*. Cambridge.
Lowrie, M. and S. Lüdemann (eds). 2015. *Exemplarity and Singularity: Thinking Through Particulars in Philosophy, Literature, and Law*. London.
Luhmann, N. 1981. *Ausdifferenzierung des Rechts. Beiträge zur Rechtssoziologie und Rechtstheorie*. Frankfurt.
Lytle, E. 2016. 'Status Beyond Law: Ownership, Access, and the Ancient Mediterranean', in T. Bekker-Nielsen and R. Gertwagen (eds), *The Inland Seas: Towards an Ecohistory of the Mediterranean and the Black Sea*. Stuttgart: 107–35.
MacLean, R. 2018. *Freed Slaves and Roman Imperial Culture: Social Integration and the Transformation of Values*. Cambridge.
MacRae, D. E. 2013. 'The Books of Numa: Writing, Intellectuals and the Making of Roman Religion', PhD diss. Harvard University.
Malcolm X. 1964. Speech at the Audubon Ballroom, Washington Heights, NY, 29 March 1964. Text available at http://www.vlib.us/amdocs/texts/malcolmx0364.html. Video at https://www.youtube.com/watch?v=3Aq2Z0i8D6A. Both accessed 26 October 2021.
Maltby, R. 1991. *A Lexicon of Ancient Latin Etymologies*. Leeds.
Maltby, R. 2012. *Terence: Phormio. Edited with Introduction, Translation and Commentary*. Oxford.
Manderson, D. 2019. 'Athena's Way: The Jurisprudence of the *Oresteia*', *Law, Culture and the Humanities* 15: 253–76.
Mankin, D. 2011. *Cicero De Oratore. Book 3*. Cambridge.
Mann, J. E. 2012. *Hippocrates. On the Art of Medicine*. Leiden.
Manson, E. 1899. 'Suicide as a Crime', *Journal of the Society of Comparative Legislation* 1: 311–19.
Mantovani, D. 2017. 'Quando i giuristi diventarono 'veteres'. Augusto e Sabino, i tempi del potere e i tempi della giurisprudenza', in S. Rocchi and C. Mussini (eds), *Imagines Antiquitatis. Representations, Concepts, Receptions of the Past in Roman Antiquity and the Early Italian Renaissance*. Berlin: 249–303.
Manuwald, G. 2009. '*concilia deorum*: Ein episches Motiv in der römischen Satire', in F. Felgentreu, F. Mundt and N. Rücker (eds), *Per attentam Caesaris aurem: Satire – die unpolitische Gattung?* Tübingen: 46–61.
Manuwald, G. 2011. *Roman Republican Theatre*. Cambridge.
Manuwald, G. 2019a. 'Plautus and Terence in their Roman Contexts', in M. T. Dinter (ed.), *The Cambridge Companion to Roman Comedy*. Cambridge: 229–40.
Manuwald, G. 2019b. *Fragmentary Republican Roman Oratory*. Cambridge, MA.
Marmorale, E. (ed.). 1950. *Naevius poeta*. 2nd ed. Florence.
Marshall, C. W. 2006. *The Stagecraft and Performance of Roman Comedy*. Cambridge.
Martelli, F. 2010. 'Signatures Events Contexts: Copyright at the End of the First Principate', *Ramus* 39: 130–59.
Martelli, F. 2013. *Ovid's Revisions: The Editor as Author*. Cambridge.

Maruotti, A. 2019. 'Sortir de soi: le parcours de Lucilius dans les «Lettres» de Sénèque', *Cahiers des Études Anciennes* 56: 177–87.

Marx, F. 1959 [1928]. *Plautus Rudens: Text und Kommentar.* Amsterdam.

Massioni, M. 1993. 'L'evocazione forense nel *Phormio* di Terenzio', *Sileno* 19: 159–77.

Matheson, S. B. 1994. 'The mission of Triptolemus and the Politics of Athens', *Greek, Roman, and Byzantine Studies* 35.4: 345–77.

Mattingly, H. B. 1960. 'Naevius and the Metelli', *Historia* 9: 414–39.

Maurach, G. 1970. *Der Bau von Senecas epistulae morales.* Heidelberg.

May, J. M. and J. Wisse (eds). 2001. *On the Ideal Orator. Translated, with Introduction, Notes, Appendixes, Glossary, and Indexes.* Oxford.

McCoskey, D. 2012. *Race: Antiquity and its Legacy.* Oxford.

McGill, S. 2012. *Plagiarism in Latin Literature.* Cambridge.

McGinn, T. 1998. *Prostitution, Sexuality, and the Law in Ancient Rome.* Oxford.

Michalopoulos, A. N. 2014. *Οβίδιος Ηρωίδες 20–21: Ακόντιος και Κυδίππη. Εισαγωγή, Κείμενο, Μετάφραση, Σχόλια.* Athens.

Michel, A. 1987. 'Esthétique et moralité dans le *Phormion*. Le *decorum* de Térence', in S. Boldrini et al. (eds), *Filologia e forme letterarie: Studi offerti a Francesco Della Corte.* Urbino: 111–26.

Milazzo, A. 2011. *Iniuria: Alle origini dell'offesa morale come categoria giuridica.* Rome.

Miles, G. 1995. *Livy: Reconstructing Early Rome.* Ithaca, NY.

Milnor, K. 2005. *Gender, Domesticity, and the Age of Augustus: Inventing Private Life.* Oxford.

Mitchell, T. N. 1971. 'Cicero and the *Senatus Consultum Ultimum*', *Historia* 20: 47–61.

Moatti, C. 1997. *La raison de Rome: naissance de l'esprit critique à la fin de la République (IIe–Ier siècle av. J.-C.).* Paris.

Moatti, C. 2015. *The Birth of Critical Thinking in Republican Rome.* Trans. J. Lloyd. Cambridge.

Momigliano, A. 1934. *Claudius: The Emperor and his Achievements.* Oxford.

Momigliano, A. 1942a. 'Camillus and Concord', *Classical Quarterly* 36: 111–20.

Momigliano, A. 1942b. Review of Lorna Robinson, *Freedom of Speech in the Roman Republic, Journal of Roman Studies* 32: 120–4.

Mommsen, T. 1888. *Römisches Staatsrecht Dritter Band. II. Abtheilung.* Leipzig.

Mommsen, T. 1899. *Römisches Strafrecht.* Leipzig.

Moore, T. J. 1998. *The Theater of Plautus: Playing to the Audience.* Austin.

Moore, T. J. 2001. 'Terence and Roman New Comedy', in S. O'Bryhim (ed.), *Greek and Roman Comedy: Translations and Interpretations of Four Representative Plays.* Austin: 243–320.

Morley, N. 2003. 'Migration and the Metropolis', in C. Edwards and G. Woolf (eds), *Rome the Cosmopolis.* Cambridge: 147–57.

Mousourakis, G. 2007. *A Legal History of Rome.* London.

Mueller M. 2016. *Objects as Actors: Props and the Poetics of Performance in Greek Tragedy.* Chicago.

Mueller, M. and M. Telò (eds). 2018. *The Materialities of Greek Tragedy: Objects and Affect in Aeschylus, Sophocles, and Euripides*. London.

Murgatroyd, P. 2000. 'Plotting in Ovidian Rape Narratives', *Eranos* 98: 75–92.

Murgatroyd, P. 2005. *Mythical and Legendary Narrative in Ovid's Fasti*. Leiden/Boston.

Murphy, C. 2007. *Are we Rome? The fall of an empire and the fate of America*. Boston.

Narducci, E. 1989. 'Cesare e la patria (Ipotesi su *Phars.* I 185–192)', *Maia* 32: 175–8.

Narducci, E. 1997. *Cicerone e l'eloquenza romana: retorica e progetto culturale*. Rome.

Nauta, R. R. 1987. 'Seneca's *Apocolocyntosis* as Saturnalian Literature', *Mnemosyne* 40: 69–96.

Ng, E. Y. L. 2008. 'Mirror Reading and Guardians of Women in the Early Roman Empire', *Journal of Theological Studies* 59.2: 679–95.

Nguyen, N. L. 2006. 'Roman Rape: An Overview of Roman Rape Laws from the Republican Period to Justinian's Reign', *Michigan Journal of Gender & Law* 13: 75–112.

Nicholas, B. 1962. *An Introduction to Roman Law*. Oxford/New York.

Nichols, M. F. 2017. *Author and Audience in Vitruvius' De Architectura*. Cambridge.

Nippel, W. 2008. 'Regel und Ausnahme in der römischer Verfassung', in M. Bernett, W. Nippel, and A. Winterling (eds), *Christian Meier zur Diskussion*. Stuttgart: 121–41.

Nissen, A. 1877. *Das Justitium: Eine Studie aus der römischen Rechtsgeschichte*. Leipzig.

Nörr, D. 1974. *Rechtskritik in der römischen Antike*. Munich.

Nörr, D. 1976. 'Der Jurist im Kreis der Intellektuellen: Mitspieler oder Außenseiter?', in D. Medicus and H. H. Seiler (eds), *Festschrift Max Kaser*. Munich: 57–90.

Norton, L. 2013. *Aspects of Ecphrastic Technique in Ovid's Metamorphoses*. Newcastle upon Tyne.

Norwood, G. 1923. *The Art of Terence*. Oxford.

Novkirishka-Stoyanova, M. 2015. 'Ius publice respondendi ex auctoritate principis', *Ius Romanum* 55: 55–82.

Nussbaum, M. 1997. 'Kant and Stoic Cosmopolitanism', *Journal of Political Philosophy* 5: 1–25.

O'Gorman, E. 2005. 'Citation and Authority in Seneca's *Apocolocyntosis*', in K. Freudenburg (ed.), *Cambridge Companion to Roman Satire*. Cambridge: 95–108.

Oksanish, J. 2019. *Vitruvian Man: Rome under Construction*. Oxford/New York.

Orestano, R. 1951. *La struttura giuridica del matrimonio romano dal diritto classico al diritto giustinianeo*. vol. 1. Milan.

Ortu, R. 2017. 'Plaut. *Rud.* 975: *Mare quidem commune certost omnibus*', *Jus-Online* 2: 160–88.

Osgood, J. 2007. 'The *Vox* and *Verba* of an Emperor: Claudius, Seneca and *Le Prince Ideal*', *Classical Journal* 102: 329–53.

Panayotakis, C. 2014. 'Ο Νέρων στην Ἀποκολοκύντωση τοῦ Σενέκα', in S. Tzounakas (ed.), *Ἐγκώμια Ἡγετικῶν Μορφῶν στὴν Λατινικὴ Γραμματεία*. Nicosia: 154–65.

Pandey, N. 2020. 'The Roman Roots of Racial Capitalism: What an Ancient Empire Can Teach Us about Diversity', *The Berlin Journal* 34: 16–20.

Paoli, U. E. 1962. *Comici latini e diritto attico*. Milan.
Paoli, U. E. 1976. *Altri studi di diritto greco e romano*. Milan.
Papaioannou, S., A. Serafim and B. Da Vela (eds). 2017. *The Theatre of Justice. Aspects of Performance in Greco-Roman Oratory and Rhetoric*. Leiden/ Boston.
Paschalis, M. 2009. 'The Afterlife of the Emperor Claudius in Seneca's *Apocolocyntosis*', *Numen* 56: 198–216.
Patterson, O. 1982. *Slavery and Social Death: A Comparative Study*. Cambridge, MA.
Peirano, I. 2013. '*Ille ego qui quondam*: On Authorial (An)onymity', in A. Marmodoro and J. Hill (eds), *The Author's Voice in Classical and Late Antiquity*. Oxford: 251–85.
Pellecchi, L. 2013. 'Per una lettura giuridica della *Rudens* di Plauto', *Athenaeum* 101.1: 103–62.
Pennitz, M. 2013. 'Zum Prozess wegen des Kaufs einer vermeintlichen Sklavin: Plautus' *Rudens* als römischrechtliche Quelle?', in P. Mauritsch and C. Ulf (eds), *Kultur(en): Formen des Alltäglichen in der Antike – Festschrift für Ingomar Weiler zum 75. Geburtstag*. Graz: 567–84.
Peppe, L. 2002. 'Le forti donne di Plauto', in L. Agostiniani and P. Desideri (eds), *Plauto testimone della società del suo tempo*. Naples: 67–91.
Petrides, A. K. 2014. 'Plautus between Greek Comedy and Atellan Farce: Assessments and Reassessments', in M. Fontaine and A. C. Scafuro (eds), *The Oxford Handbook of Greek and Roman Comedy*. New York: 424–43.
Pettinger, A. 2019. 'Rebuilding Romulus' Senate. The *Lectio Senatus* of 18 BCE', in K. Morrell, J. Osgood and K. Welch (eds), *The Alternative Augustan Age*. Oxford: 46–62.
Phillips, D. D. 2013. *The Law of Ancient Athens*. Ann Arbor.
Polt, C. 2021. *Catullus and Roman Comedy: Theatricality and Personal Drama in the Late Republic*. Cambridge.
Porter, J. I. 2006. 'Foucault's Antiquity', in C. Martindale and R. F. Thomas (eds), *Classics and the Uses of Reception*. Malden, MA/Oxford: 168–79.
Posani, M. R. 1941. 'Il Formione di Terenzio', *Atene e Roma: Rassegna Trimestrale Dell'associazione Italiana di Cultura Classica* 43: 29–55.
Posner, R. 2009. *Law and Literature*. 3rd ed. Cambridge, MA.
Price, S. R. F. 1987. 'The Consecration of Roman Emperors', in S. R. F. Price and D. Cannadine (eds), *Rituals of Royalty: Power and Ceremonial in Traditional Societies*. Cambridge: 56–105.
Pugliese, G. 1938. *La simulazione nei negozi giuridici*. Padova.
Purpura, G. 2004. '*Liberum mare*, acque territoriali e riserve di pesca nel mondo antico', *Annali del Seminario Giuridico dell'Università di Palermo* 49: 165–206.
Radicke, J. 2004. *Lucans poetische Technik: Studien zum historischen Epos*. Leiden.
Ramsby, T. 2005. 'Striving for Permanence: Ovid's Funerary Inscriptions', *Classical Journal* 100.4: 365–91.
Read, A. 2016. *Theatre and Law*. London.
Reichman, R. 2009. *The Affective Life of Law. Legal Modernism and the Literary Imagination*. Stanford.

Reinhardt, T. 2003. *Marcus Tullius Cicero, Topica (Edited with Translation, Introduction, and Commentary)*. Oxford.
Reinhardt, T., and M. Winterbottom (eds). 2006. *Quintilian, Institutio Oratoria Book 2*. Oxford.
Relihan, J. C. 1993. *Ancient Menippean Satire*. Baltimore/London.
Rich, J. W. 2012. 'Making the Emergency Permanent: *auctoritas, potestas* and the Evolution of the Principate of Augustus', in Y. Rivière (ed.), *Des réformes augustéennes*. Rome: 37–121.
Richard, C. 1995. *The Founders and the Classics: Greece, Rome, and the American Enlightenment*. Cambridge, MA.
Richardson-Hay, C. 2006. *First Lessons: Book 1 of Seneca's Epistulae Morales: A Commentary*. Bern.
Richlin, A. 1992. 'Reading Ovid's Rapes', in A. Richlin (ed.), *Pornography and Representation in Greece and Rome*. New York/Oxford: 158–79.
Richlin, A. 2017. *Slave Theater in the Roman Republic: Plautus and Popular Comedy*. Cambridge.
Riggsby, A. M. 2010. *Roman Law and the Legal World of the Romans*. Cambridge.
Rimell, V. 2015. *The Closure of Space in Roman Poetics: Empire's Inward Turn*. Cambridge.
Rives, J. 2002. 'Magic in the XII Tables Revisited', *Classical Quarterly* 52: 270–90.
Robinson, O. F. 1995. *The Criminal Law of Ancient Rome*. Baltimore.
Robinson, T. J. 2005. 'In the Court of Time: The Reckoning of a Monster in the *Apocolocyntosis* of Seneca', *Arethusa* 38: 223–57.
Roche, P. 2009. *Lucan, De bello civili, Book I*. Oxford.
Rochette, B. 1998. '*Poeta barbarus* (Plaute, *Miles Gloriosus* 211)', *Latomus* 57: 414–17.
Roller, M. B. 2001. *Constructing Autocracy: Aristocrats and Emperors in Julio-Claudian Rome*. Princeton.
Roller, M. B. 2018. *Models from the Past in Roman Culture: A World of Exempla*. Cambridge.
Rood, T., C. Atack and T. Phillips (eds). 2020. *Anachronism and Antiquity*. London.
Rose, M. 1988. 'The Author as Proprietor: *Donaldson v. Becket* and the Genealogy of Modern Authorship', *Representations* 32: 51–85.
Rose, M. 1993. *Authors and Owners: The Invention of Copyright*. Cambridge, MA.
Rose, V. and H. Müller-Strübing (eds). 1867. *Vitruvii De architectura libri decem ad antiquissimos codices nunc primum ediderunt*. Leipzig.
Rostagni, A. (ed.). 1944. *Suetonio. De poetis e biografi minori*. Turin.
Rudd, N. (ed.). 1989. *Horace, Epistles Book II and Epistle to the Pisones ('Ars poetica')*. Cambridge.
Rudd, N. (trans.). 2005. *The Satires of Horace and Persius*. New York.
Rudich, V. 1997. *Dissidence and Literature under Nero: The Price of Rhetoricization*. London/ New York.
Rüfner, T. 2016. 'Imperial *cognitio* Process', in P. du Plessis, C. Ando and K. Tuori (eds), *Oxford Handbook of Roman Law and Society*. Oxford: 257–69.

Ruhl, J. B., and T. A. J. McGinn. 2020. 'The Roman Public Trust Doctrine: What Was It, and Does It Support an Atmospheric Trust?', *Ecology Law Quarterly* 47.1: 117–78.

Rüpke, J. 2000. 'Räume literarischer Kommunikation in der Formierungsphase römischer Literatur', in M. Braun, A. Haltenhoff and F.-H. Mutschler (eds), *Moribus antiquis res stat Romana. Römische Werte und römische Literatur im 3. und 2. Jh. v. Chr.* Munich: 31–52.

Russell, A. 2016a. 'Why did Clodius Shut the Shops? The Rhetoric of Mobilizing a Crowd in the Late Republic', *Historia* 65.2: 186–210.

Russell, A. 2016b. *The Politics of Public Space in Republican Rome*. Cambridge.

Russell, D. A. 2002. *Quintilian. The Orator's Education*. Cambridge, MA.

Sabot, A. F. 1976. *Ovide, Poète de l'Amour dans ses œuvres de Jeunesse: «Amores», «Héroïdes», «Ars Amatoria», «Remedia Amoris», «De medicamine Faciei Femineae»*. Paris.

Salzman-Mitchell, P. B. 2005. *A Web of Fantasies: Gaze, Image and Gender in Ovid's Metamorphoses*. Columbus, OH.

Santangelo, F. 2015. 'Testing Boundaries: Divination and Prophecy in Lucan', *Greece & Rome* 62.2: 177–88.

Santoro, R. 2009 [1971]. '*Manu(m) conserere*' in R. Santoro (M. Varvaro, ed.), *Scritti Minori*. vol. 1. Turin: 143–221.

Sarat, A. (ed.). 2008. *Law and Literature Reconsidered*. Bingley.

Sarat, A., D. Engel, M. Constable, S. Lawrence and V. Hanset (eds). 1998. *Crossing Boundaries: Traditions and Transformations in Law and Society Research*. Chicago.

Scafuro, A. C. 1993. 'Staging Entrapment: On the Boundaries of the Law in Plautus' *Persa*', in N. W. Slater and B. Zimmermann (eds), *Intertextualität in der griechisch-römischen Komödie*. Stuttgart: 55–77.

Scafuro, A. C. 1997. *The Forensic Stage: Settling Disputes in Graeco-Roman New Comedy*. Cambridge.

Scheidel, W. 1997. 'Quantifying the Sources of Slaves in the Early Roman Empire', *Journal of Roman Studies* 87: 156–69.

Scherillo, G. 1945. *Lezioni di diritto romano: Le cose*. Milan.

Schermaier, M. J. 2009. '*Res Communes Omnium*: The History of an Idea from Greek Philosophy to Grotian Jurisprudence', *Grotiana* 30: 20–48.

Schermaier, M. J. 2012. 'Private Rechte an *res communes*?', in E. Chevreau, D. Kremer and A. Laquerrière-Lacroix (eds), *Carmina Iuris: Mélanges en l'honneur de Michel Humbert*. Paris: 773–92.

Schiavone, A. 2012. *The Invention of Law in the West*. Trans. J. Carden and A. Shugaar. Cambridge, MA.

Schiesaro, A. 2015. 'Seneca and Epicurus: The Allure of the Other', in A. Schiesaro and S. Bartsch (eds), *The Cambridge Companion to Seneca*. Cambridge: 239–52.

Schmeling, G. 2011. *A Commentary on The Satyrica of Petronius*. Oxford.

Schmeling, G. 2020. *Petronius: Satyricon. Seneca: Apocolocyntosis.* Cambridge, MA.
Schmid, K. 2017. 'How Law Evolved out of Economics: Sequential Logic and Stereometric Interpretation in Ancient Near Eastern and Biblical Law Collections', *Zeitschrift für Altorientalische und Biblische Rechtsgeschichte* 23: 115–21.
Schmitt, C. 2005 [1922]. *Political Theology: Four Chapters on the Concept of Sovereignty.* Trans. G. Schwab. Chicago.
Schmitzer, U. 2013. 'Recusatio', in H. Cancik and H. Schneider (eds), *Brill's New Pauly. Antiquity volumes*, Brill Online. http://referenceworks.brillonline.com/entries/brill-s-new-pauly/recusatio-e1019700.
Schneider, H. 1961. 'Phormio, Champion of Life', *The Classical Bulletin* 38: 27–28.
Schönegg, B. 1999. *Senecas Epistulae morales als philosophisches Kunstwerk.* Bern.
Schoonhoven, H. 1992. *The pseudo-Ovidian Ad Liviam de morte Drusi (Consolatio ad Liviam, Epicedium Drusi): A Critical Text with Introduction and Commentary.* Groningen.
Schrijvers, P. H. 1988. 'Deuil, desespoir, destruction (Lucain, la *Pharsale* II 1–234)', *Mnemosyne* 41: 341–54.
Schulz, F. 1922. 'Die Lehre vom erzwungenen Rechtsgeschäft im antiken römischen Recht', *Zeitschrift der Savigny-Stiftung für Rechtsgeschichte. Romanistische Abteilung* 43: 171–261.
Schulz, F. 1961. *Geschichte der römischen Rechtswissenschaft.* Weimar.
Schütze, R. 2019. 'Constitutionalism(s)', in R. Masterman and R. Schütze (eds), *The Cambridge Companion to Comparative Constitutional Law.* Cambridge: 40–66.
Schwind, A. 1901. *Über das Recht bei Terenz.* Würzburg.
Sealing, K. E. 1998. 'The Myth of a Color-Blind Constitution', *Washington University Journal of Urban and Contemporary Law* 54: 157–210.
Segal, E. 1986. *Roman Laughter: The Comedy of Plautus.* 2nd ed. New York/Oxford.
Segal, E., and C. Moulton. 1978. '*Contortor legum*: The hero of the *Phormio*', *Rheinisches Museum für Philologie* 121: 276–88.
Seidler, M. J. 1983. 'Kant and the Stoics on Suicide', *Journal of the History of Ideas* 44.3: 429–53.
Sharrock, A. 1996. 'The Art of Deceit: Pseudolus and the Art of Reading', *Classical Quarterly* 46: 152–74.
Sharrock, A. 2009. *Reading Roman Comedy: Poetics and Playfulness in Plautus and Terence.* Cambridge.
Shelley, P. B. 1994. *The Selected Poetry and Prose of Shelley. Introduction and Notes by B. Woodcock.* Ware.
Shelton, J.-A. 2013. *The Women of Pliny's Letters.* London/New York.
Sinfield, A. 1996. '*Poetaster*, the Author, and the Perils of Cultural Production', *Renaissance Drama* 27: 3–18.
Sjöblad, A. 2015. *Metaphorical Coherence: Studies in Seneca's Epistulae Morales.* Lund.
Skutsch, O. (ed.). 1985. *The Annals of Q. Ennius.* Oxford.
Smith, R. E. 1951. 'The Law of Libel at Rome', *Classical Quarterly* 1: 169–79.

Spencer, R. A. 1996. *Contrast in Ovid's Metamorphoses*, PhD Diss. University of North Carolina, Chapel Hill.
Spentzou, E. 2018. 'Violence and Alienation in Lucan's *Pharsalia*: The Case of Caesar', in M. R. Gale and J. H. D. Scourfield (eds), *Texts and Violence in the Roman World*. Cambridge: 246–68.
Spruit, J. E. 1966. *De juridische en sociale positie van de Romeinse acteurs*. Utrecht.
Squire, M. 2015. 'Ecphrasis: Visual and verbal interactions in ancient Greek and Latin Literature', in *Oxford Handbooks Online in Classical Studies*. https://www.oxfordhandbooks.com/view/10.1093/oxfordhb/9780199935390.001.0001/oxfordhb-9780199935390-e-58.
Stacey, P. 2011. 'The Sovereign Person in Senecan Political Theory', *Republics of Letters* 2, https://arcade.stanford.edu/rofl/sovereign-person-senecan-political-theory.
Stärk, E. 1989. *Die Menaechmi des Plautus und kein griechisches Original*. Tübingen.
Stemplinger, E. 1912. *Das Plagiat in der griechischen Literatur*. Leipzig.
Stierstorfer, K. 2018. 'The Revival of Legal Humanism', in K. Dolin (ed.), 9–25.
Straumann, B. 2016. *Crisis and Constitutionalism: Roman Political Thought from the Fall of the Republic to the Age of Revolution*. Oxford.
Stroud, S. R. 2008. 'Simulation, Subjective Knowledge, and the Cognitive Value of Literary Narrative', *Journal of Aesthetic Education* 42: 19–41.
Stroux, J. 1949 [1926]. *Summum ius summa iniuria*. Leipzig/Berlin.
Suerbaum, W. 1968. *Untersuchungen zur Selbstdarstellung älterer römischer Dichter. Livius Andronicus, Naevius, Ennius*. Hildesheim.
Sullivan, T. 2011. *Walking in Roman Culture*. Cambridge.
Sutton, E. W. and Rackham, H. 1942. *Cicero. On the Orator: Books 1–2*. Cambridge, MA.
Syme, R. 1979. *History in Ovid*. Oxford.
Tacoma, L. 2016. *Moving Romans: Migration to Rome in the Principate*. Oxford.
Tellegen, J. W. 1983. '*Oratores, jurisprudentes* and the *Causa Curiana*', *Revue internationale des droits de l'Antiquité* 30: 293–311.
Tellegen, J. W. 2003. 'The Reliability of Quintilian for Roman Law: On the *Causa Curiana*', in O. Tellegen-Couperus (ed.), *Quintilian and the Law. The Art of Persuasion in Law and Politics*. Leuven: 191–200.
Tellegen, J. W. and O. Tellegen-Couperus. 2000. 'Law and Rhetoric in the *causa Curiana*', *Orbis Iuris Romani: Journal of Ancient Law Studies* 9: 171–202.
Tellegen, J. W. and O. Tellegen-Couperus. 2013. '*Artes Vrbanae*: Roman Law and Rhetoric', in P. du Plessis (ed.), *New Frontiers: Law and Society in the Roman World*. Edinburgh: 31–50.
Tellegen, J. W. and O. Tellegen-Couperus. 2016. 'Reading a Dead Man's Mind: Hellenistic Philosophy, Rhetoric and Roman Law', in P. du Plessis (ed.), *Cicero's Law: Rethinking Roman Law of the Late Republic*. Edinburgh: 26–49.
Treggiari, S. 1969. *Roman Freedmen during the Late Republic*. Oxford.
Treggiari, S. 1988. Review of *Roman Slave Law* by Alan Watson. *Échos du Monde Classique* 32 n.s. 7.3: 434–6.

Treggiari, S. 1991. *Roman Marriage: Iusti Coniuges from the Time of Cicero to the Time of Ulpian*. Oxford.
Tuori, K. 2004. 'The *ius respondendi* and the Freedom of Roman Jurisprudence', *Revue internationale des droits de l'Antiquité* 51: 295–337.
Tuori, K. 2016a. *The Emperor of the Law: The Emergence of Roman Imperial Adjudication*. Oxford.
Tuori, K. 2016b. 'Schmitt and the Sovereignty of Roman Dictators: From the Actualisation of the Past to the Recycling of Symbols', *History of European Ideas* 42: 95–106.
Tuori, K. 2018. 'The Savage Sea and the Civilizing Law: The Roman Law Tradition and the Rule of the Sea', in H. Kopp and C. Wendt (eds), *Thalassokratographie: Rezeption und Transformation antiker Seeherrschaft*. Berlin: 201–17.
Usener, H. 1900. 'Italische Volksjustiz', *Rheinisches Museum* 64: 1–28.
Van Hoof, A. J. L. 1990. *From Autothanasia to Suicide: Self-killing in Classical Antiquity*. London/New York.
Vannini, G. 2013. 'Cesare contro Cesare. II divo Augusto nell'Apokolokyntosis', in M. Labate and G. Rosati (eds), *La construzione del mito augusteo*. Heidelberg: 197–220.
Vasaly, A. 2015. *Livy's Political Philosophy: Power and Personality in Early Rome*. Cambridge.
Vaughn, J. W. 1985. 'Law and Rhetoric in the *Causa Curiana*', *Classical Antiquity* 4: 208–22.
Versnel, H. S. 1980. 'Destruction, *Devotio* and Despair in a Situation of Anomy: The Mourning for Germanicus in Triple Perspective', in A. Brelich (ed.), *Perennitas: Studi in onore di Angelo Brelich*. Rome: 541–618.
Versnel, H. S. 1993. *Inconsistencies in Greek and Roman Religion II: Transition and Reversal in Myth and Ritual*. Leiden.
Versteeg, R. and N. Barclay. 2003. 'Rhetoric and Law in Ovid's Orpheus', *Law and Literature* 15.3: 395–420.
Vickers, B. 2002. *Shakespeare, Co-Author: A Historical Study of Five Collaborative Plays*. Oxford.
Videau, A. 2004. 'L'écriture juridique d'Ovide des élégies amoureuses (*Amours* et *Héroïdes*) aux *Tristes* de l'exil', *Ars Scribendi*. http://ars-scribendi.ens-lyon.fr/spip.php?article19&var_affichage=vf
Vincent, M. 1994. 'Between Ovid and Barthes: *Ekphrasis*, Orality, Textuality in Ovid's "Arachne"', *Arethusa* 27: 361–86.
Volk, K. 2010. 'Literary Theft and Roman Water Rights in Manilius' Second Proem', *Materiali e Discussioni per l'analisi Dei Testi Classici* 65: 187–97.
Volk, K. 2017. 'Signs, Seers and Senators: Divinatory Expertise in Cicero and Nigidius Figulus', in J. König and G. Woolf (eds), *Authority and Expertise in Ancient Scientific Culture*. Cambridge: 329–47.
Vonglis, B. 1968. *La lettre et l'esprit de la loi dans la jurisprudence classique et la rhétorique*. Paris.

von Jehring, R. 1852. *Geist des römischen Rechts auf den verschiedenen Stufen seiner Entwicklung*. Vol 1. Leipzig.

Wallace-Hadrill, A. 1982. '*Civilis Princeps*: Between Citizen and King', *Journal of Roman Studies* 72: 32–48.

Wallace-Hadrill, A. 1997. '*Mutatio morum*: The Idea of a Cultural Revolution', in T. Habinek and A. Schiesaro (eds), 3–22.

Ward, I. 1995. *Law and Literature: Possibilities and Perspectives*. Cambridge.

Ward, I. 1999. *Shakespeare and the Legal Imagination*. London.

Watson, A. 1968. *The Law of Property in the Later Roman Republic*. Oxford.

Watson, A. 1987. *Roman Slave Law*. Baltimore.

Watson, A. (trans.). 2009. *The Digest of Justinian*. Philadelphia.

Weiner, J. 2015. 'Between *bios* and *zoē*: Sophocles' Antigone and Agamben's Biopolitics', *Logeion* 5: 139–60.

Weisberg, R. 1984. *The Failure of the Word: The Lawyer as Protagonist in Modern Fiction*. New Haven.

Wharton, R. 2018. 'The Regulation of Authorship: Literary Property and the Aesthetics of Resistance', in K. Dolin (ed.), 291–307.

Wheeler, A. L. 1924. *Ovid: Tristia. Ex Ponto*. Cambridge, MA.

Wheeler, S. 1999. *A Discourse of Wonders: Audience and Performance in Ovid's Metamorphoses*. Philadelphia.

White, J. B. 1973. *The Legal Imagination*. Boston.

White, J. B. 1981–82. 'Law as Language: Reading Law and Reading Literature', *Texas Law Review* 60: 415–45.

Whitton, C. L. 2013. 'Seneca, *Apocolocyntosis*', in M. T. Dinter and E. Buckley (eds), *A Companion to the Neronian Age*. Malden, MA: 151–69.

Wibier, M. 2016. 'Cicero's Reception in the Juristic Tradition of the Early Empire', in P. du Plessis (ed.), *Cicero's Law: Rethinking Roman Law of the Late Republic*. Edinburgh: 100–22.

Wibier, M. 2020. 'On Homer and the Invention of Money: The Jurist Gaius in Servius' *Georgics* Commentary (3.306–7)', in U. Babusiaux and D. Mantovani (eds), *Le Istituzioni di Gaio: avventure di un bestseller*. Pavia: 513–29.

Wibier, M. (forthcoming). *Legal Scholarship and the World of Learning: An Intellectual History of Roman Jurisprudence in the Early Empire*. Oxford.

Wieacker, F. 1961. *Vom römischen Recht: 10 Versuche*. 2nd ed. Stuttgart.

Wieacker, F. 1967. 'The *Causa Curiana* and Contemporary Roman Jurisprudence', *Irish Jurist* 2: 151–64.

Wieacker, F. 1970. 'Die römischen Juristen in der politischen Gesellschaft des zweiten vorchristlichen Jahrhunderts', in W. G. Becker and L. Schnorr von Carolsfeld (eds), *Sein und Werden im Recht. Festgabe für Ulrich von Lübtow zum 70. Geburtstag am 21. August 1970*. Berlin: 183–214.

Wieacker, F. 1988. *Römische Rechtsgeschichte. Erster Abschnitt: Einleitung, Quellenkunde, Frühzeit und Republik*. Munich.

Wiedemann, T. 1985. 'The Regularity of Manumission at Rome', *Classical Quarterly* 35: 162–75.
Wiedemann, T. 2000. 'Reflections of Roman Political Thought in Latin Historical Writing', in C. Rowe and M. Schofield (eds), *The Cambridge History of Greek and Roman Political Thought*. Cambridge: 517–31.
Wildberger, J. 2014. 'The Epicurus Trope and the Construction of a "Letter Writer"', in J. Wildberger and M. L. Colish (eds), *Seneca Philosophus*. Berlin: 431–65.
Williams, G. 1968. *Tradition and Originality in Roman Poetry*. London.
Williams, G. D. 2009. 'The *Metamorphoses*: Politics and Narrative', in P. E. Knox (ed.), *A Companion to Ovid*, Chichester/Malden, MA: 154–69.
Williams, G. D. 2017. 'Lucan's Civil War in Nero's Rome', in S. Bartsch, K. Freudenburg and C. Littlewood (eds), *The Cambridge Companion to the Age of Nero*. Cambridge: 93–106.
Willis, I. 2011. *Now and Rome: Lucan and Vergil as Theorists of Politics and Space*. London.
Wiseman, T. P. 1998. *Roman Drama and Roman History*. Exeter.
Wisse, J. 2007. 'The Riddle of the *Pro Milone*: The Rhetoric of Rational Argument', in J. Powell (ed.), *Logos: Rational Argument in Classical Rhetoric*. London: 35–68.
Witt, P. 1971a. 'Die Übersetzung von Rechtsbegriffen, dargestellt am Beispiel der *in ius vocatio* bei Plautus und Terenz', *Studia et Documenta Historiae et Iuris* 37: 217–60.
Witt, P. 1971b. *In ius vocare bei Plautus und Terenz: Zur Interpretation römischen Rechts in klassischen Übersetzungen*. Freiburg.
Wohlleben, A. 1998. '"Conchae et umbilici": Eine motivgeschichtliche Betrachtung zu Cicero, *De oratore* 2.22f.', in J. Holzhausen (ed.), *Psyche – Seele – Anima: Festschrift für Karin Alt*. Berlin: 132–44.
Wolff, H. J. 1964. Review of Kränzlein, *Eigentum und Besitz*, *Zeitschrift der Savigny-Stiftung für Rechtsgeschichte, Romanistische Abteilung* 81: 333–40.
Wolff, H. J. 1974 [1964]. *Opuscula Dispersa*. Amsterdam.
Woodmansee, M. 1984. 'The Genius and the Copyright: Economic and Legal Conditions of the Emergence of the "Author"', *Eighteenth-Century Studies* 17.4: 425–8.
Woodmansee, M. and P. Jaszi (eds). 1994. *The Construction of Authorship: Textual Appropriation in Law and Literature*. Durham, NC.
Woods, D. 2000. 'Caligula's Seashells', *Greece & Rome* 47: 80–7.
Wright, M. 2019. *The Lost Plays of Greek Tragedy*. vol. 2. London.
Zagagi, N. 1980. *Tradition and Originality in Plautus. Studies of the Amatory Motifs in Plautine Comedy*. Göttingen.
Zetzel, J. E. G. 2003. 'Plato with Pillows: Cicero on the Uses of Greek Culture', in D. Braund and C. Gill (eds), *Myth, History and Culture in Republican Rome: Studies in Honour of T. P. Wiseman*. Exeter: 119–38.
Zetzel, J. E. G. 2018. *Critics, Compilers, and Commentators*. Oxford.

Ziegler, K. 1950. 'Plagiat', *Paulys Realencyclopädie der classischen Altertumswissenschaft* 20.2: 1956–97.

Zimmermann, R. 1996 [1990]. *The Law of Obligations: Roman Foundations of the Civilian Tradition.* New York.

Ziogas, I. 2011. 'Ovid in Rushdie, Rushdie in Ovid: A Nexus of Artistic Webs', *Arion* 19: 23–50.

Ziogas, I. 2013. *Ovid and Hesiod: The Metamorphosis of the Catalogue of Women.* Cambridge.

Ziogas, I. 2016a. 'Love Elegy and Legal Language in Ovid', in P. Mitsis and I. Ziogas (eds), *Wordplay and Powerplay in Latin Poetry.* Berlin: 213–40.

Ziogas, I. 2016b. 'Orpheus and the Law: The Story of Myrrha in Ovid's *Metamorphoses*', *Law in Context* 34: 24–41.

Ziogas, I. 2018. 'Law and Literature in the Ancient World: The Case of Phryne', in Dolin (ed.), 79–93.

Ziogas, I. 2021. *Law and Love in Ovid: Courting Justice in the Age of Augustus.* Oxford.

Index

Accius, Lucius 8, 154, 155
accountability 45, 47, 48–9, 52–3, 56, 61–2
actors 90, 95–6, 97, 209, 266
Ad Verrem (Cicero) 160
Adelphoe (Terence) 9, 10, 11
adultery 242
Aeacus 54–5, 56
Aeneid (Virgil) 28
affirmative action law 264–5
Aftsomis, Katherine 51
Agamben, Giorgio 45, 46, 67, 75, 82 n.8
   bare life 81
   biopower 81
   Homo Sacer 67, 255
   iustitium 69–70, 71, 73, 80
   sovereignty 78, 81
Agrippa, Marcus Vipsanius 128
America. *See* US
American Supreme Court 30
Amores (Ovid) 237
Ando, Clifford 4
animal aggression 233
Annales (Ennius, Quintus) 28, 33, 135, 151
Annals (Tacitus) 70, 129
Antigone (Sophocles) 17
Antiphanes 171
Antiquities (Varro) 132
Antistius Labeo, Marcus. *See* Labeo, Marcus Antistius
Apocolocyntosis (Seneca) 20, 45, 46–7
   concilium deorum (Council of the Gods) 47–54, 60
   narrative voice 61–2
   Saturnalian *princeps* 55, 57–61
   trial and punishment 47–51, 54–7
Apollodorus of Carystus
   Epidikazomenos 90, 93, 103 n.16
Appius Claudius Pulcher 77
appropriation 210, 211, 212, 213, 216
   Hegel, Georg Wilhelm Friedrich 223 n.30
   law 207, 208, 219–20

Appuleius Saturninus, Lucius 36
Aquilius Gallus, Gaius 114–15
Arachne 228–30, 232–4, 235–7, 238, 239, 240, 241–2, 243–4
architecture 198–201, 202
Archytas of Tarentum 68
Arellius Fuscus 227
Aristodemou, M. 2
Aristophanes
   Clouds 97
Aristotle 31, 68, 182 n.10
   Politics 236
Ars poetica (Horace) 29
art 233–4, 241
   *ecphrasi*s 228, 232, 233, 234, 235, 237
   regulation 241
   as tool of resistance 227, 234, 239, 241, 244
   as weapon 240
Art of Love (Ovid) 5
Artes (Celsus, Aulus Cornelius) 205 n.34
Asconius Pedianus, Quintus 160
Asinius Pollio 8
Asmis, Elizabeth 34
Athenaeus 170–1
   Deipnosophistae 171
Attic Nights (Gellius, Aulus) 132, 135, 137, 266
auctores 5–6
audiences 180, 181, 185 n.51
Augustus (emperor of Rome) 47–9, 51, 52, 60, 126
   biopower 81
   Fescennine verse 154
   immigration 260
   Labeo, Marcus Antistius 127, 128–31, 142
   legal programme 235–6
   Ovid 235, 242
   pax Romana 235–6
   power 127, 128–9
   private life 243

Res Gestae 236
shore 113
slavery 262
sovereignty 75, 230
authors 147–50
   author function 147–50, 151, 155, 157, 163
   transgression 149, 151–63
   authorship 147–8, 150, 151–2, 154, 157, 160, 163
   laws 265

Barchiesi, A.
   Poet and the Prince, The 237
bare life 81
Barthes, Roland 147
beachcombing 112–13, 116
Before the Law (Derrida, Jacques) 2
Bellum Ciuile (Lucan) 20
   Appius 77
   biopower 81–2
   iustitium. See *iustitium*
   readers of 80–2
   SCU 80
   sovereignty 75, 78–9, 81, 82
   state of exception 75, 78–9, 80, 81, 82
Bellum Histricum (Hostius) 28
Bellum Punicum (Naevius, Gnaeus) 157
Bergson, Henri 97
Bhatt, Shreyaa 81
Big Bang Theory (TV series) 97
biopower 81
birth rates 260
boats 117
body politic, the 258–9
Bourdieu, Pierre 90, 250, 253, 259
Braund, Susanna 153
Brazil 265
Breyer, Stephen 6
Brown, Henry 264
Brutus, Lucius Junius 257–8
Brutus (Cicero) 158
Buckland, W. W. and Stein, P.
   Text-Book of Roman Law 209, 210

Caecilius Africanus, Sextus 135–6, 137, 266
Caecilius Statius 8, 156

Caelius Sabinus, Gnaeus Arulenus 133, 134
Caesius Bassus 160
Caligula, Gaius 113
Calliope 238–9
Camillus, Lucius Furius 39
canons 139–40, 157
Capito, Ateius 129, 134, 140
captatio beneuolentiae 12
carnival 153, 159
   Saturnalia 55, 57, 58–9
Cassius Longinus, Gaius 7, 139
Cassius Vecellinus, Spurius 38, 39
Catilinarian conspiracy 36–41
Catilinarians (Cicero) 37, 40
Catiline (Lucius Sergius Catilina) 36, 40
Cato the Elder 34, 134
   Libri ad filium 197
   Origines 28, 151
Catullus 5
causa Curiana 96, 106–20
   Cicero 107–11
Celsus, Aulus Cornelius 205 n.34
   Artes 205 n.34
   De Medicina 205 n.34
certamen/certet/certo (contend) 230
Cicero (Marcus Tullius Cicero) 8–10, 15–16, 27, 100, 113
   Ad Verrem 160
   Brutus 158
   Catilinarian conspiracy 36–41
   Catilinarians 37, 40
   causa Curiana 107–11, 119
   constitution 27–8, 31, 32, 34–6
   De inuentione 194, 199, 242
   De legibus 31, 32, 34–6, 100
   De oratore 100, 112, 189–200, 201
   De re publica 27–8, 30, 34, 35–6, 37, 41, 42, 154
   exile 38
   ius naturale 32
   iustitium 188 n.77
   legal style 35–6
   literature 25–6
   Orator 201–2
   plagiarism 157–8
   politics 25–7
   Pro Archia 26, 29
   Pro Caelio 8–10, 11, 16, 38

Index

Pro Murena 100
Rhetorica ad Herennium 199
Somnium Scipionis 28, 37
Topica 114–15
Cincinnatus, Lucius Quinctius 39
citizenship 253, 261
  manumission 255, 256, 257–8, 260–1, 262
Claudius (emperor of Rome) 46, 47
  concilium deorum (Council of the Gods) 47–54
  as judge 50–1, 56, 60
  Saturnalian *princeps* 55, 57–61
  trial and punishment 47–51, 54–7
Claudius Pulcher, Appius 77
clementia (clemency) 10, 241, 242
Clodius Pulcher, Publius 38, 40
Clouds (Aristophanes) 97
Code of Hammurabi 251
cognitiones (judicial investigations) 56
Colognesi, Capogrossi 194
comedy 9–16, 58, 97, 161, 177, 263 see also *Phormio*
  Cicero 8–11, 15–16, 100–1
  Greek 89, 90, 177
  Greek New Comedy 89, 93
  legal system, perception of 90
  mocking the law 91, 96–101
  Plautus 98–100, 101
  theatre performances 90
Communist Manifesto, The (Marx, Karl and Engels, Friedrich) 213
concilium deorum (Council of the Gods) 47–54, 60
constitution 27–35, 41–2, 126, 250
  constitutional norms 27, 29, 31, 36, 38–40
  constitutional revisionism 36–41
  equality 249, 250, 251
  etymology 33
  interpretation 266
  US Constitution 249–50, 251, 253–5, 263
Constitution of the Roman Republic, The (Lintott, Andrew) 28
  constitutional norms 27, 29, 31, 36, 38–40
  constitutional revisionism 36–41
consultum (decree) 32
Coponius, Marcus 109, 111, 118

copyright law 148, 149, 155–8, 163 see also authorship
Cornelius Scipio Nasica Serapio 37, 38
Crassus, Lucius Licinius 107, 108, 109, 110, 118, 119
  political oratory 189–90, 191–6, 200, 201
  shore simile 107, 108, 110–11, 112, 116, 117–18
Critical Race Theory 267 n.11
cultural capital 251
Curius, Manius 109, 111

da Silva, Denise Ferreira 265
Day, Henry 67
De architectura (Vitruvius) 190–1, 198–201, 202
De Clementia (Seneca) 53, 241
De inuentione (Cicero) 194, 199, 242
De legibus (Cicero) 31, 32, 34–6, 100
De Medicina (Celsus, Aulus Cornelius) 205 n.34
De oratore (Cicero) 100, 112, 189–200, 201
De re publica (Cicero) 27–8, 30, 34, 35–6, 37, 41, 42, 154
debt 212, 213, 214, 216–17, 218, 220
deception 13
declamation 4, 208
defamation 154–5
Deipnosophistae (Athenaeus) 171
Demeter 239
demiurges 241
Derrida, Jacques 68, 220 n.2, 253
  Before the Law 2
  On Grammatology 41
  'Signature, évènement, contexte' 35
descriptive constitutionalism 31
Digest 7, 14, 30, 94, 133, 169, 178
  shore, the 114
Dio, Cassius 128, 129, 260, 262
Diphilus 172
Disciplinae (Varro) 197
dispossession 210
divinity 50, 77–8
Dolin, Kieran 3, 6
domini (owner) 195, 196, 197
drama 237
Drusus the Elder (Nero Claudius Drusus) 70, 71

economic terminology 212, 213, 214–17, 218, 220
ecphrasis (written description of work of art) 228, 232, 233, 234, 235, 237
Elmer, David
  Poetics of Consent: Collective Decision Making and the Iliad, The 73
Emathides, the 238
emperors
  divinity 50
  worship 50
Encheiridion (Pomponius, Sextus) 139
Ennius, Quintus 8, 34, 37, 42
  Annales 28, 33, 135, 151
  plagiarism 157–8
envy 237
Epictetus 215
Epicureanism 212, 213, 216
Epidicus (Plautus) 98–9, 101
Epidikazomenos (Apollodorus of Carystus) 90, 93, 103 n.16
epikleroi 91, 94
Epistles (Horace) 152–4
Epistles (Seneca) 59
Epistulae ex Ponto (Ovid) 114
equality 249, 250, 264 *see also* reparation
  Kant, Immanuel 253
  US 253–5, 261, 262, 263, 264–5
Eunuchus (Terence) 11–14, 16
Ex Ponto (Ovid) 237
exemplum 29

Fabius Pictor, Quintus 134
falsity (*falsum*) 231–2
Fasti (Ovid) 242
Favorinus 135–7, 266
Feeney, Denis 151
Fescennina licentia (Horace) 153–4, 159
Fescennine verse 153–4
festival of Liber 159
Festus, Sextus Pompeius 125, 162
fiction 3–4, 29
fishing law 171, 173, 174–5, 176, 180, 219
Fish, Stanley 2
Foner, Eric 262
fools 59–60
forensic rhetoric 10
forgiveness 15
formalism 95, 96

Fortier, M. 3
Foucault, Michel
  author function 147–50, 151, 154, 163
  biopower 81
frater (brother) 134
Freud, Sigmund 97
friendship 216–17
Frier, B. 126
Frost, Robert
  'Mending Wall' 6
Frye, Northrop 3
Fulvius Flaccus, Marcus 36
funereal mourning 67, 69, 70–3, 76
furtum (theft, extramarital affairs) 13, 156–7 *see also* theft

Gadamer, Hans-Georg 106
Gaius 7, 140, 141
  Institutes 133, 138–9
Gaius Caesar 70
Gallus, Gaius Cornelius 242
gambling 55
Gardner, J. F. 257
Geffcken, K. A. 10
Gellius, Aulus 69, 125, 131–8, 140, 141
  Attic Nights 132–3, 135, 137, 266
  Naevius, Gnaeus 159, 161
Georgics (Virgil) 159
Germanicus, Iulius Caesar 70–1
Germany, Robert 160
Goldberg, Sander 156
Goodrich, Peter 2
Gorgias 13
Gorgias (Plato) 189, 192, 196–7, 198
government
  Aristotle 31
  historical tales 29–30
Gracchus, Gaius 36, 37, 38, 39, 40
Gracchus, Tiberius 36, 37, 38, 40, 80
Gradel, Ittai 50
Gratz (and Grutter) v. Bollinger (2003) 264
Greece
  comedy 89, 90, 177
  epikleroi 91, 94
  Greek New Comedy 89, 93
  law 91–2, 93, 99, 182 n.10
  literary criticism 155–6

literature 89
   sea, the 170-2, 177, 180
Gruen, Erich 162

Habermas, Jürgen 90
Hadrian (emperor of Rome) 127
Harlan, John Marshall 264
Harries, Jill 7
Heautontimoroumenos (Terence) 15, 97-8
Hebrew works 17
Hecato 212
hermeneutics 106, 110, 118-19
Hermes Trismegistus 150
Hesiod 17
   Works and Days 233
Hippocrates 150
   On the Art of Medicine 205 n.34
historical tales 28-32
Hobbes, Thomas 84 n.41
Homer 7, 8, 150, 228
   Iliad 7-8, 73
   Odyssey 7, 8
Homo Sacer 67, 255
Honig, Bonnie 26, 251
Horace 28, 129, 150, 163, 256
   Ars poetica 29
   Epistles 152-4
   Fescennina licentia 153-4, 159
   Odes 29, 240
   Satires 129, 163
Hostius
   Bellum Histricum 28
humility 201

Iliad (Homer) 7-8, 73
immigration 260
imprudentia (lack of knowledge [of the law]) 14-15
inequality 251
inheritance law. See *causa Curiana*
iniuria (affront) 154-5
Institutes (Gaius) 133, 138-9
Institutio Oratoria (Quintilian, Marcus Fabius) 197-8, 208
intellectual property 189-90, 191-2, 194-7, 199-201, 218
   Seneca 211, 212, 213, 214, 215-16
intention 14
intentionalism 95, 96

iudices (judges, literary critics) 5
iudicium (authority) 198, 199
Iunius Brutus, Marcus 158
ius (right, justice, legal power or authority, *Recht, droit, justice*) 29, 31, 32, 36, 71
   see also *iustitium*
ius naturale See natural law
ius respondendi (right of response) 144 n.20, 144 n.33
iustitium (cessation of the legal) 67, 68, 69, 153
   chaos 71
   definition 69
   divinity 77-8
   etymology 69-70
   funereal mourning 67, 69, 70-3, 76
   legal authority 71
   SCU 80
   silence 74, 76-7
   sovereignty 67-8, 72, 75, 79, 80, 81, 82
   war 73-7

Janus 52
Jefferson, Thomas 253
Jehring, Rudolf von 178
Jerome, Saint 161
Jocelyn, H. D. 159
Judaism 30
judgment 46-54, 230-1, 249
Julius Caesar, Gaius 5, 40, 68, 75-6, 79-82, 242
Jupiter 51, 52
jurists 97, 115, 135
   Labeo, Marcus Antistius 137-41, 142
Justinian (emperor of Rome) 169, 171
Juvenal 256

Kafka, Franz
   Trial, The 4
Kant, Immanuel 253, 265
Kennedy, John F. 261
kings see also sovereignty
   fools and 59-60
knowledge 189-90, 191-2, 194-6, 197, 198-200, 218 see also intellectual property
   Seneca 215-16
Konstan, David 91, 92, 96, 176

Kornhardt, Hildegard 94–5, 96, 98
Kraus, Christina 40
Kunkel, W. 101

Labeo, Marcus Antistius 7, 117, 125–7, 141–2
  Augustus 127, 128–31, 142
  Gaius 133, 138–9, 140, 141
  Gellius, Aulus 125, 131–8, 140, 141
  jurists 137–41, 142
  Pomponius, Sextus 140, 141
  Posteriores 132–3
  reception 131–41, 142
  Twelve Tables 134, 135–6
  Ulpian 140
Laelius, Gaius 112
Laelius Felix 134
law 1–6, 20, 45, 126, 207–9, 219–20 *see also* property law
  accountability 45, 47, 48–9, 52–3
  affirmative action 264–5
  animal aggression 233
  appropriation 207, 208, 219–20
  authorship 265
  Bourdieu, Pierre 253
  cessation. See *iustitium*
  constitution 27–35, 126
  court cases 121 n.14 see also *causa Curiana*
  critique 228
  declamation 4, 208
  defamation 154–5
  definition 3
  epikleroi 91, 94
  force of 25
  formalism 95, 96
  Greek 91–2, 93
  historical tales of precedents and examples 28–2, 36–41
  inheritance. See *causa Curiana*
  intentionalism 95, 96
  interpretation 255, 266
  legal discourse 6–7, 107, 125–6
  legal rights 21
  lis 234
  litigation 173, 175
  manumission 260, 261
  marriage 91–5, 208, 236, 242–3, 260–1
  meanings of 263
  metaphor 115
  mocking 91, 96–101
  oratory 192–200, 202
  penal appropriation 149, 151–4
  poetry 6–8
  power 126
  Quintilian 208
  rhetoric 10, 106–7, 196–7
  as rule 177–8
  Saturnalia 55, 57, 58–9
  scholarship 18
  Seneca 209–12
  sovereignty 45, 75, 78–9
  as standard 178–9
  story telling 121 n.14
  terminology 93
Law and Humanities movement 2, 17
Law and Literature 17
law schools 7
Laws (Plato) 170
Lee, Robert E. 262
legal canons 139–40
legal discourse 6–7, 107, 125–6
legal norms 90, 126
legal rights 21
legal style 35–6
legal vocabulary in *Metamorphoses* 228–34
leges Iuliae 260–1
Leigh, Matthew 9, 10
Lenel, Otto
  Palingenesia 140
Lepidus, Marcus Aemilius 128, 129
lex (statute, law) 32, 36
lex Aebutia 135
lex Aelia Sentia 261
Lex Aquilia 156–7
Lex Atinia 195
lex Fufia Caninia 261
lex Iulia de ui 241
Lex Iulia et Papia 130
lex Iunia 261
lex naturale (natural law). *See* natural law
lex Papia Poppaea 260–1
lex talionis (law of retaliation) 236
libel 4–5
libertas (freedom) 128, 129, 131
liberty 209, 210

Libri ad filium (Cato the Elder) 197
Licinius Crassus, Lucius. *See* Crassus, Lucius Licinius
Liebs, D. 101
Life of Augustus (Suetonius) 128–9
Lincoln, Abraham 261, 263
Lintott, Andrew 29, 30, 31
    Constitution of the Roman Republic, The 28
lis (lawsuit) 234, 241
literature 1–6, 17, 20–1, 25, 126, 135, 244, 257, 259 *see also* poetry
    Cicero 25–6
    constitution 41–2, 126
    definitions 3–4, 107
    Derrida, Jacques 68
    fiction 3–4, 29
    force of 25
    Greek 89, 90, 93
    hermeneutics 106, 110, 118–19
    historical tales 28–32
    Homer 7, 8
    lateness of 148, 151
    legal discourse 6–7
    metaphor 115
    narrative voice 61–2
    norms 26, 28–9, 33, 37, 40 *see also* constitutional norms
    regulation 241
    rhetoric 10, 106–7, 196–7
    scholarship 18
    Seneca 211
    supplements 41–2
    synecdoche 111, 116–17
    transgression 149, 151–63
    written 148
litigation 173, 175
litus (shore) 110–18
liuor (envy) 237
Livia Drusilla (empress of Rome) 70
Livius Andronicus, Lucius 157
Livy (Titus Livius) 28, 29, 38–41, 42
    iustitium 71, 80
    manumission 257–8
Loving v. Virginia (1967) 261
Lowrie, Michèle 18, 75, 79, 107, 126, 242, 250, 251
Lucan (Marcus Annaeus Lucanus) 163
    Bellum Ciuile. *See Bellum Ciuile*

Lucilius 211, 212, 213, 215–16, 217, 220
Lucilius, Gaius 8, 63 n.15, 101, 154–5
ludi Megalenses 9, 10
Luscius Lanuvinus 11–14

McGill, Scott 155, 158
MacRae, Duncan 75
Macrobius, Ambrosius Theodosius 156
Madison, James 254
Maelius, Spurius 36, 38, 39–40, 41
magic 154
magister (teacher) 230
Malcolm X 262–3
Manlius Capitolinus, Marcus 39, 40–1
manumission 255–8, 259–61, 262
manus (marriage law) 208 *see also* marriage
Marcian, Aelius 169
marriage 91, 95, 130, 208, 236, 242–3, 260–1
    epikleroi 91, 94
Martial 156
Masurius Sabinus 7, 8, 133, 134, 138, 144 n.20, 144 n.30, 144 n.33
Menaechmi (Plautus) 100, 101
'Mending Wall' (Frost, Robert) 6
Menenius, Agrippa 258
Merchant of Venice, The (Shakespeare, William) 17
Metamorphoses (Ovid) 228, 241, 243–4
    adultery 242
    clemency 241
    envy 236–7
    legal vocabulary 228–35, 237–8, 244
    passion 236, 237
    peace 235–6
    rape 237–8, 239, 242
    suicide 239–40, 241
    tela/telas 234, 240–1
metaphor 115, 212–13, 217
Metelli, the 159–61, 163
Metellus Creticus, Quintus 160
Miles Gloriosus (Plautus) 161–2
Minerva 229–30, 231–2, 235–6, 237, 238, 239, 241
minority groups 250, 264–5
minutio 10
Mnemosyne 238–9
Molière 97

Mommsen, Theodor 80
Moral Letters (Seneca) 207, 209–19, 220
mos (custom) 32
mos maiorum (customs of the ancestors) 31, 37
mourning 67, 69, 70–3, 76
Mucius Scaevola, Quintus. See Scaevola, Quintus Mucius
Muses, the 238

Naevius, Gnaeus 148, 157–63
    Bellum Punicum 157
    Tarentilla 159
natural law 32, 36, 175, 178, 180, 216, 217–18, 219, 256
Nero (emperor of Rome) 50, 53, 163
Nerva 7
Nigidius Figulus, Publius 74–5, 78, 134
Nissen, Adolph 80
norms 26, 28–9, 33, 37, 40 see also constitutional norms

occupatio (seizure) 173–4, 175, 176, 177, 180
Octavian (emperor of Rome). See Augustus
Odes (Horace) 29, 240
Odyssey (Homer) 7, 8
oliuae (olive) 236
On Grammatology (Derrida, Jacques) 41
On the Art of Medicine (Hippocrates) 205 n.34
Orator (Cicero) 201–2
oratory 58, 189–200, 201–2, 232
originalism 255
Origines (Cato the Elder) 28, 151
ornatus (distinction in speaking) 195, 205 n.40
Ovid 20, 127, 150, 163, 227 see also Pseudo-Ovid
    Amores 237
    Art of Love 5
    Augustus 235, 242
    Epistulae ex Ponto 114
    epitaph 240–1
    Ex Ponto 237
    exile 235, 237, 242
    Fasti 242
    legal career 227
    Metamorphoses. See Metamorphoses
    Remedia amoris 237
    Tristia 237, 240
    women 227–8
ownership/title see also intellectual property
    architecture 199
    fish 171, 173–4, 175, 176, 180
    Plautus 173–7
    property law 193–7, 209
    Schermaier, Martin 178
    sea/shore 175, 176, 180, 181
    seizure (occupatio) 173–4, 80
    texts 147–8, 150, 151–2, 154, 157, 160, 163
    time 210
    uindicatio 193, 209
    Vitruvius 199

Pacuvius, Marcus 8
Palingenesia (Lenel, Otto) 140
passion 236, 237
patria potestas (power of the father) 93
Patterson, O. 256
Paul (Julius Paulus Prudentissimus) 7–8, 14, 140
pax Romana 235–6
payment 212, 213, 215, 216, 217
peace 235–6
penal appropriation 149, 151–7, 158–9, 161, 162
performance 5, 10–16, 26, 34, 35, 37, 42, 47, 53–9, 90, 96, 151, 170, 177, 180, 181, 219, 220, 232, 233, 235, 239, 242
performative force 34–5
Persephone 237, 238
Petronius 262
    Satyricon 256
Phidias 231
Philip V (king of Macedon) 256–7
philosophy 212, 215, 216, 218–19
Phoenicides 170, 171, 180
Phormio (Terence) 90–7, 100–1
plagiarism 11, 14, 16, 22 n.13, 155–8, 163
Plato 31
    Gorgias 189, 192, 196–7, 198
    Laws 170
Plaut v. Spendthrift Farm Inc (1995) 6

Plautus (Titus Maccius) 20, 89, 97, 151, 172, 221 n.12, 256
  audiences 180, 185 n.51
  Epidicus 98–9, 101
  law 177, 178
  Menaechmi 100, 101
  Miles Gloriosus 161–2
  Poenulus 99, 101, 263
  res communes omnium 169
  Rudens 116, 170, 172, 173–7, 178, 179, 180–1
Plessy, Homer Adolph 264
Plessy v. Ferguson (1896) 263–4
Pliny 63 n.18, 240
Poenulus (Plautus) 99, 101, 263
poetry 6–8, 127, 148, 150
  canon 157
  didactic function 29
  Fescennine verse 153–4
  Horace 29
  lateness of 151
  Metelli 160–1
  poetic immortality 237
  power 127
  transgression 151–63
politics 25–7 *see also* government *and* SCU
  author transgression 159
  bare life 81
  biopower 81–2
  body politic, the 258–9
  constitution 27–35
  iustitium. See *iustitium*
  oratory 189–200, 201–2
  power 126–9
  Seneca 214
  voting rights 254–5, 258, 264
Politics (Aristotle) 236
Polybius 31
Pomponius, Sextus 129, 140, 141, 142
  Encheiridion 139
population 260–1
Porcius Latro, Marcus 227
Porphyrio 129–30
Posner, Richard 4
possession (*possessio*) 193–4, 195, 196, 198, 201 *see also* dispossession
Posteriores (Labeo, Marcus Antistius) 132–3

power 126–9, 142, 243 *see also* biopower
  abuse 241
  patria potestas 93
  sovereignty 67, 82
  princeps legibus solutus est (the emperor is not bound by the laws) 46, 47
Principate, changes in society 127, 142
private/public sphere 242–3, 244
Pro Archia (Cicero) 26, 29
Pro Caelio (Cicero) 8–10, 11, 16, 38
Pro Murena (Cicero) 100
Proculus 7, 139
property law 169–70, 172–81, 190, 192–9, 210, 220 *see also* intellectual property
  Seneca 209, 211, 212, 213, 214
  uindicatio (recovery of property) 193, 209
  usucapio (ownership by possession) 195, 220
  propria (proprietary qualities) 191, 197, 198
  proprietas (ownership/title) 193, 195, 196, 195, 197, 201 *see also* ownership/title
proverbs 114
Pseudo-Acro 129–30
Pseudo-Ovid 70, 71, 74, 77
Pytheos of Priene 200

Quintilian, Marcus Fabius 8, 29, 38
  Institutio Oratoria 197–8, 208
  shore, the 114, 115

race/racism 250
  Critical Race Theory 267 n.11
  immigration 260
  reparation 251–2
  segregation 264
  US 254–5, 256, 259, 261, 262, 264
rape 232, 237–8, 239, 242
reason 32–3
recusatio/recusem (object; refuse) 231
Reichmann, R. 3
Remedia amoris (Ovid) 237
reparation 251–2
res communes omnium (things common to all) 169–70, 172, 173, 177–8, 180, 181

Res Gestae (Augustus) 236
res nullius (things belonging to no-one) 172–3, 175
resistance 227, 234
restitutio in integrum (restoration to the previous state) 93, 94–6, 100
rhetoric 10, 106–7, 196–7
　synecdoche 111, 116–17
　political oratory 189–98
Rhetorica ad Herennium (Cicero) 199
Roche, Paul 71
Rome 76
Roman Republican constitution. *See* constitution
Rousseau, Jean-Jacques 41
　Social Contract, The 214
Rudens (Plautus) 116, 170, 172, 173–7, 178, 179, 180–1

sales 7–8, 138–9, 171
salus populi suprema lex esto ('let the people's safety be the highest law') 27, 29, 31, 38
Santangelo, Federico 78
Satires (Horace) 129, 163
Saturnalia 55, 57, 58–9
Saturnalian *princeps* 55, 57–61
Saturnalicius rex 58–9
Saturninus, Lucius 36, 38, 39
Satyricon (Petronius) 256
Scaevola, Quintus Mucius 107, 108, 119
　Lenel, Otto 140–1
　political oratory 190, 191–5
　property law 192–4
　shore simile 110–11, 112, 116, 117–19
　tholepins 111, 116–18
Scalia, Antonin 6
scalmi (tholepins) 111, 116–18
Schermaier, Martin 178–9, 181
Schmitt, Carl 45, 68, 75, 78
Schreck, Heidi 254
　What the Constitution Means to Me 249–50, 265, 266
scientia (knowledge) 198–9
Scipio Aemilianus Africanus, Cornelius 28, 30, 34, 35, 36–7, 91, 112
　Naevius, Gnaeus 159
Scipio Nasica 37, 38, 80

scitum (statute, ordinance, decree, act, *Gesetz*, *loi*) 32
SCU (*senatus consultum ultimum* [ultimate decree of the senate]) 36, 37–8, 40–1, 68, 80
sea, the 169, 170–6, 177, 179, 180, 181
Segal, E. and Moulton, C. 91, 92, 96
segregation 264
seizure 173–4, 175, 176, 177, 180
Sempronius Gracchus, Gaius 36–40
Sempronius Gracchus, Tiberius 36–40, 80
Senate, the 128 *see also* SCU
senatus consultum ultimum (ultimate decree of the senate [SCU]) 36, 37–8, 40–1, 68, 80
Seneca (Lucius Annaeus Seneca the Younger) 256
　Apocolocyntosis. *See* Apocolocyntosis
　De Clementia 53, 241
　declamation 208
　Epistles 59
　Moral Letters 207, 209–19, 220
　slavery 253, 256
seruitus stillicidii (rainwater servitude) 199
Servilius Ahala, Gaius 36, 39, 40
Shakespeare, William
　Merchant of Venice, The 17
Sharrock, Alison 12, 13
shell gathering 112, 113
Shelley, Percy Bysshe 1
shore, the 107, 110–16, 117–19 *see also* property law 169, 172, 175, 176–7, 178, 180
'Signature, évènement, contexte' (Derrida, Jacques) 35
simulatio (simulation) 231, 232, 233, 242–3
slavery 56, 59, 133, 139, 209, 251, 254, 262
　manumission 255–8, 259–61, 262
　Seneca 253
　US 252, 253, 254–5, 256, 262–3
Social Contract, The (Rousseau, Jean-Jacques) 214
social hierarchies
　inverted 55–6, 57, 59, 71 *see also* carnival
Socrates 189
Somnium Scipionis (Cicero) 28, 37
songs, libellous 153–5

Index

Sophocles
  Antigone 17
  Water Carriers 170
soror (sister) 134
sovereignty 45, 75, 241
  Agamben, Giorgio 78, 81
  Bellum Ciuile 75, 78–9, 81, 82
  definition 67–8
  fools 59–60
  Hobbes, Thomas 84 n.41
  iustitium 67–8, 72, 75, 79, 80, 82
  mirror metaphor 53
  paradox of 45–6, 52, 53, 54, 55, 59–60, 68, 78–9, 244 *see also* accountability
  power 67, 82
  state of exception 75, 78–9, 80, 81, 82
spiders 228, 234
Stacey, Peter 53
state of exception 75, 78–9, 80, 81, 82
status 201, 239
Stierstorfer, Klaus 17
stigma 5
stock characters 15–16
Stoicism 212
Straumann, Benjamin 31, 36, 40
Suetonius (Gaius Suetonius Tranquillus) 5, 50, 56, 142
  Life of Augustus 128–9
suicide 229, 239–40, 241–2
Sulla (Lucius Cornelius Sulla Felix) 134
Sulpicius Rufus, Servius 138, 140–1
supplements 41–2
synecdoche 111, 116–17, 119

Tacitus 56, 70, 129, 131, 142
  Annals 70, 129
Talmud, the 30
Tarentilla (Naevius, Gnaeus) 159
tela/telas (web) 234, 240–1
telum (weapon) 234
Terence (Publius Terentius Afer) 8, 11–16, 58, 89, 151
  Adelphoe 9, 10, 11
  Eunuchus 11–15, 16
  Heautontimoroumenos 15, 97–8
  Phormio 90–7, 100–1
  plagiarism 11, 14, 16, 22 n.13, 156
  Text-Book of Roman Law (Buckland, W. W. and Stein, P.) 209, 210

texts
  hermeneutics 106, 110, 118–19
  interpretation 255
  interpreting 106–7, 108, 110, 117–19, 147
  ownership 147–8, 150, 151–2, 154, 157, 160, 163
  penal appropriation 149, 151–7, 158–9, 161, 162
textuality 5
theatre 11, 15, 90, 95–6, 159, 177, 181, 250
  audiences 11–14, 16, 180, 181
theft 10, 13, 14, 138, 139, 155–8, 163
tholepins 111, 116–18
Tiberius Caesar Augustus (emperor of Rome) 128, 144 n.33
Topica (Cicero) 114–15
Trajan (emperor of Rome) 63 n.18
Trebatius Testa, Gaius 115
Trial, The (Kafka, Franz) 4
Triptolemus 239
Tristia (Ovid) 237, 240
truth 212–14 *see also* falsity
Tuori, Kaius 50
tutela (guardianship) 235, 238
Twelve Tables 134, 135–7, 138, 151, 154

uenena (drugs) 7
uindicatio (recovery of property) 193, 209
  manumission 257–8
Ulpian 46, 130, 131, 140, 169
  property law 193
University of California v. Bakke (1978) 264
US 252, 265
  American Supreme Court 30
  Civil War 263–4
  equality 253–5, 261, 262, 263, 264–5
  race/racism 254–5, 256, 259, 261, 262, 264
  segregation 264
  slavery 252, 253, 254–5, 256, 262–3
  US Constitution 249–50, 251, 253–5, 263
  voting rights 254–5, 264
usucapio (ownership by possession) 195, 220

Valerius Maximus 28
Varro (Marcus Terentius Varro) 131, 161, 252
   Antiquities 132
   Disciplinae 197
Verres 160
Verrius Flaccus, Marcus 162
Versnel, Hank 71
Vespasian (emperor of Rome) 126–7
Vickers, Brian 150
Virgil 152, 156
   Aeneid 28
   Georgics 159
Vitruvius 113–14, 198
   De architectura 190–1, 198–201, 202
voting rights 254–5, 258, 264

Ward, Ian 2
Washington, Booker T. 259
Water Carriers (Sophocles) 170
Watson, Alan 256
Weisberg, Richard 2
What the Constitution Means to Me (Schreck, Heidi) 249–50, 265, 266
Wiedemann, Thomas 31
wisdom. *See* knowledge
women 227–8, 234, 244
   rape 232, 237–8, 239
   suicide 240
   tutela 238
   US 254
Works and Days (Hesiod) 233

X, Malcolm 262–3

www.ingramcontent.com/pod-product-compliance
Lightning Source LLC
Chambersburg PA
CBHW052149300426
44115CB00011B/1593